How to Do *Everything* with

Microsoft® Office
Access
2003

How to Do *Everything* with

Microsoft® Office
Access
2003

Virginia Andersen

McGraw-Hill/Osborne

New York   Chicago   San Francisco   Lisbon
London   Madrid   Mexico City   Milan   New Delhi
San Juan   Seoul   Singapore   Sydney   Toronto

McGraw-Hill/Osborne
2100 Powell Street, 10th Floor
Emeryville, California 94608
U.S.A.

To arrange bulk purchase discounts for sales promotions, premiums, or fund-raisers, please contact **McGraw-Hill**/Osborne at the above address. For information on translations or book distributors outside the U.S.A., please see the International Contact Information page immediately following the index of this book.

How to Do Everything with Microsoft® Office Access 2003

10 QWD QWD 01987

ISBN 978-0-07-222938-7
MHID 0-07-222938-1

Publisher:	Brandon A. Nordin
Associate Publisher	
& Editor-in-Chief:	Scott Rogers
Acquisitions Editor:	Megg Morin
Senior Project Editor:	Jody McKenzie
Acquisitions Coordinators:	Tana Allen, Athena Honore
Technical Editor:	Margaret Levine Young
Copy Editor:	Andy Saff
Proofreader:	Stefany Otis
Indexer:	Valerie Perry
Computer Designers:	Tara A. Davis, Lucie Erickson, Jim Kussow, Dick Schwartz
Illustrators:	Kathleen Fay Edwards, Melinda Moore Lytle, Lyssa Wald
Series Design:	Mickey Galicia
Cover Series Design:	Dodie Shoemaker
Cover Illustration:	Eliot Bergman

This book was composed with Corel VENTURA™ Publisher.

About the Author

When Grace Hopper, the originator of the concept of program compilers, told **Virginia Andersen** in 1948 that there was a future for women in digital computers, she responded, "In *what*?" Nevertheless, after graduating from Stanford University, Virginia pursued the idea and carved out a career applying computers to many challenging projects such as mapping the moon's surface in preparation for the Apollo landing; managing large industrial construction projects; conducting undersea surveillance; simulating navy weapon systems; and building reliability mathematical models. She also found time to teach computer science, mathematics, and system analysis at the graduate and undergraduate levels at several Southern California universities.

Since retiring from the defense industry, Virginia has written or contributed to more than 30 books about personal computer–based applications, including database management, word processing, and spreadsheet analysis. She has recently completed the story of her varied uses for computers over the last 50 years, *Digital Recall: Computers Aren't the Only Ones with Memory.*

Contents at a Glance

Contents

Acknowledgments

It has been a treat to be involved in the evolution of this new book series and it is also a pleasure to revise the How to Do Everything for Microsoft Office Access 2003. My thanks go to the great staff at McGraw-Hill/Osborne for all the help they provided. I note especially Megg Morin, my acquisitions editor, who, with skill and patience, guided me in the structure and tenor of this book. She is a pleasure to work with, as is all her staff. Tana Allen and Athena Honore, my acquisitions coordinators, skillfully juggled their many responsibilities, all the while being responsive and helpful.

I also owe many thanks to Jody McKenzie, the book's project editor, for all her help in moving the many chapters through the complex editing and production maze. Her editorial staff, including technical editor Margaret Levine Young and copy editor Andy Saff were very conscientious in pointing out glitches in the logic and lapses in the style. My sincere thanks also go to Stefany Otis for proofing, to Valerie Perry for indexing, and to Jim Kussow and Dick Schwartz for shipping this How To book. The illustrators, Melinda Lytle, Kathleen Edwards, and Lyssa Wald also did a great job with the art.

I must mention how much I appreciate the unrelenting efforts my agent, Matt Wagner of Waterside Productions, has put in to keep me from wasting my time by lolling around on the beach for the last 13 years.

Finally, I have my husband, Jack, to thank for providing quiet and peaceful surroundings, amenable to writing. I also thank him for letting me take over his computer for the duration while mine was occupied by the Office 2003 beta.

Introduction

The Microsoft Office Access 2003 database management system can be a powerful tool for you whether you need to handle business or personal information. The concept of distributing data among related tables is not new, but the way the concept is implemented in Access 2003 makes information management a snap. Access 2003 is extremely flexible and can be applied to any environment.

With Access, you can design and build complete applications with virtually foolproof data entry and retrieval functions and adaptable user-interactive vehicles.

Access's main features are the objects that you can create and combine to produce a complete information management system:

- *Tables* are the containers for the data. They consist of fields that can contain data of many different types.

- *Queries* are the questions you ask of the database. They can extract specific data from multiple tables or even perform actions such as insert, update, or delete certain records.

- *Forms* display data from one or more tables in an informative design. Forms are used for data entry and display.

- *Reports* are used for distributing printed information from one or more tables.

- *Macros* are lists of actions that work together to carry out a particular task in response to an event.

As an integral member of the Microsoft Office 2003 family, Access 2003 has become very cooperative in working smoothly with the other members. For example, it can provide the mailing list for Word's Mail Merge document or send data to Excel for analysis and charting. Access can also easily import and link to data in other program formats.

Who Should Read this Book?

This book is especially designed and written for readers who want an effective guide to all the Microsoft Office Access 2003 features, as well as for those who need a complete step-by-step walk-through to learn how to get the most out of Access. It is written for anyone who has a need to organize information efficiently and accurately, whether for personal or business objectives.

The book is appropriate for beginners to Access who are familiar with computers and other programs but who would like to become proficient in information management. It is also highly useful for beginner-to-intermediate readers who are migrating from other database management systems or earlier versions of Access.

This book focuses on how you can get the most out of Access, whether you are responsible for your company's complete information system or just want to keep track of personal information on your home computer.

What's in Each Part of the Book?

The book is divided into four parts, each of which addresses a specific aspect of Access database management in a logical sequence, from a simple beginning to complex multiple user environment.

Part I gives you a general overview of Access, and addresses the basics of creating a new database with related tables, and entering data in the tables.

Part II gets to the meat of database management by describing how to build queries to extract just the information you want, in the form you want it. Part II also shows you how to create forms and reports for displaying and distributing data. One of the chapters describes how to analyze data with visual charts and graphs.

Part III diverts from database management to discuss personalizing your workplace and improving database performance. It describes how to create custom menus and toolbars, as well as switchboards and dialog boxes. Macros are also introduced in this part.

Part IV looks outward from Access and investigates the exchange of data with other programs, including database applications. It also investigates the sharing of an Access database among multiple users, employing replication techniques, and describes various means of securing the database from intentional and unintentional disruption.

The Appendix shows how to convert a database from previous versions of Access. In addition, it describes how to deal with sharing a database across several different versions.

What Features and Benefits Are Included?

Many helpful editorial elements are presented in this book, including the chapter-opening checklist of How To topics that are covered in the chapter. If you are new to Access, you may want to start at the beginning of the book and read each chapter carefully. Work the step-by-step exercises as much as possible to gain important "hands-on" experience. If you have used earlier versions of Access, you may want to skim through the How To lists for material that is new to you.

You will find all the information you need to perform a specific task clustered together in a single chapter with cross-references to other chapters that may contain related information.

In addition to the explanations in the text, every chapter presents relevant and interesting figures and illustrations that clearly depict the activity under discussion. Other elements are included such as:

- *Tips* with graphics and text that point out alternative ways to use a feature.
- *Cautions* that warn the reader of pitfalls and workarounds that can avoid problems.
- *Notes* that contain ancillary information related to the current topic but not part of the action.
- *Shortcuts* in the form of a graphic icon that suggest ways to save time with a particular task.
- *How To* and *Did You Know? sidebars* that contain additional, peripheral information about the process at hand.

The following conventions are used in this book:

- *Menu commands* are separated by pipebars; for example, File | Open. This means select the Open command on the File menu.
- *Click* means to click an item once, using the left mouse button.
- *Double-click* means to click an item twice in rapid succession, using the left mouse button.
- *Right-click* means to click an item once, using the right mouse button.
- Procedural steps that are numbered must be carried out in the prescribed order.
- Optional choices are presented as bulleted lists from which to choose.

Let Me Hear from You

After a book leaves my domain, there is always a sense of waiting for the other shoe to drop. If you have any comments about how to make this book better, or you want to share some of your experiences with Access, I would be delighted to hear from you. I have enjoyed hearing from readers from as far away as India, China, Scotland, and Korea. Just drop me a line at my email address: VAndersenZ@aol.com.

Part I

Get Started

Chapter 1

Get Acquainted with Access 2003

How to...

- Start Access
- Open a database
- Navigate in the Database window
- Use menu commands, toolbar buttons, and shortcut menus
- Open a table
- Navigate in Datasheet and subdatasheet view
- Get help

In this, the Information Age, we are swamped by data; to use it effectively, we must store the information in such a way that we can get to it when we need it and make sense out of it. Microsoft Access 2003 is the top-notch database management system for all your information management needs, from a simple address list to a complex inventory management system. It offers all the necessary tools for storing, retrieving, and interpreting your data. Furthermore, these tools are a breeze to comprehend and employ.

Relational databases make a lot of sense. The data is distributed among tables, each table referring to a specific aspect of the database such as customers, products, and orders. The tables are closely related so you can retrieve the information you need from all of them and in any arrangement you want.

With a single copy of each data item, you need to update it in only one place, which improves the probability of correct and consistent data. In smaller, less complex, and more focused tables, information is easier to find. In a large table containing a conglomeration of information, it can be difficult to find just the information you need.

This chapter starts Access 2003 and gives you a tour of the Access workplace. If you are already an experienced user of an earlier version of Access, you might want to scan the material in this chapter to pick out the new features and move on to Chapter 2 to create a new database.

Start Access and Open a Database

You can start most software built for the Windows environment in the same way: from the Start button. Depending on how you installed Access 2003, the program's name may appear as a separate item in the Programs (or All Programs if you are using Windows XP) list or as one of the programs in the Microsoft Office menu. If you don't see Microsoft Access in the Programs list, choose Microsoft Office, then click Microsoft Access.

To start Access:

1. Click the Start button and point to Programs or All Programs in the Start menu.
2. Click on Microsoft Access 2003 in the list of programs.

When you open Access, the main window displays the Getting Started task pane with three options: access Microsoft Office Online, open one of the existing database files, or create a new database (see Figure 1-1). The upper panel contains the names of databases that have been opened recently (no doubt your list will be different).

Take a Tour of the Access Window

The Access window shows a title bar, menu bar, and toolbar common to Windows programs. Before we get to the business of creating and using an Access database, let's take a quick tour of the Access 2003 window and get acquainted with its features. It is a great advantage that many of the Access features are common to other Office programs so you may already be familiar with them.

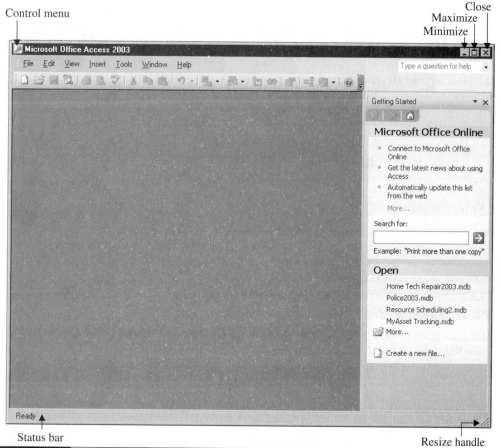

FIGURE 1-1   The Access opening window with the Getting Started task pane

The Title Bar

In addition to displaying the program name, Microsoft Access, the title bar contains buttons that you can use to manipulate the window. These buttons are common to all Windows applications. You can use them to maximize, minimize, resize, or close the window. If the window is not maximized, the lower-right corner becomes a resizing handle that you can drag to change the height or width of the window.

The Menu Bar

Most of the menu commands are dimmed and not available in the empty Database window because there's not much going on there. The File menu offers options to create a new database, open an existing one, or search for the one you want. Other options, such as the Toolbars option in the View menu, let you tailor the database workplace. All the Help menu options are available. You'll learn more about getting help later in this chapter in the "Get Help When You Need It" section.

The Toolbar

The buttons on the toolbar offer shortcuts to a lot of the commonly used menu commands. Most of the toolbar buttons are dimmed, but you can rest the mouse pointer on the button and see its name displayed below the button in a ScreenTip. The toolbar and the menu bar present different options, depending on the current activity.

The Status Bar

The status bar, located at the bottom of the Access window, provides a running commentary about the ongoing task and clues to the Access working environment. The right side of the status bar also shows boxes that indicate the presence of a filter and the status of various toggle keys such as INSERT, CAPS LOCK, SCROLL LOCK, and NUM LOCK.

Open a Database

Now let's get down to business. If the database you want to open is listed in the Getting Started task pane that appears when Access starts, you can open it by simply clicking the filename. If the one you want is not on the list, click More. The Open dialog box appears, as shown in Figure 1-2. (Your list of folders and files will be different.)

 *If Access is already running, you can open a recently opened file by choosing File on the menu bar and selecting the filename from the list.*

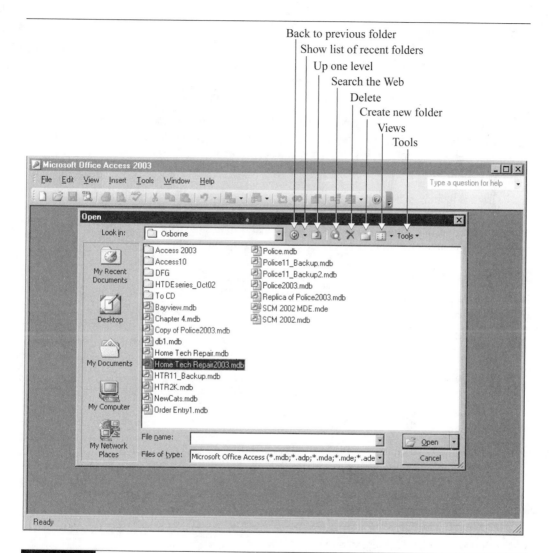

FIGURE 1-2   Choosing the database from the Open dialog box

The Groups Bar

The Groups bar at the left contains five buttons that you can click to open other folders or return to the Windows desktop:

■ **My Recent Documents**   Opens the new Recent folder, which displays the name, size, type, and date of the last modification for each database you've opened recently.

- **Desktop** Displays a list of the desktop components on your computer that you can transfer to including items such as My Computer, My Documents, and Network Neighborhood.
- **My Documents** (or the name of your personal default folder) Shows the contents of that folder. This is the default display in the Open dialog box.
- **My Computer** Displays the list of available data storage units in the system.
- **My Network Places** In Windows 2000, it displays the folders and objects you have saved in web folders. In Windows XP, you see the network drives on your LAN as well as the names of any web folders you have set up.

The trick is to know where you have stored your database. If you have used other Windows applications, such as Word or Excel, you know how to find the file you want with the Open dialog box. Use the "Look in" box to zero in on the folder that contains the database, double-click the folder name or icon to open it, then select the file you want from the list.

The Open Dialog Box

The Open dialog box contains several buttons that help you find the file you want to open. You can see the name of each button by resting the mouse pointer on the button in the command bar.

The Views drop-down list includes these options:

The Tools drop-down list includes these options:

If you want to work with a different file type, click the down arrow next to the "Files of type" box and choose from the list of 18 types or All Files. The default file type for Access 2003 is Microsoft Access, which includes all Access databases and any other Office documents that have been linked to an Access database such as an Excel spreadsheet or a Word document. Choose Microsoft Access Databases to see only the database files in the current folder or Microsoft Access Projects to see only the list of projects.

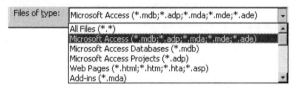

Once you have tracked down the database you want to open, double-click the name or select it and click Open.

The Open button offers other ways to open the database such as read-only, exclusive, or both. You will learn more about these options in later chapters.

Open the Sample Database

To get started working with a database in Access 2003, let's open the Northwind sample database that comes with Microsoft Office 2003. The database is installed on your hard drive during typical installation and usually is stored in the Program Files\Microsoft Office\Office\Samples folder.

TIP

If you don't have the Northwind database installed, you may need to reinstall Access and add the sample database. Also, if you don't want to be greeted by the Northwind welcoming screen every time you open the database, check the "Don't show this screen again" check box before you click OK.

The Northwind database is an order processing application that demonstrates the power and usefulness of a relational database. Although the focus seems simple enough—taking and filling orders from customers for the company products—a lot of data actually is involved.

1. To open the Northwind sample database, start Access and click More in the opening New File task pane on the right side. (Of course, if it is already showing in the list of files recently opened including the one you want to work with, just click the filename.)

2. Click the "Look in" arrow at the top of the dialog box and click on C: to revert to the root directory of your hard drive. (If Access is installed on another drive, choose that one instead.)

3. In the list of folders and files in the C: directory, double-click Program Files. Program Files now appears in the "Look in" text box, and a list of the subfolders and files in that folder shows in the window.

4. Continue to open the folders for the Program Files\Microsoft Office\Office\Samples path. If you have installed Office 2003 in a different directory, use that pathname.

5. Select Northwind and click Open. If the Northwind Traders welcoming screen appears, click OK to close the screen.

6. If you are greeted by the Main Switchboard, click the Display Database Window button to open the Northwind Database window (see Figure 1-3).

In the next section, watch for the difference between the Access window with the menu bar and toolbars and the Database window, which contains lists of all the objects in the database and has a separate command bar.

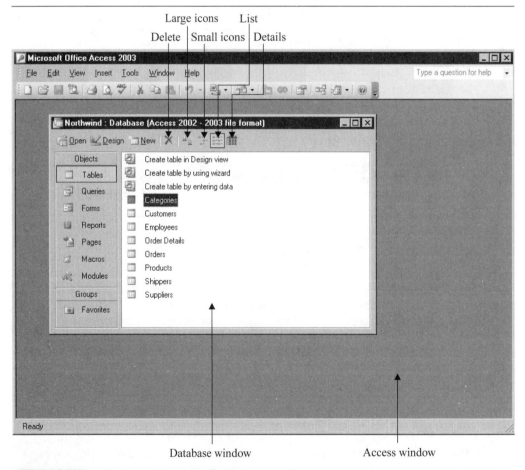

FIGURE 1-3　The Northwind sample database in the Database window

Tour the Database Window

The Database window represents the database itself. When you close the window, you also close the database. You can see all the components of the database in the Database window. The left pane of the Database window shows a set of buttons grouped under the Objects button. The buttons are labeled with the names of the Access database objects: Tables, Queries, Forms, Reports, Pages, Macros, and Modules.

Another title button named Groups includes buttons that open other folders such as the Favorites folder. Groups can be quite useful if your database is used by more than one department, such as personnel and marketing. Each department can have a group of database objects that it can use, such as favorite reports and data entry forms.

In Access 2003, you don't have to stick with Favorites; you can define and name your own custom groups. A user-defined group can contain any type of Access objects as well as objects from other Office applications, just like the Favorites group. When you click Groups, the Objects list collapses and the list of your custom groups appears in its place.

The Database window is made up of several pages, each represented by a button in the left pane under Objects. Clicking on an object button opens the page, where you can see the names of all the existing objects of that type.

The Toolbar

The toolbar you see at the top of the Database window (not the Access window) includes buttons to open an existing object to view or modify, create a new object, or delete an existing object. You also can change how the Database window lists the objects.

You can list the objects using large or small icons in alphabetical order by name or another arrangement. Additionally, with the object name, you can show details such as a description, dates created and modified, and type; viewing such details helps when you're trying to find the most recent report. Each of these options is available by clicking a button on the Database window command bar or by selecting from the View menu.

The Object Pages

Each object page also has its own toolbar with a set of buttons appropriate to that object type. All the object pages include the Design and New buttons. The first button on the toolbar depends on the object page you are on. Select the object you want to work with and click one of the buttons on the page toolbar:

- To work on an object design, click the Design button.
- To start a new object, click the New button.
- To open the table, query, form, or page, click the Open button.
- To preview the report, click the Preview button.
- To run the macro, click the Run button.

In addition to listing the objects, each object page (except the Macros and Modules pages) includes two or three shortcut items that you can double-click to start the process of creating a new object. For example, the Tables page, as shown earlier in Figure 1-3, has the following three items in the list:

- Create table in Design view
- Create table by using wizard
- Create table by entering data

You'll learn more about using these features in Chapter 3.

Look at Menu Options and Toolbar Buttons

While you are bouncing around in the Database window, you might as well take a look at the menus and toolbar buttons. The standard Database menu bar and toolbar appear in the Access window. Not all the options are available to all of the database objects, and some, such as the Save button, are not available until a table or other object is opened. It also makes sense that the Paste button is dimmed until you have copied something to the clipboard.

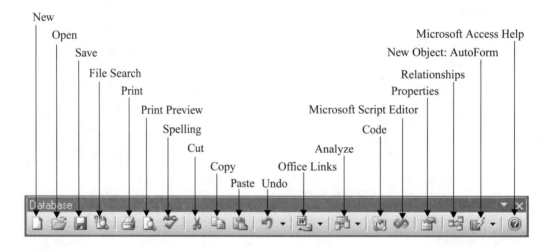

TIP *If you don't see the toolbar, right-click in the menu bar and select Database in the list of available toolbars.*

To see what a toolbar button will do, rest the mouse pointer on the button and look at the ScreenTip that appears briefly. A lot of the menu commands and toolbar buttons also have shortcut keys that might show in the ScreenTip or with the menu command name. See Chapter 16 for more information about showing shortcut keys on menus and toolbars.

You can move the menu bar and toolbar to different locations in the window. You can dock them at another edge or let them be free floating. To move either one, click the move handle located at the far-left edge of the bar (it looks like a stack of dots). Then drag the bar away from the top of the window to another edge or leave it in the center of the window. Drag the bar borders to resize the floating bar.

To restore the menu bar to the top of the screen, click and drag the move handle at the left end of the bar. To restore the floating toolbar, drag it by its title bar to the top of the window.

Use Shortcut Menus

Shortcut menus didn't get that name by accident—they really are shortcuts to a lot of actions. Shortcut menus are context-sensitive menus that appear when you click the right mouse button. The commands in the menu depend on where the mouse pointer is and what is going on when you click the button. Click anywhere outside the menu to close it.

Figure 1-4 shows the shortcut menu that appears when you right-click in a blank area of the Database window. Only the most commonly used commands are included in the shortcut menu, but they also might include commands from several different menus on the menu bar.

To choose a command from a shortcut menu, click the command or type the letter that is underlined in the name of the command, called the *access key*. If the command shows a right arrow, such as View in Figure 1-4, it is a submenu that contains more commands. Rest the pointer on the item to open the list of commands, then choose one from the list. If the command shows an ellipsis (…), as Import does, it opens a dialog box when you click it.

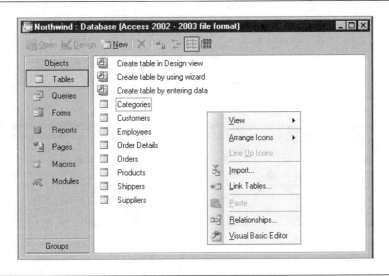

FIGURE 1-4   Choosing from the database shortcut menu

See Chapter 16 for information on how to get wild and crazy with menu bars, toolbars, and shortcut menus to create your own workplace style.

Open a Table

Nothing much happens in an empty Database window, so let's take a look at some real table data. To open one of the tables in the current database, double-click its name in the Tables page or select the name and click Open. The table appears with the data in rows and columns much like a spreadsheet. This view of table data is called *Datasheet view*.

Figure 1-5 shows the open Northwind Orders table in Datasheet view. Each row contains a single record with the information for one order. Each column contains values for one field. Each field has a unique name—for example, OrderID—and contains a specific item of data, such as the customer name or order date.

Another way to open a table is to right-click the table name in the Tables page, then choose Open from the shortcut menu. This menu features other commands that will be useful later on.

Scroll box   Scroll arrow

		Order ID	Customer	Employee	Order Date	Required Date	Shipped Date
+		10481	Ricardo Adocicados	Callahan, Laura	20-Mar-1997	17-Apr-1997	25-Mar-1997
+		10482	Lazy K Kountry Store	Davolio, Nancy	21-Mar-1997	18-Apr-1997	10-Apr-1997
+		10483	White Clover Markets	King, Robert	24-Mar-1997	21-Apr-1997	25-Apr-1997
+		10484	AB's Beverages	Leverling, Janet	24-Mar-1997	21-Apr-1997	01-Apr-1997
+		10485	LINO-Delicateses	Peacock, Margaret	25-Mar-1997	08-Apr-1997	31-Mar-1997
+		10486	HILARIÓN-Abastos	Davolio, Nancy	26-Mar-1997	23-Apr-1997	02-Apr-1997
+		10487	Queen Cozinha	Fuller, Andrew	26-Mar-1997	23-Apr-1997	28-Mar-1997
+		10488	Frankenversand	Callahan, Laura	27-Mar-1997	24-Apr-1997	02-Apr-1997
+		10489	Piccolo und mehr	Suyama, Michael	28-Mar-1997	25-Apr-1997	09-Apr-1997
+		10490	HILARIÓN-Abastos	King, Robert	31-Mar-1997	28-Apr-1997	03-Apr-1997
+		10491	Furia Bacalhau e Frutos do Mar	Callahan, Laura	31-Mar-1997	28-Apr-1997	08-Apr-1997
+		10492	Bottom-Dollar Markets	Leverling, Janet	01-Apr-1997	29-Apr-1997	11-Apr-1997
+		10493	La maison d'Asie	Peacock, Margaret	02-Apr-1997	30-Apr-1997	10-Apr-1997
+		10494	Comércio Mineiro	Peacock, Margaret	02-Apr-1997	30-Apr-1997	09-Apr-1997
+		10495	Laughing Bacchus Wine Cellars	Leverling, Janet	03-Apr-1997	01-May-1997	11-Apr-1997
+		10496	Tradição Hipermercados	King, Robert	04-Apr-1997	02-May-1997	07-Apr-1997
+		10497	Lehmanns Marktstand	King, Robert	04-Apr-1997	02-May-1997	07-Apr-1997

Orders : Table

Record: ⏮ ◀ 50 ▶ ⏭ ▶* of 830

Scroll bar   Scroll arrow

FIGURE 1-5   The Northwind Orders table in Datasheet view

Take a Tour of the Datasheet View

You probably noticed that some changes occurred in the window when you opened the table. For example, the title bar of the Database window now shows the name of the open table. The menu bar includes two new options, Format and Records, that are relevant to the open table. More of the toolbar buttons also are available. The status bar at the bottom of the Access window displays the description of the current field that is included in the table definition. For example, if the cursor is in the first field, Order ID, the status bar displays "Unique order number."

The Table Datasheet Toolbar

If you look closely, you also will notice that the Database toolbar has been replaced by the Table Datasheet toolbar, which has many new buttons.

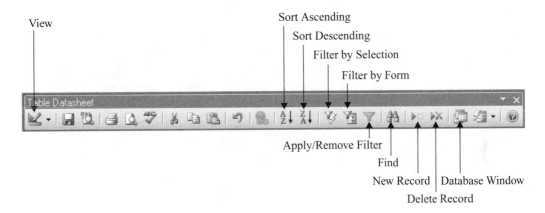

If you right-click anywhere on the toolbar, you will see that the Table Datasheet option is checked in the shortcut menu. This is a sure way to tell which toolbar is visible on the screen. You can also choose other toolbars from the list to show in addition to or instead of the default toolbar.

To scroll to a particular record in the table, drag the scroll box to that record. As you drag the scroll box, a helpful ScreenTip appears next to the pointer. It tells you the number of the current record and the total number of records in the table.

TIP

+	10578	B's Beverages	Peacock, Margaret	24-Jun-1997	22-Jul-1997
+	10579	Let's Stop N Shop	Davolio, Nancy	25-Jun-1997	23-Jul-1997
+	10580	Ottilies Käseladen	Peacock, Margaret	26-Jun-1997	24-Jul-1997
+	10581	Familia Arquibaldo	Leverling, Janet	26-Jun-1997	24-Jul-1997
+	10582	Blauer See Delikatessen	Leverling, Janet	27-Jun-1997	25-Jul-1997
+	10583	Wartian Herkku	Fuller, Andrew	30-Jun-1997	28-Jul-1997
+	10584	Blondel père et fils	Peacock, Margaret	30-Jun-1997	28-Jul-1997

Record: 326 of 830

Navigate among Records and Fields

You need to be able to get to your data if you want to enter new information or edit existing records. As always, you can choose from several ways to move the cursor around the records and fields in your table, including simply clicking in the desired location if it is visible. You should try them all and settle on the one that works for you. The other methods are as follows:

- Selecting Edit | Go To
- Clicking the record navigation buttons at the bottom of the datasheet
- Using keystrokes such as TAB and the arrow keys

Choosing Edit | Go To allows you to move to the first, last, next, previous, or an empty, new record.

The record navigation buttons at the bottom of the datasheet window give you the same options as the Edit | Go To submenu. You can also enter a specific record number (if you know the number of the record you want to see) in the text box between the navigation buttons and then press ENTER. This area also tells you what record the cursor is in and the total number of records in the table.

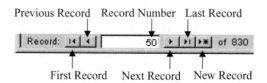

If this is a filtered subset of the table, the word "(Filtered)" appears after the total number of records, which is the number of records remaining after the filter has been applied.

Shortcut Keys

If you are mousephobic, you can use the shortcut key combinations to move around the datasheet once you get used to the correlation between the keys and the resulting cursor movement. Here are some examples of what happens when you press various key combinations:

- The up or down arrow moves to the same field in the previous or next record.
- Right arrow or TAB moves right one field in the same record. If you are in the last field in the record, the cursor moves to the first field in the next record.
- Left arrow or SHIFT-TAB moves left one field in the same record. If you are in the first field in the record, the cursor moves to the last field in the previous record.
- PGUP or PGDN moves up or down one screen of records.
- HOME or END moves to the first or last field in the same record.
- CTRL-HOME or CTRL-END moves to the first field of the first record or the last field of the last record.

Check Out the Subdatasheet

In a relational database, it is important to be able to view information related to the current data on the screen. The related data is displayed in a *subdatasheet,* which can easily be opened. If the records shown in Datasheet view display a plus sign at the left end of the row, there is additional information in another table in the database that is related to that record. To see this data, expand the subdatasheet by clicking the plus sign. The plus sign changes to a minus sign when the subdatasheet expands. To collapse the subdatasheet, click the minus sign.

You can expand as many subdatasheets as you want in a single Datasheet view. Each subdatasheet contains records that correspond to one record in the datasheet. You can expand them individually or set a table property that automatically expands all of the subdatasheets when the table opens in Datasheet view. See Chapter 3 for information about setting tables and other properties.

Figure 1-6 shows the Northwind Orders table with two subdatasheets expanded to show the products from the Order Details table, which were included in two of the orders in the Orders table. Notice the plus and minus signs that indicate the current state of the subdatasheet.

If fields have not been specified to link records in the subdatasheet with records in the datasheet, you will see all the records in the related table when you expand the subdatasheet. See Chapter 2 for more information about relating tables and what that can do for you.

Expand subdatasheet

Order ID	Customer	Employee	Order Date	Required Date	Shipped Dat.
10248 Wilman Kala	Buchanan, Steven	04-Jul-1996	01-Aug-1996	16-Jul-19
10249 Tradição Hipermercados	Suyama, Michael	05-Jul-1996	16-Aug-1996	10-Jul-19
10250 Hanari Carnes	Peacock, Margaret	08-Jul-1996	05-Aug-1996	12-Jul-19
10251 Victuailles en stock	Leverling, Janet	08-Jul-1996	05-Aug-1996	15-Jul-19

Orders : Table

Product	Unit Price	Quantity	Discount
Gustaf's Knäckebröd	$16.80	6	5%
Ravioli Angelo	$15.60	15	5%
Louisiana Fiery Hot Pepper Sauce	$16.80	20	0%
*	$0.00	1	0%

Order ID	Customer	Employee	Order Date	Required Date	Shipped Dat.
10252 Suprêmes délices	Peacock, Margaret	09-Jul-1996	06-Aug-1996	11-Jul-19
10253 Hanari Carnes	Leverling, Janet	10-Jul-1996	24-Jul-1996	16-Jul-19
10254 Chop-suey Chinese	Buchanan, Steven	11-Jul-1996	08-Aug-1996	23-Jul-19

Product	Unit Price	Quantity	Discount
Guaraná Fantástica	$3.60	15	15%
Pâté chinois	$19.20	21	15%
Longlife Tofu	$8.00	21	0%
*	$0.00	1	0%

Order ID	Customer	Employee	Order Date	Required Date	Shipped Dat.
10255 Richter Supermarkt	Dodsworth, Anne	12-Jul-1996	09-Aug-1996	15-Jul-19
10256 Wellington Importadora	Leverling, Janet	15-Jul-1996	12-Aug-1996	17-Jul-19
10257 HILARIÓN-Abastos	Peacock, Margaret	16-Jul-1996	13-Aug-1996	22-Jul-19
10258 Ernst Handel	Davolio, Nancy	17-Jul-1996	14-Aug-1996	23-Jul-19

Record: |◄| ◄| 1 |►| ►I| ►*| of 830

Collapse subdatasheet

FIGURE 1-6   Viewing subdatasheets in the Orders table in Datasheet view

Get Help When You Need It

No matter how easy Access makes database management, you can't possibly remember how to do every task. That's where the Access Help feature comes in. There are two ways to get help with what you are doing:

- Use the Ask a Question box
- Use the Microsoft Access Help task pane

The Ask a Question box is always available in the upper-right corner of the menu bar so you can always get help, no matter where you are or what you're doing in Access. It shows the "Type a question for help" message.

 The Help menu is always on the menu bar as well. The Help button is also available on all built-in toolbars.

Ask a Question

You can use the Ask a Question box to get help quickly. Simply type a key word or phrase in the box, press ENTER, and the Search Results task pane displays a list of relevant topics (see Figure 1-7).

Scroll down the list and click on the one that matches your question. The Help window opens and displays the text of the topic you chose. The topic often includes expandable items such as "Predefined calculations that use aggregate functions," as shown in Figure 1-8. To see the whole subtopic, click the expand arrow at the left of the selection.

If you want to see all the subtopics expanded, click the Show All link at the top-right of the window. In addition to the list of subtopics, you may see many terms showing in a different color, which indicates they're expandable to show definitions and other short explanations. These are also expanded when you click Show All. You can also expand them individually by clicking the colored term. To collapse a single item, click it again. To collapse all the items, click the Hide

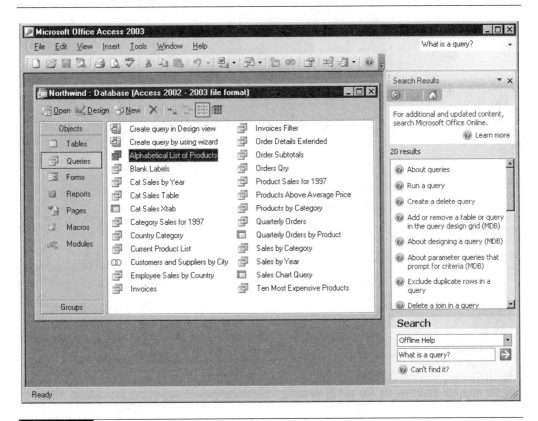

FIGURE 1-7 Looking at the Search Results task pane

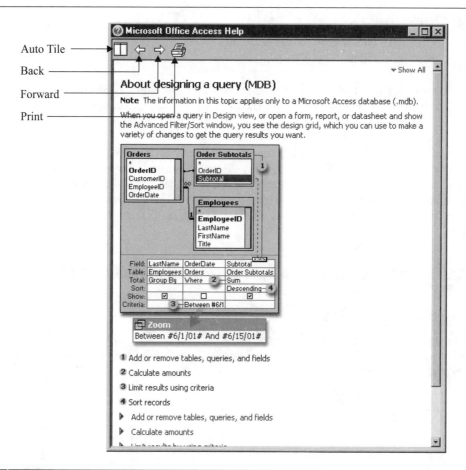

FIGURE 1-8 Viewing the selected Help topic

All button, which has replaced the Show All link. All items automatically collapse when you move to another topic.

The four buttons in the Help page do the following:

■ The Auto Tile button tiles the Help window vertically with the Search Result task pane so you can select another topic without closing the Help window.

■ The Back and Forward buttons move among recently accessed Help topics.

■ The Print button opens the Print dialog box so you can print the current Help topic.

If you are working in a different language, your version of Access may not support the Ask a Question feature.

Use the Microsoft Access Help Task Pane

You have four ways to open the Microsoft Access Help task pane (see Figure 1-9):

■ Press F1.

■ Choose Help | Microsoft Access Help.

■ Click the Help toolbar button.

■ If you already see a Task pane, click anywhere in the Task pane title bar and choose Help from the list of available Task panes.

FIGURE 1-9   Opening the Microsoft Access Help task pane

If you have selected an object or other item before pressing F1, you may see a brief definition of the selected item rather than the Help task pane.

You can use the Help task pane to search for a topic. Type specific words or phrases in the Search box and click the right-pointing arrow button.

If you want to browse through the Help file table of contents, click the Table of Contents hyperlink. The Table of Contents displays a list of topics marked with the closed book icon. Click these to expand the topics into individual Help articles (see Figure 1-10).

If you are currently connected to the Internet, you also have access to all the up-to-date Help topics. Additional online help includes assistance, training courses, the latest product updates, clip art and media, and a research library.

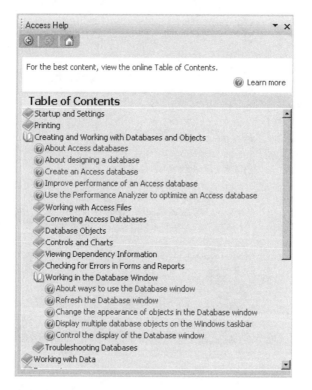

FIGURE 1-10   Viewing the Help Table of Contents

Ask the Office Assistant

If you want a little variety, you can activate the Office Assistant by choosing Help | Show the Office Assistant. When the assistant appears, click on the character to open a balloon asking "What would you like to do?" Type your question in the balloon and click Search. This functions much like typing your question in the Ask a Question box. You'll see a list of relevant topics in the same Search Results task pane as before and you can choose one to open the Help window.

NOTE   *If you have not installed the Office Assistant, you will see a dialog box asking whether you want to install it now. Click Yes and you will be prompted to insert the Microsoft Office CD.*

To remove the Office Assistant from the screen, choose Help | Hide Office Assistant or right-click the character and choose Hide from the shortcut menu. If you get tired of the paper clip, you can choose from six other characters. See Chapter 13 for information about customizing the Office Assistant and other features of the Access workplace.

Ask What's This?

Most of the Access dialog boxes include the What's This? tool, which gives you quick and short information about a specific element or choice in the box. Activating the What's This? help feature is a two-step process. First, click the ? button in the dialog box title bar. The mouse pointer changes to an arrow accompanied by a question mark. Then, click the element you want to know more about.

To return the mouse pointer to its normal state without openingWhat's This?, press ESC.

Get Help with What You're Doing

Without opening the Help window, Access gives you many hints and clues while you're working. The status bar offers information about the current activity or position of the cursor. Many design windows include hint boxes that tell you about aspects of the design. Other windows and dialog boxes include samples or previews of the selections made.

For example, when you are working in the table Design window, status bar information tells you how to move around the Design view and get help. The hint box on the right describes what should appear in the Field Name column.

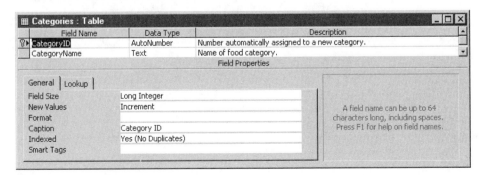

Chapter 2

Create a Database

How to...

- Design an efficient database
- Create a database with the Database Wizard
- Run the new application
- Start a new database from scratch
- Start a new database from Windows

The information in a relational database system is distributed among related tables to optimize information storage and retrieval. Common fields relate the tables so that information can be extracted and presented in useful ways. If properly designed and constructed, a database can be an essential tool in managing personal or business information.

Design an Efficient Database

The design process begins with an analysis of the tasks that will be required of the database. First, find out what the system is intended to do for the prospective users. Interview each user and get thorough descriptions of their expectations. It is essential to keep in mind that the design process also is an iterative one: as the users get used to a new system, they can think of more features they can use such as an additional data entry form, a special query, or a calculated field.

The database design process can be broken down into seven steps, each with specific goals and products, such as data entry forms, reports, analytic tools such as charts and graphs, and other end user requirements:

1. Determine what the users want from the database and what data is needed to provide the basis for those results.

2. Plan the data distribution among the related tables in the database.

3. Identify the fields for each table.

4. Assign a unique field for each table to ensure that no two records are the same.

5. Determine how the tables are related to one another.

6. Review the design and step through procedures with users.

7. Create tables and enter data.

NOTE *Although numbering the steps in a process implies that one step is completed before the next begins, in reality the design process is more fluid, with each step overflowing into the next. You can return to a previous step anywhere along the line.*

We will use the Home Tech Repair database as our first relational database example. Home Tech Repair is a small company that specializes in maintenance and improvement of home structures. Its specialties are electrical, plumbing, structural, painting, and heating and air conditioning systems in the home. Figure 2-1 shows an example of the manual record keeping system in use before the development of the Access database.

Home Tech Repair

Order #_____   Date/Time_____

Customer_____

Address_____

_____

Phone _____   Taken by_____

Description   _____

_____

_____

_____

Bid Number_____   Total Bid_____   Date_____

Supervisor_____

Work in Progress   Date Started_____

Date Finished_____   Supervisor_____

Labor			Costing Data	
Hours	Rate	Cost	Parts	_____
_____ x _____ = _____			Sales Tax _____	
_____ x _____ = _____			▬▬▬▬▬▬	
_____ x _____ = _____			Sub Total _____	
_____ x _____ = _____			Labor _____	
_____ x _____ = _____			▬▬▬▬▬▬	
Total Labor: _____			Total _____	
Cost Estimate _____ Date _____			Amount Paid_____	

FIGURE 2-1   The Home Tech Repair manual work order record

Determine the Goals of the Database

A poorly designed database is of less than no value. The more time spent on task and data analysis, the better the results will be. To begin the database design, start at the end point. Find out what the end user expects of the database, then go about structuring the design to provide these requirements.

To do so, answer the following questions:

- What do the users want to get from the database?
- What kinds of reports are needed (how do users want the information arranged and summarized)?

Then follow these directions:

- If adequate data collection forms already exist, use them as patterns for the Access forms.
- Look at other databases that address similar information management situations and see whether they can provide any guidance with the design of your own.
- Once the tasks have been defined, develop a list of the required data items.

The main purpose of the Home Tech Repair database is to maintain up-to-date information about current work orders. To do this, it must relate the individual work orders to specific customers or employees. It also must include forms for data entry and viewing of all table data.

In addition to the work order tracking, the owner would like to be able to conduct financial analyses; for example, to determine how much revenue has been generated by each employee or to review the total sales on a monthly basis. These analyses can include summary reports with charts and graphs depicting trends and proportional distributions of types of jobs over a period of time. Such studies are helpful when planning for future work.

Distribute the Data Among the Tables

Distributing data is the cornerstone of relational databases. The efficiency and effectiveness of such a database relies on the proper distribution of data among the tables that make up the database. This is not as easy as it sounds, but here are some guidelines to follow:

- The information in a table should be limited to a single subject. This allows you to maintain data about each subject independently of the others.
- Tables should not contain duplicate information among its records. With only one copy of each data item, you need to update it in only one place.

In the Home Tech Repair case, employee and customer information is repeated on several manually prepared work order sheets. To reduce the redundancy, pull out both sets of information and put them in separate tables. Keeping payments in a separate table will add flexibility, especially if the work is paid for in installments, such as a deposit at the start of the contract and the remainder while the work is being completed.

If specific parts are routinely used, such as plumbing fixtures or electrical devices, the list should be kept in a separate table. The data in the parts table can be accessed by the form or report that brings the work order expenses together.

Other peripheral data can be included in separate small tables, such as shipping or payment methods. The Home Tech Repair company information also can be kept in one separate place, accessible to the report that prints the invoice. This table can include the company address, phone and FAX numbers, Internet address, and any short standard message to include in correspondence.

Identify the Data Fields

All the fields should relate directly to the subject and not include any information that can be derived from other fields. Include all the information you need—nothing extra. Break up the information into small, logical parts, such as First Name and Last Name fields, rather than a single Full Name field. Name the fields so you will be able to locate specific records and sort by individual field values. You can always combine the fields later for finding and searching if you need to.

Table 2-1 lists the fields in each of the Home Tech Repair tables and shows the type, the size, and a brief description of the data that will be stored in the field.

After arranging the data in the tables, review the distribution carefully to remove any redundancies and make sure all fields in each table apply directly to that subject. For example, the overhead and the total work order costs are calculated fields, and thus are not included in the Workorders table.

Field	Data Type	Field Size	Description
Workorders Table			
Workorder Number	Number	Integer	Uniquely identifies work order
Customer ID	Text	50	Customer name
Bid Number	Text	5	Original bid number
Start Date	Date	N/A	Scheduled start date
Completion Date	Date	N/A	Expected completion date
Supervisor	Text	20	Name of employee in charge
Principal Worker	Text	20	Name of employee who is second in charge
Helper	Text	20	Name of helper
Material Cost	Currency	2 decimals	Cost of materials
Labor Cost	Currency	2 decimals	Cost of labor
Description	Memo	N/A	Description of work order
Drawing	Hyperlink	N/A	File of drawing, as required

TABLE 2-1   Distributing Data Among Home Tech Repair Tables

Field	Data Type	Field Size	Description
Employees Table			
Employee ID	Number	Integer	Uniquely identifies employee
First Name	Text	20	Employee's first name
Last Name	Text	25	Employee's last name
SSN	Text	10	Social Security Number
Specialty	Text	25	Special labor skills
Address	Text	50	Employee's home address
City	Text	50	City
State	Text	2	State
ZIP	Text	9	ZIP code
Work Phone	Text	12	Office phone or pager
Pager	Text	12	Home phone
Hourly Rate	Currency	2 decimals	Salary hourly rate
Billing Rate	Currency	2 decimals	Customer's billing rate
Comments	Memo	N/A	Additional information
Badge Picture	OLE Object	N/A	Employee picture
Customers Table			
Customer ID	Number	Integer	Uniquely identifies customer
First Name	Text	20	Customer's first name
Last Name	Text	25	Customer's last name
Billing Address	Text	50	Address to send bill to
City	Text	50	City
State	Text	2	State
ZIP	Text	9	ZIP code
Phone Number	Text	12	Customer's phone
FAX Number	Text	12	Customer's FAX number
Notes	Memo	N/A	Additional customer information

TABLE 2-1   Distributing Data Among Home Tech Repair Tables *(continued)*

Specify Key Fields

Each of the three main tables of the Home Tech Repair database has a field that uniquely identifies a record: Workorder Number, Employee ID, and Customer ID. The values in these fields can be entered by the user or assigned by Access in the form of an incremental AutoNumber.

If the number has no other significance, such as identifying the general location of the job, let Access enter the number and you can be sure there are no duplicates. If you don't already have a unique field, plan on asking Access to assign a special AutoNumber field to act as the primary key so you can be sure each record in the table is unique.

Define Table Relationships

To relate two tables, you use common fields. The linking field in the main table usually is the primary key field—for example, the Customer ID field in the Customers table. The linking field in the other table is called the foreign key and usually is not a primary key—for example, the Customer ID field in the Workorders table. The linking fields need not have the same names but should be the same data types and contain matching values.

The relationship between the Customers and Workorders table is one-to-many because one customer might contract for more than one job. The relationship between the Employees table and the Workorders table also is one-to-many because one employee can work on more than one job at a time and in one of three slots in a single job.

Figure 2-2 shows the Home Tech Repair tables in the Access Relationships window. The field lists have been lengthened to display all the fields. There are three instances of the Employees table in the Relationships window because it is linked to three separate fields in the Workorders table. The figure also shows a fourth table, Bid Data, which we can add later.

Chapter 4 contains information about working in the Relationships window and defining relationships.

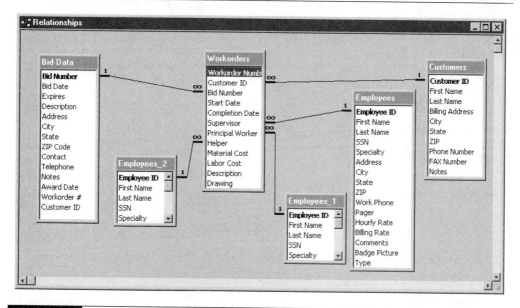

FIGURE 2-2   The Home Tech Repair tables

You Can Relate Tables Three Different Ways

One-to-Many

This is the most common relationship between tables. One record in one table can have many matching records in another table. The table on the "one" side often is called the *parent* table and the other is the *child* table. For example, the Customers table would have one record for each customer, whereas the Workorders table might have more than one work order for the same customer. Both tables would include a field with a value that represents that specific customer and links the two tables.

One-to-One

This relationship is more like a lookup tool in which each record in one of the tables has a matching record in the other table. Both tables have the same standing and neither table is designated as the parent. The key fields in both tables are the primary keys. One good use for this type of relationship is to store in the first table additional, seldom-referenced information about an item, such as an abstract of a book or the details of a work order.

Many-to-Many

The many-to-many relationship is not exactly permitted as such in a relational database. Many records in one table have the same values in the key field as many records in the second table. If you relate tables in this way using Access, you must create a third table, called a *junction table,* to place between the first two, then relate the two original tables to the junction using two one-to-many relationships. For example, the relationship between the Employees and the Customers tables is many-to-many, and the Workorders tables could serve as a junction table between them.

Complete the Database

Now is the time to consult with the users for additional comments and suggestions. Step through the operations you plan to carry out with the information. Then, armed with the "go-ahead," do the following:

1. Enter just enough data to test the application. You can complete the tables later.

2. Create the forms, reports, and queries. If the database is for inexperienced users, you can add a switchboard and other custom tools to make their jobs easier.

NOTE
A switchboard is the user's main interface with the database and displays a list of actions the user can take. Clicking on an item in the list opens a data entry form, previews a report, or offers the chance to change items on the switchboard.

3. Carefully test the entire system. Time spent refining and verifying the design can save time revising the database after it has been populated with data.

After the design is established, Access gives you three ways to create a new database:

- Starting with the Database Wizard
- Starting from scratch with a blank database
- Starting from Windows

Create a Database with the Database Wizard

If you don't want to bother designing your own database and if you need a database for a common personal or business purpose, the Database Wizard can get you started. Once you have built the database with the help of the wizard, you can add your own data and make modifications to the queries, forms, and reports that came with the turnkey application.

To start the Database Wizard, do either of the following:

- If you are just launching Access, choose Create a New File in the Open section of the Getting Started task pane and then choose On My Computer in the Other Templates section of the New File Task pane.

- If you are already running Access, whether you have another database active or not, choose File | New or click the New toolbar button, then select from the New File Task pane as previously mentioned.

The Templates dialog box has two tabs: General and Databases. The General tab initially contains the Blank Database option; a Blank Data Access Page template; and two blank project templates, one for an existing database, and one for a new database. The Databases tab (see Figure 2-3) contains ten database templates for prefabricated applications ranging from a list of categorized expenses to a complex event management system. You can also click the templates on Microsoft.com to browse online templates.

You can scroll through the sample templates on the Databases tab to find one close to the system you want. As you highlight each icon, the Preview pane shows an image reflecting the template style. Looking through the icons, it seems the Service Call Management database would match the Home Tech Repair requirements most closely.

Preview the Database Templates

The Service Call Management database used as a template in this chapter includes nine related tables to contain all the relevant data. To start the Database Wizard:

1. Double-click the Service Call Management icon on the Databases tab of the Templates dialog box, or select the icon and choose OK.

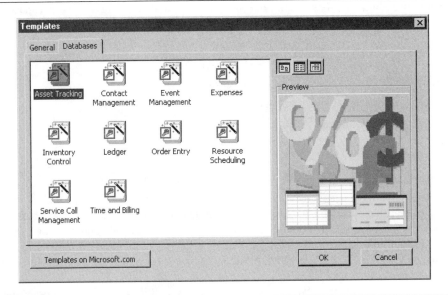

FIGURE 2-3 The Databases tab shows predefined database templates.

2. In the File New Database dialog box, specify the location for the database file and give it a name or accept the suggested name.

3. Click Create to continue with the wizard.

A blank Database window appears briefly while the wizard is looking for the database elements in the template; then a window appears listing the contents of the tables that will be in the design. Figure 2-4 shows the opening Database Wizard screen for the Service Call Management database.

If you want to see what kind of information another template has to offer, click Cancel. Then repeat the steps with the other template.

Work with the Wizard

Once you have selected the basis for your database—asset management, membership maintenance, order control, or whatever—the wizard leads you through a series of design steps. You have a chance to customize your database to a limited degree during this process. After the wizard is through, you have a lot more flexibility with the design.

To continue creating the Home Tech Repair database with the Service Management template as the basis, choose Next to accept the template.

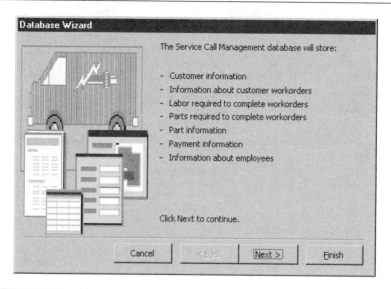

FIGURE 2-4   The information the database will include

Remember that if you change your mind or forget to select a particular option, you can always return to previous dialog boxes by clicking Back.

Add Optional Fields

The second wizard dialog box displays the list of tables that will appear in the Home Tech Repair database. You have no choice about the table list, but you can add more fields than the wizard has planned. As you highlight each table name, a list of fields appears in the right box.

The field names that appear in regular font are required fields and are already checked; optional fields appear in italic and are not checked. Checking an optional field adds it to the table. Figure 2-5 shows the CCAuthoriz. # field as an optional field that can be added to the Payment information table. Click Next to move to the third dialog box.

Choose Form and Report Styles

The next two dialog boxes give you a choice of ten different screen displays and six report styles. As you select an option, a sample appears in the Preview pane on the left.

The same screen display and report style formats also are available when you are working on a form or report design.

After choosing the screen display and report style you want, choose Next to continue with the wizard.

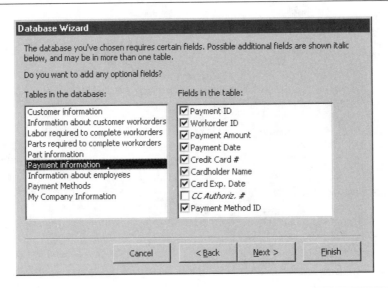

FIGURE 2-5   Adding an optional field to a table

Name the Database and Add a Picture

In the last wizard dialog box, you can give the database a special name that will appear in the switchboards and the title bar; you also can include a picture. The picture you specify in this dialog box will automatically appear in the header of all the reports generated by the wizard. If you don't select the picture in this dialog box, you have to add it individually to each report later.

To add a picture:

1. Check the "Yes, I'd like to include a picture" option and click the Picture button.

2. Browse in the Insert Picture dialog box for the folder that contains the picture you want.

3. Click OK to add the selected image and return to the previous dialog box.

4. Choose Next, then click Finish to start the new database.

As the wizard is constructing the database, you can see the process in the background behind the odometers. After a while, a message appears asking for your company name, address, and related information. Click OK and fill in the dialog box. When you close the form, the Main Switchboard for the new database appears on the screen (see Figure 2-6). This is the main user interface for working with the database.

When the wizard is finished, you have a complete database application, with all the relevant reports, forms, and queries. All you need to do is input your data.

Figure 2-7 shows the structure of the application the Database Wizard created with the Service Call Management template. The Main Switchboard leads to several forms for entering

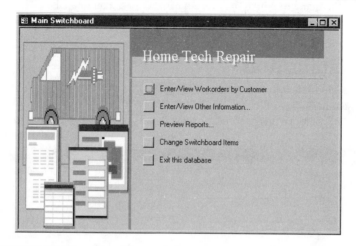

FIGURE 2-6   The Home Tech Repair Main Switchboard

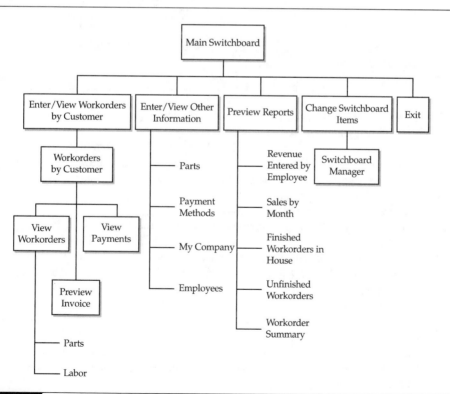

FIGURE 2-7   The application structure

and viewing table data, many of which include data from more than one table. The application also includes five reports that present and summarize current information.

Run the New Application

The Home Tech Repair application automatically displays the Main Switchboard at startup. The first option opens the main form for the application, Workorders by Customer, where you can enter new work orders, edit existing records, or view details of specific work orders.

Before trying to run the new application, you need to enter some data. Enter a few records in the Customers, Employees, and Workorders tables.

To see individual work order information, select the work order in the subform and click the Workorders command button. The information contains specifics about a single work order, including the employees who worked on the job, their billing rate, and the hours spent. The costs are calculated and displayed with payments credited to the work order and the remaining balance computed. Close this form to return to the previous form.

To see the payment history of a specific work order, select the work order and click the Payments button. To preview an invoice for the work order, click the Preview Invoice button.

The third option in the main switchboard opens a second switchboard listing the other data entry forms that you can use. Figure 2-8 shows the list of reports that are designed and included in the Home Tech Repair application. Most of them require some user entry, such as a time interval, to create the report.

Many changes are required to have the wizard's database conform to the needs of the Home Tech Repair Company. Some fields are unnecessary and should be removed; others are renamed. Additional forms and reports that depend on different queries, filters, or sort orders might be necessary. All of these changes can be made to the Home Tech Repair database built from the Service Call Maintenance template.

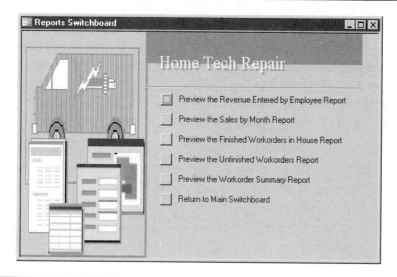

FIGURE 2-8   The Reports Switchboard

> When you let the wizard create your database, many of the components are linked together by common fields. If you try to change field names in a table, they also must be changed in any query, form, or report that refers to that field name. The wizard does not let you customize the field names during the building process.

Start with a Blank Database

If the Database Wizard doesn't have any templates that come close to the database you have in mind, you can create your own by starting with a blank one and adding the tables you need one at a time. Once you have the skeleton database, you can import objects from other databases or create the tables and other objects yourself.

First, let's start by creating a new blank database as follows:

1. Click the New toolbar button or choose File | New, then select Blank Database on the New File Task pane (or press CTRL-N).

2. As before, the File New Database dialog box opens, where you can enter a name for the new database and specify the folder in which you want to store it. Access opens the most recently opened folder or, if you have just launched Access, the My Document folder. Then it gives a unique name to the new database, such as db1, db2, db3, and so on.

3. After entering a custom name for the new database and opening the folder where you want to store the database, click Create.

An empty Database window opens (see Figure 2-9) showing the Tables page with nothing but the three startup tools. The first thing to do when starting a new blank database is to create one or more tables that will contain the data. You have already planned the distribution of data among the tables, so now is the time to build the tables. To start a new table, do one of the following:

- Click New on the Database window toolbar.
- Double-click "Create table in Design view"
- Double-click "Create table by using wizard"
- Double-click "Create table by entering data"

You'll find more information about creating and modifying tables in Chapter 4.

NOTE

If you are just starting Access and want to create a new blank database, click Blank Database in the Home Task pane.

In the next chapter, you will learn how to create and modify new table structures. The many field properties that determine the appearance and behavior of the data are also discussed. Additionally, you will learn how to improve the value of the information in a database by adding validation rules, default field values, and other features.

FIGURE 2-9   The new Database window

Chapter 3

Create and Modify Tables

How to…

■ Create a table with the help of the Table Wizard

■ Create a table from scratch in Design or Datasheet view

■ Modify a table design

■ Ensure data validity

■ Copy an existing table structure

Tables are the essential building blocks of a relational database; the development of a database begins with building the tables to store the distributed data. If you carefully design your table structures, you can have a smooth-running, error-free information system instead of a total disaster.

Create a Table with the Table Wizard

In Access, a wizard is only a click away, no matter what sort of help you want. Creating a new table is no different. The quickest way to start the Table Wizard is to double-click the "Create table by using wizard" item in the Tables page of the Database window. You can also begin a new table structure with the Table Wizard by clicking New, choosing Table Wizard from the New Table dialog box, then clicking OK.

Choose a Table and Add Fields

The Table Wizard offers help with many typical table structures in two categories: business and personal. Each of these tables comes with a list of appropriate sample fields. You can accept the fields the wizard suggests, add some optional fields that the wizard provides, then add your own special fields later in the table Design view. You also have the option of renaming the fields while you are selecting the tables and fields with the Table Wizard.

To use the Table Wizard to rename fields while selecting tables and fields:

1. Start the Table Wizard and view the list of sample tables in the first dialog box (see Figure 3-1).

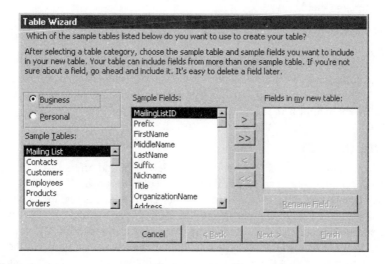

FIGURE 3-1   The first Table Wizard dialog box

2. There are actually two lists of sample tables. Click the Business or Personal radio button, whichever suits your purpose.

3. Scroll down the list of sample tables and select the one that most closely matches your requirements.

4. Add some or all of the sample fields to your new table.

5. To include (or remove) all the fields, click the double right (or left) arrow button.

6. To add (or remove) one field at a time, select the field name and click the single right (or left) arrow button.

TIP   *You are not limited to the fields in the one sample table you have chosen. Fields from other tables can be added to the new table list. Just select another sample table and choose some fields from that. Don't worry if you discover you have added unnecessary fields; they are easy to take out.*

The fields will appear in the table design in the order in which you select them from the list, so it pays to plan ahead. If you have placed them in the wrong order, you can remove one or more and reinsert them or you can rearrange them later in Design view. A field will be inserted below the currently selected field in the new field list.

You also have the opportunity to rename the fields while you are creating the table design. To rename a field:

1. Select the field in the "Fields in my new table" list.

2. Choose Rename Field.

3. Edit the name or enter a new one.

4. Click OK.

Figure 3-2 shows the Table Wizard dialog box where a new Customers table is under construction and the default ContactFirstName field is being renamed to First Name. After you have selected all the names you want to appear in the table, click Next.

Set the Primary Key

The second Table Wizard dialog box lets you name the new table and offers to set a primary key for you. You can accept the default sample table name or enter your own. If you choose for the wizard to set the primary key, it chooses an AutoNumber field if there is one in the table design. If not, the wizard adds a new AutoNumber field to the table. If you want to set your own primary key, choose the second option, "No, I'll set the primary key," then choose Next. If you choose to set your own key, the next dialog box asks you to name the field you want to use as the primary key and to specify the type of data the primary key field will contain:

■ Automatically assigned consecutive numbers

■ Numbers you will enter

■ Numbers and/or letters you will enter

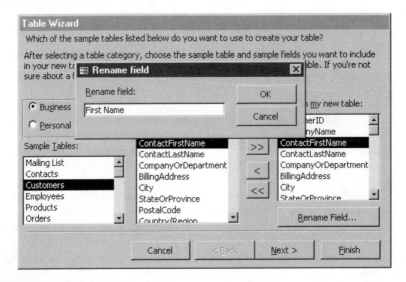

FIGURE 3-2   Renaming a field for the new Customers table

The first option defines the field you selected as an AutoNumber data type. The other two options rely on you to guarantee unique values in the primary key field.

Relate to Existing Tables

In the next dialog box (see Figure 3-3), the wizard inquires about the relationship of the new table to the tables already in your database. The wizard looks at the field names and makes a guess at the relationships between the new table and the existing tables based on the same names and data types. To define a new relationship, select the appropriate "not related to" statement and click the Relationships button.

In the Relationships dialog box, you can choose the type of relationship that will exist between the new table and the table you selected. Notice that Access is quite specific about the one-to-many relationship because it knows that the Customers table has the Customer ID field as the primary key, so it must be the parent table. The Bid Data table also has a field named Customer ID, but it is not the primary key, so it must be the child table.

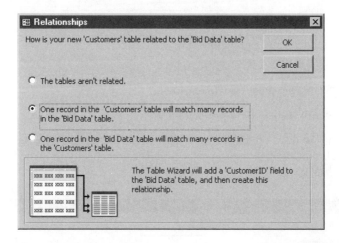

NOTE *If there is an obvious similarity between fields in the new table and those in an existing table, Access might assume a relationship exists; in this case, the dialog box will say "related to" instead of "not related to." If this happens, you can accept the link or delete the relationship by selecting the statement and clicking Relationships. If you specify a relationship between two tables that do not have a field name in common, Access copies the primary key field name to the child table to use as the foreign key and then creates the relationship.*

After clicking OK in the Relationships dialog box, return to the Table Wizard, where you can relate the new table to other existing tables.

In the final dialog box, you have three choices:

■ Go directly to the table Design view to make changes.

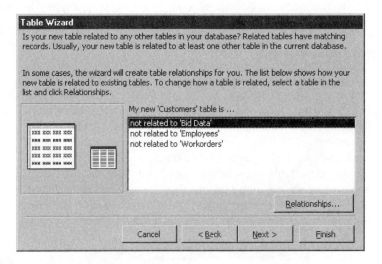

FIGURE 3-3 Examining existing relationships

- Open the table in Datasheet view to enter data.
- Use the wizard to create a form for data entry.

After making this last decision, click Finish. The wizard creates an AutoForm when the third choice is selected. This means that the data entry form is automatically formatted by the wizard. There is no data to display yet.

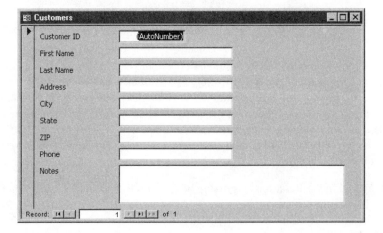

Create a Table from Scratch in Design View

The easiest way to start a new table from a blank table design is to double-click the "Create table in Design view" item in the Tables page of the Database window. You can also click the New button, select Design View in the New Table dialog box, then click OK. An empty table appears in the table Design window, as shown in Figure 3-4.

Tour the Table Design View

You have two panes to work with in the table Design window. The upper pane is the field entry area where you enter the field name, the data type, and an optional description. You can also specify in the upper pane the field that will serve as the primary key for the table. The lower pane is devoted to specifying the individual field properties for the field selected in the upper pane. Properties such as size, display appearance, validity rules, and many more appear in the list.

The list of properties you see depends on the type of field you are entering. To the right of the Field Properties pane is a description of the currently active area of the screen.

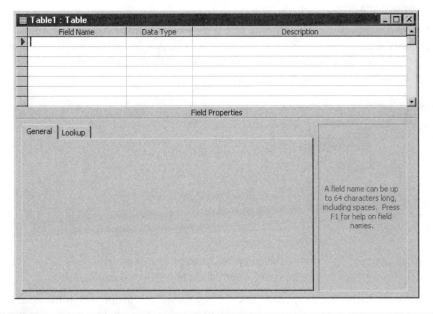

FIGURE 3-4   The empty table in the Design window

There are some new buttons on the Table Design toolbar that relate to the task of creating and modifying a table definition.

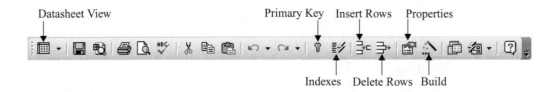

Add Fields

To begin adding fields to your new table, do the following:

1. Click in the first row of the field entry area and type the first field name. Field names can have up to 64 characters including letters, numbers, and spaces; however, do not begin a field name with a space. You also cannot use any of the characters to which Access attaches special meanings, such as a period, exclamation mark, grave accent, and square brackets.

2. Press TAB and choose an appropriate data type from the Data Type drop-down list. Because the most commonly used field type is Text, Access automatically specifies a new field as a Text field by default. To change it to another type, select from the drop-down list in the Data Type box.

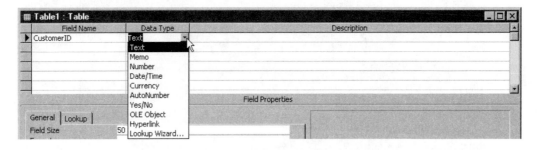

3. Enter an optional description that can provide additional information about the field. The description appears in the status bar when the field is selected in a datasheet or form.

4. Move to the Field Properties pane and change the default properties, if necessary. Otherwise, repeat steps 1 through 3 to add other fields. You can also press F6 to jump back and forth between the field list and the property pane.

TIP *Once you get used to the names of the available data types, you can simply type the first letter of the type name and Access will fill it in.*

Specify Field Data Types

Several factors come into play as you decide what data types to use; for example:

- What kind of values do you plan to allow in the field?
- What are you going to do with the data? You can count the number of records containing a specific value in a field specified as most of the data types, but you can add up values only from Number and Currency fields.
- Will you want to sort or index records? You can sort or index on any field type except Object Linking and Embedding (OLE) Objects.
- Will you want to group records for a report or query? You can group on any field type except Memo, Hyperlink, and OLE Object fields.

 You can use the Access Field Builder to help add new fields to your table. Simply click in an empty row in the table design and click the Build toolbar button (the one that looks like a magic wand). The Field Builder contains the same sample table and field lists as the Table Wizard.

The following sections introduce you to each of the ten data types and how they are used.

Text   The Text data type is the most common data type and can contain any combination of up to 255 characters and numbers. The default size is 50. You would use the Text type for storing values that contain combinations of numbers and letters such as addresses and job descriptions. If you expect the field to contain more than 255 characters, consider instead using the Memo field type, which can contain much more data.

Memo   Use a Memo field to store long but variable-length text possibly relating to the other field data. Of course, not every record will include memo data, but when one does, the text can vary in size from a few words to up to 65,535 characters.

Number   Select the Number data type when you plan to sort based on the values or use them in calculations, such as adding up the labor hours for a plumbing job or the hours that a certain employee has worked during the fall season. Fields that contain numbers but will never be used in calculations are better specified as Text data types.

If you are working with dollar sales figures, it is better to use a Currency type because you can choose from several monetary display formats.

Currency   Use the Currency type when you want to store monetary values, such as the cost and bid price of contracted jobs. You can use Currency fields, just like Number fields, in arithmetic calculations.

AutoNumber   When you specify an AutoNumber field, Access guarantees that each record in the table has a unique value in the field, thereby creating a field that you can use confidently as a primary key. Access generates a unique value for the field as you enter each new record.

Date/Time   The Date/Time type is very useful when you want to be able to sort records chronologically by the value in the field. You can also use a Date/Time field in calculations to determine elapsed time. With the Date/Time data type, you also have a variety of ways to display the data—for example, 25-Dec-2003, 12/25/2003, or December 25, 2003.

Yes/No   The Yes/No field is useful when you want the equivalent of a check mark in your records. For example, suppose you want to know if a transaction has been posted or a job has been completed. By default, a Yes/No field appears as a check box control in a datasheet and in forms and reports. You can choose to display Yes or No, On or Off, or True or False. You can also create your own custom display for Yes/No fields.

OLE Object   When you want to embed or link an object from another source in your table, use an OLE Object type field. With this type of field, you can acquire data from such objects as an Excel spreadsheet, a Word document, a graphics or sound file, or other binary data.

Hyperlink   When you want the field to jump to another location or connect to the Internet or an intranet, store the hyperlink address in a Hyperlink field. The hyperlink can link to a web address (URL), a file on your own computer, or a file on an intranet or LAN. A hyperlink field contains four parts: the text to display, the target address, a subaddress if necessary, and an optional ScreenTip.

Lookup Wizard   The Lookup Wizard is not exactly a data type. It is a wizard that creates a field that is limited to a list of valid values. When you select this option, a wizard helps you create the list and actually attaches it to your table. You can type in the values you want to use or have the Lookup Wizard consult another table for the set of valid values. When you enter table data, you can choose the value you want from a drop-down list.

Set Field Properties

You can set field properties to control how the values in the field are stored and displayed. Each type of field has a particular set of properties. For example, you might want certain currency values displayed with two decimal places, a dollar sign, and a comma as the thousands separator. Or, you could specify that the currency values be rounded off to the nearest whole dollar.

> TIP   *When you click in a field property, you can see a description of the property in the lower-right pane of the table Design view. You can also press F1 to see the related Help topic.*

Access attaches some default properties to every field. You can accept or change the settings to customize your fields. Because Text fields are the most common and most of the field properties apply to the Text data type, let's take a look at their properties first. Table 3-1 describes the properties of a Text field, most of which are also available to other types of fields, although they will have different default settings for different data types.

To specify a property setting:

1. Select the field in the field entry pane (the upper portion of the window) in Design view.

2. Click the desired property in the Field Properties pane.

TIP   *You can also press F6 to move to the Field Properties pane then use the Up and Down keys to move among the properties.*

3. If you see a down arrow next to the property, click it to display a list of property options from which you can choose. In most cases, you can also type in the setting you want.

Other properties, such as Input Mask and Validation Rule, include a Build button that appears as a button displaying three dots (...) to the right of the property text box, which you can click to get help with the property. If you don't need help building an expression, you can just type it in the property box. If the expression is invalid, Access will let you know.

Property	Effect
Field Size	Specifies the maximum number of characters allowed in the field. Default is 50. Maximum is 255 characters.
Format	Determines the display appearance, such as forcing uppercase or lowercase characters. No default format is specified for text fields.
Input Mask	Provides a template for data that follows a pattern, such as telephone numbers or Social Security Numbers, and adds literal characters to the field if you want. Used to control data entry. Default is none.
Caption	Displays a name other than the field name in datasheets, forms, and reports. Default is none.
Default Value	Automatically enters the specified value in the field. Default is none.
Validation Rule	Specifies an expression that will check for invalid data. Default is none.
Validation Text	Displays this message if the entered data fails the validation rule. Default is none.
Required	Indicates that this field may not be left blank. Default is No.
Allow Zero Length	Differentiates between a blank field and a field containing an empty string of text (""). Helpful when a value is known not to exist (such as a FAX number). Default is Yes.
Indexed	Indicates that the table is indexed on this field. Default is No.
Unicode Compression	Allows string data that now is stored in Unicode format to be compressed to save storage space. Default is Yes.
IME Mode	Sets the IME (Input Method Editor) mode for a field when focus is moved to it. IME is a program that enters East Asian text into programs by converting keystrokes into complex East Asian characters. Default is No Control.
IME Sentence Mode	Sets the type of IME sentence. Default is None.
Smart Tags	Specifies which Smart Tags to apply to the field. Smart Tags are new to Access and provide links to other information about the field.

TABLE 3-1   Text Field Properties

Choose a Field Size

The Text, Number, and AutoNumber field types are the only ones for which you can specify a field size. Access automatically sets field sizes for the other types. A text field that will contain only a few characters, such as a postal code or job number, doesn't need to take up the default 50 characters of disk space. You can change the size of the field by entering a different number in the Field Size property. Another reason to specify the field size is to prevent data entry errors by limiting the number of characters that can be entered.

Number fields are sized a little differently; they specify the name of the number layout rather than the number of characters. The options are:

- **Byte** Stores small positive integers (whole numbers) between 1 and 255
- **Integer** Stores larger positive and negative integers, between –32,768 and +32,768
- **Long Integer** Stores the default Number field size, which is used to store even larger integers between roughly –2 billion and +2 billion
- **Single** Stores single-precision floating-point numbers in IEEE format
- **Double** Stores double-precision floating-point numbers in IEEE format
- **Replication ID** Stores a global unique identifier (GUID)
- **Decimal** Makes the Precision and Scale properties available to control number entries

NOTE *AutoNumber fields are limited to Long Integer and Replication ID field sizes.*

If you change the size of a Number field, you change only the way that numbers are stored, not the appearance of the numbers. To change their appearance, you need to change the Format property.

Format Field Data

The Format property is used to specify the appearance of the value when displayed; it has no effect on the way the value is stored nor does it check for invalid entries. A format makes sure that all the field values look alike no matter how you entered the data.

When you set a field's Format property in Design view, Access applies that format to the values in Datasheet view and in any new forms and reports based on the table. Fields that were added to the form or report design prior to setting the custom formats are unaffected. Table 3-2 describes the custom formatting symbols that can be used with all data types.

Other custom formatting symbols are valid for only specific data types as described in the following paragraphs.

Text and Memo Fields Text and Memo fields use the same format symbols, some of which are character placeholders that apply to individual characters; others affect the entire entry. Table 3-3 describes the symbols you can use with Text and Memo field data.

3

Symbol	Effect
!	Enters characters from left to right instead of right to left, forcing left alignment.
(Space)	Enters a space as a literal character when the SPACEBAR is pressed.
"xyz"	Displays the characters or symbols within the quotation marks.
*	Fills available space with the character that follows.
\	Indicates that the character that follows should be treated as a literal character. The back slash is often used with reserved symbols and characters.
[color]	Displays the field data in the color contained within the brackets. You can use black, blue, green, cyan, red, magenta, yellow, or white.

TABLE 3-2   Custom Formatting Symbols

Custom Text and Memo format settings can have two sections, separated by a semicolon. The first section applies to fields containing text and the second to fields that are blank.

The following are some examples of using the Text and Memo format settings:

Format Setting	Entered As	Displays
@@@@-@@-@@@@	123456789	123-45-6789
@@@@@@-&&&&	92118	92118-
>	Jimmy	JIMMY
<	JIMMY	jimmy
@@\!	Hello	Hello!
@@;"No Data"	horse	horse
@@;"No Data"	(blank)	No Data

Number and Currency Fields   You can format your Number and Currency data with one of Access's predefined formats or create your own using the special formatting symbols. The Format property of a Currency field is automatically set to Currency but you can change it to any of the other settings. The Format property of a Number or Currency field displays a list of the predefined formats as described in Table 3-4.

Symbol	Effect
@	Indicates that a character or a space is required
&	Indicates that a character or a space is optional
<	Converts all characters to lowercase
>	Converts all characters to uppercase

TABLE 3-3   Text and Memo Format Symbols

Setting	Effect
General Number	Displays the number as entered. This is the default setting for Number fields.
Currency	Displays the number with a currency symbol and thousands separator. Negative values appear in parentheses. Default is two decimal places. This setting is the default for Currency fields.
Euro	Displays the number with the Euro currency symbol and a thousands separator. Negative values appear in parentheses. Default is two decimal places.
Fixed	Displays at least one digit. Default is two decimal places.
Standard	Displays the thousands separator. Default is two decimal places.
Percent	Displays the value multiplied by 100 with an added percent sign (%). Default is two decimal places.
Scientific	Uses standard scientific notation with exponents. For example, 243 displays as 2.43E+02.

TABLE 3-4   Number, AutoNumber, and Currency Predefined Formats

TIP   *When you specify the Percent format for a number field, you have to change the Field Size property from the default Long Integer to Single. Otherwise, the field displays only the integer portion of the number you enter and leaves off the fraction. For example, if you enter 1, the field will display "100.00%," but if you enter 1.25, the field will still display "100.00%."*

Date/Time Fields   Date/Time fields include seven predefined format settings and some symbols you can use to create your own custom formats. Table 3-5 describes the formats that Access

Setting	Description
General Date	Combines Short Date and Long Time settings. This is the default setting. If no time is specified, then only the date is displayed; if no date is displayed, only the time is displayed. Examples: 5/21/04 3:30:00 PM (US) 21/5/04 15:30:00 (UK)
Long Date	Uses the Long Date Regional setting. Examples: Monday, May 21, 2004 (US) Monday, 21 May 2004 (UK)
Medium Date	Example: 21-May-04
Short Date	Uses the Short Date Regional setting. Examples: 5/21/04 (US) 21/5/04 (UK)
Long Time	Example: 3:30:00 PM
Medium Time	Example: 3:30 PM
Short Time	Example: 15:30

TABLE 3-5   Date/Time Predefined Format Settings

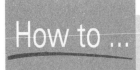

Include Literal Characters with Date/Time Values

You can use characters other than the date and time separators with the Date/Time values, to present dates and times with text. Enclose the text and spaces in quotation marks. Some examples of using these special formatting symbols are:

Setting	Displays
ddd", "mmm d", "yy	Thurs, Jan 15, 04
dddd", "mmmm d", "yyyy	Thursday, January 15, 2004
h:n:s AM/PM	9:15:35 AM

In addition, you can add other characters to the display format by enclosing them in quotation marks. For example, entering the value **5/21/04** in a field with the format setting

"Today is " dddd " in week number " ww "."

displays

Today is Friday in week number 21.

Notice the spaces within the quotation marks that separate the characters in the string from the date values and the period added to the end of the expression.

provides. Date and Time format settings are specified according to the setting in the Regional Setting Properties dialog box in the Windows Control Panel.

You can create almost any display format using special characters to represent the hour, minute, and second in a time format and the day, week, month, and year in a date format. For example, the letter *d* can display the day of the month as one or two digits or as the full name, depending on how many *d*'s you use in the string. The letter *m* can also be used to represent the month from one or two digits to the full name. Refer to the Access Help topic "Format Property–Date/Time Data Type" for details of the many formatting symbols you can use with Date/Time fields.

Yes/No Fields   Access automatically displays a default check box control when you specify a Yes/No data type and ignores any format settings you make.

To change a Yes/No field Display Control property:

1. Open the table in Design view.

2. Select the Yes/No field.

3. Click the Lookup tab in the Field Properties pane.

4. Select Text Box from the Display Control list.

5. Return to the General tab to choose the desired display format.

The Yes/No custom format contains up to three sections separated by semicolons. The first section is not used, but you still need to enter the semicolon before entering the second section. The second and third sections specify what to display when the value is Yes and No, respectively. For example, the format

```
;"Yes, indeed!"[Green];"No, never!"[Red]
```

displays

```
Yes, indeed!
```

in green when the value is Yes, and

```
No, never!
```

in red if the value is No.

 If you choose Combo Box as the Display Control property instead of Text Box, more properties appear on the Lookup page, where you can set the appearance and values of the list that the combo box will display. For more about using combo boxes and lookup lists, see Chapter 5.

Set the Number of Decimal Places

The Field Size, Format, and Decimal Places properties of Number and Currency fields are all related. The Field Size property determines whether the number is stored as an integer or with fractional values and specifies the degree of mathematical precision.

The Format property adds display features such as dollar or percent signs and commas as thousands separators.

The Decimal Places property determines how many digits to display to the right of the decimal point in a Number or Currency field. The default Decimal Places setting for Number and Currency fields is Auto, which displays two decimal places for fields with Format property settings of Currency, Fixed, Standard, Percent, and Scientific. If you want to change the number of Decimal Places in the display, click the arrow in the Decimal Places property box and choose a number from the list or just enter the number you want. The Decimal Places setting has no effect on the precision of the stored number, only on the display.

If the value is stored as an integer (Byte, Integer, or Long Integer data type), you will see only zeros to the right of the decimal point—whatever you set in the Decimal Places property. If you kept the default Long Integer property, the values will be rounded to the nearest integer no matter how many decimal places you specify for the display.

To change the number of decimal places stored in the field, change the Field Size property to one of the settings for real numbers, such as Single, Double, or Decimal.

Include a Caption

If someone else will be using the database and you think the field names are not descriptive enough, you can use the Caption property to change the column heading in the Datasheet view. A caption can contain up to 2,048 characters in any combination of letters, numbers, special characters, and spaces.

The new caption will also appear in queries and replace the text in the field labels attached to controls in report and form designs. The field names remain the same; only the labels show the new caption text.

 If you rename the field later in Datasheet view, the Caption property is deleted. To prevent this, rename fields only in table Design view.

Choose a Primary Key

In a relational database system, it is important to be able to gather and retrieve related information from separate tables in the database. To do so, each record in one table must be unique in some way. The field or fields that contain the unique value is the *primary key*. Access does not permit duplicate values in the primary key nor does it permit blanks. There must be a valid, unique value in the primary key in every record.

Set a Single-Field Primary Key

You saw how the Table Wizard picked a primary key; now it's your turn. If your table has a field that you are sure will not contain any duplicate values, you can use that field as the primary key. The AutoNumber field type is an Access tool that can guarantee unique records in a table.

Designating an AutoNumber field as the primary key for a table probably is the simplest way to set the key. You don't have to worry about inadvertently entering duplicate values because Access uses unique numbers to identify each record. Once the number is generated, it can't be changed or deleted.

 In the table Design view, click in the field row that you want to use as the primary key, then click the Primary Key toolbar button or choose Edit | Primary Key. To remove the primary key designation, repeat the step.

Set a Multiple-Field Primary Key

If you can't guarantee that the values in a single field will be unique throughout the table, you can combine two or more fields as the primary key. For example, a list of customers might include several with the same last name (or even some with the same first and last names); this field cannot be used as a primary key, but you can combine first and last names with date of birth to create unique values.

To set a primary key that combines two or more fields:

1. Hold down CTRL while you select each field. If the fields are contiguous in the list, select the top field row and hold down SHIFT while you select the last field you want to include.

2. Click the Primary Key button. Key icons appear in each row that is included in the multiple-field primary key. The table has a three-field primary key that includes the first and last names with the ZIP code.

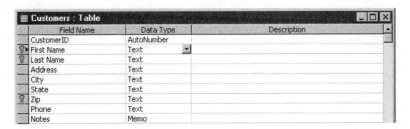

The multiple-field primary key is constructed in the same order as the fields in the table structure. If a different field order is necessary, you can rearrange the fields in the Indexes window. Read more about working in the Indexes window in the section "Modify or Delete an Index."

Create Other Indexes

Indexes help Access find and sort records faster just as an index helps you find topics in a reference book: an index contains a pointer to the location of the data rather than the data itself. The primary key in a table is automatically indexed, so the indexes that you can create are secondary indexes created with other fields. An index can include a single field or multiple fields.

To help you decide which fields to use as indexes, look at the fields you expect to search frequently or by which you will want to sort. Also, if you expect to use a field to create a relationship with another table, you might want to create an index on the field to improve performance.

A field that has many records containing the same value is not a good candidate for an index because an index on such a field won't speed things up much.

Add a Single-Field Index

To set a single-field index, simply change its Indexed property to Yes and decide whether to permit duplicate values.

To take a look at the indexes that have been specified for a table, click the Indexes toolbar button or choose View | Indexes. The Customers table includes two currently defined indexes. The primary key, Customer ID, is listed with the key icon as the first index and a single-field index based on the customer's last name as the second. Notice that the primary key properties, shown in the Index Properties pane, specify the index as Primary with Unique values and that the Ignore Nulls property is marked No.

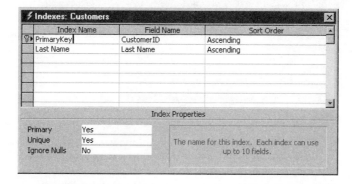

Create a Multiple-Field Index

Often, you might want to search or sort records based on more than one field at once. Creating a multiple-field index allows you to do just that. When you sort records using a multiple-field index, the records are sorted initially by the first field in the index. If Access finds duplicate values in the first field, it sorts by the next field, and so on. For example, you want to see records for customers in particular areas of the city. To do this, you can create an index using both the City and ZIP code fields.

To create a multiple-field index, follow these steps:

1. With the Customers table open in Design view, click the Indexes toolbar button.

2. Click in the first empty row in the Indexes window.

3. Enter a name for the new index, such as **City Region**, then press TAB to move to the Field Name column.

4. Click the down arrow and select City from the list of available fields.

5. Accept Ascending as the sort order for the City field and click in the Field Name in the next row (leaving the Index Name blank because both fields will be used in the same index).

6. Choose ZIP from the field list and change the sort order, if necessary.

7. If the index is intended to be the primary key, set the Primary property to Yes. (You will have to click the first row of the index containing the index name to display the Index Properties pane.) If you want the index to contain unique values for each record, change the Unique property to Yes. If you want the index to ignore Null values, change the Ignore Nulls property to Yes.

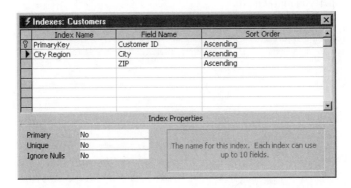

8. Close the Indexes dialog box and then save the changes to the table.

You can specify up to ten fields in one index with a mixture of ascending and descending orders for the fields.

Create a Table in Datasheet View

You don't have to be in Design view to create a new table; you can do it right in Datasheet view by entering data directly into a blank datasheet. Access automatically analyzes the data you enter and assigns the appropriate data type and format to the field. If there is any ambiguity, the field is considered to be a Text field.

To begin a new table in Datasheet view:

1. Double-click the "Create table by entering data" item in the Database window.

2. A blank datasheet opens displaying ten columns and 21 rows. The columns are named Field1, Field2, and so on.

3. Enter the field names in each column by double-clicking the column header and replacing the default Field*n* caption. If you enter the fields in the wrong order, you can change the order in Design view later.

4. Enter the field data for each record, then click Design view.

5. Switch to Design view, then save and name the table. Access will offer to assign a primary key when it saves the new table or you can designate one in Design view.

Figure 3-5 shows the design of a table created in Datasheet view.

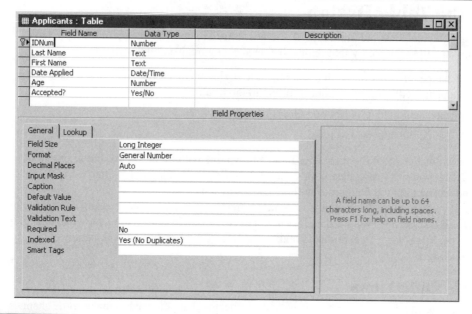

FIGURE 3-5 The design of a table created in a Datasheet view

Access has automatically assigned data types to the fields depending on the data you entered. The excess fields have been eliminated from the design.

Save the Table Design

The table design does not have to be complete before you save it. In fact, it is a good idea to occasionally save the design during the design process to guard against catastrophes. But Access does require you to save the design before you can switch to Datasheet view to enter data. To save the table design, click the Save button or choose File | Save. The first time you save a new table, Access prompts you for a name.

The table name can have up to 64 characters in any combination of letters, numbers, and spaces. It may not begin with a space, however. You can include special characters except those that have a special meaning to Access, such as a period (.), exclamation point (!), accent grave (`), or brackets ([]). You cannot use any control character with an ASCII value between 0 and 31.

TIP *If you want to undo the changes you have just made to the table design, close the table design and respond No when Access asks whether you want to save the changes.*

Modify the Table Design

Even though you have tried to include all the necessary features and properties in your table design, you will undoubtedly find things that need changing. You might want to:

- Change the order of the fields in the table so that the ones you want to see most often appear on the screen without scrolling to the right.
- Add a new field or delete one that is not needed.
- Change the field size or type.

You can make any of these changes to an empty table with no problems, but after you have entered data, you risk losing data with some of the changes. Adding fields, increasing a field size, and rearranging the field order will not cause any data loss.

But if you decide to delete a field or reduce a field size in a table that already contains data, Access will display a warning if data loss might occur. Problems can also occur when changing a field type. It is always a good idea to make a backup of the data before making any changes to the table design.

Switch Table Views

If you are entering data in Datasheet view and you decide that you need to make some changes in the table structure, you can quickly return to the Design view by clicking the View (Design) button or choosing View | Design View.

Add or Delete Fields

You can add a new field to the bottom of the list of fields or insert one anywhere among the existing fields. To add one to the bottom, click in the first blank field and enter the field definition. To insert a field among existing fields, click in the row below where the new one is to appear, then click the Insert Rows toolbar button or choose Insert | Rows.

The new blank field row is inserted above the row that contains the cursor, and all the fields below are moved down one row. The insertion point is in the new row.

> **TIP**
>
> *Another way to add a new field, one that will inherit the same properties as one already in your table, is to copy the existing field to the clipboard, then paste it in an empty row. Of course, you must change the new field's name before you can save the table because no two fields can have the same name. Only the field definition is copied; previously entered data is not.*

If you want to add several rows at once, select the number of contiguous rows in the table design equal to the number of new fields you want to insert, then click Insert Rows. A number of new blank rows equal to the number of rows you selected appear above the top selected row.

When you delete a field from the table design, you are not only deleting the field name but any data that has been entered in the field. Before deleting a field that contains data, Access warns that you will permanently lose the data and asks whether you really want to delete the field.

To delete a field, in Design view click the row selector for the field (the gray button to the left of the field name) and click Delete Rows or choose Edit | Delete Rows. To delete several rows at once, select them all and delete them as a group.

 You can cause a problem by deleting a field that you have used in a query, form, or report. Be sure that you remove from the other objects any references to the field you are about to delete before you try to delete it. Access will not let you delete a field that is a link in a relationship to another table without deleting the relationship first.

Change the Field Order

If you want to change the order of fields in both the stored table and the Datasheet view, you can rearrange them in Design view. To move a field to a new position in the table design, click the row selector to select the row, then drag the row selector to move the field to its new position.

You can move several contiguous fields at once by selecting them all, then dragging them as a group. To select more than one, click in the top field row selector and drag through the row selectors until all are selected or click the top field row selector and hold down SHIFT while you click the field row at the end of the group.

Although you can select noncontiguous field rows by holding down CTRL as you select the rows, you cannot drag the group to a new position.

If you want to keep the field order in the stored table but would like to view them in a different order in the datasheet, you can rearrange the datasheet columns without disturbing the table design. See Chapter 5 for information about changing the appearance of a datasheet.

Change a Field Name or Type

You saw earlier how to change the name that appears in the column heading in Datasheet view by changing the field Caption property. You can also change the actual field name in the design. Changing the field name has no effect on the data already entered into the field. However, it might cause problems with references to the field in other objects such as queries, forms, and reports, or in an expression. To change a field name in Design view, simply type the new name. After changing the name, you must save the table again.

If there is no data in the table, you can safely change any field data type, but it is a little more complicated if the table already contains data. You might be trying to convert to a type quite different from the data already in the table. For example, you try to convert a text field to a number data type but the text fields contain alphabetic characters that are not permitted in number fields. Some types convert easily to another type, but other conversions might result in loss of data.

If data will be lost, then before making the changes, Access displays a message showing the number of values that will be affected. If you have used the field in an expression, you might need to change the expression as well.

To change a field type:

1. Click in the Data Type column.

2. Click the arrow and select the new data type.

3. Save the table design. If Access displays a warning message, respond No to cancel the changes or Yes to go ahead and make the changes. If you have no data in the table, Access doesn't display any warnings.

You will not encounter any difficulties converting other data types to text. Memo fields that are too long are truncated. Number fields convert to text with a General Number format, whereas Date/Time fields convert to text with the General Date format. Currency fields convert accurately to Text fields but without the currency symbols. Converting from text to other data types requires only that the text values conform to the new data type.

If the field you are converting is a primary key field or a unique index and the conversion would result in duplicate values, Access deletes the entire record. Access warns you first so you can prevent the deletion.

Change a Field Size

Changing the Field Size property has no effect on the data if you are increasing the size. Obviously, if you want to reduce the field size, especially for a Number field, you should make sure no values are larger than permitted by the new field size. If the values are too large to fit the new field size, they are replaced with Null values. If the new field size doesn't permit the number of decimal places currently specified, the values are rounded off.

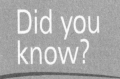

About Name AutoCorrect?

Starting with Access 2000, you no longer needed to be so careful about changing the names of fields that are used in forms and other database objects. The Name AutoCorrect feature automatically corrects most side effects that occur when you rename fields, tables, queries, forms, reports, and controls that are included in form and report designs. When you open a form or other object, Access searches for and fixes any differences between the form and the fields and controls on which the form depends. By checking the date/time stamp for the last revision of the table and the form, Access can tell whether any names have changed since the last time the form was saved. If the stamps are different, Access automatically performs Name AutoCorrect.

By default, Name AutoCorrect is automatically set on in any database you create in Access 2003. If you convert a database from a version of Access before 2000, you must turn it on in the Options dialog box. In Chapter 13, you can find more information about Name AutoCorrect and other options to customize the workplace.

Modify or Delete the Primary Key

You might find that the primary key does not always have a unique value after all and decide to use a different field or create a primary key with two or more fields.

To change the primary key, select the row you want as the primary key and click the Primary Key button. The key icon is removed from the old key field and appears in the new one.

To add another field to the existing primary key, select both the old and new key fields, then click the Primary Key button. The key icon appears in the row selector of both rows.

There might be times when you want to temporarily disable the primary key—for example, when importing records from another table, some of which might contain values that duplicate your original table. You must remove any duplicates in the new data before restoring the primary key. This has no effect on the data stored in the field designated as the key; it just removes the key field feature temporarily.

To remove the primary key designation effectively, select the primary key field and click the Primary Key button. If the key is used in a relationship, you must delete the relationship before you can remove the key.

Modify or Delete an Index

To delete a single-field index, change the field's Indexed property to No. This removes only the index; it has no effect on the field itself or the underlying data.

In the Indexes dialog box, you can add or delete fields from a multiple-field index, change the sort order for any field in the index, or change the index properties. You can also change the field order in the index.

- To remove a field from a multiple-field index, display the Indexes dialog box, select the field row, and then press DEL.

- To remove the entire index, display the Indexes dialog box, select all the rows in the index, and then press DEL.

- To insert an additional field into the index, display the Indexes dialog box, select the field below where you want the new field to appear, press INSERT, and then enter the new field name.

- To change the field order in a multiple-field index, select and drag the field selector to the desired position in the index definition.

- To change the sort order for any of the fields in the index, choose from the Sort Order list.

After making changes to the table's indexes, you must save the table.

Ensure Data Validity

You have seen how Access can ensure that the values entered in your database are valid. For example, the data type you choose for the field can limit the values to date and time values. You can also limit the number of characters in a Text field and prevent duplicate values. A direct way to ensure valid data is to set some rules that the values must obey.

You can specify two kinds of data validation rules: *field validation* and *record validation.* A field validation rule can limit the value to a few specific values or to a range of values. Access checks the rule when you try to move to another field in the same or another record. For example, a rule could limit a numeric value to a range between 1 and 100 or insist that a date value fall in 2003.

A record validation rule is handy for comparing the values in two fields in the same record. The rule is checked when you move out of a record and Access attempts to save the record. Access will not save a record with a conflict between fields. For example, a record validation rule could prevent saving a record in which the job cost is greater than the bid price. Another record validation rule could ensure that the elapsed time between dates in two separate fields does not exceed a specific value.

When either type of rule is broken, Access displays a message in a warning box that explains the violation and alerts you that you can't move to another field or record. The message you want to display is the Validation Text property in the table or field property. If you don't enter message text, Access creates a standard default message such as the one shown here.

Define Field Validation Rules

To define a field validation rule:

1. Select the field name in the upper pane of the Design window, then click Validation Rule in the Field Properties pane.

2. Type the expression you want in the property box. For example, if the value must not exceed 100, enter **<=100** (less than or equal to 100).

3. Then move to the Validation Text property box and enter the message you want to display when the rule is broken.

NOTE *The Validation Rule property has a Build button that you can use to open the Expression Builder if you need help with the expression. See Chapter 7 for information about using the Expression Builder.*

You can also include wildcards in the expression. These are the same placeholders that are used in search strings: ? stands for a single character, and * stands for any number of characters. When you enter an expression with a wildcard, Access converts it to an expression using the Like operator and adds quotation marks.

For example, if you type **C*** in the property text box, it turns into Like "C*" when you move out of the property box. This expression means that all values entered in the field must begin with the letter *C* or *c*. The expression is not case sensitive.

How to ... **Build Validation Rules**

You can set more than one criterion in a validation rule for the same field by combining them using the And or Or operators. Here are some examples of validation rules, the corresponding Access expression, and an appropriate Validation Text message:

Rule	Access Version	Typical Message
<>0	<>0	Value must not be 0 but it might be negative.
100 Or 200	100 Or 200	Value must be either 100 or 200.
C*	Like "C*"	Value must begin with "C."
C* Or D*	Like "C*" Or Like "D*"	Value must begin with "C" or "D."
C??t	Like "C??t"	Value must be four characters long, begin with "C," and end with "t."
>=01/01/04 And <01/01/05	>=#1/1/04# And <#1/1/05#	Value must be in 2004.
Not CA	Not "CA"	Field can contain any value but "CA."

A validation rule defined for a Date/Time field also includes special symbols when translated by Access. To enter a rule specifying that the date entered must be earlier than January 1, 2004, you type **<01/01/04** and Access converts it to <#01/01/04# to make sure it is not confused with a Number value.

Figure 3-6 shows the Bid Data table structure with a validation rule added to the State field. The rule specifies that the State value must be CA, AZ, or NV; if the rule is violated, the message "Bid contracts only in California, Arizona or Nevada" displays in an information box.

NOTE   *The State validation rule in the example will also cause a violation if the field is left blank because it insists on one of three values. If you want to be able to leave the field blank, add Null to the list of valid values. You can also create a more complex record validation rule that insists on a value only if there is no value in the corresponding City field (to allow for customers who deal solely over the Internet instead of by mail).*

Define a Record Validation Rule

A record validation rule is a table property rather than a field property. You can define only one record validation rule for a table, but if you want to apply more than one criterion, you can combine them in an expression using the AND or OR operators.

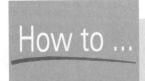 **Test the Rules**

As you add validation rules to a table, you can test them against existing data to see whether any of the field values will violate the new rule. To do this, choose Edit | Test Validation Rules or, if the Design window is not maximized, right-click in the Design window title bar and choose Test Validation Rules from the shortcut menu.

Access warns you that the process also will check the Required and Allow Zero Length properties and might take a long time and asks whether you want to do it anyway. If you respond Yes, you are told you must save the design before testing the rules. Choose Yes to save the design and continue testing. If Access finds no violations, it displays a message saying that all the data was valid for all the rules you have defined. If a violation is found, Access stops checking and displays a message indicating which rule was violated and asks whether you want to continue with the rule testing. You can then build a query to find any records that violate the rule.

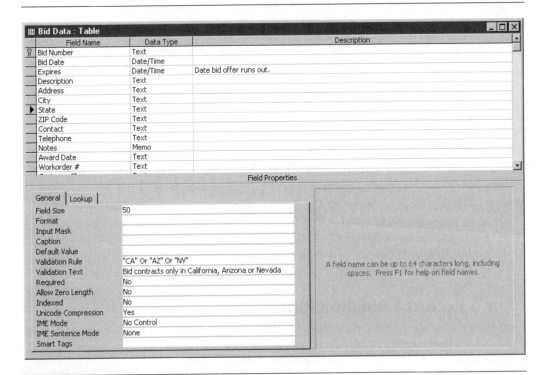

FIGURE 3-6 Setting new State field properties

The record validation rule is applied whenever you enter or edit table data. When you move to another record, Access checks the new record against the rule you defined. As with field validation rules, if you define a record validation rule for a table that contains data, Access will ask whether you want to apply it to the existing data when you save the table.

To add a record validation rule to a table:

1. Choose View | Properties or right-click in the field entry and choose Properties from the shortcut menu to open the Table Properties dialog box.

2. Enter the validation rule expression in the Validation Rule property; for example, **[Bid Date]<[Expires Date]**. Enclose the field names in brackets so Access knows you are referring to fields in your table.

3. Enter the text to display when the rule is violated in the Validation Text property— for example, **Bid date must be prior to Expires date**.

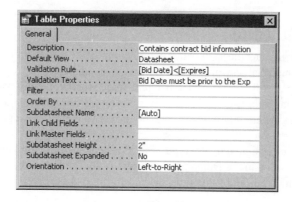

Require an Entry and Prevent Duplicates

One of the field properties is Required, which is set to Yes or No. The default value is No, but you can change it to Yes if the field should never be left blank. For example, every employee record must have a Social Security Number, so you would change the field's Required property to Yes.

You can use the Indexed property to help prevent duplicate values. A single-field primary key field already requires unique values, but you can have only one such field in a table. To require other fields to contain unique values, change the field's Indexed property to Yes (No Duplicates). If you open the Indexes window, you will see the new single-field index with its Unique property set to Yes. This works with multiple-field indexes, too. Once the index is created, change the Unique property in the lower pane of the Indexes window to Yes; then no two combinations of the values in these fields can be the same.

Handle Blank Fields

In a database, blank fields can pose quite a problem if not handled properly. It is very important to understand why the field is blank and to correct or prevent blank fields when they cause a problem.

You can use two special field properties to control how blank fields are handled. The Required property determines whether or not a blank field is acceptable. The Allow Zero Length property, when set to Yes, permits zero-length strings.

These two properties work together as follows:

- If you want to be able to leave the field blank and don't care why it is blank, set both the Required and Allow Zero Length properties to No.

- If you never want to leave a field blank, set Required to Yes and Allow Zero Length to No. You cannot leave the field without entering a value, even if it is only "Don't know" or "None."

- If you want to be able to tell why the field is blank, set Required to No and Allow Zero Length to Yes. Then you would leave the field blank if the information is not known or enter quotation marks ("") to indicate that the field doesn't apply to the current record (there is no pager).

Assign a Default Value

If one of your fields usually has the same value—for example, the City field in a list of local customers—use the Default Value property to have that value automatically entered when you add a new record. You can still change it to a different value when you enter data, but a default value can save time during data entry, especially if it is a long value such as Sacramento or Indianapolis. A newly assigned default value does not affect values already entered in the table, only new entries.

A default value can be assigned to any type of field except an AutoNumber or OLE Object. To assign one, enter the value in the Default Value property for the field. The type of value you enter depends on the data type. The value must also conform to the property settings and data type requirements.

If you assign or change a default field value after entering record data, you can change the existing values to the new value by pressing CTRL-ALT-SPACEBAR with the insertion point in the field.

Copy an Existing Table Structure

If you already have a table with a structure similar to what you need now, you can save time by copying the structure to a new table without the data. Then change the field names and properties as necessary.

To copy the table structure:

1. Select the existing table name in the Database window.

2. Click Copy on the toolbar or choose Edit | Copy.

3. If you want to copy the structure to a different database, close the current one and open the target database; otherwise, keep the Database window open.

4. Click Paste or choose Edit | Paste to open the Paste Table As dialog box.

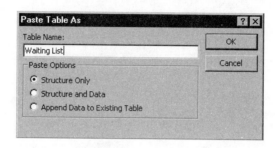

5. Enter a name for the new table and choose Structure Only, then click OK.

The new table inherits the field properties from the original table.

Chapter 4

Relate Tables

How to...

- Define a relationship
- View all relationships
- Modify and delete relationships
- Print the database relationships

There are many advantages to relating tables in a database. At the top of the list is the reduction of data redundancy. Having a single copy of each piece of information not only reduces required disk space but also speeds up processing and helps prevent errors caused by inconsistent data. You need to update the data in only one place and it is available to all forms and reports.

You can define relationships between tables at any time but the best time is when the tables are new and contain no data. When you design the database, an important step is to decide on the relationships between the tables and which fields they have in common. As you create new tables, the Table Wizard can help you define relationships or you can wait until you have all the table structures built and define all the relationships at once.

Define a Relationship

To define a relationship between two tables, specify which fields the tables have in common. In a one-to-many relationship, the field in the parent table is called the *primary key* and must be either the table's primary key or a unique index. The field in the child table is called the *foreign key* and does not need to have a unique value; however, data retrieval is faster if the child table is indexed on the foreign key.

TIP *Defining table relationships at the table level keeps the relationships active and makes the database easier to use. You can link two tables temporarily in a query when you want to draw information from more than one table, but the permanent relationship is preferred—you can break it later if necessary.*

Use Ready-Made Relationships

If you used the Table Wizard to create a new table, you might already have defined relationships with other tables in your database. As you saw in Chapter 3, when you add a new table to your database with the help of the Table Wizard, one of the dialog boxes asks you to specify how the new table is to relate to the existing tables in the database.

The database shown in the following diagram was created by adding tables to a blank database with the Table Wizard. The relationships created by the Table Wizard link the existing Employees and Customers tables to the newly created Time Billed table. The Employees and Customers tables were not linked until the Time Billed table was added to the database.

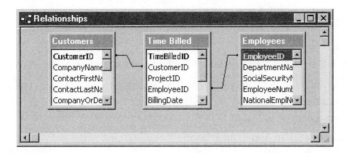

4

TIP *The sequence in which you add tables to the database determines which relationships the wizard automatically builds. If you add the Time Billed table before the Employees table, Access will not relate the Employees table to the Time Billed table.*

Use the Relationships Window

The Relationships window has all the tools you need to add a table to the relationship, relate the tables, specify the type of relationship, set up the referential integrity rules, and choose the join type. To open the Relationships window, choose Tools | Relationships or click the Relationships button on the Database toolbar.

If no relationships have been defined in the current database, the Show Table dialog box appears in a blank Relationships window. The dialog box displays a list of all the tables and queries in the current database. The Invoices table you see in the list was created from the table Design window without the help of the Table Wizard and added to the database.

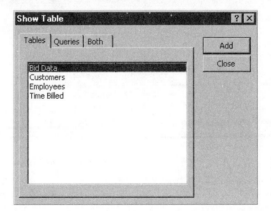

NOTE *If you have already examined the relationships between tables in this database, Access goes directly to the Relationships window without displaying the Show Table dialog box.*

To add the tables you want to relate from the list in the Show Table dialog box, do one of the following:

- Double-click the table's name or select the table and click the Add button.
- To select multiple adjacent tables, select the first table to be included, then hold down SHIFT as you select the last table in the list to be included, then click the Add button. If the table names are not adjacent in the list, hold down CTRL while you select the names.
- Click the Queries tab to add a query to the Relationships window.
- Click the Both tab to have access to a combined list of tables and queries.

When you have added all the tables and queries you want to work with in the Relationships window, click Close.

Tour the Relationships Window

The Relationships window shows the field lists of the tables you have chosen. The lists display the primary key field in boldface. Use the scroll bars to see all the fields, or resize a field list box by dragging the bottom border to see more names or the right border to see complete field names.

You also can drag the field list boxes around in the window for better viewing. In the following diagram, all four tables appear in the Relationships window; three were created earlier by the Table Wizard, and the Invoices table was created from scratch. Relationships exist only among the first three.

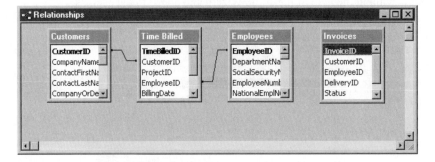

Before going on to join the tables, take a look at the new toolbar buttons on the Relationships toolbar and menu options in the Relationships window.

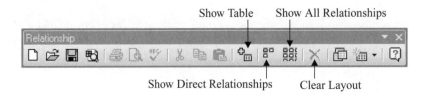

- Show Table opens the Show Table dialog box
- Show Direct Relationships displays the relationships for the selected table
- Show All Relationships displays all relationships in the current database
- Clear Layout removes the display of all tables and relationships from the Relationships window but does not affect the relationships themselves

Draw the Relationship Line

It couldn't be easier to relate two tables. You simply drag a field (usually the primary key) from one table and drop it on the corresponding field (the foreign key) in the other table. The field names do not need to be the same but they usually need to be the same data type and contain the same kind of information. If you intend to enforce referential integrity, the fields must be the same data type. If the fields are Number fields, they also must have the same Field Size property.

There are two exceptions to the requirement to match data types in the related fields:

- An AutoNumber field with the New Values property set to Increment can be linked to a Long Integer Number field. AutoNumber values are stored as four-byte numbers, so for the foreign key to have a matching value, it must contain a number of the same size— a Long Integer.

- An AutoNumber can be linked to a Number field if both fields have the Field Size property set to Replication ID.

> **TIP** *Dragging the foreign key field from the related table to the primary key field in the primary table creates the same relationship.*

To relate the Customer table to the Invoices table by CustomerID:

1. Click the CustomerID field in the Customers field list and drag it to the CustomerID field in the Invoices field list.

2. Drop the linking field into the child table. The Edit Relationships dialog box opens.

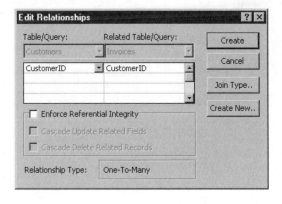

> **TIP**   *Notice that Access recognizes this relationship as one-to-many because one of the fields is a primary key and the other is not. If both fields are primary keys, Access recognizes the relationship as one-to-one. If neither field is a primary key nor has a unique value, Access calls the relationship Indeterminate.*

3. Verify the field names that relate the tables, then do one of the following:

■ If you want to change the field at either side of the relationship, select a different field from the drop-down field list under the table name.

■ If you want to add another relationship between the same tables that relates two different fields, move to an empty row in the grid, click the down button, and choose from the list for each table.

■ If you have chosen the wrong foreign key, choose Cancel in the Edit Relationships dialog box and start again in the Relationships window.

> **TIP**   *If you type the first few letters of the field name in the Edit Relationships dialog box grid, Access will fill in the rest for you.*

4. To complete the relationship, choose Create and return to the Relationships window. Figure 4-1 shows the Relationships window with the new link drawn between the tables.

5. Repeat the preceding procedure to draw the relationship line from the EmployeeID field in the Employees field list to the EmployeeID field in the Invoices field list.

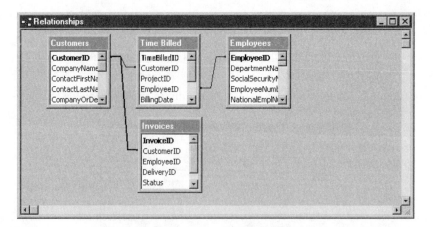

FIGURE 4-1   A relationship line is drawn between two tables.

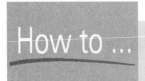 **Relate to Two or More Foreign Keys**

If you need to create relationships from a primary table to two or more foreign keys in the same table, Access will create additional instances of the table in the Relationships window. You do not have two copies of the table in the database—only in the Relationships layout. Here is a Relationships window with three copies of the Employees table with the EmployeeID primary key field relating to the Supervisor, Principal Worker, and Helper foreign keys in the Workorders table.

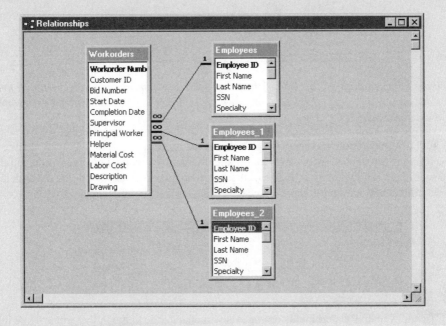

Enforce Referential Integrity

Referential integrity is a set of rules that keeps a database complete, with no loose ends. No related records can exist without a parent. When you want Access to enforce the referential integrity rules on the relationship you are defining, check Enforce Referential Integrity in the Edit Relationships dialog box.

Two options that let you override some restrictions become available: Cascade Update Related Fields and Cascade Delete Related Records. When you set these options, you can perform delete and update operations that normally would not be allowed.

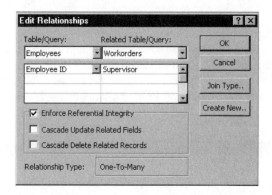

 *If the tables already violate one of the rules, such as when related fields are not of the same data type, Access displays a message explaining the violation and does not apply the enforcement.*

With both of these options checked, if you delete a record from the parent table or change one of the primary key values, Access will automatically make equivalent changes to the child table to preserve referential integrity. If one of these options is not checked and you try to delete a parent record that still has child records, Access displays a warning message.

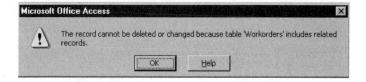

The Cascade Update Related Fields option lets you change the value in the primary key field in the parent table, and Access automatically changes the foreign key value in the child table to match. For example, if you change the CustomerID value in the Customers table, all records for that customer in any related table will automatically be updated to the new value. This option preserves the relationship.

 If the primary key in a table serves as a link to more than one table, you must set the Cascade Update Related Fields property for each of the relationships.

The Cascade Delete Related Records option allows you to delete a parent record; Access then automatically deletes all the related child records. When you try to delete a record from the parent table of a relationship with this option selected, Access warns you that this record and the ones in related tables will be deleted.

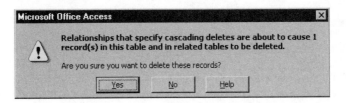

 Setting the Cascade Delete Related Fields property can be dangerous. If you delete records using a Delete query, Access automatically deletes the related records without issuing the warning.

Create a One-to-One Relationship

There might be times when you want to store information about an employee separate from the main pieces of information. For example, you might have data about an employee such as name, address, and Social Security Number readily available in one table but keep other data such as the resume and employment history in another table. These two tables are related by primary keys using a one-to-one relationship because only one record in each table matches one record in the other table.

To relate two tables in a one-to-one relationship, do the following:

1. Choose Tools | Relationships or click the Relationships toolbar button in the Database window.

2. If the tables you want to relate do not appear in the Relationships window, click the Show Table button.

3. Select each table in the Show Table dialog box and click Add; then choose Close.

4. Drag the primary key field from one table and drop it on the key field on the other table. It doesn't matter which direction you go; the same one-to-one relationship is created.

Specify the Join Type

One of the most powerful Access tools is the query that extracts and brings together data from more than one source. For example, you might want to see how much time each employee spends working on service for each current customer. To do so, you need information from the Time Billed, Employees, and Customers tables. Once the data is extracted, the query adds up the hours for records with matching employees and customers.

When you define the relationship, you also can specify the type of join you want for the tables. The join type specifies which records to display in a query based on related tables when they don't correspond exactly. For example, do you want the customer record to appear only if

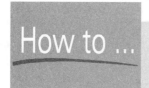

Create a Many-to-Many Relationship

In a many-to-many relationship, a record in one table (call it Table A) can have several matching records in another table (Table B) and vice versa. Neither table is considered the parent table because the linking field is not the primary key in either table. The only way you can create such a relationship is by creating a third table, called a *junction table*. This new table has a primary key that actually is a combination of at least the primary keys from tables A and B. The junction table acts as a bridge between the two tables when you build two one-to-many relationships among them. You can add other fields to the junction table like any other table. Here is a junction table linking the Orders and Products tables.

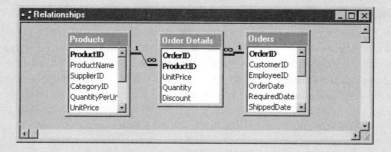

Because several products could be included in a single order and several orders could include the same product, this represents a many-to-many relationship. To define the relationship in Access, the junction table Order Details was created with a primary key that combines the foreign keys from the Products table (ProductID) and from the Orders table (OrderID). Both field names appear in boldface in the Order Details table, indicating that together they constitute the primary key; thus two one-to-many relationships link the Products and Orders tables to the Order Details table.

there are corresponding invoice records or do you want to see all customer records even if there are no related invoices?

NOTE
The join type does not affect the relationship; it simply tells Access which records to include in a query.

To modify the relationship between the Employees and Invoices tables and set the join type:

1. In the Relationships window, right-click in the middle of the relationships line joining the Customers table with the Invoices table and choose Edit Relationship from the shortcut menu. The Edit Relationships dialog box opens.

2. Click the Join Type button to open the Join Properties dialog box.

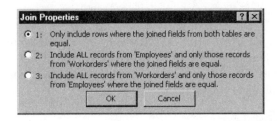

3. Select option 2 as the type of join for this relationship because you want to see all the Customers records even if they have no related records in the Invoices table. Notice that the explanatory text is specific to the tables you have related.

Understanding Joins

You can specify three types of joins through the Join Properties dialog box:

- Option 1 includes only records where both parent and child have the same values in the linking fields (no orphans and no childless parents). This is called an *inner join* or an *equijoin,* and it's the default join type.

- Option 2 includes all the records from the table on the left, even if no corresponding values are in the other and only the matching records from the table on the right. This is called a *left outer join* (all parents, including the childless, but no orphans).

- Option 3 is the opposite of option 2 and includes all the records from the table on the right and only matching records from the left table. This is called a *right outer join* (all children but no childless parents). If Referential Integrity is enforced, there will be no children without a parent.

If you have trouble deciding which table is the "left" in the relationship, look at how we read a sentence: from left to right. Read a relationship from primary table (left) to related table (right). Physical positioning in the layout doesn't matter.

If you select an outer join, an arrow at one end of the relation line points to the table whose value must match to be included in the query results. In a one-to-many relationship, the "one" side is considered the left table and the "many" side is the right table.

4. Click OK in the Join Properties dialog box.

5. Click OK in the Edit Relationships dialog box.

Figure 4-2 shows the completed layout for four tables in a database that tracks customer billing and prepares invoices. The relationships that include referential integrity show a 1 on the "one" side and an infinity sign (∞) on the "many" side. Relationships with no referential integrity enforcement appear as lines with small dots at each end.

Relationship lines with no arrows represent inner joins. An arrow on a relationship line means the join is an outer join and the arrow points to the table whose values must match to be included in the query results. The relationship between Employees and Time Billed tables is a left outer join with referential integrity enforced.

Save the Relationships Layout

All relationships are saved when you create them. You also can save the arrangement of the field lists in the Relationships window (the layout). Saving the layout has no effect on the tables in the database. To save the layout, right-click anywhere in the Relationships window (except on a field list) and choose Save Layout from the Relationships shortcut menu, or choose File | Save.

If you have made changes in the layout and try to close the Relationships window without saving the layout, Access prompts you to save it. If you want to discard the changes, choose No. When you open the Relationships window again, the previously saved layout is displayed. When defining relationships, you can always call for help by typing a specific question in the "Type a question for help" box in the Access title bar and pressing ENTER.

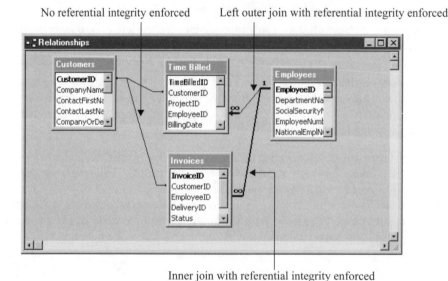

FIGURE 4-2   A layout containing four related tables

View and Edit Relationships

You have a choice of viewing all the relationships that you have set in your database or only those involving a specific table. In the database window, click the Relationships toolbar button or choose Tools | Relationships.

In the Relationships window, do one of the following:

■ To view all the relationships in the current database, click the Show All Relationships toolbar button.

■ To see only the relationships for the table selected in the database window, click the Show Direct Relationships.

If all the relationships already appear in the Relationships window and you want to see only one table's relationships:

1. Clear the layout by clicking the Clear Layout toolbar button.

2. Click the Show Table button, double-click the table name in the Show Table dialog box, then choose Close.

3. In the Relationships window, click the Show Direct Relationships button.

Hide or Delete a Table

If the Relationships window becomes too crowded, you can hide a table or delete it from the layout. To hide the table temporarily, choose Relationships | Hide Table, or right-click the table and choose Hide Table from the shortcut menu. The next time you view the Relationships window, all the tables will reappear unless you save the layout with the changes.

To delete the table from the layout, select the table and press DEL, or choose Edit | Delete. This affects only the display of the layout and does not remove the relationship or the table from the database.

To restore the relationship's layout to its previous arrangement, close the window without saving the changes. When you reopen the window, the old layout returns. If you want to keep the window open and restore the relationships, click the Show All Relationships toolbar button or choose Relationships | Show All Relationships.

Modify or Delete a Relationship

Relationships are not cast in concrete. There will be times when you need to make some changes such as altering the linking field or modifying the type of join. You can use the same Relationships window to edit a relationship that you used to create one.

To modify an existing relationship:

1. Open the Relationships window as before.

2. If you don't see the relationship you want to change, choose Show Table from the Relationships menu, double-click the missing table, and choose Close.

3. Double-click the relationship line or right-click the line and choose Edit Relationship from the shortcut menu to open the Relationships dialog box.

4. Make the changes you want, then click OK.

To delete a relationship, click the join line to select it and press DEL or choose Edit | Delete. You also can right-click the line and choose Delete from the shortcut menu.

Access asks for confirmation before permanently deleting the relationship no matter which method you use.

 *Pressing DEL with a table selected only removes the table from the layout, whereas pressing DEL with a relationship line selected permanently removes the relationship between the tables.*

Change a Table Design from the Relationships Window

You might need to make a change in a table design to be able to create the relationship you want. For example, the primary key might be a Text field and the foreign key a Number field. This design may suffice unless you want to enforce referential integrity, which requires the same data type in both fields. You can open the child table design and change the field type to Text.

If you have already set a relationship between the tables, you must delete the relationship before you can change the table design. You also might want to add a secondary index on the foreign key in the child table to speed up processing.

To switch to the Table Design view from the Relationships window, right-click anywhere in the table's field list box and choose Table Design from the shortcut menu. When you finish changing the table design, save the changes and close the window; then return automatically to the Relationships window.

Print the Relationships

Documentation is always helpful, especially if you work with several databases or develop applications for others. Once you have defined all the relationships for the database, it is easy to document the structure graphically by printing it.

To print the table relationships diagram:

1. In the Relationships window, right-click in an empty area and choose Show All.

2. When all tables appear in the layout, choose File | Print Relationships. Figure 4-3 shows the printed layout of the Home Tech Repair database relationships.

Although the primary key fields do not appear in bold in the printed diagram, you can use the join line symbols as a guide to the linking fields.

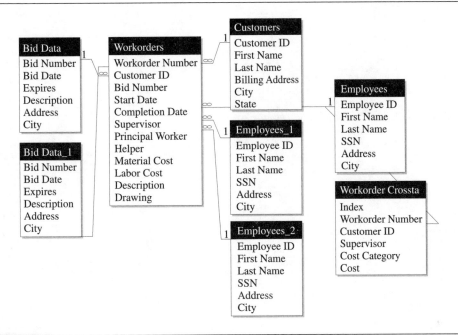

FIGURE 4-3 Printed database relationship diagram

> **TIP** *You might need to run Page Setup and reduce the left and right margins or change to landscape orientation to be able to print the entire diagram on one page.*

If you want more precise information about the relationships you have established in the database, including the attributes such as referential integrity and the relationship type, you can use the Documenter, one of the Access analytical tools. See Chapter 14 for information about using the Documenter and other analysis tools.

Chapter 5

Enter and Edit Data

How to...

- Enter new data
- Customize data entry
- Change the datasheet appearance
- Edit data in a table
- Find and replace data

Once you have figured out how to distribute your data and built the tables to hold it, it's time to enter the data and get to work. In the last chapter, you saw some design features that keep errors out of your database. This chapter discusses more tools that block data errors and speed up the data entry process.

Enter New Data

 When you open a new table, it appears in Datasheet view, ready for data entry. To add a new record, click the New Record toolbar button or click the New Record navigation button. If you prefer menus, choose Edit | Go To | New Record or Insert | New Record.

 *You can also simply scroll down to the blank record at the end of the table and start typing.*

When the insertion point moves to an empty field, type in the data. If you have specified a custom display format, the entered value will adapt to that format when you move to the next column. If you have created an input mask for that field, the mask appears when you enter the field. See the section "Add Custom Input Masks" later in this chapter for details about input masks and how they compare with display format settings.

You can enter date/time data in any valid format; Access will then convert it to the format you've specified in the field property. However, do not try to enter decimal fractions in number fields that are defined as integers because you will lose the decimal by the rounding off to the integer equivalent.

Copy and Move Data

Access provides some shortcuts for entering repetitive data by copying or moving existing data. You can copy or move all the data from one record to another or to individual fields or you can move or copy specific items using the Edit menu or toolbar buttons. You also can display the clipboard side pane and use it to copy and paste items:

- Click Copy to add the selected item to the clipboard, then choose Edit | Copy or press CTRL-C.

■ Click Cut to move the selected item to the clipboard, then choose Edit | Cut or press CTRL-X.

When you collect items by copying or cutting them from their source, they are placed on the Office clipboard, which is shared by all Office programs. The Office 2003 clipboard is a Task pane that can hold up to 24 items with previews of the text or pictures that have been copied (see Figure 5-1). You can paste them to a new location singly or as a group. If you place a 25th item on the clipboard, the first item is deleted.

The first item on the Office clipboard is also on the Windows clipboard, and you can paste it into almost any other Windows program. Similarly, cutting or copying from a non-Office program puts an item on the Windows clipboard, and you can paste it into any Office program, including Access.

■ To paste a selected item from the clipboard, place the insertion point where you want to paste it and click Paste, choose Edit | Paste, or press CTRL-V.

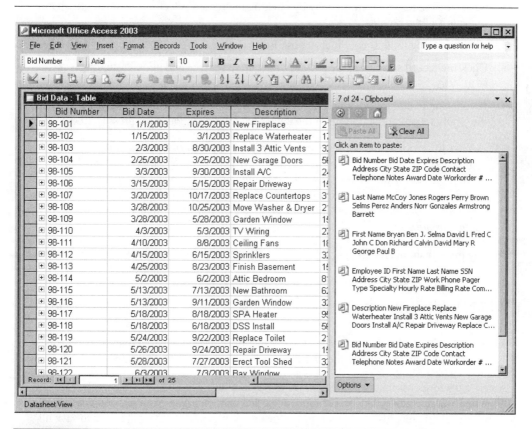

FIGURE 5-1   Copying items to the Office clipboard

- To delete an item from the clipboard, move the mouse pointer to the item, then click the down arrow to the right of the item and choose Delete from the menu.
- To close the clipboard side pane, click the Close button in the upper-right corner.
- To display the clipboard later, choose Edit | Office Clipboard.

 The Options button at the bottom of the clipboard gives you control over the behavior of the clipboard. The options include Show Office Clipboard Automatically, Show Office Clipboard When Control-C Pressed Twice, Collect Without Showing Office Clipboard, Show Office Clipboard Icon On Taskbar, and Show Status Near Taskbar When Copying.

Copy and Move Within the Same Table

You can copy or move one or more records within the same table. Once you copy a record, you can add it to the table or replace an existing record with the one you copied.

To copy a record within the same table:

1. Select the record you want to copy by clicking the record selector (the small gray button to the left of the record).
2. Click the Copy toolbar button or choose Edit | Copy (or press CTRL-C).

3. Click the record selector in the record you want to replace and click Paste (or press CTRL-V).

4. If you want to add the copy as a new record rather than replace an existing one, select the empty record at the bottom of the datasheet, then click Paste (or press CTRL-V).

Access tries to save the copied record when you move out of it. If the table has a primary key or a unique index, Access won't let you leave the new record until you have replaced the duplicate value with a unique one. If the primary key field is an AutoNumber data type, Access automatically increments the number rather than copying the original number—another good reason to use an AutoNumber field as the primary key.

To copy more than one record:

1. Select all the records you want to copy before clicking Copy.

2. When replacing records, select the same number of existing records as you have placed on the clipboard, then click Paste.
3. To append the new records to the table instead of replacing existing ones, select the new empty row at the bottom of the datasheet and click choose Edit | Paste Append.

Access asks for confirmation when you try to paste multiple records.

If the table has a primary key or a unique index that is not an AutoNumber, you will not be able to paste multiple records until you remove the key or index. Access would have to save all but one of the records, rather than paste a single record, and this would create duplicate values in the field. If you try, Access objects by displaying the information message shown here.

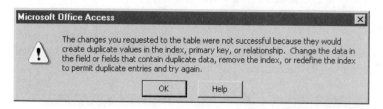

> **TIP**   *If you just want to repeat the value in a single field to the next record while you are entering data in a new record, you can quickly copy the value by pressing CTRL-' (apostrophe) after moving to the field.*

If you want to move one or more records rather than create another copy of the data in the record, click Cut instead of Copy. This removes the record completely and places it on the clipboard. Then use the same paste or append process as described previously for copying records.

Copy and Move from Another Table

If you want to copy or move records from another table, select the records in the source table and click Copy or Cut. (If you click Cut, you will be asked to confirm that you wish to delete the record or records from the source table.) Switch to the destination datasheet and select the blank row at the bottom of the datasheet. When you click Paste, the new records are added to the destination datasheet.

> **CAUTION**   *The fields in the copied records are pasted in the same order as they appeared in the original datasheet, regardless of the field names. You might need to rearrange the columns in the destination datasheet before pasting so they will correspond with the incoming fields. Inconsistent data types or sizes between the incoming and the destination records can result in problems.*

If you want to replace certain records in the destination datasheet with records from another table, select the records you want to replace before clicking Paste. To append records from another table to the existing datasheet, choose Edit | Paste Append. If the source table has more fields than the destination table, the excess fields are not pasted.

Insert Pictures

The Home Tech Repair Employees table has a field reserved for the employees' badge pictures. The Badge Picture field is an OLE (Object Linking and Embedding) Object data type and will store a file containing the digitized photograph. The Badge Picture photos are OLE Objects created by a scanner and contained in image files such as .tif, .gif, or .pcx. Because the photos

 **Fix Paste Problems**

When errors occur during a paste operation, Access creates a Paste Errors table and displays a message advising you of the errors as each is added to the table.

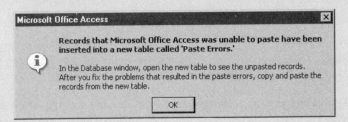

To view the Paste Errors table, double-click the table name in the Tables page of the Database window. When you open the Paste Errors table, you might be able to paste the data in the destination table field by field.

Here are some of the problems you might encounter when trying to paste data into a datasheet:

- Values are incompatible with the destination data types.
- The value is too long for the destination field.
- The destination is in a hidden column.
- A value violates one of the destination field property settings.

are not expected to change, they are embedded in the table. Additionally, they represent the value stored in the Badge Picture field, which means they are bound to the table records.

 Objects you expect to be edited often are better left in the source program and linked to your table. You can store the pathname or filename of the picture or other object in the Text field and won't have to reimport it when changes occur.

To insert an image in the Badge Picture field:

1. Place the insertion point in the Badge Picture field and choose Insert | Object, or right-click the field and choose Insert Object from the shortcut menu.

2. In the Insert Object dialog box, choose Create from File.

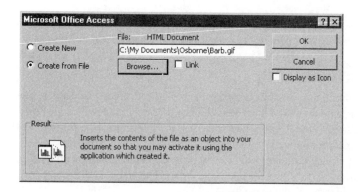

5

3. Type the path and filename of the image file in the File box or click Browse and look for the object.

4. Choose OK to embed the picture in the field.

 When you return to Datasheet view, the field now contains the name of the source of the OLE object. To see the image, create a form by clicking New Object: AutoForm. Figure 5-2 shows an Employee record with the badge picture embedded.

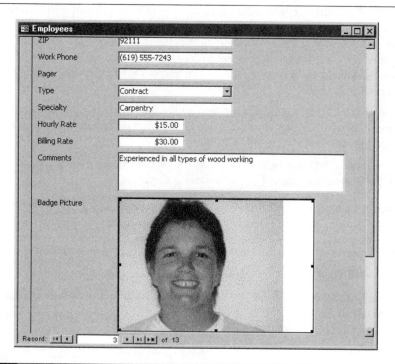

FIGURE 5-2   The employee's badge picture inserted

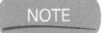 *You might need to double-click the added object to activate the OLE source program associated with that type of file before you can see the image.*

Insert Hyperlinks

A *hyperlink* is a connection to an object in the same or another Access database, a document created in another program, a document on the Internet, or your local intranet. The *hyperlink field* contains the address of the target object, and when you click the hyperlink, you jump to it. If the object is the product of another application, that application is automatically started.

In the Home Tech Repair database, the Workorders table contains a hyperlink field that contains the engineering drawings for that work order. The scanned drawings are saved as .gif files in the same folder as the database itself.

Define the Hyperlink Address

A hyperlink address can contain up to four parts, separated by the pound sign (#), as in *displaytext#address#subaddress#screentip,* of which only the address is required. If you want the hyperlink to jump to a specific location in the target object, a subaddress is also required.

- The *displaytext* is optional and can be displayed in the field in place of the actual address. If you don't include display text, the hyperlink address or subaddress appears instead.

- The *address* is either a *Uniform Resource Locator* (*URL*) such as a web address, or *Universal Naming Convention* (*UNC*) path to the document. An *absolute path* starts with \\ and describes the exact location on the system or local area network (LAN). A *relative path* is related to the current path or the base path specified in the database properties. An address is required unless you added a subaddress that points to an object in the current database.

- The *subaddress* contains a named location within the target object, such as a bookmark in a Word document, a particular slide in a PowerPoint presentation, or a cell range in an Excel spreadsheet.

- The *screentip* is the text that appears when you rest the mouse pointer on the hyperlink. If you don't specify a ScreenTip, the address is displayed.

The scanned drawings for the Workorders Drawing field are stored in the Home Tech folder with the database. To use the Insert Hyperlink tool to enter the hyperlink address:

1. Place the insertion point in the Drawing field in the Workorders datasheet.

2. Click Insert Hyperlink or choose Insert | Hyperlink (see Figure 5-3).

3. Click the Existing File or Web Page button under Link to: if not already chosen. Then do one of the following:

- ■ Type the path to the drawing file in the Address box; for example, **c:\My Documents\Osborne\fireplace.gif**.

- ■ If you have accessed the target of this hyperlink before, you can select it from the list of Recent Files or Browsed Pages.

- ■ Click the Browse for File button (the open folder) and locate the file in the Link to File dialog box and click OK.

4. Enter the text you want to show in the field in place of the address in the "Text to display" box. For example, you could enter **Fireplace**.

5. If you want to show a ScreenTip, click the ScreenTip button and enter the text in the Set Hyperlink ScreenTip dialog box, then click OK.

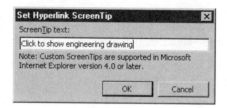

Browse the Web

Move up one folder | Browse for file

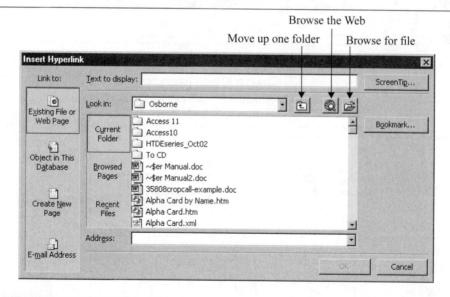

FIGURE 5-3 The Insert Hyperlink dialog box

5

6. Click OK to finish inserting the hyperlink and return to the Workorders datasheet where the hyperlink appears in the Drawing field. When you rest the mouse pointer on the hyperlink, you will see the ScreenTip.

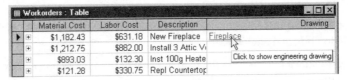

		Material Cost	Labor Cost	Description	Drawing
▶	+	$1,182.43	$631.18	New Fireplace	Fireplace
	+	$1,212.75	$882.00	Install 3 Attic V	Click to show engineering drawing
	+	$893.03	$132.30	Inst 100g Heate	
	+	$121.28	$330.75	Repl Countertop	

7. Click the hyperlink to test it; Microsoft Picture Library (or whatever program handles your .gif files) opens, displaying the scanned fireplace drawing, as shown in Figure 5-4.

Edit and Delete Hyperlinks

Editing a hyperlink address is a little different from editing normal text because if you click on the address, you jump to the target. There are two ways to edit the address:

- Right-click the hyperlink, point to Hyperlink in the shortcut menu, and click Edit Hyperlink in the submenu; edit the address directly in the Edit Hyperlink dialog box.

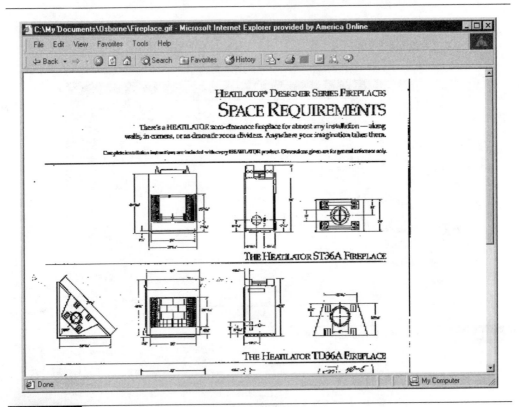

FIGURE 5-4 The target of the fireplace hyperlink

■ Press TAB to move to the field and press F2 to switch to Edit mode.

| TIP | *An easier way to change only the displayed text is to right-click the hyperlink, choose Hyperlink | Display Text, and edit the text in the box.* |

To delete a hyperlink from a field, right-click the hyperlink and choose Cut from the shortcut menu. You can also point to Hyperlink in the shortcut menu and click Remove Hyperlink. If you want to delete all the hyperlink addresses you have inserted in a field, delete the field from the table design.

Customize Data Entry

Access offers many tools that help improve the efficiency and accuracy of data entry. Some minimize the process, others assist in navigation in a datasheet or give you access to special symbols. For example, input masks guide the user with data input and help to prevent data errors, and lookup fields offer a list of valid values for selection.

Add Custom Input Masks

An *input mask* is a field property similar to the Format property but with a different purpose. An input mask displays a fill-in blank for data entry whereas a format is used to display field data with a consistent appearance. Setting the Format property affects how data is displayed after it is entered and offers no control over or guidance for the data being entered. Input masks can be used with Text, Number, Date/Time, and Currency fields. An Input Mask Wizard can help you with Text and Date/Time fields.

To decide between a Format property and an Input Mask property, use the following guidelines:

■ If you just want to make sure the field values look the same when displayed, use the Format property to specify the desired appearance.

■ If you want to guide data entry and make sure it is entered properly, use an input mask.

An input mask appears before any data is entered, when the insertion point reaches the field. The mask displays fill-in blanks with literal characters separating them. When you use an input mask, you can be sure the data will fit the specifications you set by limiting the number of fill-in spaces. Depending on the characters you use in the mask, you can leave some fill-in spaces blank but you cannot enter more characters than there are spaces.

To create an input mask with the Input Mask Wizard:

1. Move the insertion point to the field in the table Design view.

2. Click in the Input Mask property, then click the Build button (...).

3. Select a mask in the Input Mask Wizard dialog box, as shown in Figure 5-5, and click Next.

4. You can make changes to the mask, such as changing the placeholder that displays as the fill-in blanks (the default is an underline character). Then click Next.

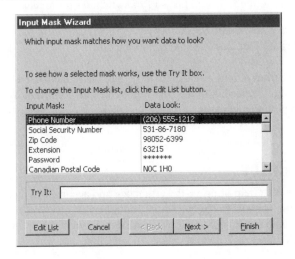

FIGURE 5-5 Predesigned input masks

5. Choose to store the literal characters with the data, if desired, by adding them to the Input Mask text box. This uses more disk space but the symbols are already available when you want to use the value in a form or report.

6. Click Finish to close the wizard.

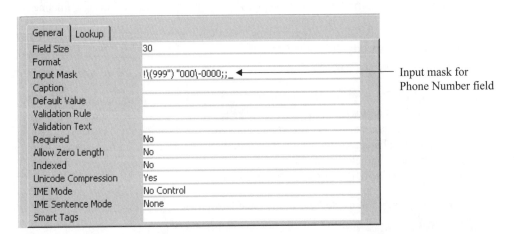

If you have a customized field that is not part of the Input Mask Wizard's repertoire, you can easily create your own mask manually using special symbols. The special symbols are placeholders that specify which entries are required and define what type of characters can be entered at each position in the mask. You can even add a custom mask to the wizard's list of predefined input masks. You cannot create an input mask for a Memo, AutoNumber, Yes/No, OLE Object, or Hyperlink field.

To build an input mask manually, enter the desired characters directly in the field's Input Mask property in Design view. Table 5-1 describes the symbols you can use in an input mask and indicates whether they will require an entry in that position.

Here are some examples of the effects of input masks:

Input Mask	Description	Sample Valid Value
00000-9999	Uses zeros to represent required entries. The 9s are optional.	92118-2450 or 92118-
(999) AAA-AAAA	Allows letters or digits. The area code is optional.	(301) 555-CALL
!>L0L 0L0	Converts all letters to uppercase, and fills the mask from left to right.	N0C 1H0
>L<?????????	Converts required initial letter to uppercase. Other characters are optional and converted to lowercase.	Henrietta
>LL0000-000	Converts the two required letters to uppercase, which are followed by the seven required digits.	BT5430-115

To make a change in one of the wizard's masks, select the mask first in the Input Mask Wizard dialog box, then click Edit List and proceed as in the preceding examples to make the desired changes.

Symbol	Entry	Entry Required?
0	Displays a digit (0 through 9) with no + or – sign. Blanks display as zeros.	Yes
9	Displays a digit with no + or – sign. Blanks display as spaces.	No
#	Displays a digit with + and – signs. Blanks display as spaces.	No
L	Displays a letter (*A* through *Z*).	Yes
?	Displays a letter.	No
A	Displays a letter or digit.	Yes
a	Displays a letter or digit.	No
&	Displays any character or space.	Yes
C	Displays any character or space.	No
<	Converts letter to lowercase.	N/A
>	Converts letter to uppercase.	N/A
!	Fills the mask with the characters that the user types into the mask, from left to right. Can appear anywhere in the mask.	N/A
\	Treats the next character as a literal.	N/A

TABLE 5-1   Input Mask Symbols

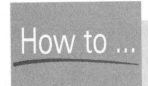

How to ... Create a Custom Input Mask

If you have a field that commonly appears in your tables or forms, such as the Canadian postal code, you can create a new input mask and save it in the Input Mask Wizard's list of predefined masks, as follows:

1. In table Design view, click the Input Mask property for the field, then click the Build button to open the Input Mask Wizard dialog box.

2. Click Edit List. The Customize Input Mask Wizard dialog box shows the Phone Number input mask.

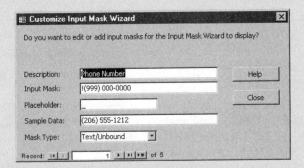

3. Click the New Record navigation button at the bottom of the dialog box to show a blank form.

4. Enter a description of the new mask, the mask itself, the symbol you want to use as the placeholder, and a sample of the data you intend to enter into the field.

5. Select the Text/Unbound Mask Type. The definition for the Canadian postal code input mask is complete.

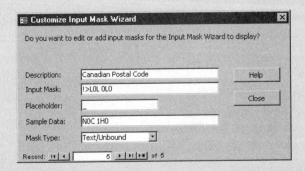

6. Click Close. The new definition appears in the list of predefined masks.

Create Lookup Fields

A *lookup field* is an Access tool that makes entering data quicker and more accurate. A lookup field displays a list of values from which to choose. The most common type of lookup field, called a *lookup list,* gets its values from an existing table or query. The advantage of this type of lookup field is that the tables actually are related and as the source list changes, the current values are available to the lookup field.

The second type of lookup field gets its values from a list that you type in when you create the field. This type is called a *value list* and is best used when the list is limited to a few values that do not change often, such as a short list of product categories or employee status.

You can add either type of lookup field in Design or Datasheet view. If the field already exists in the table design and you want to change it to a lookup field, you must change the data type in Design view. To add a new lookup field to a table, do one of the following:

- In Design view, add a new field row and select Lookup Wizard from the Data Type list.

- In Datasheet view, click in the column to the right of where you want the new lookup field, then choose Insert | Lookup Column.

Both methods start the Lookup Wizard, which displays a series of dialog boxes where you specify the details of the lookup field. In the first dialog box, decide which type of lookup field to create: a lookup list that relates to a table or query, or a value list that you type in.

Specify a Lookup Column

As an example of defining a lookup field that gets its values from another table, let's insert a new field in the Workorders table of the Home Tech Repair database. The Workorders information is easier to enter and read if a lookup field is used for the Supervisor, Principal Worker, and Helper fields. The Last Name will be displayed, but the Employee ID will be stored.

To add a lookup field to the Workorders table:

1. Open the Workorders table in Design view and insert a field named Supervisor between Completion Date and Principal Worker, choosing the Lookup Wizard data type.

2. In the first Lookup Wizard dialog box, choose the first option, "I want the lookup column to look up the values in a table or query." Click Next.

3. Select Employees from the list of tables and click Next. You could also select a query as the source of the values.

4. In the next dialog box, double-click the Employee ID and Last Name fields in the list of available fields in the Employees table (see Figure 5-6). Click Next.

5. In the next dialog box, you can specify the sort order for the fields in the lookup list. Click Next.

6. The next dialog box (see Figure 5-7) shows you how the field values will look in the lookup column. Drag the right edge of the column header to adjust the width if necessary. Also check the "Hide key column (recommended)" option so you need not view the Employee ID key value, only the last name. If you have no data in the column yet, accept the default column width. Click Next.

5

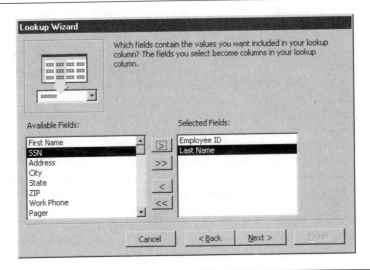

FIGURE 5-6 Selecting the fields for the lookup field

7. Accept the name Supervisor for the lookup column and click Finish. Access prompts you to save the table so that the relationships can be completed.

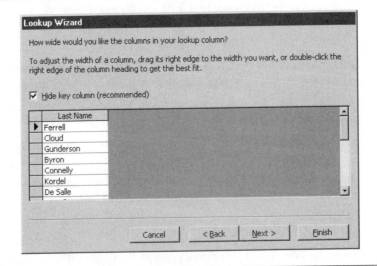

FIGURE 5-7 Changing the lookup column appearance

8. Choose Yes. Access returns you to the table Design view.

The Lookup Wizard has set the properties for the new field based on your selections in the dialog boxes, which you can view on the Lookup tab of the Field Properties pane.

General Lookup	
Display Control	Combo Box
Row Source Type	Table/Query
Row Source	SELECT [Employees].[Employee ID], [Employees].[l
Bound Column	1
Column Count	2
Column Heads	No
Column Widths	0";1"
List Rows	8
List Width	1"
Limit To List	Yes

Take a look at the Lookup properties that specify the appearance and behavior of the lookup field when it appears in a datasheet or a form. As you click in each property on the Lookup tab, look at the description in the right pane.

The Workorders table shows the new lookup field used to locate employee names in the Employee table. The lookup field links the Employee table to the Workorders table by the Employee ID field. The employee's last name is displayed; the foreign key (Employee ID) is not displayed but it is stored in the field.

Workorders : Table

Workorder Num	Customer ID	Bid Number	Start Date	Completion Dat	Supervisor	Principal Worke	He
+ 001	1032	98-101	2/25/2003	3/10/2003	Ferrell	Howell	
+ 002	1033	98-103	3/15/2003	3/18/2003	Ferrell	Gikas	
+ 003	1034	98-105	3/10/2003	3/5/2003	Cloud	Dobbins	
+ 004	1035	98-107	4/15/2003	4/20/2003	Gunderson	Howell	
+ 005	1036	98-108	5/10/2003	5/15/2003	Byron	Dobbins	
+ 006	1037	98-111	5/12/2003	5/25/2003	Connelly		
+ 007	1038	98-113	1/15/2003	9/15/2003	Kordel	Kordel	
+ 008	1033	98-116	6/15/2003	7/1/2003	De Salle	Gikas	
+ 009	1039	98-117	6/25/2003	6/26/2003	Howell	Howell	De Sal

Specify a Lookup List

A list of acceptable values can be helpful when entering data in the Employees table. Because only a few values are valid in the Specialty field, it is a good candidate for streamlining. Start with the Lookup Wizard as before, and in the first Lookup Wizard dialog box, choose the second option "I will type in the values I want." Then move to the next dialog box, shown here, where you enter the values for the list.

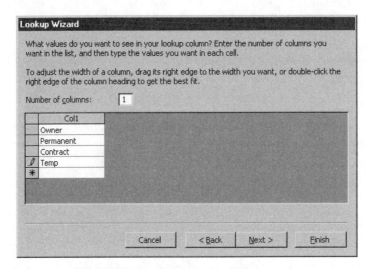

The Row Source property on the Lookup tab for the Specialty field now shows the list of values you typed in instead of a SELECT statement.

Change the Datasheet Appearance

Datasheet properties include the layout of the fields and records—the order in which the fields appear, the dimension of the rows and columns, and the column headings. Other properties are the font size and style, the colors of the text, the background, and special cell effects such as raised or sunken.

You also have the option of hiding some fields from view if the data shouldn't be visible to all users of the database. Finally, if you have too many fields to view on the screen at once, you can keep one or more key fields on the left of the screen as you scroll right so some information is always in view.

All of these changes in datasheet appearance also can be applied to subdatasheets.

Move and Resize Columns and Rows

Access displays the data fields in columns in the same order as the fields appear in the table design unless you change the column order. By default, the columns are all the same width, so you might not be able to see the whole field name or value. Other columns might be wider than necessary and waste screen space. The rows also are standard height. You can change any of these datasheet properties using the elements of the datasheet itself.

Row sizing lines   Field selectors   Column sizing lines

	Workorder Num	Customer ID	Bid Number	Start Date	Completion Date	Supervisor	Principal Worke	H
001	1032	98-101	2/25/2003	3/10/2003	Ferrell	Howell	
002	1033	98-103	3/15/2003	3/18/2003	Gunderson	Gikas	
003	1034	98-105	3/10/2003	3/5/2003	Byron	Dobbins	
004	1035	98-107	4/15/2003	4/20/2003	Gunderson	Howell	
005	1036	98-108	5/10/2003	5/15/2003	Ferrell	Dobbins	
006	1037	98-111	5/12/2003	5/25/2003	Byron		

Rearrange the Columns

To move a column, click the field selector, release the button, and move the mouse pointer to the field selector. When the mouse pointer changes shape to an arrow with a small rectangle, click and drag the column to the desired position.

As you move the column, a dark vertical line moves with it, showing you where the left boundary of the moving column is at that moment. Release the mouse button to reposition the column. Changing the relative position of a column in the datasheet has no effect on the way the fields appear in the table design or the way they are stored on the disk.

Change the Column Width

There are three ways to change a column width:

- Drag the sizing line at the right border of the field selector button
- Double-click the column sizing line to fit the contents
- Set the precise width in a dialog box

TIP   *If you drag the boundary all the way left until it reaches the left boundary, the column disappears. This is one way to hide a column. You will learn more about hiding columns in the section "Freeze and Hide Columns."*

If you need to specify a column width more precisely, you can set the exact width in the Column Width dialog box after selecting one or more columns:

1. Select one or more columns.

2. Choose Format | Column Width or right-click the field selector and choose Column Width from the shortcut menu.

3. Type a new value in the Column Width text box or click Best Fit. The Best Fit option resizes the selected column or columns to fit the longest data string currently in the field or the text in the column heading, whichever is longer.

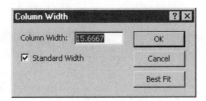

Change the Row Height

You can change column widths individually; however, rows are all the same height, thus when you change the height of one, you change them all.

To change the row height:

1. Move the mouse pointer to any one of the row sizing lines in the record selector area.

2. Click and drag the line until the rows reach the desired height.

3. Release the button. All rows will be the same height.

To set a more exact row height, choose Format | Row Height to open the Row Height dialog box. (The insertion point can be anywhere in the datasheet.) You also can right-click in a selected row or a row selector and choose Row Height from the shortcut menu. The Row Height dialog box is similar to the Column Width dialog box except there is no Best Fit option. The height is measured in points; the default height depends on the default font size.

Freeze and Hide Columns

Two other properties of a datasheet deal with the display of the data. *Freezing* a column keeps the data on the screen as you scroll right to see other fields in a long record. *Hiding* a column keeps the data from displaying in the datasheet. Again, neither of these properties changes the way the data is stored, only the way it is displayed.

Freeze and Unfreeze Columns

When you freeze a column on the screen, the column and its contents are automatically moved to the left of the datasheet and kept on the screen as you scroll right.

To freeze a column:

1. Place the insertion point anywhere in the column you want to freeze.

2. Choose Format | Freeze Columns, or right-click in the column header and choose Freeze Columns from the shortcut menu.

To freeze several adjacent columns, select them all before choosing Freeze Columns. If you want to freeze non-adjacent columns, freeze them one at a time in the order you want them to appear at the left of the screen. Access will move them one by one to the left side of the datasheet. To unfreeze the columns, choose Format | Unfreeze All Columns.

Unfortunately, Access doesn't return the thawed column to the position it was in before you froze it and moved it to the left. You have to move it back yourself or close the table without saving the changes in the layout to restore the original arrangement.

Hide and Unhide Columns

If your table contains information that is not relevant to the current activity, you might not want it to take up space on the screen. In this case, you can hide one or more columns from view. Again, this changes only the appearance of the datasheet, not the data that is stored in the table. To hide a column, place the insertion point anywhere in the column, then choose Format | Hide Columns.

You can also right-click in a selected column or in the field selector and choose Hide Columns from the shortcut menu. The column immediately disappears from the screen. If you want to hide several adjacent columns, select them all first. If you want to hide non-adjacent columns, reposition them so they are adjacent, then hide them as a group or one at a time.

NOTE   *If you try to copy or move records to a datasheet that currently has hidden columns, the data will not be entered and you will get paste errors. Be sure to unhide all the hidden columns before attempting to copy or move records.*

To return the hidden columns to the datasheet display, choose Format | Unhide Columns. The Unhide Columns dialog box appears with a list of all the fields in the datasheet. Check marks next to the field names indicate the fields currently in view. If a field does not show a check mark, it is currently hidden. To return a field to the datasheet display, check the box next to its name. Choose Close when you have returned all the desired fields to the display.

TIP   *While you are unhiding columns with the Unhide Columns dialog box, you can hide columns at the same time by removing the check marks next to the columns you want to hide.*

Change the Font

Access uses 10-point Arial as the default font for datasheets. The font setting applies to all the characters in the datasheet—data and captions alike. You might want to reduce the font size to get more data on the screen or enlarge it to make it more visible if a group will be viewing the screen from a short distance. The row height and column widths are automatically adjusted to accommodate the font changes.

To change the datasheet font, choose Font from the Format or shortcut menu to open the Font dialog box (see Figure 5-8). Select the font, size, and effects you want, then click OK.

5

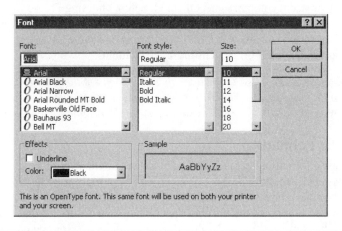

FIGURE 5-8   The Font dialog box

You can use the Formatting (Datasheet) toolbar buttons to change the font properties. You also can use the Formatting toolbar to change the appearance of the datasheet gridlines and cells. Any changes you make affect the entire datasheet.

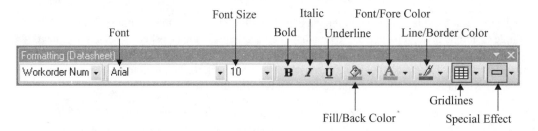

Change Grid Lines and Cell Appearance

Now comes the fun part: making some dramatic changes to the appearance of the datasheet with colors and special effects. The *grid lines*—the horizontal and vertical lines that separate the datasheet into rows and columns—are displayed by default, but you can remove the horizontal or vertical lines, or both. The *cells* are the boxes at the intersection of the rows and columns. In addition to changing the appearance of the grid lines, you can apply special effects to the cells to make them appear raised or sunken.

To change the datasheet properties, choose Format | Datasheet. The Datasheet Formatting dialog box opens, as shown in Figure 5-9.

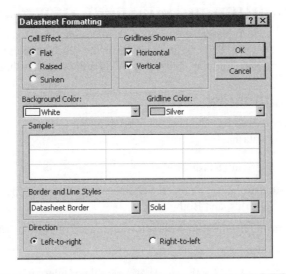

FIGURE 5-9   The Datasheet Formatting dialog box

In the Datasheet Formatting dialog box, you can make the following changes; as you make changes, the combined effects are shown in the Sample panel:

- Set a special cell effect, such as Raised or Sunken
- Show or hide the horizontal and vertical gridlines
- Change the color of the grid lines and the cell background
- Change the style of the borders and grid lines to weights ranging from transparent to double-solid
- Change the column display direction from left-to-right (the first field appears in the first column, the second in the column to the right, and so on) to right-to-left (the first field appears in the rightmost column, the second in the column to the left, and so on)

Set Datasheet Default Options

To save the new datasheet appearance, save the layout with the table. To create a custom datasheet layout for use with all the tables in the database, change some of the default datasheet options. Choose Tools | Options to open the Options dialog box, then click the Datasheet tab. The same formatting options from the Datasheet Formatting dialog box are available in the Options dialog box in addition to Show Animations, which turns on the animation features, such as the columns sliding over to make room when you insert a new column. There is also an option to show Smart Tags on the datasheet, which, when checked, displays a purple dotted line under text to indicate a Smart Tag.

Change Table Definition in Datasheet View

Although the best place to modify the table definition is in Design view, you can make some limited changes in Datasheet view. You can insert or delete the subdatasheets that display records from related tables, add or delete columns, and change field names in Datasheet view.

Insert/Delete a Subdatasheet

You can use the Insert menu to add a subdatasheet to a table.

To insert or delete a subdatasheet:

1. Open the table or query in Datasheet view.

2. Choose Insert | Subdatasheet. The Insert Subdatasheet dialog box opens showing three tabs: Tables, Queries, and Both.

3. Click the tab that contains the datasheet you want to use for the subdatasheet.

4. Select the table or query name in the list.

5. Choose the foreign key field for the subdatasheet table or query in the Link Child Fields box.

6. Choose the primary key or matching field for the open datasheet in the Link Master Fields box and click OK.

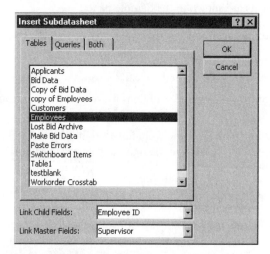

To remove a subdatasheet from a table or query, open the table or query in Datasheet view and choose Format | Subdatasheet | Remove. The subdatasheet is removed only from the display. The data is not affected and the relationship remains intact.

Insert/Delete a Column

To insert a column in the datasheet, place the insertion point in the column to the right of where you want the new one, then choose Insert | Column. A new blank column appears and the columns to the right move over. Double-click the field selector, usually labeled Field1, and rename the column with the appropriate field name.

If you want to change the data type that Access assumes for the field, define a validation rule, or change other properties, you must switch to Design view.

5

As discussed earlier in this chapter, the Insert menu offers two special columns: Lookup and Hyperlink. If you choose Lookup Column, the Lookup Wizard starts. Choosing Hyperlink Column inserts a new blank column, but the field is automatically specified as the Hyperlink data type.

To delete a column in Datasheet view, click anywhere in the field and choose Edit | Delete Column. Access warns you that the deletion will be permanent. This is one of those cases where Undo doesn't work. Choose Yes to go ahead with the deletion or No to cancel. You can delete only one column at a time in Datasheet view.

NOTE *You cannot delete a field that is part of a relationship without first deleting the relationship. Either open the Relationships window to delete the relationship or accept Access's offer to delete it for you.*

Change Field Names

In Datasheet view, you have three ways to rename an existing column. All three methods place the insertion point in the field name text, where you can replace or edit the existing name. Be warned that this also deletes the caption you might have specified:

- Double-click the text in the field selector and type the new name.
- Select the column and choose Format | Rename Column.
- Right-click the field selector and choose Rename Column from the shortcut menu.

Edit Record Data

You can use the Edit | Go To submenu or the navigation buttons at the bottom of the datasheet or form to move to another record: Next, Previous, First, Last, or New. The TAB key and the RIGHT ARROW and LEFT ARROW keys move to another field.

NOTE *All the Office Spelling and AutoCorrect features are available to you in Access. You can use these tools to help with Text and Memo field data.*

When the table contains many fields, some of them are not always visible. Instead of scrolling right and left to enter data in long records, you can use the Go To Field box on the Formatting (Datasheet) toolbar, which contains a list of all the fields in the current datasheet. Click the arrow next to the box to display the list of fields in the current table. When you click on a field name in the list, the insertion point moves to that field in the current record.

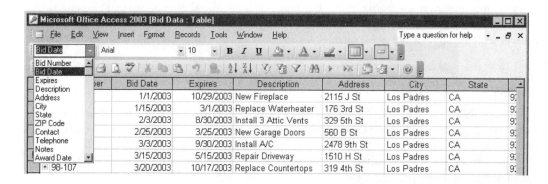

To change the entire value in a field, select the field and enter the new value. To edit only part of the value, change to Edit mode by clicking in the field or pressing F2. Once in Edit mode, the RIGHT ARROW and LEFT ARROW keys move the insertion point through the characters instead of among the fields.

You can tell you are in Edit mode when the insertion point is in the text and the whole value isn't selected. If the whole value is selected, you are not in Edit mode. Then you can press HOME and END to move to the beginning and end of the value respectively.

Locate Records

If your table doesn't contain a lot of records, you probably can find the record you want by scrolling down through the records in the datasheet or form, especially if the records are sorted by the field you are searching. However, if your table contains hundreds of records, that method is rather time-consuming, so Access provides the Find feature. You just tell Access what you want to find and where and how to search for the value. The search can apply to the complete value in the field or only certain characters within the field.

If you are looking for values in a datasheet with a subdatasheet or a form with a subform, Access searches only the object that contains the insertion point.

Find an Exact Match

When you want to edit a specific value in a field in the table, you need a method to locate all the records that contain that value. You can find them one at a time and make the changes you want or ask Access to make the changes for you automatically.

To find a record with a specific value in one of the fields:

1. Place the insertion point anywhere in the column.

2. Click the Find toolbar button or choose Edit | Find or press CTRL-F.

3. Enter the value to look for in the Find What box.

4. Click Find Next. The insertion point moves to the next record with that value (see Figure 5-10).

5. Click Find Next again to find subsequent records with the same value in the field. After Access has found the last record that matches the value, choosing Find Next displays an information dialog box indicating that there are no more records with that value.

6. Click Close.

Limit or Expand the Search

By default, Access searches only the specified field in all the records. In the Look In box, you have a choice between the field that contains the insertion point or the entire table. By choosing the whole table, you can have Access search for the value in all the Text and Memo fields in the table. This is slower than limiting the search to a single field but it comes in handy for finding

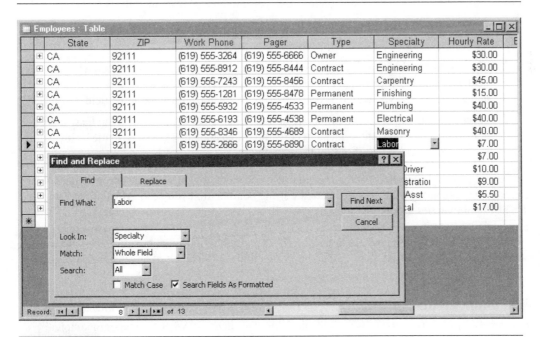

FIGURE 5-10   Finding records with Labor in the Specialty field

specific values in all fields, especially when you want to replace one value globally with another. The Search option drop-down list includes:

- **All** Is the default setting; begins at the current record, searches to the end of the table, and begins again at the first record until all records are examined
- **Up** Searches from the current record toward the first record
- **Down** Searches from the current record through the remaining records

The Match Case option, when checked, treats upper- and lowercase letters as different characters. For example, if you enter the value **labor** in the Find What box and check Match Case, Access will not find *Labor.* The Search Fields As Formatted option looks for the field based on the displayed format rather than the stored value.

Find an Inexact Match

Access offers two ways to find an inexact match in a Text or Memo field: setting the Match option to limit the search to only part of the field or using wildcards in the search string. The Match options specify whether to require a complete and exact match or to accept a match with only part of the field. The Match options that you can choose from include:

- **Whole Field** Is the default and finds only records containing values that exactly match the search string.
- **Any Part of Field** Finds records whose field contains the search string anywhere in the field. For example, if you want to find all work orders that have the word *heater* somewhere in the description, you would ask Access to find a match anywhere in the field.
- **Start of Field** Specifies the first one or more characters to match with the field values. For example, if you want to locate records for all customers whose last name begins with *A*, you would use the Start of Field Match option.

Several wildcard characters can be used in the search string to represent one or more characters. You can mix and match wildcards to create the string combination you need. Most of them can also be used in queries and expressions, as you will see in Chapter 7. Look at Table 5-2 for ways to use wildcards.

Wildcards can appear anywhere in the search string in the Find What box. For example, you can enter the string **12##*[BC]*** to find all addresses in the 1200 block of any street that begins with *B* or *C.*

Find Blank Fields

You can use Find to locate records with blank fields. This is useful when you enter incomplete record data because all the information wasn't available. Then, when more data arrives, you can quickly look for the records that need to be filled in.

To find blank fields, enter Null or Is Null in the Find What text box. When Access finds a record with a blank in the field, the record selector moves to the record but the field is not

Look for Wildcard Characters

The field value you are looking for might include one of the characters Access recognizes as a wildcard, such as an asterisk (*), a question mark (?), a number sign (#), an opening bracket ([), or a hyphen (-). If you use the character directly in a search string, Access handles it as a wildcard.

When you use wildcards in a string to look for one of these characters, you must enclose the item you are looking for in brackets. For example, to find a value that begins with *?B,* you would use the string **[?]B***.

But if you are looking for a hyphen along with another wildcard character, you must treat it a little differently. Access interprets a hyphen or tilde as an indication of a sequence of acceptable characters. You must put such a character before or after all the other characters inside the brackets, not between them. If you have placed an exclamation point (!) inside the brackets to indicate a match excluding the characters within the brackets, place the hyphen right after the exclamation point.

If you are searching for an exclamation point or a closing bracket, you don't need to use the brackets at all. Just place the characters in the string with the rest.

highlighted. When you close the Find and Replace dialog box, the insertion point appears in the blank field, ready for you to enter data.

If you have created a custom format for a Text or Memo field that specifies a certain display when the field contains a Null value and a different display when it contains a zero-length string, be careful how you apply the Search Fields As Formatted option.

Wildcard	Matches	Example
*	Any number of characters.	**b*** finds *bird, belt,* and *blueberry*
?	Any single character.	**b??l** finds *ball, beal, bell, bowl,* and so on
[]	Any character within the brackets.	**b[aeo]ll** finds *ball, bell,* and *boll,* but not *bill* or *bull*
!	Any character not in the brackets.	**b[!ae]ll** finds *bill, boll,* and *bull* but not *ball* or *bell*
- (hyphen)	Any character in the specified range of characters. The range must be in ascending order.	**B[a-d]t** finds *bat, bbt, bct,* and *bdt*
#	Any single numeric character.	**10#** finds *100, 101, 102,* and so on but not *10A*

TABLE 5-2   Wildcard Characters

Also, be sure to select Whole Field in the Match box when you are looking for either a Null value or a zero-length string.

Find and Replace Data

A variation of the Find feature is the Replace tool, which lets you specify a value that you want in the field in place of the one that is already there. The search options are the same. The only difference between the Find tab and the Replace tab is the addition of the Replace With box where you type the replacement value. For example, to replace all occurrences of the word *Lost* in the Award Date field of the Bid Data with the words *Not Awarded*:

1. Place the insertion point in the Award Date column.

2. Choose Edit | Replace to open the Replace tab of the Find and Replace dialog box.

3. Enter **Lost** in the Find What box and **Not Awarded** in the Replace With box.

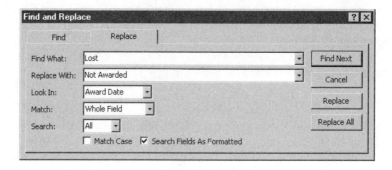

4. Click Find Next, then do one of the following:

   ■ Choose Replace to replace this instance of *Lost.* Access replaces the value and moves automatically to the next occurrence.

   ■ Choose Find Next to skip replacing this occurrence and move to the next.

   ■ Choose Replace All to replace all the values without reviewing them.

5. Access displays a message when it has finished searching the records. Click Cancel to close the dialog box.

Delete Data

To delete individual characters, place the insertion point in the field and press DEL to remove the next character or press BACKSPACE to remove the previous character. To delete all data in the field, select the field and press DEL or BACKSPACE. You can restore characters deleted from a field by choosing Edit | Undo Delete.

To delete an entire record, select the record and press DEL or choose Edit | Delete. A deleted record cannot be restored, so Access warns you before deleting the record. To delete several records, select them all, then proceed as previously described. To delete a record without selecting it, place the insertion point anywhere in the record and click Delete Record.

TIP

If you have a lot of records to delete, you can save time by using a delete query. See Chapter 8 for information about this special query.

5

Part II

Retrieve and Present Information

Chapter 6

Sort, Filter, and Print Records

How to...

- Sort records by values in one or more fields
- Filter records
- Use the Advanced Filter/Sort feature
- Remove/delete or save a filter
- Preview and print filtered or sorted table data

Once you have stored all the information in the related tables of your database, you must be able to retrieve specific data and arrange it in meaningful ways. The Access Sort and Filter features help you do that. Sorting arranges the records in a specified order; filtering hides records. Combining these two tools gives you the power to display only the records you want, in the order you want.

Sort Records

Access automatically sorts records by the value in the primary key field. During data retrieval and presentation, there will be times when you will want to arrange the records in a different order. In Datasheet view, you can sort up to 255 characters in one or more fields to achieve a sort within a sort. In Form view, records can be sorted by only one field with the Sort feature. In ascending order, Yes/No fields sort by Yeses first, then by Nos. Use descending order to reverse the order of the sort. You can sort on Memo fields using the first 255 characters. Access sorts hyperlink fields by the Text to Display (if any) or the address. You cannot sort on OLE Object fields.

Sort on a Single Field

To see records grouped together in Datasheet or Form view, you can sort the records based on the value in a specific field. To sort by a single field in a datasheet or form, click in the field by which you want to sort, then do one of the following:

- Click Sort Ascending or Sort Descending.
- Choose Records | Sort | Sort Ascending or Records | Sort | Sort Descending.
- Right-click in the field and choose Sort Ascending or Sort Descending from the shortcut menu.

To restore the records to their original order, choose Records | Remove Filter/Sort or right-click in the datasheet and choose Remove Filter/Sort from the shortcut menu.

To sort records in a subdatasheet, display the subdatasheet by clicking the expand indicator (the plus sign in the left margin), then proceed as with a datasheet. When you specify a sort order for one subdatasheet in Datasheet view, all the subdatasheets of that level are also sorted accordingly.

Sort by Two or More Fields

To sort by more than one field, the fields must be adjacent in the datasheet. Access uses a sort precedence from left to right so the records are sorted first by the values in the left column. If duplicate values appear in that column, a secondary sort is performed on those records by the values in the next column.

If the columns involved in the sort are not adjacent or are in the wrong relative position in the datasheet or subdatasheet, move the columns before sorting the records. When all are in position, select the columns you want to sort on and click one of the Sort buttons as before or choose from the Records or the shortcut menu.

NOTE
When you sort records by two or more fields, Access performs a "simple" sort in which all the values in the fields are sorted in the same order, ascending or descending. To mix sort orders, you must use the Advanced Filter/Sort operation described in the section "Filter with Advanced Filter/Sort" later in this chapter. Or use a query instead, as described in Chapter 8.

6

Save the Sort Order

If you close the table after sorting the records, Access asks if you want to save the changes to the design (which includes the sort order). Responding Yes saves the sort order with the table; the next time you open the table, the records will appear in that order. Responding No saves the table in the original, primary key order.

Filter Records

When you want to see only certain records in your datasheet, subdatasheet, or form, you can filter out the ones you don't want to see. The *filter* process does just that: it screens the records and lets through only those that meet your criteria. A filter doesn't actually delete any records, it just hides them. The *criteria* are a set of specified conditions that limit the display to a certain subset of records.

The difference between finding records and filtering records is that when Access finds a record, the cursor moves to the record and leaves all the rest on the screen. With a filter, the non-compliant records are removed from the screen, leaving only the records you want to see.

In Access, you have five ways to filter records, depending on the conditions you want to set and whether you want the records sorted in a particular order.

- **Filter By Selection**   Leaves only the records with the same value as the one you select in one of the records

- **Filter Excluding Selection**   Leaves only the records that do not include the same value as the one you select in one of the records

- **Filter By Form**   Screens records with the criteria you enter into a table skeleton

- **Filter For**   Displays a box in the shortcut menu where you enter the filter criteria directly
- **Advanced Filter/Sort**   Gives you, in addition to filtering, the capability to sort the records by two or more fields using different orders, ascending or descending

Filter By Selection

Filtering by selection is the most commonly used and easiest filtering method. You just select the value you want to use as the match for the records and click a button. The records that remain on the screen are only those that contain the selected value. You can Filter By Selection on a value in any type of field except OLE Object fields.

Specify the Filter Value

To set the filter value, place the insertion point in the field that contains the value you want to filter for and apply the filter in one of the following ways:

- Choose Records | Filter | Filter By Selection
- Click Filter By Selection on the toolbar
- Right-click the desired value and choose Filter By Selection from the shortcut menu

The way you select the filter value determines what records pass the filter. Table 6-1 describes the various ways of selecting values for filtering and matches them with comparable settings in the Find dialog box, as discussed in Chapter 5.

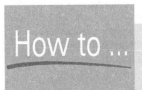 **Pick a Filter Type**

To decide what type of filter you should use, look at what you want it to do:

- If you want to search for records that meet more than one criterion at once (combined with AND), you can use any of the five types of filters. Using Filter By Selection, you must specify and apply the criteria one at a time.

- If you want to combine criteria with the OR operator or enter expressions as criteria, you must use Filter By Form, Filter For, or Advanced Filter/Sort.

- If you also want the records sorted as part of the filter process, you must use the Advanced Filter/Sort. You can, however, sort the results of the other types of filters after applying the filter by clicking one of the Sort buttons on the toolbar.

Selection	Returns Records Where	Find Match Equivalent
Entire value; or, you can place the insertion point in the field without selecting any characters.	Whole field matches the selected value.	Whole Field Match option.
Part of the value, including the first character.	Field starts with the selected characters.	Start of Field Match option.
Part of the value, not including the first character.	Field includes a matching value anywhere in the field.	Any part of Field Match option.

TABLE 6-1 Value Selections for Filtering

6

Let's try out a few filters on the Home Tech Repair tables. First, filter the Workorders table to show records for jobs supervised by Ferrell.

1. With the Workorders table open in Datasheet view, place the insertion point in a Supervisor field with the value Ferrell.

2. Click Filter By Selection. Only four records remain on the screen, all with Ferrell in the Supervisor field.

Microsoft Office Access 2003

File Edit View Insert Format Records Tools Window Help   Type a question for help

Remove Filter

Workorders : Table

	Workorder Number	Customer ID	Bid Number	Start Date	Completion Date	Supervisor	Principal Worker
▶ ⊞	001	1032	98-101	2/25/2003	3/10/2003	Ferrell	Howell
⊞	005	1036	98-108	5/10/2003	5/15/2003	Ferrell	Dobbins
⊞	009	1039	98-117	6/25/2003	6/26/2003	Ferrell	Howell
⊞	010	1032	98-119	6/26/2003	6/26/2003	Ferrell	
✳							

Record: ◄ ◄   1   ► ►I ►✳ of 4 (Filtered)

NOTE *Access reminds you that you are not viewing the entire table. The status bar shows FLTR, indicating that a filter is in effect, and the navigation bar gives you the number of records qualified by the word (Filtered). The Apply Filter toolbar button appears pressed and the ScreenTip for the button has changed to Remove Filter.*

3. Click Remove Filter. All the records return to the datasheet or subdatasheet.

TIP *After you have removed the filter and restored all the records to the display, you can reapply the most recently used filter by clicking the Apply Filter toolbar button or choosing Records | Apply Filter/Sort.*

As an example of filtering to a partial value, filter the Bid Data table so you see only records that contain the word "heater" in the Description field.

1. In the Bid Data datasheet, select the "heater" part of Replace Waterheater in the Description field of the Bid Number 98-102 record.

2. Choose Records | Filter | Filter By Selection. Two records remain, both with the word "heater" at the end of the Description field.

		Bid Number	Bid Date	Expires	Description	Address	City	State
▶	+	98-102	1/15/2003	3/1/2003	Replace Waterheater	176 3rd St	Los Padres	CA
	+	98-117	5/18/2003	8/18/2003	SPA Heater	952 C St	Los Padres	CA
*								

Record: ◄ ◄ | 1 | ► ►I ►* | of 2 (Filtered)

3. Click Remove Filter. All filters are removed and all records return to the datasheet.

Filter By Selection applies only one filter condition at a time. If you need to filter based on a combination of two or more values, you can apply the second Filter By Selection criterion to the records that remain after the first filter is applied. This is equivalent to combining the filter criteria with an AND operator.

Use an Exclusion Filter

Instead of telling Access which records you want to see, sometimes it's easier to specify which ones you don't want to see. In this case, you can use the Filter Excluding Selection option, which screens out the records with the value you select.

Filter Excluding Selection works much like Filter By Selection: you select the value or partial value in the datasheet or form, then choose Records | Filter | Filter Excluding Selection, or right-click the selection and choose Filter Excluding Selection from the shortcut menu.

Filter By Form

Filter By Form is not much different from Filter By Selection. Instead of selecting a value from the datasheet or subdatasheet as a filter criterion, you enter the value in a filter grid. The grid is a table skeleton that resembles a blank record showing all the filterable fields in the table with space to enter filter values.

One advantage of using Filter By Form is that you can combine filter criteria in one operation. You can specify two or more conditions so that a record must meet any one or all of them to survive the filter. The multiple criteria can apply to a single field or to more than one field.

Enter Filter Criteria

When you choose Filter By Form, the table grid appears on the screen. The most recent filter that has been saved with the table shows in the filter grid.

To create a new filter, click Clear Grid to remove any existing filter and move to the field where you want to specify a value. When you move the insertion point to a field in the grid, an arrow appears in the field. Clicking this arrow displays a list of unique values that currently exist in the field, sorted in ascending order. Here you see a list of values in the Completion Date field in the Workorders table.

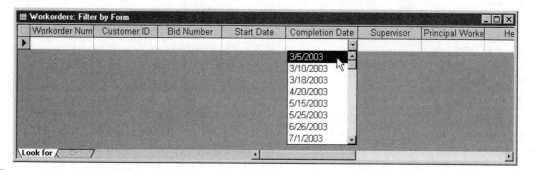

6

To filter on one of these values, select the value and click Apply Filter. This is equivalent to using Filter By Selection.

If you don't see the value list in the table skeleton, the option might be turned off. Check the options on the Edit/Find tab of the Options dialog box. In addition, if the table is large and has a long list of unique values, you may see only two choices: Is Null and Is Not Null.

Now try filtering the Workorders records by using an expression to show only those whose scheduled completion date is before July 1, 2003:

1. In the Workorders datasheet, click Filter By Form on the toolbar.

2. If there are entries in the filter grid, click Clear Grid to remove them.

3. Place the insertion point in the Completion Date field and select 7/1/2003 from the value list. Access automatically adds the date/time delimiter symbols (#) to the date you select from the list.

4. Place the insertion point at the beginning of the date and enter < (less than).

Workorder Num	Customer ID	Bid Number	Start Date	Completion Date	Supervisor	Principal Worke	He
				<#7/1/2003#			

5. Click Apply Filter. Only the eight records of Workorders scheduled to be completed before July 1, 2003 remain on the screen.

	Workorder Num	Customer ID	Bid Number	Start Date	Completion Date	Supervisor	Principal Worke
▶ ⊞	001	1032	98-101	2/25/2003	3/10/2003	Ferrell	Howell
⊞	002	1033	98-103	3/15/2003	3/18/2003	Gunderson	Gikas
⊞	003	1034	98-105	3/10/2003	3/5/2003	Byron	Dobbins
⊞	004	1035	98-107	4/15/2003	4/20/2003	Gunderson	Howell
⊞	005	1036	98-108	5/10/2003	5/15/2003	Ferrell	Dobbins
⊞	006	1037	98-111	5/12/2003	5/25/2003	Byron	
⊞	009	1039	98-117	6/25/2003	6/26/2003	Ferrell	Howell
⊞	010	1032	98-119	6/26/2003	6/26/2003	Ferrell	
*							

Workorders : Table

Record: 14 ◀ 1 ▶ ▶I ▶* of 8 (Filtered)

6. Click Remove Filter or choose Records | Remove Filter/Sort to restore all the records.

Use Wildcards and Expressions in a Filter

You can use wildcards in filter criteria for Text and Memo fields; refer to Chapter 5 for examples of using wildcards. In a search, wildcards can be applied only to character strings. You can use wildcards to replace individual characters or groups of characters.

You can also enter an expression as the filter criterion, such as the earlier example of <7/1/2003 entered in the Completion Date field in the Filter By Form grid. To use an expression as a criterion, enter it directly in the filter grid. Open the Access Help topic, "Examples of expressions used in queries and filters," to see some useful expressions. However, there are a few rules you must obey when entering expressions in a filter condition, whether you're using the Filter By Form, Filter For Input, or Advanced Filter/Sort method:

- ▣ If a Text field value contains a space, any punctuation, or an operator character, the value must be enclosed in quotation marks. If the entry is one of the values in the list, Access adds the quotation marks for you after you leave the criteria grid.

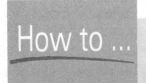

How to ... Filter Memo, OLE Object, and Hyperlink Fields

When you apply Filter By Selection to a Memo, OLE Object, or Hyperlink field, you can see all the records with the same values in the field. With the other filter operations, you can filter based only on whether the field has a value or is empty. When you click the drop-down list in one of these fields, the only available values are Is Null and Is Not Null.

- To filter a Memo field, use the asterisk (*) wildcards to filter on embedded text.

- For Number, Currency, and AutoNumber fields, do not include characters such as the currency symbol or the thousands separator. Decimal points and minus signs are okay.

- For Date/Time field values, abide by the options set on the Date tab of the Regional Settings Properties dialog box of the Windows Control Panel. These options control the sequence of the month, day, and year values within the field. Access encloses the date or time value in pound signs (#).

- For Yes/No fields, you can enter Yes, -1, On, or True to filter for Yes values, and No, 0, Off, or False for No values.

Combine Filter Criteria with AND

To combine two filter conditions with the AND operator and limit the records to those that meet both conditions:

1. In the Workorders datasheet, click Filter By Form on the toolbar.

2. Click Clear Grid to remove the previous filter conditions and click in the Material Cost field.

3. Type **<=1000** and press TAB to move to the Labor Cost field and type **>=500**, then press ENTER.

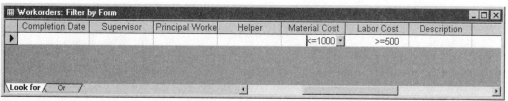

4. Click Apply Filter. Four records meet the combined filter conditions that show the labor-intensive contracts.

 TIP *If your filter doesn't return any records, you might have set conflicting criteria that were impossible to meet.*

5. Click Remove Filter to restore all the records in the datasheet.

Combine Filter Conditions with OR

The OR operator expands the resulting record set by including records that meet either of the conditions, not necessarily both. The Filter By Form window contains two tabs at the bottom of the window: Look For and Or. Enter the first filter condition and any others you want to combine with it using AND on the Look For page.

How to ... **Use AND in one Field**

The preceding example combines filter conditions in different fields with the implied AND operator. You also can combine filter conditions in the same field with AND by typing **AND** between the expressions. For example, if you enter the filter condition **>=500 AND <=1000** in the Material Cost field, you would see only the records for work orders requiring between $500 and $1,000 worth of materials, inclusive. Another way to express the same criterion is to use the Between…And…operator: **Between 500 And 1000**.

If you want to add an OR filter condition, click the Or tab and enter the condition on the second page. If you change your mind and want to delete the Or tab, select it and choose Edit | Delete Tab.

NOTE *Another Or tab appears when you begin to add a filter to the first Or page.*

To combine two filter conditions with OR so that you can see all the Workorders records for jobs on B or H Streets:

1. In the Bid Data datasheet, choose Records | Filter | Filter By Form. The Filter window opens showing the last filter condition in the grid.

2. Click Clear Grid, then enter *** B*** (with a space before the *B*) in the Address field on the Look for page and press ENTER. Access translates the expression to *Like "* B*"*.

3. Click the Or tab at the bottom of the window. The Or page opens with the same empty grid as the Look For page. Notice a third tab now shows at the bottom of the window.

4. Place the insertion point in the Address field and enter *** H***, then press ENTER. The expression is changed to *Like "* H*"*.

5. Click Apply Filter on the toolbar. The datasheet now shows the five jobs with addresses on B or H Streets.

Bid Number	Bid Date	Expires	Description	Address	City	State
⊞ 98-104	2/25/2003	3/25/2003	New Garage Doors	560 B St	Los Padres	CA
⊞ 98-106	3/15/2003	5/15/2003	Repair Driveway	1510 H St	Los Padres	CA
⊞ 98-118	5/18/2003	6/18/2003	DSS Install	560 B St	Los Padres	CA
⊞ 98-120	5/26/2003	6/26/2003	Repair Driveway	1510 H St	Los Padres	CA
⊞ 98-123	6/5/2003	7/5/2003	Porch Roof	560 B St	Los Padres	CA

Record: 1 of 5 (Filtered)

6. Click Remove Filter to restore all the records.

TIP *If you don't include a space before the* H *in the filter criterion, you will see all records with the letter* H *anywhere in the Address field. Examples include addresses on any street with* th, *such as 5th or 6th.*

Filter For

The Filter For option lets you filter records by entering the condition right in the open Datasheet or Form view. You can use the same conditions and expressions as in the Filter By Form grid.

To apply the filter, right-click in the field whose values you want to filter and type the value or expression in the Filter For box and press ENTER. For example, you might want to see only records in the Bid Data table that have expiration dates before July 1, 2003.

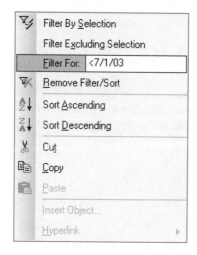

If you want to apply the filter and keep the shortcut menu open to specify additional criteria, press TAB instead. Repeat to add as many criteria as you need to refine the filter to just the records you want to see. This is equivalent to applying successive filters with Filter By Selection or combining conditions with AND in Filter By Form.

To filter more than one value in the same field, enter an expression that combines the criteria with an OR operator. You cannot combine criteria in different fields with an OR operator using Filter For Input.

Filter with Advanced Filter/Sort

The Advanced Filter/Sort feature is the most flexible and comprehensive of the Access filtering tools. It includes all the features of Filter By Form and allows you to specify mixed sort orders for different fields in the table. You enter all of the filtering and sorting specifications in a single window.

The Advanced Filter/Sort window is divided into two parts very similar to a Query Design window. The upper part contains the field list. The lower part is the design grid where you specify which fields you want to filter, the values to use as filters, and how you want the records sorted in the resulting recordset. If you have applied a filter recently, the criteria will appear in the Criteria row of the grid. Click Clear Grid to remove it.

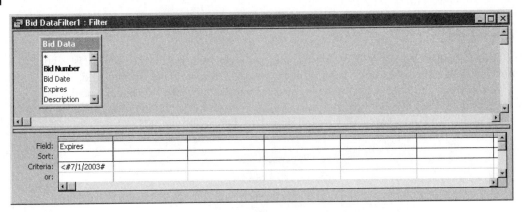

The process of creating an Advanced Filter/Sort is nearly identical to that of creating a query. Chapter 7 contains all the details for creating queries that you can use to build an Advanced Filter/Sort that can accomplish tasks such as the following:

- Selecting the fields to filter or sort
- Specifying filter criteria
- Setting the sort orders

Apply the Advanced Filter

At any time during the design of an advanced filter, you can apply it to see if you are getting the data you want. Access gives you three ways to apply the filter:

- Click Apply Filter on the toolbar.
- Choose Filter | Apply Filter/Sort.
- Right-click anywhere in the upper section of the Design window and choose Apply Filter/Sort from the shortcut menu.

Bid Number	Bid Date	Expires	Award Date	Description	Address	City
98-103	2/3/2003	6/1/2003	3/1/03	Install 3 Attic Vents	329 5th St	Los Padres
98-105	3/3/2003	7/2/2003	4/1/03	Install A/C	2478 9th St	Los Padres
98-107	3/20/2003	7/19/2003	4/10/03	Replace Countertops	319 4th St	Los Padres
98-108	3/28/2003	7/27/2003	5/1/03	Move Washer & Dryer	2111 J St	Los Padres
98-109	3/28/2003	5/28/2003	Lost	Garden Window	156 8th St	Los Padres
98-106	3/15/2003	5/15/2003	Lost	Repair Driveway	1510 H St	Los Padres
98-104	2/25/2003	3/25/2003	Lost	New Garage Doors	560 B St	Los Padres

Record: 1 of 7 (Filtered)

Notice that the toolbar and the navigation key area both warn you that this is a filtered record set. Remove the advanced filter the same way as other filters.

Filter by Lookup Fields with Advanced Filter/Sort

Filtering on a field that gets its value from a lookup list with Advanced Filter/Sort can present a slight problem. When you choose to filter records by values in a Lookup field in Filter By Form, you pick from the value list that contains all the values in the lookup list created by the Lookup Wizard. What you don't see in the list are the values that are actually stored in the field. It is the value in the primary key field of the lookup list that is stored instead of the more informative displayed value.

When you use Advanced Filter/Sort, you do not choose from the lookup list because there is only one table in the Filter window. This means that you must enter the stored value in the Criteria row to filter on a Lookup field. For example, using Filter By Form to filter on Ferrell in the Supervisor field of the Workorders table, you can select Ferrell from the list or type **Ferrell** in the grid. To do the same in Advanced Filter/Sort, you must enter **10**, Ferrell's Employee ID number, in the Criteria row.

Save a Filter

The most recent filter is saved with the table—not as a separate object—if you respond Yes to save the table changes. When you reopen the table, the filter is no longer in effect but you can reapply it by any of the methods discussed earlier.

If you want to have more than one filter available to a table or want to save a filter permanently, you must save it as a query, which is stored as a separate Access database object. When you want to use the filter again, you can bring it back from the query to the Filter window or simply run it as a query.

To save an advanced filter as a query and load it again in the Filter window:

1. With the Filter window displayed, click the Save As Query button or choose Save As Query from the shortcut menu or the File menu.

2. Name the query and choose OK.

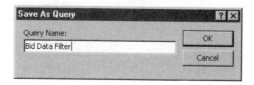

3. To restore the specifications to the Filter window, open a blank Advanced Filter/Sort window and click the Load From Query button. You can also choose Load From Query from the shortcut menu or the File menu.

4. The Applicable Filter dialog box shows a list of all the queries that are based on the Bid Data table.

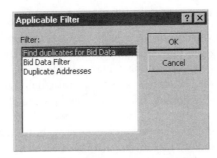

5. Choose the query you want and click OK. All the filter parameters are returned to the grid, where you can choose to apply the filter or make changes to it.

 If all you want to do is filter the records, simply run the query you saved from the filter.

Remove and Delete Filters

There is a difference between removing and deleting a filter. Removing a filter simply returns all the records to the datasheet or form; you can reapply it later. Deleting the filter erases the filter criteria, and the filter cannot be reapplied without reconstructing it. You saw earlier how to remove a filter.

To delete a filter entirely, clear the filter grid and apply the empty filter to the datasheet by the following method:

1. Switch to the Advanced Filter/Sort window. It doesn't matter how you created the filter; you can still see it in the filter grid.

2. Click Clear Grid or choose Clear Grid from the Edit or the shortcut menu.

3. Click Apply Filter.

4. Click Close to close the datasheet and respond Yes to save the changes.

When you open the table again, the Apply Filter button is dimmed indicating the filter has been removed.

Preview and Print Sorted or Filtered Table Data

You don't have to create a fancy report to print your table data. You can print the datasheet as it appears in the Datasheet view or print in the default report format, called the AutoReport. To print a single copy of the entire datasheet, click the Print button. Without opening the table, right-click the table name in the database window and choose Print from the shortcut menu.

If you want to see how the filtered or sorted table data will look when it is printed, use the Print Preview. To open the Print Preview window, do the following:

1. Open the table in Datasheet view.

2. Apply the filter or sort order.

 3. Choose File | Print Preview or click the Print Preview button.

The Preview window toolbar includes some buttons that offer options for viewing the printout. The Preview window shortcut menu contains many of the same options. See Chapter 11 for details of how to use the Print Preview window.

Figure 6-1 shows the Bid Data datasheet previewed in three pages. If you change the page orientation to landscape, it will need only two pages.

If you want to adjust the margin settings, the paper size, or the page layout, use the Page Setup dialog box. If you want to choose other print options such as multiple copies or selected pages, open the Print dialog box. See Chapter 11 for information about running Page Setup and setting Print options.

6

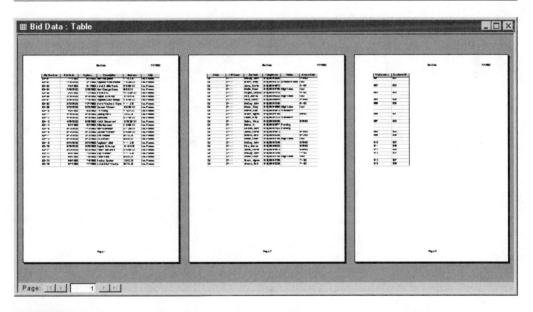

FIGURE 6-1   Previewing the Bid Data printout

Chapter 7

Extract Information with Queries

How to...

- Create a select query with help from the Query Wizard
- Create a select query without the wizard
- Add selection criteria
- Set query properties
- Modify a query
- Perform calculations with a query
- Create special queries with the Query Wizard

When you work with information in an Access datasheet, you can filter and sort the records in many ways, but you have even more flexibility with queries. You can limit the records to a specific subset and specify only the fields you want to see in the result.

An Access query is a set of explicit specifications that tell Access exactly what information you want to see and how you want it arranged or manipulated in the results. Access provides several types of queries ranging from the popular *select query,* which extracts specific data to the more exotic *action queries,* which can insert, update, and delete records.

The results of both filters and queries can be used as the source of data for forms and reports. You can also sort the results of both and save the sort order for use in a later work session. Both methods let you edit the data displayed in the results if editing is otherwise permitted.

Before getting down to business, you need to understand a few new terms. When you run a query, the resulting group of records is called a *recordset* which may or may not be editable, depending on the type of query that produced the recordset. If the records can be edited, the result is called a *dynaset.* Simple select queries produce dynasets. If not editable, it is called a *snapshot.* Crosstab queries and any queries with groupings or calculated fields produce snapshots. See the Access Help topic, "When can I update data from a query?" for more information.

 **Decide between a Query and a Filter**

Usually you will use a filter to view or edit records temporarily in a datasheet or form. If you want to return to the subset of records later, you should use a query. Queries are separate database objects that appear in the Database window whereas a single filter is saved with a table.

Use either a query or a filter when you want to do the following:

- Use the results as a basis for a form or report
- Edit data in the result if editing is allowed

Use a query if you want to do the following:

- Add another table and include those records in the result
- Select only specific fields to include in the result
- Store the data as a separate Access object in the database
- See results without opening the underlying table, query, or form
- Include calculated values in the result

The results of both filters and queries can be used as the source of data for forms and reports. You also can sort the results of both and save the sort order for use in a later work session. Both methods let you edit the data displayed in the results if editing is otherwise permitted.

Create a Select Query

As usual, Access gives you a choice of methods to begin a new query design:

- Click the New command button on the Queries page in the Database window.

- Click the arrow next to the New Object toolbar button and select New Query from the drop-down list.
- Choose Insert | Query.

All three approaches open the New Query dialog box. As you can see, there are wizards to help with several types of queries. If you want to create a select query, you can start from scratch by selecting Design View in the New Query dialog box or choose one of the wizards to help you. Choosing Design View takes you to the Query Design window, which looks a lot like the Advanced Filter/Sort Design window. To create a select query with the wizard, choose Simple Query Wizard, which will guide you through choices about the basic design of the select query. You can then go to the Design window to customize the query design if necessary.

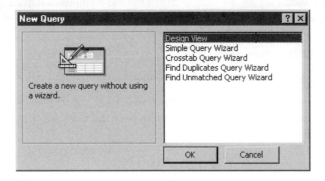

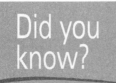

Specific Types of Select Queries

The Access select queries include the following:

- **Simple Select queries**   Display data from one or more tables sorted in a specific order. You also can perform many types of predefined or custom calculations on values in all records or within groups of records.

- **Parameter queries**   Display all records that match a criterion you enter at a prompt.

- **Find Duplicate queries**   Display all records with duplicate values in one or more specified fields.

- **Find Unmatched queries**   Display records in one table that have no related records in another table.

Use the Simple Query Wizard

The Simple Query Wizard displays a series of dialog boxes in which you specify the fields and records you want to include in the query and enter a name for the same query. You can include fields from any of the tables or other queries in your database.

Let's use the Simple Query Wizard to build a list of current work orders and include information from the Workorders and Bid Data tables:

1. In the Database window, click Queries, then click New.

2. Select Simple Query Wizard from the New Query dialog box or simply double-click "Create query by using wizard" in the Queries pane.

3. You can also run this wizard by double-clicking "Create query by using wizard" in the Queries pane of the Database window. Select Table: Workorders from the Tables/Queries list box (see Figure 7-1) and use one of the following methods to move the Workorder Number, Supervisor, Material Cost, Labor Cost, and Description fields to the Selected Fields list.

    - Double-click the field name.

    - Select the field in the Available Fields list and click the right arrow (>).

TIP   *To add all the fields from a table, click the double right arrow (>>). If you change your mind about including a field, double-click it in the Selected Fields list or select it and click the left arrow (<).*

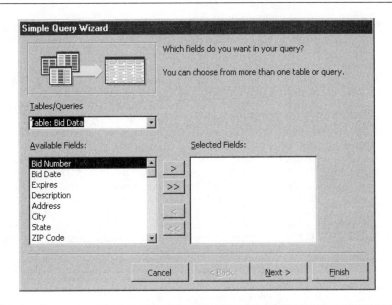

FIGURE 7-1   Choose the fields in the Simple Query Wizard dialog box.

4.   Select Table: Bid Data from the Tables/Queries list box and add the Address, Bid
     Number, and Principal fields to the Selected Fields list.

5.   Click Next and accept the Detail option, which will show every field of every record,
     then click Next.

6.   Enter Current Workorders as the name for the new query and accept the default option to
     open the query to view information.

7.   Click Finish. The query results appear in a datasheet showing not only the eight fields
     you selected but all the records (see Figure 7-2). The column widths and record height
     have been adjusted in the figure to show all the information.

The wizard has helped you with the basic query definition; now it is up to you to add the
final touches, such as adding selection criteria to limit the records, changing the query and field
properties, adding another table, specifying a sort order, or adding calculated fields.

Tour the Query Design Window

A query, like a table, can be viewed as a datasheet or a design. The Datasheet view shows you
the data that results when you run the query. The Design view is where you can look at the query
structure and make changes to the query design or even create a new one. The third query view is

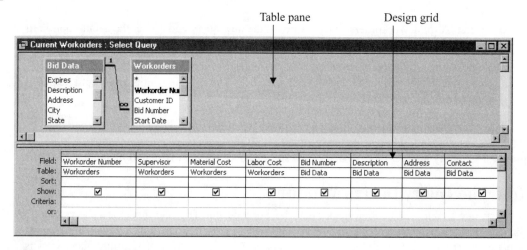

Current Workorders : Select Query

Workorder Num	Supervisor	Material Cost	Labor Cost	Bid Number	Description	Address	Contact
001	Ferrell	$1,072.50	$572.50	98-101	New Fireplace	2115 J St	McCoy, John
002	Gundersor	$1,155.00	$840.00	98-103	Install 3 Attic Vents	329 5th St	Jones, David
003	Byron	$850.50	$126.00	98-105	Install A/C	2478 9th St	Rogers, Ohykki
004	Gundersor	$115.50	$315.00	98-107	Replace Countertops	319 4th St	Perry, Oliver
005	Ferrell	$262.50	$252.00	98-108	Move Washer & Dryer	2111 J St	McCoy, John
006	Byron	$750.00	$800.00	98-111	Ceiling Fans	186 G St	Brown, Agnes
007	Connelly	$2,500.00	$7,200.00	98-113	Finish Basement	1520 8th St	Selms, Harry
008	Gundersor	$400.00	$750.00	98-116	Garden Window	329 5th St	Jones, David
009	Ferrell	$1,100.00	$450.00	98-117	SPA Heater	952 C St	Anders, Bob
010	Ferrell	$175.00	$100.00	98-119	Replace Toilet	2111 J St	McCoy, John
011	Kordel	$300.00	$1,300.00	98-120	Repair Driveway	1510 H St	Norr, James
012	Ferrell	$280.00	$480.00	98-121	Erect Tool Shed	329 5th St	Jones, David
013	Byron	$400.00	$1,100.00	98-122	Bay Window	2111 J St	McCoy, John
014	Gundersor	$75.00	$300.00	98-124	Soaker System	186 G St	Brown, Agnes
015	Gundersor	$420.00	$100.00	98-125	Install Dish Washer	952 C St	Anders, Bob

Record: ◄ ◄ 1 ► ►I ►* of 15

FIGURE 7-2 The results of the Current Workorders query

the SQL view, which shows the SQL statements that Access creates behind the scenes to implement the query. The SQL view has no counterpart with table objects.

 To switch to Design view, click the View toolbar button and choose Design View from the drop-down list or choose View | Design View.

■ The upper pane is the table pane, which displays the field lists for all the tables in the query and shows the relationships among the tables.

■ The lower pane is the design grid, which shows the elements of the query design.

The design grid shows the field names you selected in the wizard dialog box and includes the name of the table they came from. Here is where you specify which fields to include, any filter criteria or sort orders, and whether to show the field in the query result. The check marks in the Show row indicate which fields are to appear in the query result. Clearing the check mark hides the field from the query result. This is helpful when you want to filter or sort the results based on a field that you don't want to appear in the query results.

The Query Design toolbar has some new buttons; the menu bar also includes new options.

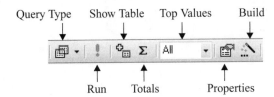

Without the Wizard

To bypass the wizard and create your query from scratch, select Design View from the New Query dialog box. The Show Table dialog box opens; there you will select the tables or queries you want to question.

As an example of creating a new query without the wizard, Home Tech Repair needs a list of work orders showing the following fields from the Bid Data and Workorders tables arranged in the following order:

■ Bid Number (Bid Data)

■ Supervisor (Workorders)

■ Job Address (Bid Data)

■ Description (Workorders)

■ Award Date (Bid Data)

■ Start Date and Completion Date (Workorders)

Later we will add the customer's Last Name and Phone Number from the Customers table. We'll also add the cost data; compute the total cost; and add criteria based on start date, total cost, and other factors to limit the records in the result.

To create the new query:

1. Choose New in the Queries tab of the Database window.

2. Select Design View and click OK. The Show Table dialog box opens with three tabs that display a list of Tables, Queries, or Both in the current database.

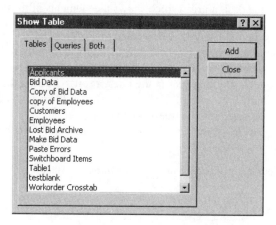

3. Select Bid Data (if it is not already selected) and choose Add. You can see the field list added to the query table pane behind the dialog box.

4. Double-click Workorders in the Tables list and choose Close. Figure 7-3 shows the query design with the two tables. (Field lists have been resized in the figure so you can see the linking fields.)

5. Keep the Query window open to add fields to the design grid.

The next tasks are to choose the fields that you want to appear in the query result and arrange them in the desired order; let's first take a look at the relationships that Access shows for the two Home Tech Repair tables and add a third table to the design.

Relate Multiple Tables in a Query

To add a table to an existing query, click Show Table, choose Query | Show Table, or right-click the table pane and choose Show Table from the shortcut menu. If the tables are already related at the table level, Access automatically displays the join lines when you add the table to the query design. You can tell by the appearance of the line whether referential integrity is enforced, and which table is the "one" side and which is the "many."

If the tables are not related before you add them to the query, Access often assumes a relationship between them based on fields with the same name and data type, especially if one is a primary key. When Access joins the tables, referential integrity is not enforced.

In the Home Tech Repair database the relationship between the Bid Data and the Workorders table was defined as one-to-many, linked by Bid Number, with referential integrity enforced. The Workorders table is related to the Bid Data table by Customer ID but referential integrity is not enforced. You can see these relationships in the query table pane.

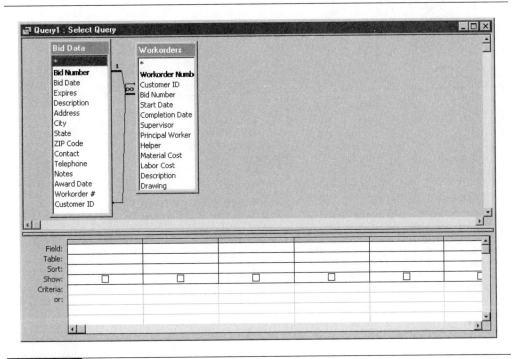

FIGURE 7-3 Tables added to the query design

Let's add the Customers table to the new query and include the Last Name and Phone Number in the results so we won't have to look them up to reach the customer.

To add the Customers table:

1. Click Show Table to open the Show Table dialog box.

2. Double-click the Customers table and click Close. Referential integrity is enforced on the relationship with the Workorders table but not on the relationship with the Bid Data table (see Figure 7-4). (The tables have been rearranged slightly in the figure to show the relationships more clearly.)

NOTE *To remove a table from the query design, click on the field list in the table pane and press DEL or right-click the field list and choose Remove Table from the shortcut menu. The table is removed from the query design but remains untouched in the database. Any fields from that table that you have already placed in the design grid are also removed.*

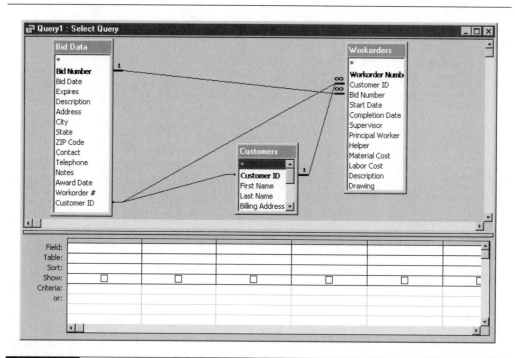

FIGURE 7-4   A third table is added.

Add/Remove Fields

You can add all the fields at once, add a selected group of fields, or add one field at a time. To add all the fields in a table to the grid at once, do one of the following:

- Double-click the asterisk (*) at the top of the field list. This method places the table or query name in the Field row of the column followed by a period and an asterisk, as in the following example: Customers.*

- Drag the asterisk from the field list to an empty column in the grid. This method does the same as the previous one.

- Double-click the field list title bar to select all the fields and drag the group to the grid. Access places each field in a separate column across the grid in the order in which they appear in the field list.

TIP   *There is an advantage and a disadvantage to using the asterisk method of adding all the fields to query. The advantage is that if fields are added or deleted from the underlying table or query, this query will automatically make corresponding changes to the design. The disadvantage is that if you want to sort or filter using one of the fields, you must add it separately to the grid.*

To add fields to the grid one at a time, do any of the following:

- Double-click the field name to place it in the first empty column.

- Drag the field to an empty column or insert it between filled columns.

- Select the field name from the Field row drop-down list. The list in a blank column contains all the fields in all the tables in the table pane and the table names with a period and asterisk.

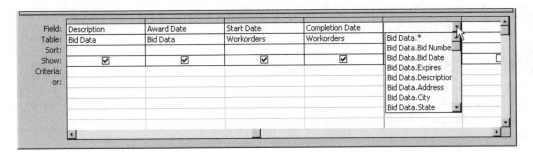

To add a group of fields to the grid at once, select them and drag them as a group. The standard use of SHIFT and CTRL to select adjacent and non-adjacent field names works here the same as with filters. When you drag the block of selected field names to the grid, Access spreads them to empty columns, beginning where you drop the group. If there are already fields in the grid, the ones to the right of where you drop the group move over to make room.

To delete a field from the grid, click the column selector and press DEL or choose Edit | Delete Column. If you remove the check mark from the Show cell in a column with no Sort or Criteria entries, the field will be removed from the grid the next time you open the query.

You can adjust the column widths and drag a column to a new position just as in a datasheet. Changing the column width has no effect on the query results datasheet unless you reduce the column width to zero.

 To adjust a column width to fit its longest visible entry in the design grid, move the mouse pointer to the right edge of the column selector and double-click when the pointer changes to a two-way arrow. If you enter a longer value in the column later, you will need to readjust the width to see it all.

Figure 7-5 shows the new query, still unnamed, with all the required fields in place. The columns have been resized to fit their contents and some are out of sight.

Run and Save the Query

As you progress with the query design, it's a good idea to run the query now and then to see if you are getting the information the way you want it. You have three ways to run the query:

 ■   Click Datasheet view

- Click Run
- Choose Query | Run

When you try to close the query from the Design view or one of the query result views, Access will prompt you to save the design. To save the new query design before adding the sort order and filter criteria:

1. Return to the Query Design view and click Save.
2. Enter **Workorder Cost Sheet** in the Save As dialog box, then choose OK.

Hide and Show Fields

There might be one or more fields that you want to use in filtering or sorting the query results but don't want to appear in the results. The check box in the Show cell of the design grid determines whether the field values will be displayed. Clear the check mark to hide the field; check it to show the field.

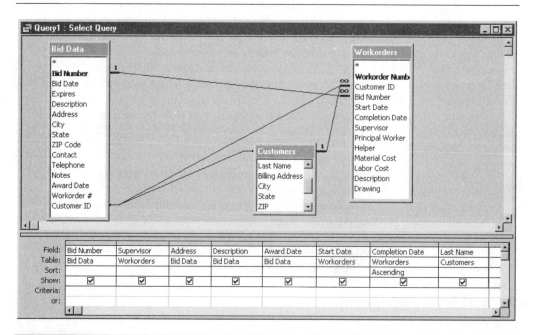

FIGURE 7-5 Fields added to the new query

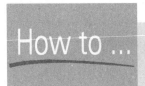

How to ...   **Optimize Query Performance**

If you have created an important query but it seems to take a long time to run, there might be ways to streamline it:

- ■ Make sure all the foreign keys in the related tables are indexed. If a field cannot be indexed, try not to sort on it.
- ■ Include in the design grid only those fields that are necessary in the results. Extra fields take more time to display.
- ■ Make sure you are not using exorbitantly large data sizes. Unnecessarily large fields waste disk space and slow processing.

TIP   *When you reopen the design of a query in which you have hidden some of the fields, you might think they have been removed. Actually, Access moves the hidden fields to the rightmost columns in the design grid when you save the query, so they might be off the screen. However, if there are no Criteria or Show entries, the field indeed is removed from the design.*

Specify the Record Order

To set a sort order in the query design, choose from the Sort cell list box in the column containing the field by which you want to sort. If you want to sort on more than one field, make sure you have the fields arranged in the proper order from left to right; they need not be adjacent.

A sort order will be saved with the query if you specify it in the design. Any new form or report based on the query then inherits the sort order. The order need not be applied but it is an inherited property of the form or report.

Sorting on a lookup field can have confusing results. For example, Figure 7-6 shows the results of sorting the Workorder Cost Sheet records first by Supervisor, then by Completion date. The lower window shows the underlying query grid with both fields sorted in ascending order.

The Completion Dates are in the correct order within the set of records for a given Supervisor. However, the Supervisor fields do not appear to be in alphabetical order, either ascending or descending. When you specify a sort in the query grid, Access sorts on the stored value, which in this case is the Employee ID number, not the employee name. If you want the records sorted by the displayed value, sort in the Datasheet view, which has access to the related lookup list values.

NOTE   *You could include the employee Last Name field in the query and sort on that, but you would run the risk of showing two or more employees' names.*

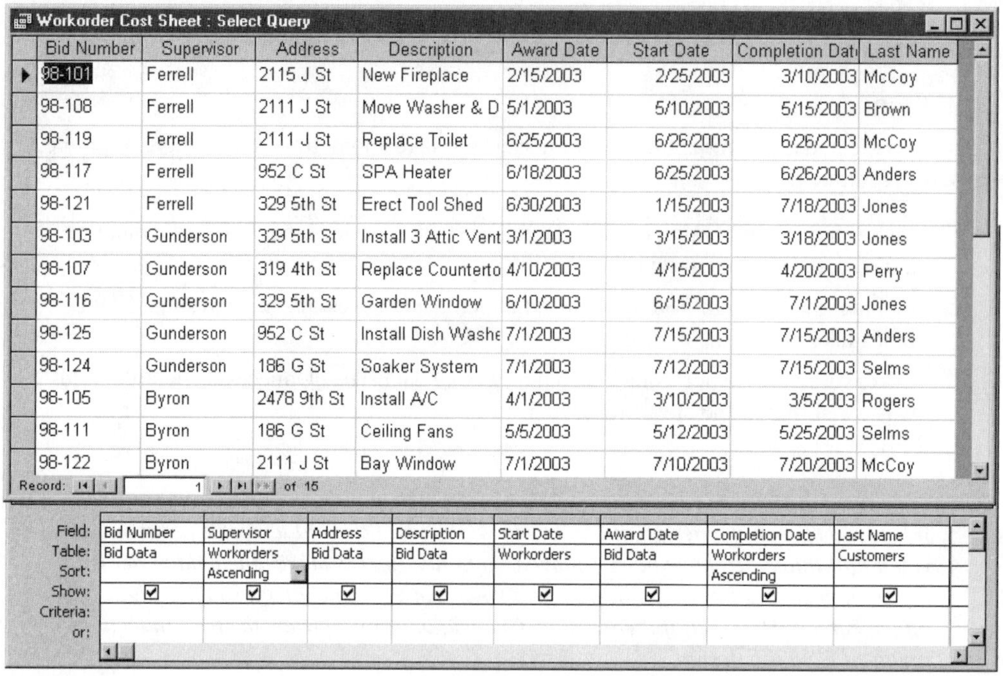

Bid Number	Supervisor	Address	Description	Award Date	Start Date	Completion Dat	Last Name
98-101	Ferrell	2115 J St	New Fireplace	2/15/2003	2/25/2003	3/10/2003	McCoy
98-108	Ferrell	2111 J St	Move Washer & D	5/1/2003	5/10/2003	5/15/2003	Brown
98-119	Ferrell	2111 J St	Replace Toilet	6/25/2003	6/26/2003	6/26/2003	McCoy
98-117	Ferrell	952 C St	SPA Heater	6/18/2003	6/25/2003	6/26/2003	Anders
98-121	Ferrell	329 5th St	Erect Tool Shed	6/30/2003	1/15/2003	7/18/2003	Jones
98-103	Gunderson	329 5th St	Install 3 Attic Vent	3/1/2003	3/15/2003	3/18/2003	Jones
98-107	Gunderson	319 4th St	Replace Counterto	4/10/2003	4/15/2003	4/20/2003	Perry
98-116	Gunderson	329 5th St	Garden Window	6/10/2003	6/15/2003	7/1/2003	Jones
98-125	Gunderson	952 C St	Install Dish Washe	7/1/2003	7/15/2003	7/15/2003	Anders
98-124	Gunderson	186 G St	Soaker System	7/1/2003	7/12/2003	7/15/2003	Selms
98-105	Byron	2478 9th St	Install A/C	4/1/2003	3/10/2003	3/5/2003	Rogers
98-111	Byron	186 G St	Ceiling Fans	5/5/2003	5/12/2003	5/25/2003	Selms
98-122	Byron	2111 J St	Bay Window	7/1/2003	7/10/2003	7/20/2003	McCoy

Record: 1 of 15

Field:	Bid Number	Supervisor	Address	Description	Start Date	Award Date	Completion Date	Last Name
Table:	Bid Data	Workorders	Bid Data	Bid Data	Workorders	Bid Data	Workorders	Customers
Sort:		Ascending					Ascending	
Show:	☑	☑	☑	☑	☑	☑	☑	☑
Criteria:								
or:								

FIGURE 7-6 Sorting on a lookup field

As with a sort order, you can apply a filter to the query results instead of making it a part of the query design. This will have the same effect as adding the criteria to the design, but the filter will not be saved with the query.

Show Highest or Lowest Values

Limiting the results to the few highest or lowest values in a field can be handy for isolating the more labor-intensive jobs or finding the employees who could use a raise. For example, you can ask Access to display only the records with the 15 highest or lowest values in a field or the records with the highest or lowest 15 percent of values.

Use the Top Values box on the toolbar to specify how many or what percentage of the records to include in the results. The Top Values list includes 5, 25, and 100 records and 5 percent and 25 percent of the values to choose from as well as All. You can also type any percentage or number of values you want directly in the box.

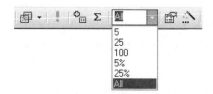

Access selects the records starting from the top of the list, so before you select the Top Values setting, you must sort (descending) on the field you want to display the highest values. If you want the lowest values, sort in ascending order. If you have specified a sort on any other field in the query, make sure that field (or fields) is to the right of the top values field so it will be subordinate to the Top Value list.

Add Selection Criteria

The selection criteria in queries are expressions that define a condition that must be met for the record to be included in the subset. An *expression* is a combination of symbols, values, identifiers, and operators that are used for many purposes, many of which you have already seen; others will be discussed in later chapters, including

- **Symbols**   Quotation marks, colons, asterisks, and other special characters that are used in expressions
- **Values**   Literal values, constants, results of a function, or identifiers
- **Identifiers**   The values of a field, controls in a form or report, or properties
- **Operators**   Symbols or words that indicate an operation that is to be performed on one or more elements in the expression

Use Wildcards and Operators

If you want to set a criterion for a text field and you want to match only part of the field, you can use the same wildcards you used in filters: **?** to represent a single character and ***** to represent any number of characters. For example, to find all Bid Data records for jobs on J Street, enter the expression ***J St*** in the Criteria cell in the Address column and press ENTER. Access examines the expression and completes the syntax by adding special characters such as Like "*J St*".

Operators are the key to more flexible expressions. Access has several classes of operators: *arithmetic, comparison, concatenation,* and *logical*.

- Arithmetic operators include + (addition), - (subtraction), * (multiplication), and / (division).
- Comparison operators include Equals, Greater Than, Less Than, Is Null, Is Not Null, and Like.
- The concatenation operator usually is the & (ampersand) symbol.
- Logical operators include And, Or, and Not.

Use a Single Criterion

To see information from the Workorder Cost Sheet for only those jobs that are supervised by Gunderson:

1. Open the Workorder Cost Sheet query in Design view and enter **12** (the Employee ID number for Gunderson) in the Criteria cell of the Supervisor column, then press ENTER. Access adds quotation marks around 12 because the field is a text data type.

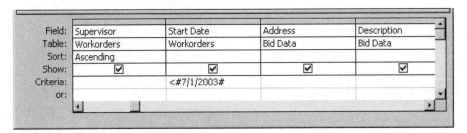

Field:	Bid Number	Supervisor	Address	Description	Award Date	Start Date
Table:	Bid Data	Workorders	Bid Data	Bid Data	Bid Data	Workorders
Sort:						
Show:	☑	☑	☑	☑	☑	☑
Criteria:		"12"				
or:						

2. Switch to Datasheet view to display the five records for Gunderson's jobs.

3. Now you want to see the records for all jobs that were started before July 1, 2003 without regard to the supervisor. Return to Design view and delete the Supervisor criteria by selecting the expression and pressing DEL.

4. Enter **<7/1/03** in the Start Date Criteria cell and press ENTER. Access adds the date delimiters.

Field:	Supervisor	Start Date	Address	Description
Table:	Workorders	Workorders	Bid Data	Bid Data
Sort:	Ascending			
Show:	☑	☑	☑	☑
Criteria:		<#7/1/2003#		
or:				

5. Run the query to see the records for jobs started before July 1, 2003.

Use Multiple Criteria

To apply more than one selection criterion, combine them with the AND or OR operators, using the same logic as with filters:

■ Use AND to require that both criteria be met to include the record in the query result.

■ Use OR to extract records that satisfy either expression.

NOTE *If you want to select records based on field values, the field must be in the design grid even if you don't show it in the results.*

Where you enter the expressions in the design grid depends on how you want them applied:

- In a single field using OR, enter one expression in the Criteria row and the second expression in the OR row.

Field:	Bid Number	Supervisor	Start Date	Address
Table:	Bid Data	Workorders	Workorders	Bid Data
Sort:				
Show:	✔	✔	✔	✔
Criteria:		"12"		
or:		"10"		

- In a single field using AND, enter both expressions in the Criteria row combined with the AND operator.

TIP

If the expression is wider than the input area, press SHIFT-F2 with the insertion point in the cell where you are entering the expression. This opens the Zoom box where you can enter and edit the expression. Even though the text wraps to multiple lines in the Zoom box, the expression is only one line.

- In two fields using OR, enter one expression in the Criteria row of one column and the other expression in the OR row of the other column. It doesn't matter which is which.

Field:	Bid Number	Supervisor	Start Date	Address
Table:	Bid Data	Workorders	Workorders	Bid Data
Sort:				
Show:	✔	✔	✔	✔
Criteria:		"12"		
or:			<#7/1/2003#	

- In two fields using AND, enter both expressions in the Criteria row.

Field:	Bid Number	Supervisor	Start Date	Address
Table:	Bid Data	Workorders	Workorders	Bid Data
Sort:				
Show:	✔	✔	✔	✔
Criteria:		"12"	<#7/1/2003#	
or:				

7

■ In three fields using both AND and OR, enter one pair of AND expressions in the Criteria row and the other pair in the OR row.

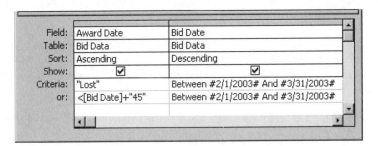

Field:	Bid Number	Supervisor	Start Date	Address	Description
Table:	Bid Data	Workorders	Workorders	Bid Data	Bid Data
Sort:		Ascending			
Show:	☑	☑	☑	☑	☑
Criteria:		"12"	<#7/1/2003#		
or:			>#6/1/2003#	Like "*J St*"	

The Advanced Filter/Sort we saved as a query in the last chapter provides an example of a slightly different arrangement of multiple selection criteria in the design grid.

Field:	Award Date	Bid Date
Table:	Bid Data	Bid Data
Sort:	Ascending	Descending
Show:	☑	☑
Criteria:	"Lost"	Between #2/1/2003# And #3/31/2003#
or:	<[Bid Date]+"45"	Between #2/1/2003# And #3/31/2003#

If you are using a field name in a criterion and it contains a space or any special character, you must enclose it in square brackets.

The criteria specified in the Look For tab in the Advanced Filter/Sort appear in the Criteria row of the query design grid, and the expressions entered in the OR tab appear in the OR row. The Bid Date column has been widened to show the entire expression.

When working with expressions, you can use the Cut, Copy, and Paste buttons as shortcuts to entering criteria.

Get Help from the Expression Builder

When entering a complicated expression in a query design as a selection criterion for constructing a calculated field, you can call upon the Expression Builder for help. To open the Expression Builder, click in the cell where you want to enter an expression, then click Build. You can also right-click in the cell where the expression will go and choose Build from the shortcut menu.

If the cell already contains an expression, it is copied to the Expression Builder. For example, the Builder shows a Date criterion left over from an earlier query. Notice the Workorder Cost Sheet folder is open and a list of fields is displayed in the center of the lower section.

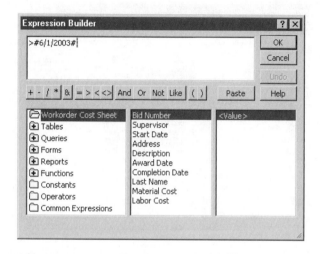

The upper pane of the Expression Builder is where you enter the expression. The lower pane consists of expression elements divided into three levels. The leftmost panel contains all the groups of elements that you can include in an expression. When you open a folder in this panel, the contents of the selected item are listed in the middle panel.

Selecting an item in the center panel opens a list of individual elements in the right panel. You can add one of these to the expression by double-clicking the name or selecting it and clicking Paste. The row of buttons between the upper and lower panes gives you a quick way of adding many of the commonly used operators and symbols.

For example, suppose you want to use the Month() function to define a selection criterion on the Start Date field in the Workorder Cost Sheet query to display only records for jobs started in June. To accomplish this, do the following:

1. In the Query Design view, right-click in the Criteria cell of the Start Date column and choose Expression Builder from the shortcut menu. Delete any expression already in the upper pane.

2. Double-click the Functions folder to open two subfolders: Built-In Functions and Home Tech Repair.

3. Open the Built-In Functions folder. A list of function categories appears in the center panel.

4. Choose Date/Time. The right panel shows a list of all the date- or time-related built-in functions.

5. Scroll down the list and select Month, then choose Paste. The Month() function is copied to the upper pane with the correct syntax.

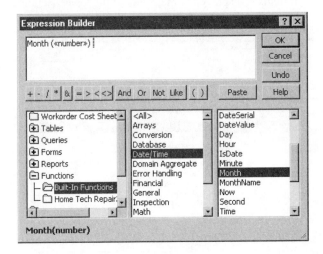

6. The Month() function requires an argument, a number, to tell Access which month you want to specify in the expression. Click to highlight <<number>> in the parentheses and enter **6** (for June).

7. Click OK. Month(6) now shows in the Criteria cell of the Start Date column.

You will see more of the Expression Builder in Chapter 15 when you add condition expressions to macros.

Set Query Properties

Like all other database objects, a query has a set of properties that control its appearance and behavior. To open the Query Properties dialog box (see Figure 7-7), place the insertion point in the table pane and do one of the following:

■ Click Properties.

■ Choose View | Properties.

■ Right-click anywhere in the design window outside the field lists and choose Properties from the shortcut menu.

■ Click in the table pane and press ALT-ENTER.

To see a description of a property, place the insertion point in the property box and press F1. If you click in a field in the table grid, the property sheet shows the properties of that field instead of the query.

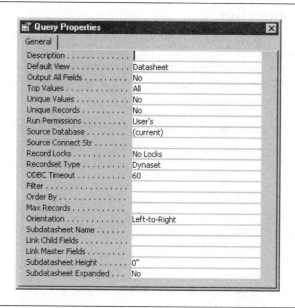

FIGURE 7-7   Set query properties in the Query Properties dialog box.

Modify a Query

You can add or delete a field, rearrange the columns, show or hide any of the fields, change the resulting records sort order, and add one or more selection criteria. To open a query for modifying the design, select the query in the Queries page of the Database window and click Design. If you want to view the results of the query first, click Open, then switch to Design view. You can also right-click the query name and choose Open or Design from the shortcut menu.

Insert a Field and Change the Field Order

If you want to add another field to the grid, drag the field name to the Field row of the column where you want the field. The field is inserted and the other columns move to make room.

> **TIP**   *If you double-click the field name, Access puts it at the end of the line in the first empty column.*

Moving a field in the design grid works the same as in a datasheet. Select the field by clicking the column selector (the mouse pointer changes to a down arrow). Release the mouse button and click again when it changes to a left upward arrow. Now drag the column to a new position.

When you see the dark vertical line where you want the column's left margin to appear, release the mouse button. The column moves and the other columns slide over to oblige.

Change Field Properties

The fields that appear in the query results inherit the properties from the table design. However, you might want the field to look different or show a different name in the query results, especially if you are going to use the results as the basis for a custom form or report. You cannot change all of a field's properties, only those that appear in the field's property sheet in the query.

To rename a field in the query design:

1. Place the insertion point left of the first letter of the name in the grid.

2. Type the new name followed by a colon (:). If you are replacing Expr1 or another Access-assigned name, replace only the name, not the expression following the colon.

3. Press ENTER.

 *If you want to keep the name in the grid but show a different name in the datasheet, change the field's Caption property in the property sheet.*

 To change other field properties, click in the field on the grid and click Properties or press ALT-ENTER. Entries in the field property sheets are blank; they do not contain the settings defined in the table design. Any entries you make in the Query Design window will override the preset properties.

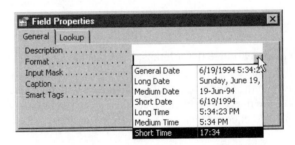

The field property sheet has two tabs: General and Lookup. The General tab shows four properties that you can change in the query design, as follows:

- **Description** Presents the text that is displayed in the status bar when you click the field in the Datasheet view. Any text entered here replaces the Description entered in the table definition. You can enter up to 255 characters.

- **Format** Shows a list of applicable formats for the field. A Text field has no list but you can enter a custom format.

- **Input Mask** Creates a data entry skeleton. You can either type the mask in the box or click Build to start the Input Mask Wizard.

- **Caption** Specifies the column header for a datasheet, form, or report in place of the field name.

■ **Smart Tags**   Specifies which available Smart Tags are attached to the field.

■ **Decimal Places**   Appears in the property sheet if the field is a Number field and specifies the number of digits right of the decimal point.

If the field is a lookup field, the Lookup tab has one option that can change the display control to a text box, list box, or combo box. The other properties on the Lookup tab are the same as those in the table design. If the field is not a lookup field, this tab is blank. Changing field properties in a query design has no effect on the underlying table design.

> TIP   *If you want to change properties of several fields or even a query property, keep the property sheet open and the options will change when you click another object in the query design.*

Perform Calculations in a Query

You can perform many types of calculations in a query that are recomputed each time the query is run so data is always current. The results of the calculations are not stored in the table. In a query, there are two types of calculations: aggregate calculations and calculated fields.

The aggregate calculations are predefined operations that are performed on groups of records and provide totals, counts, averages, and other information about field values in all records or in groups of records. Think of these aggregate calculations as vertical computations. For example, you can add up the number of jobs on J Street or calculate the average labor cost for all jobs.

The calculated fields actually create new fields in a record by combining the values in other fields in the record, producing a horizontal computation. You can create new numeric, date, or text fields for each record using custom calculations. For example, use the expression:

```
[Completion Date]-[Start Date]
```

to create a new field named Job Time. After creating a calculated field, you can use the aggregate calculations to further analyze the data. For example, after finding the Job Time for each job, you can compute the average time over all jobs or even add a selection criterion to limit the records to jobs in a specific area or supervised by a specific employee.

Add a Calculated Field

To add a new field that displays the results of a calculation based on other fields in the grid, click in the Field row of an empty column and enter an expression. The field names in the expression must be enclosed in brackets so Access recognizes them as fields.

For example, add a calculated field to a query of the Home Tech Repair Workorders table that shows the total cost of each current job:

1. In the Query Design view, drag the fields you want to see in the result to the grid, including Material Cost and Labor Cost.

2. Click in the Field cell on the first empty column and enter the expression **[Material Cost]+[Labor Cost]**, then press ENTER.

3. Move the insertion point to the left in the Field cell and replace Expr1 with **Total Cost**, keeping the colon.

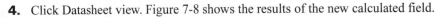

4. Click Datasheet view. Figure 7-8 shows the results of the new calculated field.

If you want to see the total cost of each job, including a 15 percent markup for overhead expenses, add another calculated field using the expression:

```
[Total Cost]*1.15
```

> **TIP** *If you misspell a field name in an expression when running the query, Access assumes it is a parameter needed by the query and asks you to enter the value. Click Cancel to close the Enter Parameter Value dialog box and return to the grid to correct the field name. See Chapter 9 for information about query parameters.*

You are not limited to Number and Currency fields in calculated fields. Text fields are easily combined with the concatenation operator (&). For example, to create a new field showing employees' complete names in one field, use the following expression as the Field in the query grid:

```
Full Name:[First Name]&" "&[Last Name]
```

Current Workorders : Select Query

Material Cost	Labor Cost	Description	Address	City	State	Contact	Total Cost
$1,072.50	$572.50	New Fireplace	2115 J St	Los Padres	CA	McCoy, John	$1,645.00
$1,155.00	$840.00	Install 3 Attic Vents	329 5th St	Los Padres	CA	Jones, David	$1,995.00
$850.50	$126.00	Install A/C	2478 9th St	Los Padres	CA	Rogers, Ohykki	$976.50
$115.50	$315.00	Replace Countertops	319 4th St	Los Padres	CA	Perry, Oliver	$430.50
$262.50	$252.00	Move Washer & Dryer	2111 J St	Los Padres	CA	McCoy, John	$514.50
$750.00	$800.00	Ceiling Fans	186 G St	Los Padres	CA	Brown, Agnes	$1,550.00
$2,500.00	$7,200.00	Finish Basement	1520 8th St	Los Padres	CA	Selms, Harry	$9,700.00
$400.00	$750.00	Garden Window	329 5th St	Los Padres	CA	Jones, David	$1,150.00
$1,100.00	$450.00	SPA Heater	952 C St	Los Padres	CA	Anders, Bob	$1,550.00
$175.00	$100.00	Replace Toilet	2111 J St	Los Padres	CA	McCoy, John	$275.00
$300.00	$1,300.00	Repair Driveway	1510 H St	Los Padres	CA	Norr, James	$1,600.00
$280.00	$480.00	Erect Tool Shed	329 5th St	Los Padres	CA	Jones, David	$760.00
$400.00	$1,100.00	Bay Window	2111 J St	Los Padres	CA	McCoy, John	$1,500.00
$75.00	$300.00	Soaker System	186 G St	Los Padres	CA	Brown, Agnes	$375.00
$420.00	$100.00	Install Dish Washer	952 C St	Los Padres	CA	Anders, Bob	$520.00

Record: 1 of 15

FIGURE 7-8 Displaying the new Total Cost field

The quotation marks between the field names add a space between the names.

Field:	Full Name: [First Name] & " " & [Last Name]	SSN	Address	City
Table:		Employees	Employees	Employees
Sort:				
Show:	☑	☑	☑	☑
Criteria:				
or:				

To include only the employees' initials and add some text to the display, you can use an expression such as the following:

```
"Supervised by: " & Left([First Name],1) & Left([Last Name],1)
```

The Left function extracts characters from the left of the field value. The integer argument in the function indicates how many of these characters you want to see—only one in this case. The result of this calculated field looks like this:

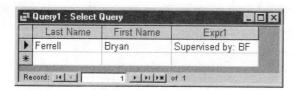

If you need help with a more complex expression, click Build to open the Expression Builder as described earlier.

Summarize with the Wizard

The second wizard dialog box offers two choices: Detail, in which all records are shown, and Summary. To include a summary:

1. Choose Summary and click the Summary Options button (see Figure 7-9).
2. Choose Avg in both the Material Cost and Labor Cost rows.
3. Choose Sum in both the Material Cost and Labor Cost rows.
4. Click the Count Records in Workorders check box in the Summary Options dialog box.

5. Click OK, then click Finish.

Supervisor	Sum Of Material Cost	Avg Of Material Cost	Sum Of Labor Cost	Avg Of Labor Cost	Count Of Workorders
Ferrell	$2,890.00	$578.00	$1,854.50	$370.90	5
Gunderson	$2,165.50	$433.10	$2,305.00	$461.00	5
Byron	$2,000.50	$666.83	$2,026.00	$675.33	3
Connelly	$2,500.00	$2,500.00	$7,200.00	$7,200.00	1
Kordel	$300.00	$300.00	$1,300.00	$1,300.00	1

Record: 1 of 5

Summarize in the Query Design

The summaries work with values in a field from multiple records, whether from all records in the result or a group of records based on a specific field value. A summarizing query produces a snapshot instead of a dynaset, and none of the fields in the result can be edited.

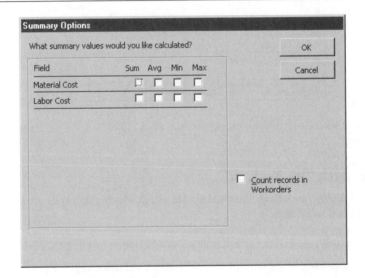

FIGURE 7-9   The Summary Options dialog box

Summarize All Records

To summarize field values in a query, start with a select query, add the field you want to summarize, then specify the way you want the fields summarized. For example, to find the total and average Material Cost for current work orders, do the following:

1. Start a new select query of the Workorders table and drag the Material Cost field to the grid.

2. Click Totals to add the Total row to the grid. You can also choose View | Totals or right-click in the grid and choose Totals from the shortcut menu.

3. Click the Total cell in the Material Cost column and choose Sum from the drop-down option list.

4. To summarize on the same field in two ways, drag another copy of the Material Cost field to the next empty column and choose Avg from the Total list.

5. Switch to Datasheet view to see the results. This example is summarized over all the records in the table.

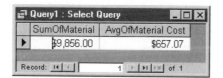

Summarize by Group

When you add fields to the grid with the Total row visible, the default entry is Group By. To group records with the same value in that field, leave the Group By option in the Total cell. For example, to count the number of work orders under control of each supervisor:

1. Start a new select query with the Workorders table and drag the Supervisor, Workorder Number, and Labor Cost fields to the grid.

2. Enter the expression **Avg([Labor Cost]+[Material Cost])** and press ENTER.

3. The Total cell still holds the Group By option. Change this to **Expression** and press ENTER.

4. Change the default Expr1 name to **Average Total**.

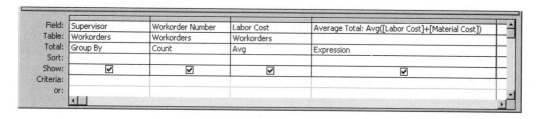

Field:	Supervisor	Workorder Number	Labor Cost	Average Total: Avg([Labor Cost]+[Material Cost])	
Table:	Workorders	Workorders	Workorders		
Total:	Group By	Count	Avg	Expression	
Sort:					
Show:	☑	☑	☑	☑	
Criteria:					
or:					

5. Run the query.

Supervisor	CountOfWorkorder Number	AvgOfLabor Cost	Average Total
Ferrell	4	$343.63	$996.13
Gunderson	5	$461.00	$894.10
Byron	2	$463.00	$1,263.25
Connelly	1	$1,100.00	$1,500.00
Kordel	1	$1,300.00	$1,600.00
Howell	1	$480.00	$760.00
Dobbins	1	$7,200.00	$9,700.00

Record: 1 of 7

NOTE *You can also sort the groups by the values computed in the summaries. For example, you could reorder the preceding records in descending order of the average total cost of the work orders assigned to each supervisor.*

Add Criteria

You can add selection criteria to summary queries to limit the result in three ways:

- To limit the records before they are included in the group and before the group calculations are performed, add the field whose records you want to limit, then enter the criterion. For example, you could include in the Supervisor's group only those work orders whose labor costs exceed $500. If you are calculating any totals in the same query, change the Total cell in that column to Where.

- To limit the groupings after the records are included in the group but before the group calculations are performed, enter the criterion in the Group By field. For example, you could include a summary for specific Supervisors.

- To limit the results of the group summaries, enter the criterion in the field that contains the calculation. For example, you could display results only for Supervisor groups whose average total cost exceeds $1,000.

Create Special Queries with the Query Wizard

As you saw in the New Query dialog box, there are more Query Wizards than the Simple Select Wizard. The list includes wizards that create crosstab queries, queries that find duplicate records, and queries that find unmatched records in related tables.

Create a Find Duplicates Query

A Find Duplicates query locates and displays records in which the specified field has the same values. To display all the bids that were made on jobs at a particular address:

1. Click New in the Queries page of the Database window and double-click Find Duplicates Query Wizard in the New Query dialog box.

2. Choose Bid Data and click Next.

3. In the next dialog box (see Figure 7-10), double-click Address in the Available Fields list to add it to the Duplicate-value fields list, then click Next.

4. Select all the fields you want to display in addition to the field in which duplicates might occur—for example, Bid Number, Bid Date, Description, and Principal. Click Next.

5. In the last dialog box, enter **Duplicate Addresses** as the name for the query and click Finish. The query result shows records for all addresses that are duplicated in the Bid Data table.

NOTE *If you want to sort the results or modify the query in some other way, choose to modify the query in the last wizard dialog box rather than view the results.*

7

Create a Find Unmatched Query

With the Find Unmatched Query Wizard, you can locate and display records in one table that have no match in a related table. For example, you can find customers who have no work orders so you can send them a letter reminding them of your services.

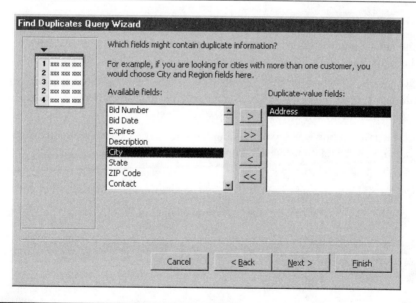

FIGURE 7-10 Choosing the Duplicate-value field

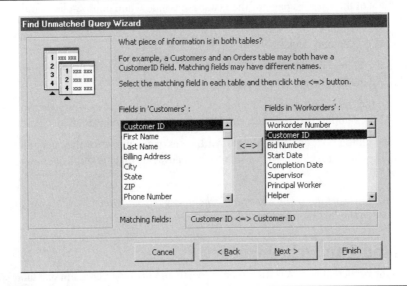

FIGURE 7-11 Specifying the joining field

To create a Find Unmatched query:

1. Start a new query with the Find Unmatched Query Wizard.

2. In the first dialog box, choose Customers as the table whose records you want to display and click Next.

3. In the next dialog box, choose Workorders as the table you want to match with the Customers table. If there are any customers with no corresponding work orders, the Customer record is included in the result. Click Next.

4. In the next dialog box, specify the joining field. If the fields have the same name, Access predetermines the relationship (see Figure 7-11). Choose the field from each list and click the <=> button to join them. Click Next.

5. Select the fields you want to see in the result, such as name, address, and phone number.

6. Accept the query name as Customers Without Matching Workorders and click Finish.

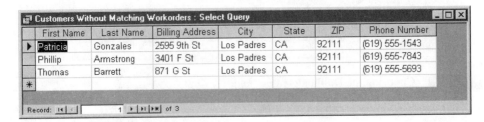

Create a Crosstab Query

A crosstab query is a special type of summary query that correlates summary values between two or more sets of field values, such as sales of types of products within certain sales regions or categories of work order costs correlated with the active supervisor. One set of facts is listed vertically as row headings at the left of the crosstab; the other is listed as column headings across the top. The summarized values—whether sums, averages, or counts—are contained in the body of the crosstab.

To create a crosstab, you need at least three output fields: row headings, column headings, and values. You can create a crosstab query from scratch or with the help of the Crosstab Query Wizard. The result of running a crosstab query is a snapshot, and none of the data in the results is editable.

As an example of creating a crosstab query, use the table named Workorder Crosstab, which has all the costs in one field and a field that indicates the category of the cost: labor or material. To use the Crosstab Query Wizard to correlate the category of cost with the job supervisor:

7

1. Click New on the Queries page of the Database window and choose Crosstab Query Wizard from the New Query dialog box. Then click OK.

2. In the first dialog box (see Figure 7-12), choose the Workorder Crosstab table as the basis for the query and click Next. (This is just an example; the table name needn't include the word "Crosstab.")

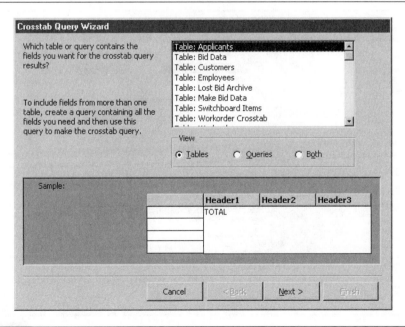

FIGURE 7-12   The first Crosstab Query Wizard dialog box

3. In the next dialog box, double-click Supervisor as the field to use as the row heading (see Figure 7-13) and click Next.

4. In the next dialog box, choose Cost Category as the column heading and click Next.

5. In the next dialog box, select Cost as the value field and Sum in the Function list. Clear the check mark next to "Yes, include row sums," if you don't want to see a Total of Costs column (see Figure 7-14). The sample pane shows how the fields will be arranged in the crosstab. Click Back to return to a previous dialog box to make changes or click Next to finish the query.

6. Enter the query name, Workorder Costs by Category and Supervisor, in the final dialog box and click Finish.

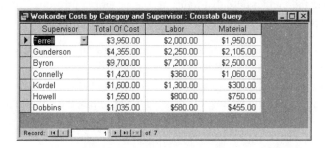

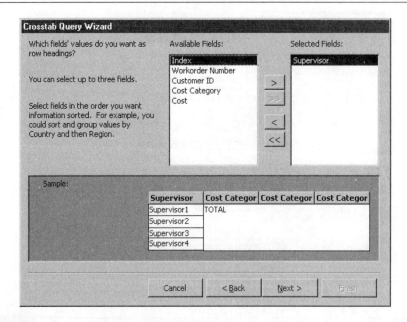

FIGURE 7-13   Choosing the row heading

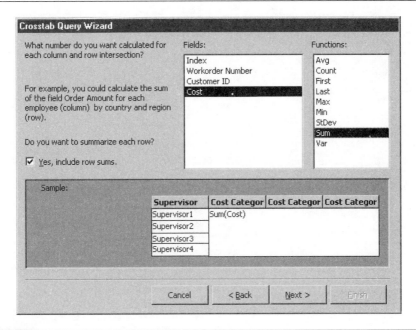

FIGURE 7-14   Choosing the values for the crosstab

   The icon that accompanies the query name in the Database window indicates that it is a crosstab query.

   You can also create a crosstab query from the Design view by starting a new query based on the same table: Click Query Type and choose Crosstab Query. The crosstab row is added to the design grid.

You can make changes to the query design after the wizard is finished with it. For example, you can limit the records included in the crosstab by adding the field on which you want to set the limit and setting the Total cell to Where. Leave the Crosstab cell blank and enter the expression in the Criteria cell.

If you want to change the column headings in the crosstab, return to the query design and open the query property sheet. Enter the titles you want for the columns in the Column Headings property in the order they are to appear in the result. Separate the headings with semicolons (;). You can also type the list of column headings enclosed in double quotation marks and separated with commas.

You can have up to three row heading fields. The additional row headings effectively become subgroupings of the data. Each additional row heading multiplies the number of records in the result: Two row headings double the records in the result; three headings triple the result.

7

Chapter 8

Create Advanced Queries

How to...

- Create a parameter query that requests user input
- Create an AutoLookup query that fills in table data
- Create an action query
- Create a SQL query
- Create a subquery for an existing query

Queries are the primary means of retrieving information stored in an Access database. In addition to providing the popular select query discussed in the previous chapter, Access offers more flexible ways to retrieve data such as permitting the user to specify which records to extract at run time and automatically filling in field data during data entry. Queries can also perform data management operations such as adding, updating, or deleting data.

Create Special Purpose Queries

When you want to specify quickly which group of data you want, use a parameter query. This is much the same as a common select query except that Access prompts for one or more of the selection criteria before running the query. You can use a parameter in any field in which you can type text in the Criteria row.

Another special query, the AutoLookup query, can save data entry time by looking up the value you enter in the matching field and automatically entering the corresponding information into fields in the related tables.

Parameter Queries

To create a parameter query, start with a normal select query and instead of entering the criteria in the Criteria cell, enter the text for the prompt enclosed in brackets ([ ]). The text you enter becomes the prompt in a dialog box, so be sure it is informative enough for the user to know how to respond. You cannot use the field name as the prompt but you can include it in the prompt text.

To create a parameter query that allows the user to specify which customer's work orders you want to see:

1. Click New in the query page of the Database window, choose Design View in the New Query dialog box, and click OK.

2. Hold down CTRL and choose the Workorders, Bid Data, and Customers tables from the Show Tables dialog box. Click Add, then click Close.

3. Drag the Supervisor, Description, Start Date, and Address fields from the field lists to the grid. Add the customer's Last Name field, which is the parameter the user will enter.

4. Type **[Enter customer's last name]** in the Criteria row of the Last Name column.

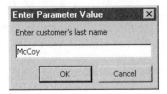

Field:	Supervisor	Description	Start Date	Address	Last Name	
Table:	Workorders	Workorders	Workorders ▼	Bid Data	Customers	
Sort:						
Show:	☑	☑	☑	☑	☑	
Criteria:					[Enter customer's last name]	
or:						

5. Click Run. The Enter Parameter Value dialog box appears.

6. Enter the desired Last Name (**McCoy** in this example) and click OK.

7. Run the query. The result shows three current work orders for customer McCoy.

8

You also can use a parameter query to find records that have a range of values such as a time period. For example, you can show all the work orders that were started in the month of June. To do this, include parameters in a Between…AND expression in the Criteria row. Access will prompt for each parameter in a separate dialog box.

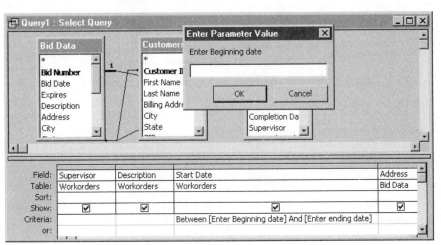

After entering 6/1/03 in the first prompt box and 7/1/03 in the second, Access runs the query and displays records for the four work orders that began in June.

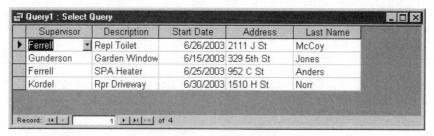

Supervisor	Description	Start Date	Address	Last Name
Ferrell	Repl Toilet	6/26/2003	2111 J St	McCoy
Gunderson	Garden Window	6/15/2003	329 5th St	Jones
Ferrell	SPA Heater	6/25/2003	952 C St	Anders
Kordel	Rpr Driveway	6/30/2003	1510 H St	Norr

By default, the data type of a parameter is Text but you can specify a different data type by opening the Query Parameters dialog box while in the Query Design view:

1. Choose Query | Parameters or right-click in the table pane and choose Parameters from the shortcut menu.

2. In the Query Parameters dialog box, enter the parameter exactly as it appears in the Criteria row (without the brackets).

3. Choose the data type from the Data Type drop-down list.

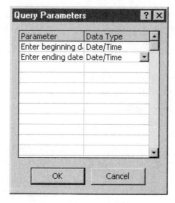

4. Repeat steps 2 and 3 for each parameter for which you want to specify a data type.

5. Click OK.

Sometimes Access prompts for a parameter in a field you have not designated as a parameter. This can be caused by misspelling the field name or changing the name in the table but not changing it in other database objects. If you have checked the Name AutoCorrect option, field name changes are projected to all objects that include that field.

*If you want to return all records with a parameter query, place the parameter prompt in the Criteria cell in the query grid for the field used as the parameter, move to the Or cell, and enter the same parameter prompt followed by **Is Null**.*

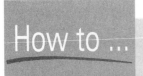

How to ... Display the Parameter in the Results

If you want to display the entered parameter value itself in the query result, add a calculated field with the parameter's name. For example, if you want to see the beginning date in the result of the previous query, enter the following expression in the Field row of an empty column: **Job Start:[Enter beginning date]**. The value will be the same in all the records in the result.

You can use the Format function to customize the parameter display. For example, use the expression **Job Start:Format([Enter beginning date],"d mmm yyyy")** to display the date as 1 Jun 2003 in the query result such as a query, form, or report.

AutoLookup Queries

The AutoLookup query was invented to save time during data entry by pulling field values from the parent table into the form or datasheet. For example, when you enter a valid Customer ID, the query will fill in all the rest of the customer information in the datasheet or form. An AutoLookup query is actually a special-purpose select query containing data from related tables.

> **NOTE** *An AutoLookup query is different from a lookup field in that the query automatically fills in the data for you whereas the lookup field merely displays a list from which to choose.*

To create an AutoLookup query:

1. Create a new query based on the Customers and Workorders tables.

2. Drag the Customer ID field from the Workorders table (the "many" side of the relationship) to the grid.

3. Drag the Last Name, First Name, and Billing Address fields from the Customers table to the grid.

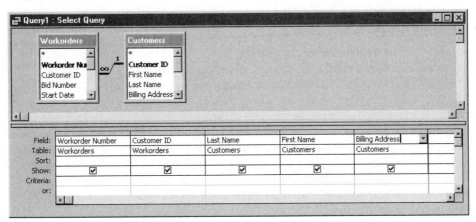

The field on the "many" side that you add to the query grid must not be a primary key or a unique index; the linking field on the "one" side must be a primary key or unique index, but do not add it to the query design. You can add other fields from either table to the query design.

In the query result datasheet, when you add a new record or change the value of the join field on the "many" side, Access automatically looks up and displays the associated values from the table on the "one" side. Here a new record is being entered in which the Customer ID value, 1033, was entered and TAB was pressed. Access filled in the remaining three fields.

010	1032	McCoy	John, C	2115 J St
011	1040	Norr	James	1510 H St
012	1033	Jones	David	329 Fifth
013	1032	McCoy	John, C	2115 J St
014	1037	Selms	Harry	1520 8th St
015	1039	Anders	Bob	952 C St
016	1033	Jones	David	329 Fifth

Record: 14 ◀ 16 ▶ ▶I ▶* of 16

Design Action Queries

Action queries are used to perform global data management operations on one or more tables at once. The four types of action queries reflect the most common database activities: updating field values, adding new records, deleting existing records, and creating new tables.

The results of action queries cannot be used as a record source for forms or reports. Nor can you create an AutoForm or AutoReport from the result of an action query. However, if you save the result as a table first, you can use the table as a record source.

Before undertaking any kind of action query, make a backup copy of the tables that will be involved. If several tables will be changed, back up the entire database. An additional safety precaution when designing an action query is to switch to Datasheet view to check your progress instead of running the query. Showing the results in Datasheet view does not actually run the query and carry out the intended action, so no data is changed.

Update Query

Update queries are used to change one or more field values in many records at once. You can add criteria that screen the records to be changed or update records in more than one table. Update queries can use most types of expressions to specify the update.

In the Home Tech Repair database, several bids have expired but can be renewed. To renew the bids, the company must increase the costs slightly to reflect inflation and set a new expiration date. For example, renewing bids might involve finding records in the Bid Data table whose Expires date is before August 15, 2003, and making changes to the related Workorders table to increase the Material Cost and Labor Cost values. If there is no corresponding Workorder record, the update query does not change the Expires value because the relationship is defined as an inner join.

To create this update query, start with a new query design with the Bid Data and Workorders tables, then do the following:

1. Click Query Type and choose Update Query from the list.

2. Drag the Bid Number field from the Bid Data table to the grid.

3. Drag to the grid the Expires field from the Bid Data table and the Material Cost and Labor Cost fields from the Workorders table.

4. Enter the expression **<8/15/03** in the Criteria cell in the Expires column to limit the records. Access adds the pound sign (#) date delimiters.

5. Enter the following update expressions in the Update To row:

   ■ **Bid Number** in the Bid Number column; Access adds the quotation marks

   ■ **[Expires]+90** in the Expires column

   ■ **[Material Cost]*1.05** in the Material Cost column

   ■ **[Labor Cost]*1.05** in the Labor Cost column

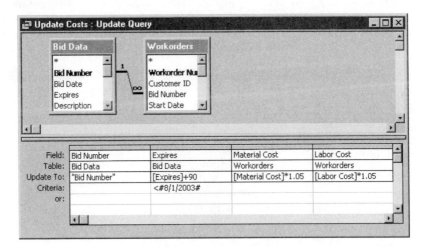

8

6. Click Datasheet view to see which records will be affected by the update query. If the selection is not correct, return to the Design view and make changes.

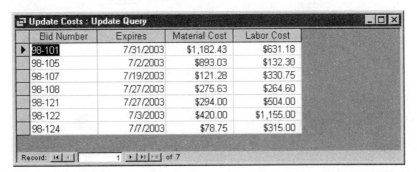

7. Click Design view to return to the Query Design window and save the query as **Update Costs**, then click Run or choose Query | Run. Access displays a message warning that the update is irreversible.

8. Choose Yes to update the records or No to abandon the process.

Figure 8-1 shows a comparison of the updated Bid Data records with the backup copy. The four of the seven updated records that appeared in the datasheet of the update query show the Expires Date updated in the left table. You can see the others if you scroll down the datasheet.

NOTE   *You can see in the figure that there are still several records in the Bid Data table, for example numbers 98-102 and 98-104 whose Expires date is prior to August 15, 2003. This might seem confusing or an error; however, as mentioned earlier, they are not updated because there is no matching record in the Workorders record and the join is an inner join, which includes in the result only those records that have matching values in the join field. If you have enforced referential integrity between related tables in the database and checked the Cascade Update Related Records option on the "one" side, Access will apply the updates to the matching fields on the "many" side even if they are not included in the query.*

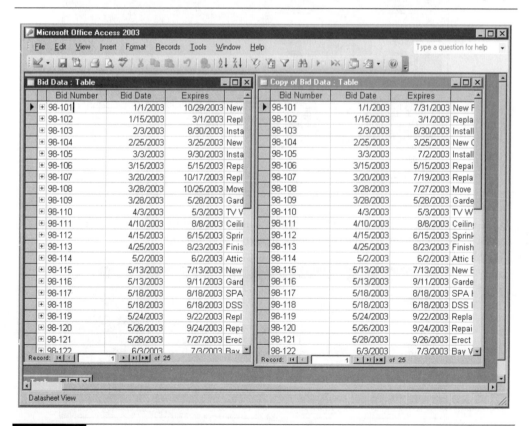

FIGURE 8-1   Comparing updated and backup tables

Append Query

When you want to add records from one or more source tables to other tables, you first must decide which fields you want to append, then locate the target table and determine which fields in the target table correspond to the fields from the source. The field values are only copied to the target table, not moved.

To be matched, fields need not have the same names but do need to be of the same data type. Also, the target table need not have exactly the same structure as the source table.

For example, the Home Tech Repair Bid Data table will become large and cumbersome if none of the outdated records are removed. The bids that have been lost are no longer needed in the current table but they might be useful in an archive history of past bidding. Before you can archive the records, you must create a new table with the same design as the Bid Data table to hold the records using the following steps.

1. Right-click the Bid Data table name in the database window and choose Copy.

2. Right-click in the Tables page and choose Paste.

3. In the Paste Table As dialog box, name the new table **Lost Bid Archive**, choose Structure Only, then click OK.

Now create the append query:

1. Start a new query, adding only the Bid Data table.

2. Click Query Type and choose Append Query.

3. In the Append dialog box, enter the table name, **Lost Bid Archive**, in the Table Name box and choose Current Database, then click OK.

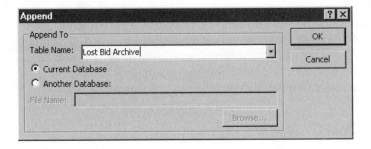

4. Drag the asterisk (*) from the Bid Data field list to the grid. If you do not want all the fields appended, drag the fields individually to the grid.

5. To add the Lost criteria, drag the Award Date field to the grid and enter **"Lost"** in the Criteria cell.

6. Remove the field name from the Append To cell of the Award Date column so you won't append two copies of the Award Date field.

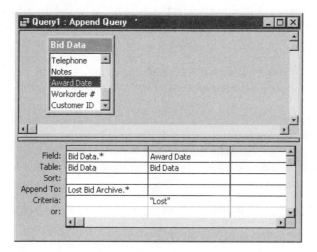

7. Switch to Datasheet view and check for Lost in the Award Date field to make sure the right records will be appended, then switch back to Design view and save the query as **Add to Archive**.

8. Click Run. Access displays a message asking for confirmation to append six records.

9. Choose Yes to complete the addition or No to cancel the operation.

Once you have copied the Lost Bid data records to the archive, the next step is to remove them from the original table.

Delete Query

The delete query might be the most dangerous action query of all. No action queries can be reversed, but deletion seems to be the most drastic—all the more reason to make a backup copy of all the tables before you begin a delete query.

A delete query removes entire records from the table, not just the specified fields. You can remove records from a single table, multiple tables related one-to-one, or multiple tables related one-to-many.

Delete from a Single Table

Deleting records from a single table or from several one-to-one tables is straightforward: add the tables to the query design and specify the criteria for deleting the record—for example, the account is paid in full, the work order is completed, or the house has been sold.

To delete records from a single table with a Delete query:

1. Start a new query with the table from which you want to delete records such as a copy of the Bid Data table.

2. Click Query Type and choose Delete Query or choose Query | Delete Query.

3. Drag the asterisk from the field list to the grid; the Delete row now shows From.

4. Drag the field containing the value that indicates the record is to be deleted (for example, the value Lost in the Award Date field) and enter the criteria expression in the Criteria row.

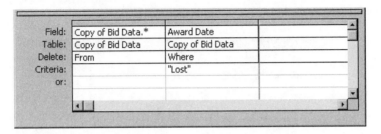

5. Switch to Datasheet view to preview the records that will be deleted and make any necessary changes in the query design.

6. Return to Design view and run the query. Respond Yes to proceed or No to cancel the operation.

8

Delete from Related Tables

If you have Cascade Delete Related Records enabled for the relationship, all matching records on the "many" side are deleted with the records on the "one" side. If the option is not selected, you must run two delete queries to accomplish the job. First delete the records from the tables on the "many" side, then go after the records on the "one" side.

To delete records from multiple related tables, start a new query with all the involved tables, and then do the following:

1. Click Query Type and choose Delete Query.

2. Drag the field to use for criteria to the grid.

3. Drag the asterisk (*) from all the field lists of the tables on the "many" side of the relationships to the grid. Do not drag the "one" table to the grid yet.

4. Click Datasheet view to preview the records that will be deleted.

5. Return to Design view and click Run.

6. Remove the "many" side tables from the Query window.

7. Drag the asterisk (*) from the "one" table to the grid and run the same query again to delete the records from that table.

Make-Table Query

The make-table query does just what it advertises: makes a new table out of records from one or more existing tables or queries.

 *Make-table queries copy the data to the target table. The source tables and queries are unaffected.*

To build a make-table query, start a new query with the tables and queries from which you want records, then do the following:

1. Click Query Type and choose Make-Table Query.

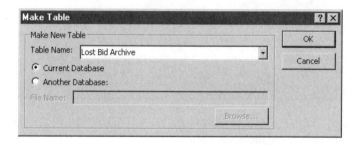

2. Do one of the following:

■ If the target table is in the same database, enter the table name and click OK or choose the table name from the drop-down list. Be aware that the query will replace the records in the existing table.

■ If you want the new table in a different database, select Another Database and type in the full path- and filename of the database; then enter the table name and click OK. If the target is not an Access database, follow the database name with the name of the application, such as **Paradox**.

3. You can also click Browse to navigate to the other database. Drag the fields from the field lists to the design grid and include record selection criteria the same as you do with a select query.

4. Click Datasheet view to preview the records that will be included in the new table.

5. Return to the Design window and click Run.

6. If you are replacing records in an existing table, Access asks for confirmation before proceeding. Respond Yes or No to the final confirmation box that completes the make-table query.

Although you cannot undo an action query (including the make-table query), if the new table isn't what you want, you can delete it and start over.

 The only field properties that are inherited by the table created with a make-table query are the field size and data type. All other properties, including the primary key, format, default values, and input masks, are not inherited and must be reset in the new table or in the form or report that uses the new table as a record source.

Make-table queries create snapshots of the data as it was at the time it was run and as such are not updatable manually. If the data in the source tables changes, run the query again to update the values.

Look at Structured Query Language (SQL)

SQL is the language Access uses behind the scenes to program query operations. It is composed of statements, each complying with specific language syntax and conventions. To view or edit SQL statements while working on a query, switch from Design view to SQL view by choosing View | SQL View.

You can enter a SQL statement in most places where you would enter a table, query, or field name such as the record source for a form or report. If you use a wizard to create a form or report, the record source is a SQL statement created by Access.

Review SQL Statements

Without going too far into the details of the language, look at some simple examples of SQL statements. The SELECT statement is the most common statement in SQL and the most important. All select queries start with the SELECT statement. For example, if you create a query that retrieves all the fields in records from the Bid Data table with "Lost" in the Award Date field, the SQL version would look like this:

8

```
ELECT *
FROM [Bid Data]
WHERE [Award Date]="Lost";
```

- The SELECT * command means to include all the fields, as does SELECT ALL.
- The FROM clause names the table that contains the records to retrieve.
- The WHERE clause specifies the selection criteria. This is the same value you entered in the Criteria row of the Award Date column. Include the WHERE clause only if you have used the complete FROM clause.

SQL statements always end with a semicolon (;). All the queries result in SQL statements, which can be viewed by switching to SQL view. Choose SQL view from either the View button or the View menu. Figure 8-2 shows the SQL views of a few of the queries in the Home Tech Repair database including the action queries from the previous section.

Take a look at the Customers Without Matching Workorders (shown in the upper-left corner in Figure 8-2). This query was created to locate records in the Customers table that had no matching records in the Workorders table. The entire SQL statement is shown here:

```
SELECT DISTINCTROW Customers.[First Name], Customers.[Last Name],
Customers.[Billing Address], Customers.City, Customers.State,
Customers.ZIP, Customers.[Phone Number]
FROM Customers LEFT JOIN Workorders ON Customers.[Customer ID] =
Workorders.[Customer ID]
WHERE (((Workorders.[Customer ID]) Is Null));
```

This statement has two clauses in addition to the SELECT command: FROM and WHERE. Each clause begins on a separate line for readability; Access treats the entire statement as a single line.

■ **SELECT**   Determines which fields are included in the query result. Because there are two tables involved in the query, field names must be qualified with the table name separated by a period (.).

■ **FROM**   Shows the table name and specifies the join type that relates the Customers table with the Workorders table using the Customer ID as the matching field.

■ **WHERE**   Sets the criteria that limit the result to Customer records with no matching records in the Workorders table. That is, the Customer ID field has a Null value because there is no matching record.

Like all programming languages, SQL has strict conventions and grammatical syntax. The more sophisticated the language, the more complex the rules and procedures become. For the complete details of the SQL language, refer to the many Help topics that Access provides.

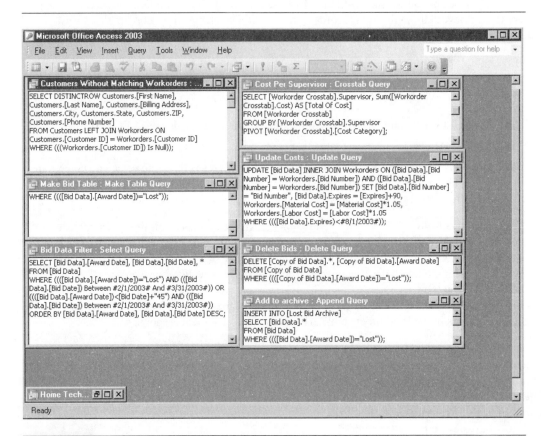

FIGURE 8-2   SQL views of existing queries

Create a Subquery

Subqueries are select queries within other select or action queries. You can use a subquery to specify a criterion for selecting records from the main query or to define a new field to be included in the main query. Using subqueries is like layering filters to close in on the data you need, except that the subquery runs first and results in a single criterion value that is used in the main query.

Define a Criterion

To define a criterion, enter the SELECT statement directly in the Criteria cell in the query design grid or in a SQL statement in place of an expression in a WHERE or HAVING clause.

For example, suppose you want to see fields from the Workorders table for all the jobs run by supervisors who have at least one job incurring more than $1,000 in material costs. Start a new query and add the Workorders table, then place the Workorder Number, the Bid Number, Supervisor, and Material Cost fields in the grid.

To place this subquery in the query grid, type **IN (SELECT Supervisor FROM Workorders WHERE [Material Cost]>1000)** into the Supervisor field Criteria cell. Be sure to enclose the SQL statement in parentheses. If you switch to SQL view, you can see both the main query and the subquery that were created from the criteria:

```
SELECT Workorders.[Workorder Number], Workorders.[Bid Number],
Workorders.Supervisor, Workorders.[Material Cost]
FROM Workorders
WHERE (((Workorders.Supervisor) In (SELECT Supervisor FROM Workorders WHERE
[Material Cost]>1000)));
```

Supervisor Ferrell has four jobs listed, two of which have Material Cost over $1,000. Gunderson has five jobs, only one of which has Material Cost over $1,000; Dobbins has only one. You can compare the results of this query/subquery to the full Workorders table to see how it works.

8

Workorder Num	Bid Number	Supervisor	Material Cost
001	98-101	Ferrell	$1,182.43
002	98-103	Gunderson	$1,212.75
004	98-107	Gunderson	$121.28
005	98-108	Ferrell	$275.63
007	98-113	Dobbins	$2,625.00
008	98-116	Gunderson	$420.00
009	98-117	Ferrell	$1,100.00
010	98-119	Ferrell	$183.75
014	98-124	Gunderson	$78.75
015	98-125	Gunderson	$441.00

Query1 : Select Query

Record: 1 of 10

Define a New Field

To use a subquery to define a new field, type the statement in the Field cell of an empty column. For example, the following subquery adds the field Address from the Bid Data table to the grid.

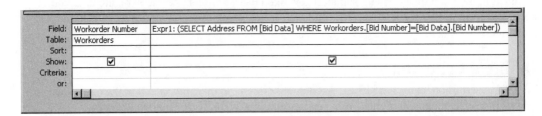

You can return to the Field cell and change the Expr1: default field name to a more informative one. Be sure to keep the colon (:), however.

Workorder Num	Expr1
▶ 001	2115 J St
002	329 5th St
003	2478 9th St
004	319 4th St
005	2111 J St
006	186 G St
007	1520 8th St
008	329 5th St
009	952 C St
010	2111 J St
011	1510 H St
012	329 5th St
013	2111 J St
014	186 G St
015	952 C St

Record: 1 of 15

Although this is a simple example, you can see that using subqueries to define fields based on values found in other tables can reduce the number of tables you need in a query. In this case, we don't have to add the related Bid Data table to the query design to include the job address.

NOTE *You cannot calculate totals with, or group records by, fields defined with subqueries.*

Chapter 9

Understand Form and Report Design Basics

How to...

- ■ Use the AutoForm and AutoReport Features
- ■ Look at form and report design elements
- ■ Work in the form or report Design window
- ■ Add controls to a form or report design
- ■ Modify or delete controls
- ■ Add other objects to a form or report design
- ■ Modify form or report properties

Now that you have seen how to store data efficiently in a relational database and retrieve the information in the arrangement that will be most helpful to you, it is time to learn how to present the information. Information can be displayed on the screen in forms suitable for viewing, editing, or entering data accurately.

If you need to print the information (such as for an annual report or form letter) or simply wish to transport the information to the outside world, Access offers a variety of reporting features.

Use AutoForm and AutoReport Features

When you click the New Object button to use AutoForm and AutoReport, there are no format or style options.

AutoForm produces a columnar arrangement of data from a single table or query. If there is a subdatasheet with the table, the AutoForm also includes a subform. AutoReport creates a quick report of all the data in a table or query.

The report is not fancy but it is useful for checking and verifying the data in your table. No style is applied and no report title, page numbers, or dates are included. Figure 9-1 shows the default AutoForm and AutoReport for the Workorders table.

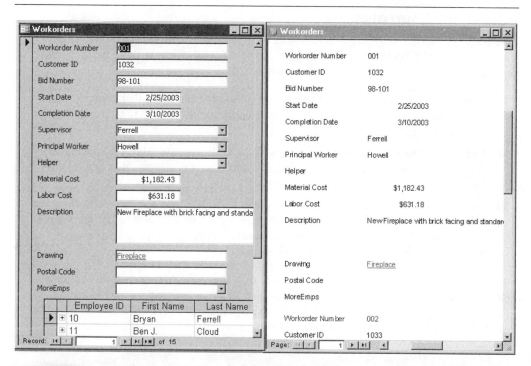

FIGURE 9-1 The default AutoForm and AutoReport

When you click New on the Forms page of the Database window, the New Form dialog box offers five choices of AutoForm style: Columnar, Tabular, Datasheet, PivotTable, and PivotChart. There is also more flexibility when you create an AutoReport by selecting from the New Report dialog box; there is a choice of Columnar or Tabular styles. You must select a table or query as the basis before Access will create an AutoForm or AutoReport.

After creating the AutoReport, you can print it as it appears or switch to Design view and make changes. An AutoReport is so quick and easy; unless you plan to use it quite often, don't bother to name and save it. To close the form or report without saving the design, choose File | Close and respond No when asked if you want to save the changes.

Common Form and Report Design Elements

The design elements that are common to forms and reports include the record source that contains the data and the graphic objects that are added to the design. The Record Source is where you find the data you want in the form or report. It can be a table, a query, or a SQL statement. The individual fields in the underlying tables and queries become elements in the design.

Understand Controls

A *control* is a graphical object that you place on a form or report to display data, perform an action or enhance the appearance of the form or report. Controls come in three basic types, depending on their relationship to values in the tables:

- **Bound control**   Gets its value from a field in the table and as the data changes, the value of the bound control changes with it. The data fields you add to a form design are examples of bound controls.

- **Unbound control**   Has no tie to the underlying table data and retains the parameters you used to create it. Examples of unbound controls are lines, rectangles, labels, and images.

- **Calculated control**   Gets its value from values in the table and actually is an expression that produces a result. Expressions contain functions, operators, and fields. The value shown in a calculated control changes as the values in the underlying fields change, but you cannot directly edit a calculated control.

Here are some examples of the many typical controls you will add to your form and report designs. The option group contains a set of option buttons but in this case they could also be check boxes or toggle buttons. The combo box is shown expanded to display the value list. All controls are accessible from the toolbox that you can display in the Design window.

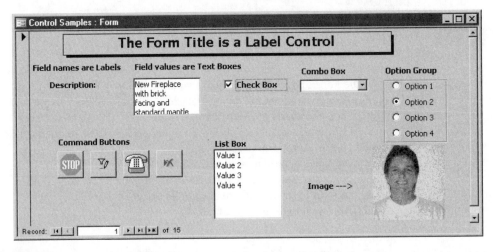

In Chapter 10, you will learn about more special controls you can add to forms, including hyperlinks.

Work in the Design Window

Similarities also exist in the form and report Design windows. The toolbars and menus are nearly identical and the design surface looks the same. The only difference between them shows up at the beginning of a new design. The report Design window shows the page header and footer sections by default, but in the new form Design window, only the detail section is shown at the outset. You can add the headers and footers to the form design if needed.

Start a New Design

Because the two Design windows are so similar, the following paragraphs will focus on the form Design window and point out any significant differences in the report Design window. To start a new form, choose Forms in the Objects pane in the Database window and do one of the following:

- Double-click the Create form in the Design view shortcut item on the Forms page. This opens a blank form design that is not based on any existing table or query.

- Double-click the Create form by using the wizard shortcut item on the Forms page. This starts the Form Wizard.

- Click New on the Forms page. This opens the New Form dialog box.

- Choose Insert | Form. This also opens the New Form dialog box.

Let's start a new form design by building a data entry form for Home Tech Repair to enter new work order data. To start the new form, click Forms in the Objects bar in the Database window, then do the following:

1. Click the New button in the Forms page of the Database window or click the arrow next to New Objects on the toolbar and choose Form from the list. The New Form dialog box opens.

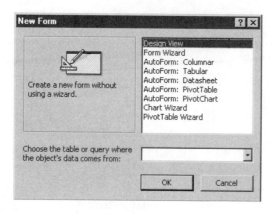

2. Choose Design View.

3. Click the drop-down arrow in the lower box and choose Workorders from the list of existing tables and queries, then click OK.

4. Click the Field List and Toolbox buttons or choose both from the View menu.

5. Keep the form design open (see Figure 9-2) for adding fields and titles.

Tour the Design Window

As you see in Figure 9-2, the form Design window has many new features, including two toolbars, a toolbox, property sheets, and a field list. All of these are used to create form and report designs.

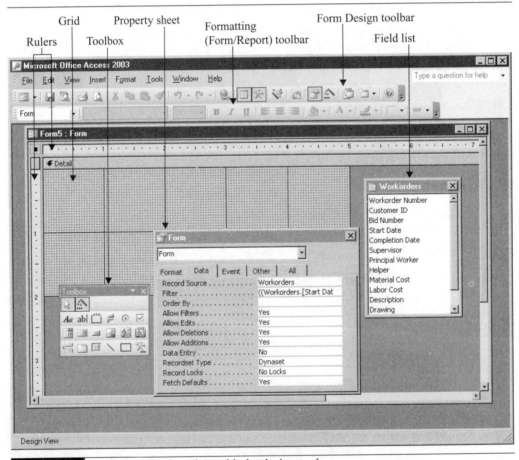

FIGURE 9-2   The form Design view with the design tools

Did you know?

About Form and Report Sections

A new form consists only of the detail section where most of the information will be displayed. If you want to display some text or other information in a form header or footer, add the section by choosing View | Form Header/Footer. You also can right-click in the form design and choose Form Header/Footer from the shortcut menu; both sections are added to the design.

If you want a header or a footer but not both, you can shrink the unwanted section to nothing. Report designs automatically include page headers and footers in addition to the detail section. You can add report headers and footers by choosing View | Report Header/Footer.

You also can add page headers and footers to forms. In a form, the information placed in the page header and footer appears only when the form is previewed or printed, not when it is open in Form view. Choose Page Header/Footer from the View menu or the shortcut menu to add a form page header and footer.

The buttons on the toolbars are used for form and report designing and formatting while the buttons on the toolbox contain tools for adding elements to the design. The property sheet shows tabs for categories of form, report, and control properties. The field list contains all the fields that you have included in the underlying table or query.

9

The Toolbars and Toolbox

The Form Design toolbar includes buttons that change the current view, display the toolbox, change the design style, or insert a hyperlink in the design.

TIP   *If you rest the mouse pointer over the button, a ScreenTip appears displaying the name of the button.*

The Report Design toolbar has most of the same buttons with only two exceptions:

- The Print Preview button shows instead of the Form View button.

- An additional button, Sorting and Grouping, appears between the Toolbox and AutoFormat buttons.

The Formatting toolbar includes buttons for customizing the appearance of the elements in both form and report designs. The buttons on the Formatting toolbar become available when one or more controls are selected in Design view.

Both design toolbars open automatically when you are working in form or report Design view. To display the toolbox, click the Toolbox button or choose View | Toolbox. You can also right-click in a toolbar and choose Toolbox from the list of available toolbars.

Most of the buttons on the toolbox represent controls you can add to the design. To add a control, click on the desired button, then click in the design where you want the control. For some controls, you can draw an outline to specify the size of the control.

The first two toolbox buttons are special, however. When the first button, Select Objects, is pressed in, you can click one of the control object buttons then click in the design to add the control to the design. The second button is the Control Wizards button, which automatically invokes one of the Control Wizards when you add its control to the design. Wizards are available for adding list boxes, combo boxes, option groups, command buttons, subforms, and subreports. If the Control Wizards button is deactivated, a wizard will not appear when you add one of those controls.

The toolbox is usually a floating window, which means you can drag it by the title bar to any location on the screen to get it out of the way. You can vary the height and width of the floating toolbox by dragging the borders. You also can dock it on one side, the top, or the bottom of the Design window by dragging it all the way to the side, top, or bottom of the window. To remove the toolbox from the screen, click the Close button.

The Property Sheets

Property sheets list all the properties that pertain to the form or the selected form section or control. The properties are grouped by category into four tabs with a fifth tab showing the entire list. The categories are Format, Data, Event, and Other.

Use the property sheets to view the properties that are set for the controls and make any necessary changes. Some properties have drop-down lists of valid settings, others include the Build option.

If you have selected more than one control, the property sheet shows only those properties that the group has in common. If the selected controls have no properties in common, the sheet is blank.

The Field List

The field list resembles the lists you saw in the Relationships window and in a query design but without the asterisk. Use the field list to add fields to a design by dragging the name to the design grid. A text box control in the design displays the field value, and an attached label shows the field caption, which might be different than the field name.

The Alignment Tools

The horizontal and vertical *rulers* help you place controls accurately in the design. The rulers are optional and you can show or hide them by selecting View | Ruler while you are in Design view. The single command, Ruler, applies to both the vertical and horizontal rulers. You also can right-click in an empty area of the form design and choose Ruler from the shortcut menu.

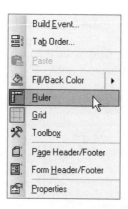

The *grid* shows as faint dots and lines in the design background. To show or hide the grid, choose View | Grid. One of the settings you can choose from the Format menu is Snap To Grid. With this setting selected, Access automatically aligns the controls to the nearest grid mark.

Add Controls

You can add all types of controls to the design with the toolbox, but it is easier to use the field list to add text box controls for the table fields. In the following subsections, you will see how to add fields from the Workorders table, add a form title and subtitle, and include some calculated fields.

From the Field List

The field list contains the names of all the fields in the record source. When you add a field from the list to the design, Access creates a new text box control that shows field values in the Form view. There are three ways to add fields from the list to the design:

- Drag a field name from the list to the design. Dragging the field name to the design looks much like dragging a field name to the query grid. When you drop the button, the control appears showing the new control with its attached label.

- To add all the fields to the design at once, double-click the field list title bar to select all the names, then drag the group to the design. The text boxes and attached labels appear in a tight column in the form design.

- Use the standard SHIFT-click or CTRL-click to select contiguous or dispersed field names, then drag the group to the design.

The field list remains open until you click the Close button or click the Field List button again or choose View | Field List.

9

To get back to the Home Tech Repair data entry form and add fields from the Workorders table:

1. Click on the Workorder Number field in the field list and drag the button to the design at about the 1-inch mark on the horizontal ruler.

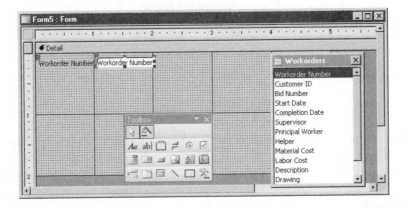

2. To make room for more fields, drag the form's right border to the 6.5-inch horizontal mark and the lower border to the 3-inch vertical mark.

3. Drag the other fields from the field list to positions in the design resembling Figure 9-3.

Once you have all the fields you want in the design, close the field list to make more room on the screen. Next, add a form header and use the toolbox to add a title and subtitle to the header.

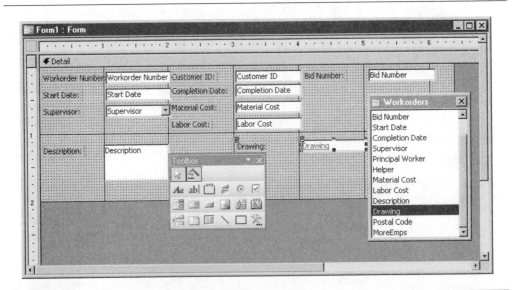

FIGURE 9-3   Other Workorder fields are added

From the Toolbox

To add a control, click the appropriate button and draw the control outline in the design. What happens next depends on the type of control you are adding. To add a title in the Workorders form header:

1. Choose View | Form Header/Footer.

2. Move the mouse pointer to the dividing line between the Form Header and Detail sections; when it changes shape to a double vertical arrow, click and drag the line down 1 inch on the vertical ruler.

3. Click the Label toolbox button and draw an outline in the Form Header across the form. The outline appears with the insertion point at the left.

4. Type **Home Tech Repair** and press ENTER or click outside the label box; click it again to select the label control.

5. Use the Formatting toolbar to change the font size to 18 points, italic, and centered. Figure 9-4 shows the form design with the new header.

6. Click the Label toolbox button and draw a box beneath the title, then type **Data Entry Form — Workorders** in the label control.

7. Use the Formatting toolbar to customize this text so that it is bold and font size 10.

8. Click the View button or choose View | Form View to switch to Form view to see how the design looks now (see Figure 9-5).

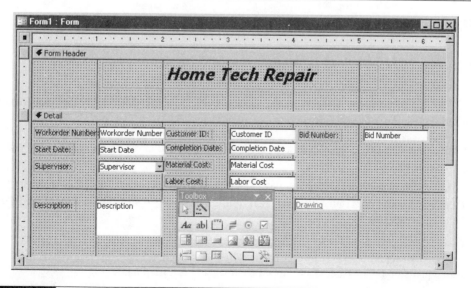

FIGURE 9-4   Adding a title in the form header

9

Home Tech Repair

Data Entry Form -- Workorders

Workorder Number: 001	Customer ID: 1032	Bid Number: 98-101
Start Date: 2/25/2003	Completion Date: 3/10/2003	
Supervisor: Ferrell	Material Cost: $1,182.43	
	Labor Cost: $631.18	
Description: New Fireplace	Drawing: Fireplace	

Record: 1 of 15

FIGURE 9-5 The Workorders Data Entry Form in Form view

Add Calculated Controls

A calculated control contains values from multiple text, number, currency, or date fields in the record source. For example, in Chapter 7 you saw how to combine text values from first and last name fields into a single whole name field.

You also can combine currency or date fields; for example:

- **[Birthday]-Date()** Displays the number of days you have to wait until your next birthday.

- **[Price]*1.07+[Shipping&Handling]** Computes and displays the sales price plus 7 percent tax and adds the shipping and handling charges.

Add two calculated fields to the Workorders data entry form that will display the total cost of the job and the number of days estimated to complete the work:

1. Click the Text Box control button in the toolbox and click in the area to the right of the Material Cost field.

2. Double-click the new control or click the Properties button to open the property sheet for the new unbound text box. You can also right-click a control and choose Properties from the shortcut menu.

3. Click the Data tab and enter the following expression in the Control Source property box: **=[Material Cost]+[Labor Cost]**. Notice that you must start the expression with an equal sign (=) or Access assumes the expression is a field name.

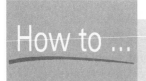

Dress Up with Lines and Rectangles

Although not essential, lines are useful in forms and reports to create a visual separation between parts of the design. A heavy line can help focus attention on a specific area. You can draw a line anywhere in a form or report section.

To draw a line, click the Line toolbox button and click where you want the line or drag the pointer to draw the line. If you just click in the design, Access draws a solid horizontal line 1 inch long and 1 point thick. When you drag to draw the line, you can drag it in any direction and to any length. To make sure the line is horizontal or vertical when you draw it, hold down SHIFT while you draw.

Rectangles come in handy as boxes that group related data or as a means to emphasize another control. For example, in a form you can draw a box around a set of command buttons to set them off from the rest of the design.

To draw a rectangle, click the Rectangle toolbox button and draw the box in the design. After drawing the line or rectangle, you can use the Formatting toolbar buttons to change the line or border thickness, choose colors, and add a special effect. You also can use the property sheet to change the line or rectangle border style; for example, to a dashed or dotted line.

> **NOTE** *If you draw a rectangle around other controls and add a background color, you might obscure the other controls. To cure this, select the rectangle and choose Format | Send To Back to place it behind the others.*

---

4. Double-click the attached label that shows Text*n* and type **Total Cost**, where *n* is the sequentially numbered label.

5. Repeat steps 1 through 4 to add another calculated field to show estimated work time with the expression **=[Completion Date]-[Start Date]** and label it **Work Time (days)**.

6. Switch to Form view to see the design with the new calculated fields.

Completion Date:	3/10/2003	Work Time (days)	13
Material Cost:	$1,182.43	Total Cost:	1813.6125
Labor Cost:	$631.18		

You can see that although the two cost fields retain the currency format with the dollar sign and two decimal places, the Total Cost field does not. A later section in this chapter, "Use Property Sheets," discusses how to correct this.

9

Modify Controls

You can customize the controls you add to a form or report design to present information in just the right way. Controls can be moved about in the design or resized, and any of the properties can be changed to create the appropriate effect. To change any control, you first must select the control to focus Access on the object with which you want to work.

Select Controls and Other Objects

There are many ways of selecting the form or report design, one of the design sections, or one or more controls. The Object button on the Formatting toolbar displays a complete list of every element of the design: the form (or report); each of its sections; and all the controls in the design, including any added lines and text. The list is in alphabetical order. To select one of these, choose from the list. You might need to scroll down the list to find the element you want to select.

Select the Form or a Form Section

Once the form or form section is selected, you can view and change any of the properties, including the record source, in the form or report property sheet. You can select the form itself in the following ways:

- If the rulers are displayed, click the form selector (the small square in the upper-left corner where the horizontal and vertical rulers meet)

- Choose Edit | Select Form (or Report) or press CTRL-R
- Click anywhere in the plain gray background, within the window, but outside the form design

In addition to choosing from the Object list, you can do one of the following to select a form or report section:

- Click the section selector (the small box in the vertical ruler opposite the section bar)

- Click in the section bar
- Click anywhere in the gray background of the section

When a section is selected, the section bar, the horizontal divider that contains the section title, appears shaded.

Select Controls

That leaves the controls themselves. To select one control, you can simply click in the control or choose the control name from the Object list on the Formatting toolbar. When you select a control, a set of small dark squares called *handles* appear around the control. You use these handles to move and resize the controls. The larger squares are the *move handles* and the smaller ones are the *sizing handles*. You'll learn more about moving and resizing later in this chapter.

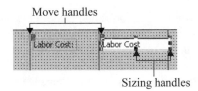

If you want to make the same change to several controls at once, you can select more than one of them in one of the following ways:

- Hold down SHIFT as you click each control.
- To select a column of controls, click the selection arrow in the horizontal ruler above the controls.
- To select a row of controls, click the selection arrow in the vertical ruler to the left of the controls.
- To select a block of controls, click the selection arrow in one of the rulers and drag to draw a rectangle around the controls. This selects all the controls that are inside or partially within the rectangle.
- To select a block of controls within the design but not a complete column or row, click in the design outside of any control and draw a rectangle around the controls.
- To select all the controls in the design, choose Edit | Select All or press CTRL-A.

To remove the selection, click anywhere outside the selected objects. To remove only a few controls from a group of selected controls, hold down SHIFT and click each of the controls you want to exclude.

A text box control is a special case because it contains two parts that can be treated together or separately. The attached label usually is the field name, and the edit region displays the field value. If you click the edit region to select a text box control, you can change the text box properties. If you click the attached label, only the label is selected and you can change its properties.

You can tell by the size and number of handles that appear around the control whether you have selected them both or only the label. Two text box controls are shown in the following illustration; both the label and the edit region of the Labor Cost control are selected whereas only the label of the Material Cost control is selected.

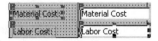

Once you have selected the controls you want to work with, you can move, resize, align, or space them equally or change any of their properties.

Group Controls

If you have several controls that you want to look and behave alike, you can define them as a single group and format them all at the same time. To create the control group, select all the controls you want to include, including the labels for the text box controls, and choose Format | Group. A frame appears around the set of controls but does not show up in Form view.

The new form shown in the following illustration contains the cost fields in a single group. To remove the group designation, choose Format | Ungroup.

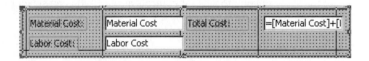

Move and Resize Controls

One reason to select a control is to change its size or move it to a different position in the design. As mentioned earlier, when you select a control, handles appear around the control. These handles are used to move and resize a control or a selected group of controls.

Move Controls

To move a control in the design, move the mouse pointer to the move handle (the larger square in the upper-left corner of a selected control). When the pointer changes shape to an open hand, click and drag the control to the desired position. You can drag it over other controls to place it where you want it.

Again, the text box control is a special case because it has two move handles. If the pointer shows as an open hand, the control and its label move together. If the mouse pointer changes to a pointing hand instead of an open hand, you can move the edit region by itself.

When you move the mouse pointer to the move handle of the attached label, it always changes to a pointing hand so you can move the label by itself. You can't move both parts with the move handle in the label unless you have also selected the label.

Dragging a control by its move handle can be inaccurate, so if you want to move a control a smaller or more precise distance, hold down CTRL and press the appropriate arrow key. Each key press moves the control one-fourth of a grid unit in the direction of the arrow. Holding down CTRL while you drag a control temporarily turns off the Snap To Grid feature.

If you have selected more than one control, you can drag any one of them and all will move together.

Resize Controls

A selected control has seven sizing handles, one on each side and one at each corner (except the move handle corner). Dragging one of the side handles changes the width or height whereas dragging a corner handle can change both height and width at once.

If you have selected several controls, all will change size the same when you drag the sizing handle of one of them.

If you need to make more precise adjustments in the size of the selected control, hold down SHIFT while you click the appropriate arrow key. Each keypress increases or decreases the size of the control by one grid unit.

9

The Format and shortcut menus also have options that help you size one control or a group of controls so that they match in length or width. First select the controls you want to resize, then choose Format | Size or right-click and point to Size in the shortcut menu.

The first command, To Fit, resizes a control to fit its contents. For example, if you have drawn a long label control and entered short text, choose the To Fit command to reduce the size of the control to fit the entered text. The second command, To Grid, automatically adjusts the size of the control so that all four corners fall on the nearest grid points.

Double-clicking one of the sizing handles automatically resizes the control to fit the contents.

The remaining four commands adjust the size of each control in a group of controls relative to the tallest, the shortest, the widest, or the narrowest of the group.

Align and Space Controls

Lining up the controls in a form gives the form or report a professional look. To align a group of controls, select them first, then choose Format | Align or right-click and point to Align in the shortcut menu.

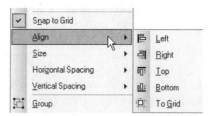

The last command in the Align menu, To Grid, places the upper-left corner of all the selected controls on a grid mark. If you have Snap To Grid checked, this is automatically done.

 *When aligning controls, be sure to select only those in the same row or same column. If you have controls in the group from a different area of the form, they will be aligned with the rest, creating a confused appearance.*

When you have a row or column of controls that you want uniformly spaced across or down the form or report, you can use the Horizontal Spacing or Vertical Spacing commands in the Format menu. These commands also are used to increase or decrease the spaces evenly between the controls. Each time you choose Increase or Decrease, the spacing is changed by one grid interval.

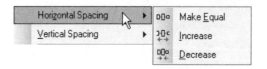

Use Property Sheets

Properties establish the characteristics of form and report design elements. Everything in a form or report design has properties—controls, sections, and even the form or report itself. Control properties set the structure, appearance, and behavior of the controls. Properties also can determine the characteristics of the text and data contained in a control.

Property sheets contain lists of all the properties that pertain to the selected control or group of controls. To open a property sheet for a control, do one of the following:

- Double-click the control
- Select the control and choose View | Properties
- Select the control and click Properties on the toolbar
- Select the control and press ALT-ENTER
- Right-click the control and choose Properties from the shortcut menu

The list of properties will depend on the current selection. The All tab of the property sheet for the Workorder Number text box control lists all the control's properties. As you can tell by the scroll bar, there are more properties in the list. The properties are grouped in the sheet by type: Format, Data, Event, Other, and All. Click on the tab that will show the properties you want to change, or stay with All to see the entire list.

To change a property, click the property in the list, then do one of the following:

- Type the desired setting in the property box
- If an arrow appears in the property box, select the desired setting from the list
- If a Build button (…) appears, click it to display a builder or a dialog box with a choice of builders, depending on the type of control

When you click a property in the property sheet, you can see a description of the property in the status bar. If you need more information about the property or how to use it, press F1.

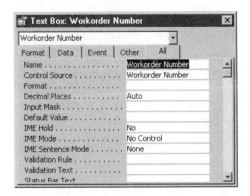

9

The calculated field, Total Cost, which we added to the Workorders data entry form earlier, needs to show currency symbols. To set the format property:

1. In the form Design window, double-click the edit region of the Total Cost text box control.

2. Click the arrow in the Format property box and choose Currency from the list.

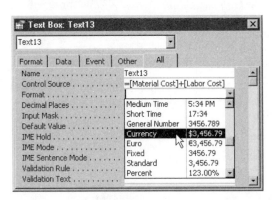

To apply the same property settings to a group of controls of the same type, select them all, then open the property sheet. Only those properties common to all members of the group are visible in the sheet.

Once you open a property sheet, it remains on the screen until you close it. To set properties of a different object in the design, select the object from the drop-down list at the top of the property sheet or select the control in the design.

Assign a Default Value

When you assign a default value to a bound control in a form or report design, the value you enter overrides any default value set in the underlying table design. The default value you assign is stored in the field when a new record is entered in the form unless you enter a different one. For example, if you are entering new bid data and one of the fields in the form is the date, you can assign the current date as the default value. This automatically stores the current system date in the new record. To assign the current date as the default value, type **=Date()** in the control's Default Value property box.

Change Default Control Properties

Access provides a default set of properties for each type of control. The set specifies the general appearance and behavior of that type of control. For example, the default properties for a text box control determine the font size and alignment of text within the attached label. Another default text box property automatically includes the field name as an attached label. This set of properties is called the *default control style* for that control type.

 If you think you will want different default control styles, you can save time by making the changes before starting to create the form.

If you find that you are making the same changes to most of the controls of a certain type, you can change the default property setting. For example, if you usually want a larger font size in your text boxes, change the Font Size from the default size of 8 to a larger size. Or, if you don't want the attached labels for every text box, change the Auto Label property on the Format tab to No.

 When you change a default setting to the one you use most, you save space. Access doesn't need to store both the default and the custom settings.

To change a default property setting:

1. Click the tool in the toolbox for the desired control type.

 2. Click Properties on the toolbar. The property sheet for that control type opens, but the title bar indicates that these are the default settings instead of the settings for a particular control in the design.

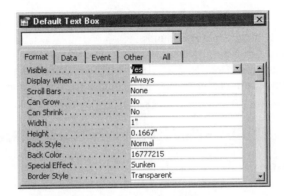

3. Change the setting in the default property sheet.

If you have already made changes to a control and like what you see, there is a quick way to copy the changes to the control type's default style. Any new controls now will use the properties from the existing control as a default control style. Select the control that has the characteristics you want as defaults for subsequent controls, then choose Format | Set Control Defaults.

Use the Formatting Toolbar

The Formatting toolbar is a quick way to change the appearance of the text in selected controls. The toolbar is optional when you are designing a form or report. To see the Formatting toolbar, choose View | Toolbars and check Formatting (Form/Report). You also can right-click in any menu bar or toolbar and choose Formatting (Form/Report) from the shortcut menu.

The Formatting toolbar has, in addition to the Object button we've already discussed, eight buttons for formatting text in the design. These eight buttons change the font name, size, and style and align the text within the control boundaries. The last five buttons give you a quick way to change the color and style of many elements in the design.

The three color buttons each display a color palette you can use to change the color of the background, the font, or the border of a control. The fourth button changes the thickness of the selected control's border and the last button adds special effects to a control or an entire section such as raised, sunken, shadowed, etched, chiseled, and flat effects.

> **TIP** *If you want to apply the same formatting property changes to a group of similar controls, select them all, then change the common property.*

Format Conditionally

Conditional formatting was introduced in Access 2000. You can use it with text boxes and combo boxes to specify a default format for the control and up to three additional formats to be applied under special conditions: the current value of the field, when the field gets focus, or when an expression evaluates to True. The expression can refer to the values in other fields in the same record. For example, if the date in a field is more than 30 days ago, display the value in this field underlined and in red on a light green background.

To activate conditional formatting, select the control you want to apply it to and choose Format | Conditional Formatting. The Conditional Formatting dialog box shows two areas: one for setting the default format and one for specifying a conditional format to be applied under specific conditions.

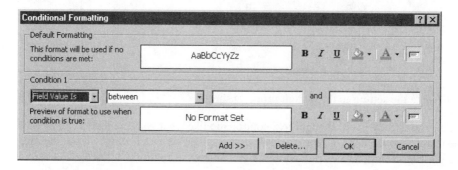

The formatting choices include bold, italic, and underline as well as text and background colors. The button on the right end of the condition box enables or disables the control. When a control is enabled, you can reach it by pressing TAB. If it is disabled, it is skipped in the tab order. The box in the middle displays an example of how the chosen formatting will look.

To set conditional formatting, set the default format, then move to Condition 1. In the first box, you have a choice of conditions:

- **Field Value Is**   Defines the value or range of values for which to apply the format settings
- **Expression Is**   Applies the formatting if the expression you enter evaluates to True
- **Field Has Focus**   Applies the formatting to the field as soon as it gets focus

Depending on which selection you make in the first condition box, other specifications can be made in the other boxes. If you choose Field Value Is in the first box, you have a choice of several comparison operators.

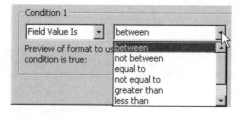

If you choose Expression Is, you have only one box in which to enter the expression. Field Has Focus requires no additional criteria.

After defining the condition, use the formatting buttons to set the format you want to apply if the condition is met. Choose Add to add another condition. You can specify up to three conditional formatting scenarios for each text box or combo box control. The conditions are ranked with the first one taking precedence. If the first condition is not met, the second is evaluated, and so on. Figure 9-6 shows the Conditional Formatting dialog box with settings for the Total Cost text box control. The three conditions are

- If the Total Cost exceeds $5,000
- If the Total Cost is less than $1,000
- If the Labor Cost is greater than the Material Cost

If you want to remove a condition, choose Format | Conditional Formatting again and click Delete in the dialog box. The Delete Conditional Format dialog box opens. In this dialog box, you can check the conditions you want to delete. Then click OK.

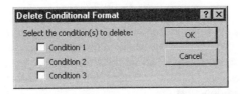

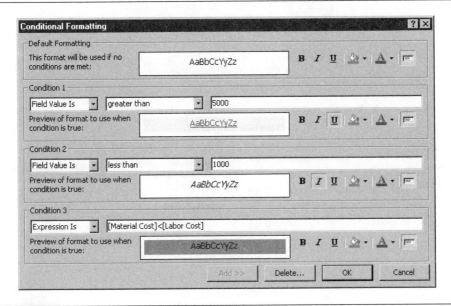

FIGÚRE 9-6   Conditionally formatting a text box

Change a Control Type

When you change your mind about what type of control you want in the form or report, Access lets you change the control type dynamically. Not all types can be converted and you are limited to the types you can convert to, depending on the original control type.

To change a control type, click the control you want to change and choose Format | Change To. You can also right-click the control and point to Change To in the shortcut menu. A list appears displaying the list of controls to which the selected control can be changed. Click on the new type of control. If a control type is dimmed in the list, you cannot change the selected control to that type. Table 9-1 describes the types of conversions permitted by Access.

When you change to another type of control, the applicable properties are copied from the original control to the new control. If the original control has property settings that don't exist for the new control, they are ignored. If the new control has properties that were not used in the original control, Access assigns the default settings for the new control.

Delete Controls

To delete a control, select the control and press DEL or choose Edit | Delete. If you change your mind, you can restore the control by clicking Undo on the toolbar (or choosing Edit | Undo). You can delete more than one control by selecting them all, then pressing DEL. With the Office 2003 stacked Undo/Redo, you don't have to act immediately to reverse an action. You can select the action from the Undo drop-down list.

Original Control	Permitted Conversions
Label	Text box
Text box	Label, list box, combo box
List box	Text box, combo box
Combo box	Text box, list box
Check box	Toggle button, option button
Toggle button	Check box, option button
Option button	Check box, toggle button

TABLE 9-1 Permitted Control Conversions

Modify Form or Report Properties

Forms and reports have many properties in common such as Record Source, Filter, Order By, Width, and several event properties. Each of these can be changed in the object's property sheet; some can also be changed in Design view.

Change the Record Source

When you have created a useful form or report design using one set of data, you can easily reuse the design with other data by changing the Record Source property to the new data. To change a form or report record source:

1. Click the form or report selector, then click Properties.

2. Click the Data tab and click the down arrow in the Record Source property.

3. Choose the new record source from the drop-down list of all tables and queries in the current database.

You can also click the Build button to the right of the Record Source property box to start the Query Builder where you can create a new query to use as the record source.

When you change the record source, some of the bound text boxes no longer represent fields in the underlying record source. You will immediately see a marker in the upper-left corner of the text box edit region and a tag next to it because no field exists in the new record source with that name.

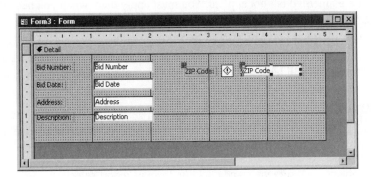

When you rest the pointer on the tag, you can see the reason for the marker. To see how to fix it, click the tag and choose from the drop-down list. This is a big improvement over earlier versions of Access that simply displayed #Name? or #Error? with no clue as to what was wrong.

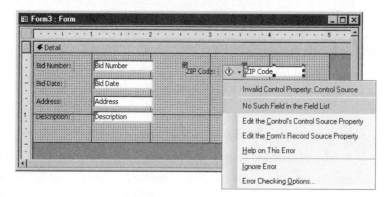

Apply Filters and Sort Orders

When you create a form or report based on a table or query with a filter or a specified sort order, both are included in the object's properties. The sort order is automatically applied but the filter may or may not be, depending on how you created the form or report:

- If you created the form or report from a table not open in Datasheet view, the filter and sort order are inherited but not applied. You must apply them when you need them.

- If you created the form or report from a table that is open in Datasheet view and contains filtered data, the filter is applied every time you open the report but only the first time you view the form in Form view. After you save and close the form, the next time you open the form, you will have to apply the filter yourself by clicking Apply Filter.

Use AutoFormat

Access has provided several attractive formats for forms and reports that add style to the design. To apply the style to a form or report under construction or already completed:

1. Open the object in Design view and click the form or report selector.

2. Click the AutoFormat button or choose Format | AutoFormat.

The report AutoFormat list of styles is different. The Options button has been clicked in the illustration to show that you can apply the font, color, and border attributes selectively.

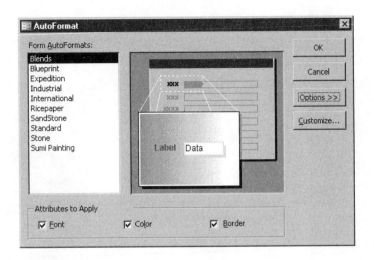

If you click Customize, you open another dialog box where you can create a new AutoFormat based on the form design you are working on, modify the selected AutoFormat in the AutoFormat dialog box with attributes in the current form design, or delete the selected AutoFormat completely. This last option is handy if you create a custom AutoFormat and then decide it is no longer useful.

If you want to apply AutoFormat to just one section in the form or report design, click the section selector before opening the AutoFormat dialog box. You can also use AutoFormat for a single control.

Add a Background Picture

Adding a picture in the background of a form or report is a little different from adding one as a control. A background picture is a property of the form or report and is found on the Format tab of the form or report property sheet. To add a background picture:

1. Select the form or report with one of the following methods:
    - ■ Click the form selector
    - ■ Choose Edit | Select Form (or Report)
    - ■ Choose Form or Report from the Object list on the Formatting toolbar

2. Open the property sheet and click in the Picture property box on the Format tab.

3. Click the Build button, select the picture you want from the Insert Picture dialog box, then click OK.

Figure 9-7 shows the title page of a report with a picture of Home Tech Repair equipment in the background.

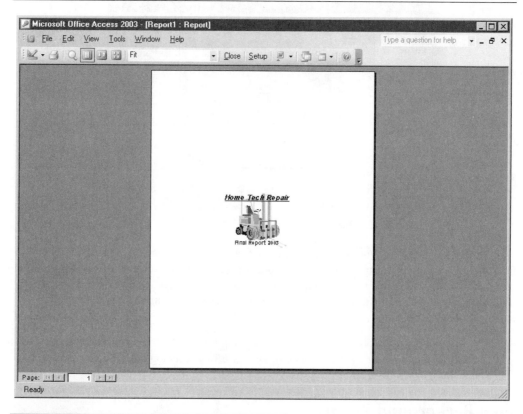

A report showing a background picture

In some designs, you might want to overlap controls with one in the foreground and the other behind. The Format | Bring To Front and Format | Send To Back commands determine which of the controls is in the foreground.

Chapter 10

Create Custom Forms and Subforms

How to…

- Create a new form design
- Modify the form
- Use the form for data entry
- Create a multiple-page form
- Add calculated and special fields
- Create a hierarchical form
- Add custom user guidance
- Control data entry

Create a New Form Design

Access forms usually are used for viewing and entering data. It is important to design a form that will make data entry as foolproof as possible and present the data so that it is easily understood. For example, arrange the data in a logical sequence in the form or group related information together on the screen.

Although the Access Form Wizard will do most of the work for you, it does only what you ask; so it pays to plan ahead. Design the form on paper before invoking the wizard. If a manual data entry form has already proved efficient, the design can be repeated in an Access form.

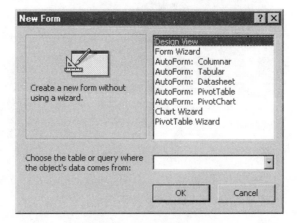

FIGURE 10-1   Choosing from the New Form dialog box

To start a new form, open the New Form dialog box (see Figure 10-1) using one of the following techniques:

■ If you want to base the form on a single table, select the table or query name in the Tables or Queries page of the Database window and click the New Object toolbar button, then choose Form from the list.

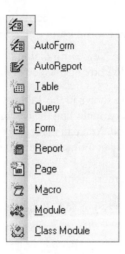

10

 ■ To start a new form with a table or query open in Datasheet or Design view, click the drop-down arrow next to the New Object toolbar button and choose Form from the menu.

NOTE   *If you create a new form while the table or query is open in Design view, you will not be able to see the form in Form view until you close the underlying table or query.*

■ In the Database window, click the Forms button in the Objects bar and choose New.
■ Click anywhere in the Database window and choose Insert | Form.

If you select a table or query name before opening the dialog box, that name is displayed in the dialog box. If not, you can choose one from the drop-down list or wait and choose one in the wizard's first dialog box. Choose the type of form you want to create or one of the wizards and click OK.

You also can start a new form by double-clicking one of the shortcut items in the Forms page:

■ Create form in Design view
■ Create form by using wizard

Use the Form Wizard

When you choose Form Wizard from the New Form dialog box or double-click the shortcut item, the first wizard dialog box opens where you choose the fields to add to the form. If you haven't selected a table or query, you can do that here too.

To start a new form design based on the Current Workorders query:

1. Select the Current Workorders query in the Queries page of the Database window, then click the New Object button and choose Form (not AutoForm).

2. Double-click Form Wizard in the New Form dialog box or select Form Wizard and click OK. The first Form Wizard dialog box opens (see Figure 10-2).

The Current Workorders query name shows in the Tables/Queries box and the Available Fields list shows all the fields in the query, including the calculated fields. The fields appear in the same order as in the query design grid. You can place any or all of the fields in the form design in the desired order. Add them one at a time in the sequence you want them to appear in the form.

To continue with the Current Workorders form:

1. Click the double right chevrons (>>) to add all the fields from the Current Workorders query to the Selected Fields list.

2. Click Next. The Form Wizard's second dialog box opens.

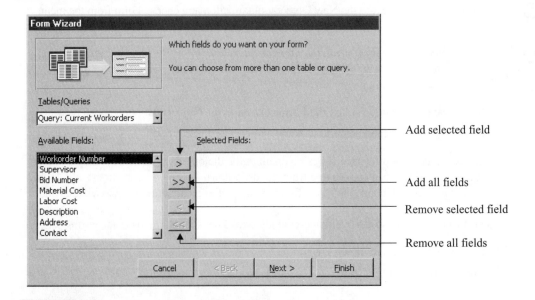

FIGURE 10-2   Choosing fields for the form

If the fields in the Available Fields list are not in the order you want to see in the form, choose the fields one at a time in the order you want them to appear. To insert a field name into the Selected Fields list, select the field name above where you want the new one, select the field from the Available Fields list, and click the right chevron. By selecting the fields in the right order in the Form Wizard dialog box, you avoid moving the controls around in the form design.

If you select fields from more than one table or query, the Form Wizard will create a main form with one or more subforms. The "Create a Hierarchical Form" section discusses this subject in more detail.

The second Form Wizard dialog box offers a choice of six form layouts: Columnar, Tabular, Datasheet, Justified, PivotTable, and PivotChart (see Figure 10-3).

For the Current Workorders form, select the Columnar layout and click Next.

The next dialog box shows a list of ten styles from which to choose. These are the same styles you see when you click the AutoFormat toolbar button, as shown in the previous chapter. Choose a style and click Next to reach the final Form Wizard dialog box, where you name the form and decide whether to view the data in the new form or go directly to the Design view to modify the design.

After entering the form name, click Finish to save and open the form. Once the wizard is finished, you can go about customizing the form for your special needs.

10

Current Workorders				
Workorder Numl	001		Extended Cost	$2,085.65
Supervisor	Ferrell			
Bid Number	98-101			
Material Cost	$1,182.43			
Labor Cost	$631.18			
Description	New Fireplace with brick facing and standard mantle			
Address	2115 J St			
Contact	McCoy, John			
Total Cost	$1,813.61			

Record: |◄| ◄| 1 |►| ►| |►*| of 15

Create a Form Without the Wizard

You don't need the help of a wizard to create your form. You can start a new form by one of the following methods:

- Double-click Create A Form In Design View in the Database window
- Choose Design View in the New Form dialog box

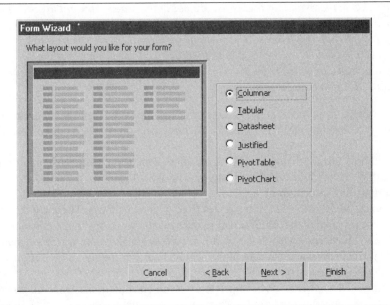

FIGURE 10-3   Choose the form layout

When you start a new custom form without the help of the Form Wizard or one of the AutoForm templates, you begin with an empty Design view window. If you have chosen a table or query in the New Form dialog box to use as the basis for the form, you can display the field list and drag the fields into the form design. If you have not already chosen the basis for the form, you can define it in Design view by selecting the table or query from the form's Record Source property list; then you can add other controls and set properties as before.

Modify the Form Design

Although the Form Wizard does a good job of creating a form, there are a lot of things you can do to improve the result. For example, you can

- Add a form header with a title
- Resize the form to fit the window or the window to fit the form
- Add special controls such as the current date, a calendar, or an AutoDialer
- Change the text of attached labels
- Add lines and rectangles for emphasis
- Change the progression of the cursor through the controls when TAB is pressed (the tab order)

Add Form Header and Footer Sections

By default, a form created by the wizard from a single table or query has a detail section and form header and footer sections in which the user can specify information that will appear at the top and bottom of the form. This information remains on the screen as you scroll through records in the detail section. You also can add page header and footer sections to hold information such as a title, graphics, or column headings. Page sections appear only when you preview or print the form, not in Form view.

The thin form header section appears above the detail section. If you scroll down the form design, you will also see the footer section. Both sections are shrunken but appear in the form design. To increase the size of the form header section, move the mouse pointer to the detail section bar; when the pointer changes to a black plus sign with up and down arrows, click and drag the bar down.

To add a title to the form:

1. Open the toolbox and click the Label control button, then draw a frame in the form header section.

2. Type **Current Workorders** in the new label.

3. Click outside the label control, then click it again to select it.

4. Using the Formatting toolbar, change the font size to 18 and make it bold and centered.

5. Right-click the label and choose Size | To Fit from the shortcut menu or choose Format | Size | To Fit. The label box frame shrinks to the size of the text in it.

Figure 10-4 shows the Current Workorders form design with a title in the new header section.

TIP *When you click View | Form Header/Footer, both sections are added to the form design. If you have no information to put in the footer and don't want the section to take up room in the form, you can drag the bottom form border up to reduce the footer section space to zero.*

All the sections in a form have the same properties. Double-click one of the section selectors to open the property sheet for the section. Form sections have fewer properties than the form itself. Most of the section properties apply to formatting.

For example, the Can Shrink and Can Grow properties resize the section to fit the data in it. The Force New Page property can start printing the form section on a new page rather than on the current page, before or after printing the current section.

Place and Customize Data-Related Controls

In the last chapter, you saw how to add bound text box controls to a form design by dragging the field names from the field list. In addition to the text box controls in which you enter and edit data, list and combo boxes enable you to choose from a list of values.

10

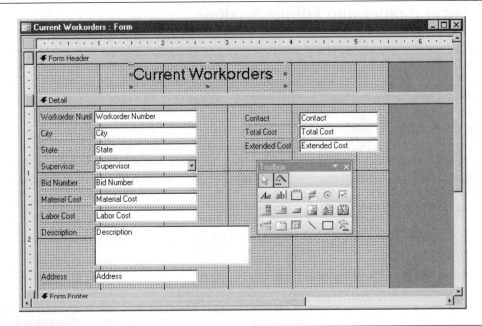

FIGURE 10-4 Adding a title to the form header section

List boxes limit your choice to values in the list but combo boxes usually let you type entries and choose from the list. Either of these can be bound or unbound. If the control is bound, the selected or entered value is stored in the field to which it is bound. If it is unbound, the value is not stored in a table but can be used by another control or as a search criterion.

Add New Text Box Controls

The Current Workorders query does not have all the fields we would like to see in the Current Workorders form. To add more bound text box controls, change the query that is the form's Record Source property and include the additional fields. If you are using a table as the record source, you may need to create a query that includes the fields from the original table plus the additional fields from related tables.

To add more fields from the related tables that are used in the query, open the form in Design view and do the following:

1. If the property sheet is already visible, click the form selector or select Form from the drop-down list. If not, click the form selector, and then click the Properties button.

2. Click in the Record Source property box on the Data tab, and then click the Build button. This starts the Query Builder, which looks much like the query design grid except that the words "Query Builder" appear in the title bar.

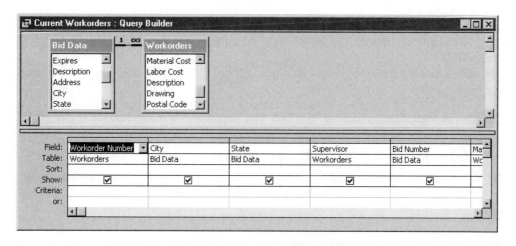

3. Hold down CTRL while you select the City and State fields in the Bid Data field list and drag the group to the grid. The position in the grid is unimportant right now.

4. Click Save, then click the Close button to return to the form design.

The additional fields now are available to the form and the field list is displayed. Follow the next steps to complete the addition of the City and State fields:

1. Select Bid Number in the field list and drag it to the 4-inch mark on the horizontal ruler in line with the Workorder Number field.

2. Select the City field in the field list and drag it to a position in the design below the Bid Number field, and then drag the State field next to the City field.

3. Resize the City and State labels to fit the text, then resize the State text box because it will contain only two characters. Move the State text box next to its attached label.

4. To make the three address fields the same height, click in the vertical ruler level with the row of text boxes to select all three and choose Format | Size | To Tallest.

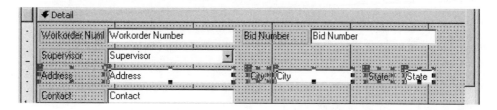

5. Align the boxes by choosing Format | Align | Top while they are still selected.

You can also add a line to separate the material and labor cost from the calculated fields that show the total and extended costs. First, move the two calculated fields down a little to make room for the line. Then click the Line control button and draw a line across under the Labor Cost text box. You can change the line thickness, style, and color by selecting from the Border properties lists.

The last control to add to the Current Workorders form is the current date, which will appear in the form header section. To add the date:

1. Choose Insert | Date and Time. The Date and Time dialog box appears (see Figure 10-5).

2. Check Include Date (if it is not already checked) and select the middle date format (Medium Date), which displays dates as *dd-mm-yy*.

3. Clear the Include Time check box and click OK. The expression = *Date()* appears in the upper-left corner of the form header section.

4. Drag the date control down to just above the detail section bar.

Figure 10-6 shows the completed Current Workorders form in Form view.

TIP *When you switch to Form view, choose Window | Size to Fit Form to resize the window. This works only if the form Design view is not maximized.*

Create List and Combo Boxes

It often is quicker and safer to select a value from a list than to try to remember the correct value to type. List boxes and combo boxes consist of rows of data with one or more columns that can appear with or without headings. One of the columns contains the values you want to store in the

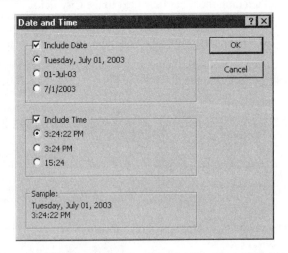

FIGURE 10-5 Setting date and time properties

FIGURE 10-6   The completed Current Workorders form

10

field (the bound control) or use for other purposes (the unbound control); the other columns contain explanatory information.

When you compare text, list, and combo boxes, you see that the list box is always open but is limited to the size you draw in the form design. If the list is wider or longer than the space allowed, Access adds scroll bars. The combo box list is by default the same width as the control in the design, but you can change the width to fit the list. Scroll bars also are added to combo boxes when necessary.

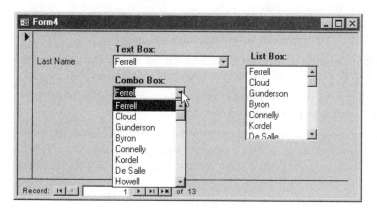

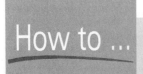

How to ... Decide Between a List Box and a Combo Box

Selecting a value from a list is often quicker and safer than trying to remember the correct value to type. Because list and combo boxes are similar, how do you decide which type of control to use in the form?

■ The values in a list box are always visible and you are limited to the values in the list. To choose from the list, click the entry and press ENTER or TAB. You also can choose one of the values by typing the first letter of the value and pressing ENTER or TAB. (If you have more than one value starting with the same letter, the first one is selected.) You cannot enter a value that is not on the list. List boxes are best when you are limited to just a few values; otherwise the list box takes up valuable viewing space.

■ The values in a combo box are not displayed until you click the arrow to open it, so it takes up less room on the screen than a list box. As with the list box, you can select one of the values by clicking it or by typing the first few characters of the value into the text box area of the combo box. You also can type in values that are not in the list unless you have set the Limit To List property to Yes.

To add a list box or combo box to a form design based on the Employees table, open a blank form in Design view and do the following:

1. Make sure the Control Wizards button is pressed, then click the List Box or Combo Box tool in the toolbox.

2. Click in the form design or draw an outline where you want the control to appear. The wizard's first dialog box opens (see Figure 10-7). For both the List Box Wizard and the Combo Box Wizard, the first dialog boxes are nearly identical.

3. Choose one of the options (both wizards offer the same options):

■ **I want the combo (or list) box to look up the values in a table or query.** If you choose this option, the box displays field values from the table or query you choose.

■ **I will type in the values that I want.** If you choose this option, the list contains values you type into the next dialog box.

■ **Find a record on my form based on the value I selected in my combo box.** This option is used to create a combo box that acts as a search string to find a specific record and display it in the form. This option creates an unbound control.

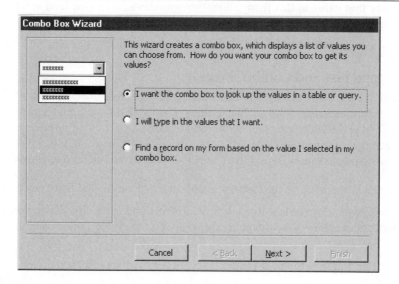

FIGURE 10-7   The first Combo Box Wizard dialog box

4. After making a choice in the first dialog box, click Next. Depending on your choice in step 3, do one of the following:

- If you chose the first option, select the table or query that contains the values the box will display. Click Next, select the fields you want to see in the list, and click Next again.

- If you chose to type in the values, enter the number of columns you want to see and the values to display. Choosing this option skips the next dialog box.

TIP *If you are typing in the values, press TAB to move to the next row in the list of values. If you press ENTER, you will advance to the next wizard dialog box. In that case, click Back to return to the value list dialog box.*

- If you chose the third option, choose the field whose values you want to see. The value you choose in Form view acts as a search value. Click Next.

5. In the next dialog box, adjust the column widths to show the values and decide to show or hide the primary key field. Click Next.

6. The next dialog box asks what you want Access to do with the value you select in the list box or combo box:

- **Remember the value for later use**   Saves the value for use by a macro or procedure. When you close the form, the value is erased.

10

- ■ **Store that value in this field** With this option, you select the field in which you want to store the selected value.

7. If you want a label attached to the box, type it in the last dialog box and click Finish.

Create Unbound List and Combo Boxes

An unbound list or combo box can display either a set of fixed values that you enter when you create the box or specific values from a table or query. The value chosen from the control list is not stored in a field in the underlying table. You can use the value for other purposes such as looking up a record with that value in a field.

To add a combo box to an Employee form that will display the record for a selected employee:

1. Start a new form based on the Employee table and add the desired fields to the form.

2. Start the Combo Box (or List Box) Wizard as before and in the first dialog box, choose the third option, "Find a record on my form based on the value I selected in my combo box." Click Next.

3. Choose Last Name as the field value to show in the list and click Next.

4. Choose Hide key column (recommended) and click Next.

5. In the final dialog box, enter **Show record for:** as the control label and click Finish.

When you use the combo box in Form view, select a value from the list; Access will move to the first record with that value in the corresponding field. This option offers a quick way to move to a specific record in Form view.

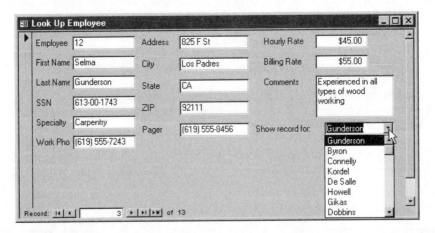

Set List and Combo Box Properties

If your form contains a bound list box or combo box, the control inherits most of its properties from the field properties you set in the table design. When you use a wizard to create such a control, Access sets certain other properties for you. You can modify these properties by changing the settings in the property sheet to make them work just the way you want.

For example, Auto Expand automatically fills in the remaining characters with a value in a combo box when you type the first few characters of the value. Limit To List prevents entering values that are not in the list. The Row Source is another important property. If the Row Source Type property is set to Table/Query or Field List, Row Source specifies the name of the table or query or a SQL statement. If the Row Source Type property is set to Value List, the Row Source property displays a list of items separated by semicolons. If the Row Source Type is a user-defined function, this property is blank. See the related Help topics for complete descriptions of the control properties.

Add Yes/No Controls

Three different types of controls can be used to view or enter a Yes/No value in the underlying table or query. They are check boxes, option buttons, and toggle buttons. When you have a limited number of alternative choices in one field, you can also group the controls together in an option group. The grouped options work as a single control; only one can be selected. The option group can display the list of choices as any of the three types of Yes/No controls.

When you select or clear a check box, option button, or toggle button, Access displays the value in the table or query according to the format property set in the table design (Yes/No, True/False, or On/Off). Here's how the various Yes/No controls appear when the values are Yes and No.

Option groups are a little different. An option group offers a limited set of mutually exclusive alternatives, usually four or less. The option group control consists of a frame around a set of check boxes, option buttons, or toggle buttons.

If the option group is bound to a field, the frame itself is the bound object, not the individual controls in the group. When you create an option group, you specify the values of the options in terms of numbers that are meaningful to the underlying field. When you select an option in the group, that value is stored in the field. If the group is not bound to a field, Access uses the value of the option you choose to carry out one of a list of actions, such as to print the report you choose or open another form.

Although you can create an option group without the help of the wizard, it is a lot easier to take advantage of the wizard. To create an option group, make sure the Control Wizard button is pressed in on the toolbox, then do the following:

1. Click the Option Group tool and click in the form design where you want the upper-left corner of the group to appear. The wizard draws a 1-inch square box. Click Next.

2. In the first wizard dialog box, enter the text you want to see as choices in the group.

3. Press TAB or DOWN ARROW or click the record selector to move to the next row. After entering all the values, click Next.

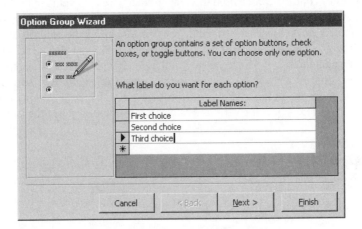

4. In the second dialog box, set the default option (if desired) and click Next.

5. Specify the Option Value property for each of the options in the group. This property must always be a number. This is the value that is passed to the field when the option is selected. By default, the values are consecutive integers: option 1 has the value 1, option 2 has the value 2, and so on. Click Next.

6. The next dialog box asks in which field you want to store the value (bound) or if you want Access to save the value for later (unbound). If the form does not have a record source, the wizard skips this dialog box.

7. Choose the type of control and the style you want to see in the option group and click Next.

Option Group Wizard

Sample
- ⦿ First choice
- ⚪ Second choice
- ⚪ Third choice

What type of controls do you want in the option group?

- ⦿ Option buttons
- ☐ Check boxes
- ☐ Toggle buttons

What style would you like to use?

- ⦿ Etched   ⚪ Shadowed
- ⚪ Flat   ⚪ Sunken
- ⚪ Raised

| Cancel | < Back | Next > | Finish |

8. In the final wizard dialog box, enter the name you want as the label for the group. This text will appear in the group frame. Click Finish.

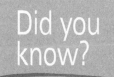

Did you know?

About Events and Event Properties

10

Access is an object-oriented, event-driven application. Nothing happens until the user tells it what to do by pressing a key or clicking the mouse button. An *event* is an occurrence that is recognized by an Access object. You can define a response to events by setting the object's or control's event property.

Examples of events include

- Pressing or releasing a key
- Opening or closing a form
- Moving the cursor to or away from a control
- Applying a filter to records in a form
- Changing or deleting the value in a control

The action Access takes depends on the event property that has been specified. For example, clicking the Open command button (the event) in the Database window opens the selected object (the response). When you move to another record after entering or editing data, the event causes Access to automatically check any validation rules and, if there is no violation, save the record. This system triggers these actions based on the built-in event properties.

Add User-Interactive Controls

Because often a form is used to enter data, the user is constantly interacting with the form and the controls it contains. Some of the controls are directly associated with table data such as text boxes, list boxes, and combo boxes; others accept user actions.

The most common control unrelated to data is the command button, which is used in Form view to perform an action. When the user clicks a command button, Access recognizes this event and carries out the response you have specified for the event.

Add Command Buttons

The Command Button Wizard is on hand to help create more than 30 different types of command buttons that accomplish tasks ranging from moving to the next record to closing the form. The wizard helps you select the category of action you want and the specific procedure to execute. It also enables you to identify the button with text or a picture.

To add a command button to the Current Workorders form that prints the current record:

1. Make sure the Control Wizards button is pressed in, then click the Command Button tool and click in the form design. The first Command Button Wizard dialog box appears (see Figure 10-8).

2. Select the Record Operations category, then select the Print Record action and click Next.

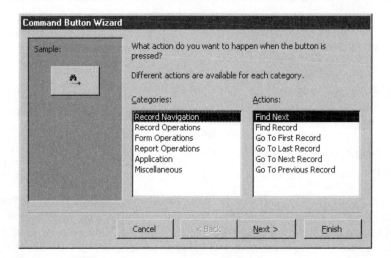

Choose the type of command button

3. The next wizard dialog box lets you choose between text and a picture for the button. Accept the default picture and click Next.

4. Enter a name for the button or accept the default name. Click Finish.

Figure 10-9 shows the Current Workorders form with the new Print Record command button. When the Command Button Wizard builds the button for you, it writes an event procedure containing Visual Basic code to store with the form.

Add Hyperlinks

In Chapter 5, you saw how to add a hyperlink field to a table and how to insert a hyperlink address in the field. A hyperlink in a table can jump to a different address for each record. For example, the hyperlink field Drawing in the Home Tech Repair Workorders table contains addresses of files containing scanned engineering drawings. If you don't need to tie the hyperlink address to a record, you can add it to the form in Design view as an unbound label or an image control.

To add a hyperlink as a label control to the Home Tech Repair Roster form that will jump to the Employees table:

1. With the form open in Design view, click the Insert Hyperlink toolbar button or choose Insert | Hyperlink. The Insert Hyperlink dialog box opens.

10

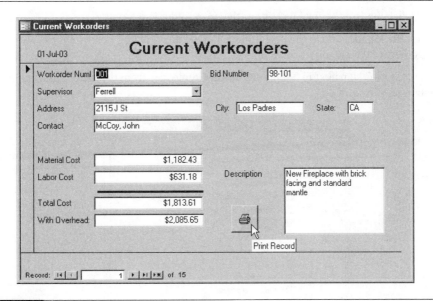

FIGURE 10-9 A Print Record command button added to a form

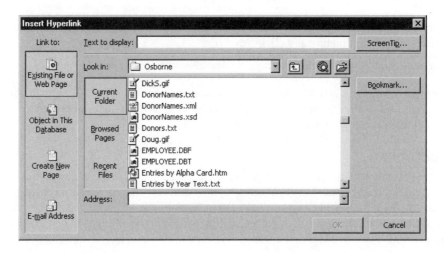

2. Enter the filename for the hyperlink, a Web address (URL), or a local area network address (for example, *computername**pathname*) in the Address text box as follows:

   ■ Select the file from the list

   ■ If the file you want to jump to is in the current folder, type the filename preceded by two periods and a back slash; for example, **..\\HomeTech Repair.mdb**

   ■ If you are not in the current path, type the entire path and filename

   ■ Click the Browse for File button (the open folder icon)

3. Click Bookmark to open the Select Place in Document dialog box where you can specify the object to which you want to jump.

4. Click the plus sign next to Tables and select Employees from the list of tables in the database. Click OK.

5. Enter **Lookup Employees** in the Text To Display box to see it in the hyperlink instead of the address.

6. Click ScreenTip and enter **Display Employees table** in the Set Hyperlink ScreenTip dialog box, and then click OK. The default is the complete hyperlink address.

7. Click OK to close the Insert Hyperlink dialog box. Access creates the hyperlink in the upper-left corner of the form.

8. Drag the hyperlink control to the position you want in the form design.

You can test the new hyperlink in the form design by right-clicking and choosing Hyperlink | Open Hyperlink from the shortcut menu. When you switch to Form view, the hyperlink appears as an underlined label. Rest the mouse pointer on the hyperlink to see the ScreenTip. Click on it to open the Employees table in Datasheet view.

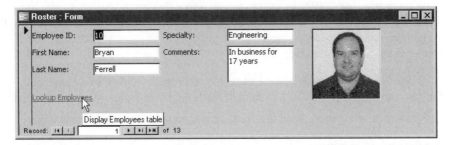

Use the Form for Data Entry

Forms are the principal user interface with the database information. The user can view all the data, search for specific records, enter new records, and edit existing records. To accomplish these tasks efficiently, the user must know how to get around in the form and how to move through the records in Form view.

To open a form in Form view where you can view and edit data, double-click the form name in the Forms page of the Database window or select the form name and click Open. In Form view, you can add a new record by clicking the New Record button to show a blank form. You also can edit existing records using the navigation tools or the Edit menu.

Size the Form

If your form isn't maximized to fill the Access window, you can adjust the form window to fit the form. In Design view, drag in the form boundaries to fit the contents of the form, switch to Form view, and do the following:

1. If the form window is maximized, click the Resize button in the title bar to reduce it.

2. Choose Window | Size To Fit Form. Access adjusts the window around the form boundaries.

3. Click Save to save the new form size.

If the form's Default View property is set to Single Form, the window is cropped or expanded to fit the displayed record. If a single record is too large for the screen, Access expands the window to display as much of the record as possible.

If the Default View is set to Continuous Forms, Access crops any partial record showing at the bottom of the screen. If only one record fits in the window, Access expands the form window to display as much of the record as possible.

Navigate in the Form

As with datasheets, you can operate in two different modes in a form: navigation and editing. In navigation mode, the cursor moves to other fields; in editing mode, it moves among characters in a field. The keypresses have different consequences depending on the current mode. For example, in editing mode, pressing RIGHT ARROW moves the insertion point one character to the right. In navigation mode, it moves the cursor to the next field and usually selects the value.

To change modes, do the following:

- To switch from editing mode to navigation mode, press F2 or click in a field label. You also can press TAB or SHIFT-TAB to leave editing mode and move to another field.

- To switch from navigation mode to editing mode, press F2 or click in the text box.

Clicking the navigation buttons at the bottom of the form moves the cursor to the first, previous, next, or last record. You can enter a specific record number to move to that record. Choosing from the Edit | Go To menu also moves the cursor to other records. These methods move the cursor to the same field in another record.

Change the Tab Order

Each time you press TAB in Form view, the cursor moves to another field. The progression of the cursor through the fields in the form is called the *tab order*. Each text box control is assigned a tab index number indicating its position in the sequence. The first control in the order has 0 as the tab index number; the second, 1; and so on. Access sets the tab order to match the order in which the fields were added to the design.

To change the tab order so that the cursor moves more logically through the records:

1. Open the form in Design view and click in the detail section.

2. Choose View | Tab Order. (The Tab Order command can be in the expanded View menu.) The Tab Order dialog box opens showing a list of all the text box controls in the detail section.

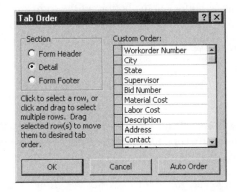

3. To reposition a control in the tab order, move the mouse pointer to the row selector and drag the row to a new position. You can also select a group of rows and reposition them as a group.

4. Repeat step 3 until you have the order the way you want it, then click OK.

Clicking the Auto Order button in the Tab Order dialog box rearranges the controls in order from left to right and top to bottom. If this is the way you want the cursor to move through the fields, click Auto Order instead of moving the controls by hand.

Locate Records

Searching for specific records by examining the value in one or more fields is just the same in a form as in a datasheet. Use the same Find and Replace dialog box to specify the search string and the scope of the match, whether you want to search all of the field or only part of it.

To display a specific record in the form, place the insertion point in the field that has the value you are looking for and click Find or choose Edit | Find. If you want to replace the current field value with another, choose Edit | Replace or click the Replace tab in the Find and Replace dialog box. Refer to Chapter 5 for more information about using Find and Replace.

Sort and Filter Data in a Form

Once you are viewing data in the form, you can filter the records just as in a datasheet: use Filter By Selection, Filter By Form, Filter For Input, or Advanced Filter/Sort. To sort records in the form, place the cursor in the field you want to sort on and click one of the Sort buttons. You can also enter filter and sort expressions in the form's property sheet.

If the form is based on a table or query that already has a sort order or filter saved with it, the form inherits both properties. A sort order is automatically applied to the records in the form. Whether the filter is automatically applied to the records in the form depends on the status of the table or query when you created the form.

- If the table or query was open and the filter applied when you created the form, the filter is automatically applied to the records in the form. The word "(Filtered)" will appear to the right of the navigation buttons at the bottom of the form and "FLTR" appears in the status bar to remind you of the filter. To remove the filter, click the Remove Filter button, which appears pressed in when a filter is applied, or choose Records | Remove Filter/Sort.

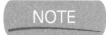   *The filter is not saved with the form. Therefore, if you close and reopen the form, you see all the records.*

- If the table or query was closed and saved with the filter, the filter is inherited by the form but is not automatically applied. Click the Apply Filter button or choose Records | Apply Filter/Sort.

   *To disable all filtering of records in the form, set the Allow Filters property to No. This disables the Filter By Selection, Filter By Form, Filter For Input, and Advanced Filter/Sort.*

View Multiple Records

If you want to see more than one record on the screen, you can switch to the form's Datasheet view or change the form's Default View property from Single Form to Continuous Forms. When you choose Form View from the View button or from the View menu, the form appears with as many records as will fit on the screen. Home Tech Repair uses a form named Roster as a quick way to look up employees. When the Roster form is set to Single Form, only one record appears on the screen, as shown in the following illustration. The user has resized the Form view window to fit the form by choosing Window | Size to Fit Form.

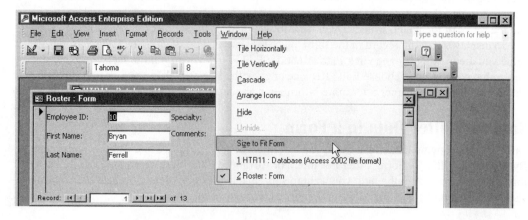

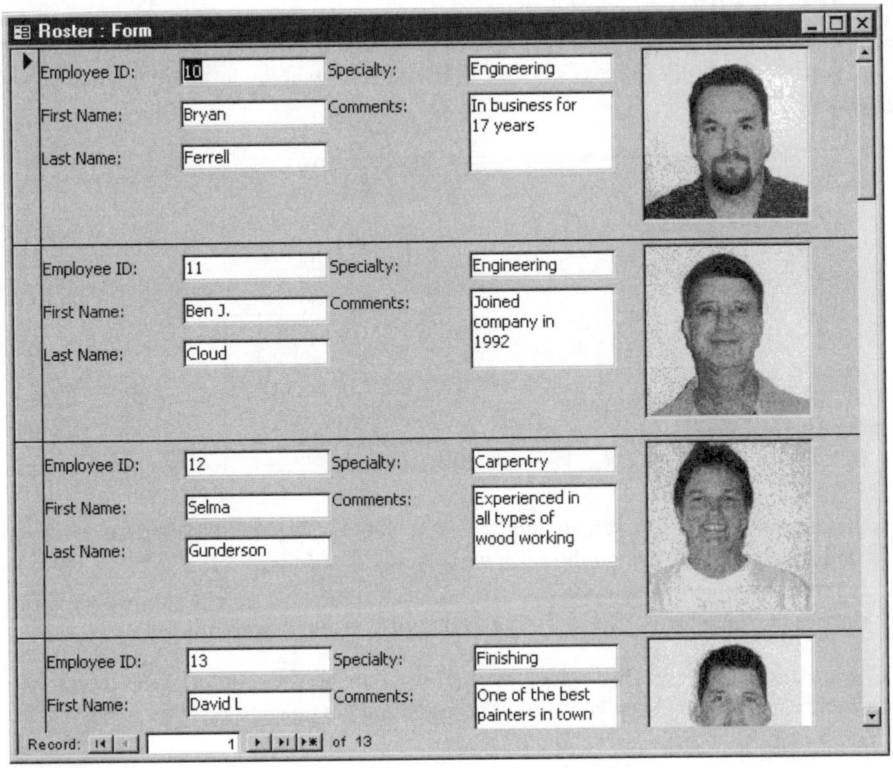

FIGURE 10-10   The Roster continuous form

Figure 10-10 shows the same Roster form with the Default View set to Continuous Forms.

Create a Multiple-Page Form

Access offers two ways to create a multiple-page form: inserting a page break control or adding a tab control. A page break separates the form horizontally into two or more pages, which are separate controls. To move sequentially among the pages, press PGUP or PGDN. Tab controls produce multiple-page forms that combine all the pages into a single control. To move between pages in a tab control, click the desired tab.

Add a Page Break

To insert a page break, click the Page Break Control tool in the toolbox, then click in the form where you want the split. Access shows a short dotted line at the left border where the break occurs.

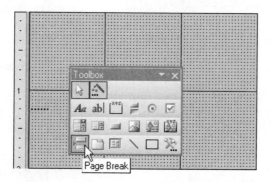

Pages are not necessarily full-screen height. If you want every page to be the same size and show only one page at a time, design the form with evenly spaced page breaks. Use the vertical ruler to help place the page breaks evenly.

After placing the page break, change some of the form properties as follows:

- Change the Cycle property on the Other tab from the current default All Records to Current Page, which keeps you from moving to the next page when you press TAB at the last control in the tab order on one page.

- Change the Scroll Bars property on the Format tab from Both to Horizontal Only to remove the vertical scroll bar. This prevents scrolling to a different page. If the form is not wider than the screen, you can set the property to Neither and remove both scroll bars.

Switch to Form view and press PGDN and PGUP to see if the page breaks are properly placed.

Add a Tab Control

Tab controls are easier and more efficient than page breaks because all the pages in the form belong to a single control. Tab controls are useful for presenting groups of information that can be assembled by category. They are also widely used in dialog boxes.

To add a tab control to the Roster form:

1. Open the Roster form in Design view and maximize the window.

2. Drag the lower form border down to make room for the tab control.

3. Click the Tab Control tool in the toolbox and draw a tab control frame in the lower half of the form design across the width (see Figure 10-11).

4. Press SHIFT and select the Employee ID, First Name, Last Name, Specialty, and Picture fields in the Roster form and click Copy on the toolbar.

5. Right-click in the tab control and choose Paste from the shortcut menu. The controls from the Roster form appear in the first page of the tab control.

6. Click the Field List button if the list is not already showing, then click the tab for the second page in the tab control and drag the SSN, Hourly Rate, and Billing Rate fields from the field list.

7. Copy the Comments field from the form to the second page.

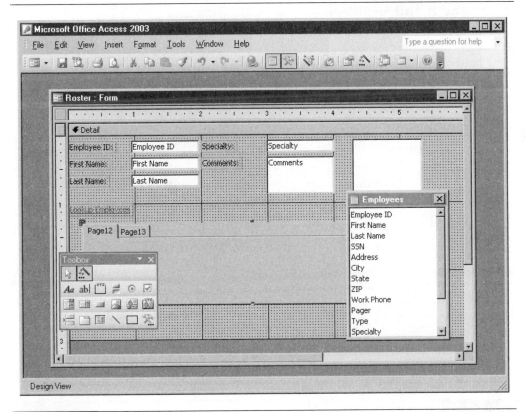

FIGURE 10-11 A new tab control

8. Double-click in the first page to open the property sheet and change the Caption property to read Employee Info, then click in the other page and change its caption to read Rates and Comments.

9. Select the Picture control and change the Size Mode property to Stretch.

10. Delete the controls from the upper half of the form and reduce the form height to show just the tab control, then switch to Form view. Figure 10-12 shows two copies of the form so you can see both pages.

To add another tab or delete a tab, right-click the tab control border and choose Insert Page or Delete Page. When you delete a page this way, the last page to be inserted is deleted. You can also right-click on the tab of a page and choose Delete Page to remove that page.

Customize a Tab Control

Two property sheets are used to customize a tab control: the tab control property sheet and the page property sheet. To customize the tab control as a whole, double-click the control border

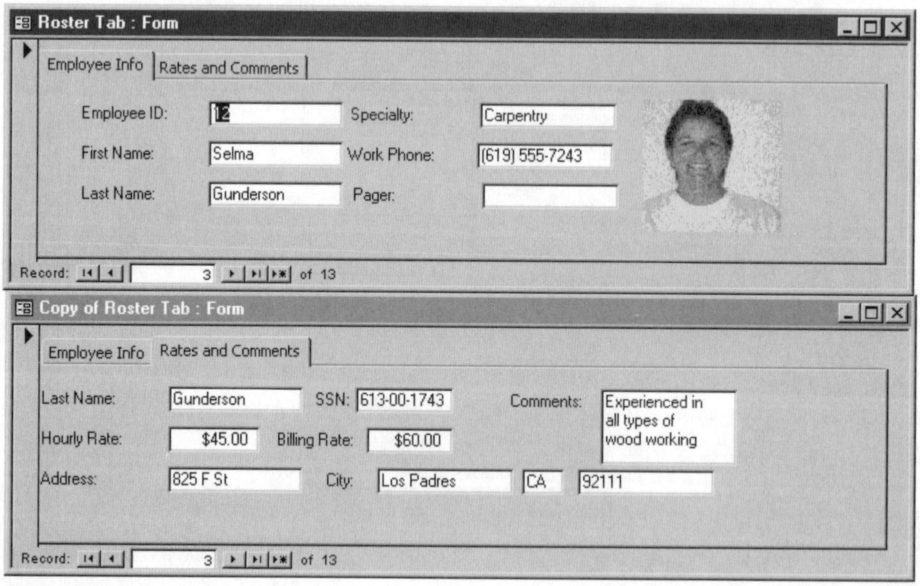

![Two Access form windows showing a two-page tab control. The top window titled "Roster Tab : Form" shows the Employee Info tab with fields: Employee ID: 12, First Name: Selma, Last Name: Gunderson, Specialty: Carpentry, Work Phone: (619) 555-7243, Pager: (blank), and a photograph of a person. Record 3 of 13. The bottom window titled "Copy of Roster Tab : Form" shows the Rates and Comments tab with fields: Last Name: Gunderson, Hourly Rate: $45.00, Address: 825 F St, SSN: 613-00-1743, Billing Rate: $60.00, City: Los Padres, CA, 92111, Comments: Experienced in all types of wood working. Record 3 of 13.]

FIGURE 10-12   A two-page tab control

outside of a page to open the property sheet. For example, you can change the style to show tabs or buttons and specify multiple rows of tabs. To set individual page properties, double-click in the page area. You can enter the text you want to show on the tab or even add a graphic to it.

Add Special Controls

In addition to images, unbound option groups, lines, and rectangles, there are other special controls that you can add to a form design to enhance its appearance or provide additional information. Calculated controls can combine data from more than one field into processed or summary information. As you saw in Chapter 9, there are also many ActiveX controls you can add to a form.

Add Calculated Controls

It often is helpful to include a calculated field in a form or report. For example, in the last chapter, we used a query to add two calculated fields to the Current Workorders form. You can also add a calculated field to a form directly without using a query.

An unbound text box control usually is used for a calculated field but you can use any control that has a Control Source property, which tells Access where to get the information to display. Combo boxes, list boxes, bound and unbound object frames, toggle buttons, option buttons, and check boxes all have a Control Source property.

After adding the control to the form design, enter the expression in the Control Source property box. You can also type the expression directly into the calculated control box. Be sure to precede the expression with an equal sign in both cases.

Add an AutoDial Control

You can use the Command Button Wizard to create a command button that you can click to dial a selected phone number automatically. To use the AutoDialer, you need to have a dial-up modem connected to your computer and a regular telephone connected to the same line. To add this special control:

1. Open the form in Design view.

2. Make sure the Control Wizards button in the toolbox is pressed in, then click the Command Button tool.

3. Click in the form where you want the button.

4. In the first Command Button Wizard dialog box, click Miscellaneous in the Category box, then click AutoDialer in the Actions box. Click Next.

5. Choose one of the pictures of a telephone and click Finish.

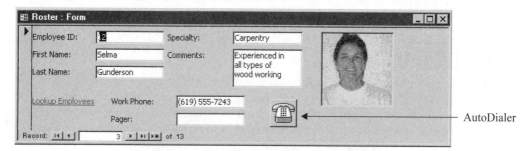

When you click the button in Form view, the AutoDialer dialog box opens. If you have moved the cursor to a telephone number field before clicking the button, the number appears in the box. If not, you can enter a number in the empty Number box. Choose OK to dial the number.

The Setup button in the AutoDialer dialog box opens a dialog box where you can set the modem properties. Also note that you need a dial-up modem connected to your computer and a regular telephone connected to the same line. People with broadband Internet connections no longer have their dial-up modem jacks connected to anything!

Create a Hierarchical Form

A hierarchical form usually consists of a main form and one or more subforms. The main form shows data from records on the "one" side of a one-to-many relationship; the subforms show related data from records on the "many" side. You can use the Form Wizard to help you create the form and subform at the same time or, if you already have the subform designed separately, you can simply add it to the main form design.

Use the Form Wizard

You can create a form and a subform at the same time using the Form Wizard by choosing fields from related tables. For example, to create a hierarchical form showing the list of work orders currently active for each customer, choose fields from both tables. The Form Wizard will figure out how the tables are related, and decide which data goes in the main form and which in the subform.

To create the Workorders By Customer hierarchical form:

1. Start the Form Wizard with the Customers table and in the first dialog box choose the Customer ID, First Name, Last Name, and Billing Address from the Customers table.

2. Choose the Workorders table in the Tables/Queries list and add the Workorder Number, Bid Number, Start Date, Completion Date, Supervisor, Material Cost, and Labor Cost fields. Click Next.

   The second dialog box (see Figure 10-13) asks how you want to view the data—in other words, which records go in the main form and which in the subform. Access has assumed that the Workorders data (on the "many" side of the relationship) goes in the subform. The other two options in the dialog box let you specify whether the data is to be arranged as a single form with a subform or as two separate forms linked by a common field value.

3. Accept the default options and click Next. The next dialog box offers four layouts for the subform: Tabular, Datasheet, PivotTable, and PivotChart. Choose Datasheet and click Next.

4. Choose the style for the form in the next dialog box.

5. Enter the name **Workorders by Customer Form** for the main form, leave the default name for the subform, then click Finish.

Figure 10-14 shows the completed hierarchical form with a few modifications such as a title in the form header. The columns in the subform also have been resized to fit the screen. You can

10

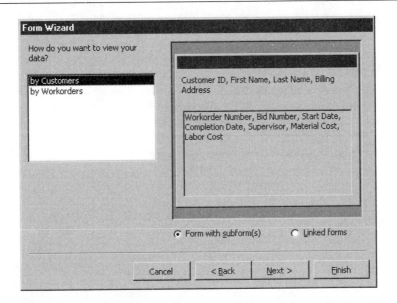

FIGURE 10-13   Creating a form with a subform

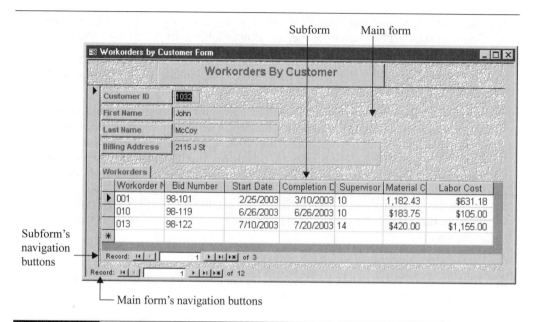

FIGURE 10-14   The completed hierarchical form

modify the subform in place. To modify the subform design, open the main form in Design view and click the subform selector or any of the controls in the subform. Modify the subform and its controls the same as in the main form.

Use the Subform Wizard

You can use the Subform Wizard to create and insert a new subform or insert an existing subform into a main form. To use the wizard to add the Workorders Subform to a form based on the Employees table:

1. Create a new form named Workorders by Supervisor based on the Employees table.

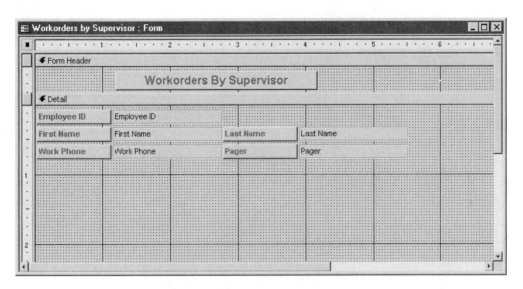

2. Make sure the Control Wizards button is pressed in and click the Subform/Subreport tool in the toolbox.

3. Click in the form design and draw an outline where you want the subform. Usually you will want the subform to span the width of the detail section in the form below the information in the main form. Once the wizard starts, do one of the following:

■ If you are creating a new subform, click "Using existing tables and queries" and click Next. Choose from the Tables/Queries list and fields lists just as when creating a regular form with the Form Wizard. Click Next.

■ If you have already created and saved the form you want to insert, click the Forms tab and select Workorders Subform from the drop-down list, then click Next.

4. In the next dialog box, you can choose from a list of links provided by Access or define your own. If you choose to define your own, the dialog box includes boxes where you can choose the fields that link the main form to the subform. Choose the Employee ID field from the Workorder by Supervisor form and Supervisor from the Workorders Subform, then click Next.

5. Enter a name for the subform or accept Workorders Subform and click Finish.

10

6. Open the property sheet and click the subform border (not the label).

7. Click the Data tab and make sure the Link Child Fields property refers to the foreign key in the subform and the Link Master Fields property refers to the linking field in the main form.

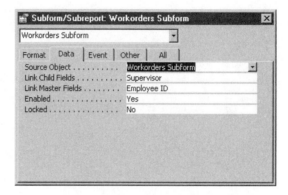

8. Select the subform label and press DEL.

9. Delete Supervisor from the subform and move the other controls to fill the space.

10. Switch to Form view and double-click the column dividers in the subform to resize the columns (see Figure 10-15). You can also drag the column dividers to get the size you want.

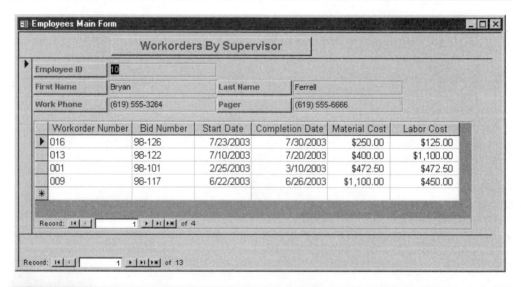

FIGURE 10-15   The Workorders by Supervisor form with a subform

How to ...   Add a Subform Without the Wizard

If you have already created and saved the form you want to insert into the main form as a subform, the easiest way to insert it is to drag it to the form design from the Database window. To do this, open the main form in Design view and tile the window vertically with the Database window. Drag the subform icon from the Forms page of the Database window to the detail section of the main form. After placing the subform, check the Source Object and linking properties as before.

Use the Hierarchical Form

To move from the main form to the subform, click in the subform, usually in a record selector or an editable area. To return to the main form, click an editable control or its label. When you are working in Navigation mode, special key combinations move the cursor from the subform back to the main form; for example:

- **CTRL-TAB**   Moves the cursor through the sequence of editable controls in the main form, then moves to the first record in the subform. Pressing the combination again moves to the first control of the next record in the main form.

- **CTRL-SHIFT-TAB**   Moves the cursor to the previous control in the main form or, if anywhere in the subform, it moves the cursor to the last control in the tab order of the main form.

- **CTRL-SHIFT-HOME**   Moves the cursor to the first editable field in the main form even if it was pressed while the cursor was in the subform.

Each form has its own set of navigation buttons that you can use to move among the records. The subform also has a vertical scroll bar to move other records into view. You can add new records, or edit or delete existing records in either the main form or the subform using the standard data entry techniques. You can also sort records and set filters to limit records in either the main form or the subform using standard sorting and filtering methods.

 Make sure the cursor is in the right place—in the main form or the subform—before you try to add or delete records.

Modify a Subform

The complete subform design is included with the main form design. You can make changes to it in place. Select the control in the subform that you want to change and change as usual. If you

10

want to work on the subform in its own window, right-click the subform and choose Subform in New Window from the shortcut menu. You can also choose View | Subform in New Window.

 *The subform control in the main form is a separate control and has different properties than the subform object. To select the subform control, click on one of the subform boundaries. To select the subform for making changes in the subform itself, click the form selector for the subform.*

Add Custom User Guidance

You have already seen some of the ways you can get help from Access. When you move the mouse pointer over a toolbar button, a ControlTip pops up displaying the name of the button. The status bar displays messages related to the current activity or object, including the description you entered for the fields in your table design. When you design your own application, there might be times when a quick reminder can help with entering data, creating a filter, or printing a report. Access lets you create your own custom tips and status bar messages as properties of a form or report.

The ControlTip Text property specifies the message that appears when you rest the mouse pointer over a control in the form. Short tips are best but you can enter up to 255 characters. To create a ControlTip, select the control and type the message in the ControlTip Text property box on the Other tab.

A status bar message is a good way to display instructions for entering data in a control or explaining the options in an option group. Status Bar Text is a control property for any control on a form that you select. The message displays when the control gets focus. To specify a message to display in the status bar, type the text in the Status Bar Text property box on the Other tab. You can enter up to 255 characters but the amount of text displayed is limited by the space across the status bar.

Add Data Validation

Access offers several ways to validate or restrict data that is entered in forms. You can create controls such as check boxes that limit the data to Yes/No values or a list box that requires a value be picked from the list. You can also set certain form and control properties that will do the job.

Validate with Properties

When you designed your tables, you set field properties that would help ensure valid data. You created input masks, entered validation rules, and specified default values for some of the fields. This is the preferred way to validate data because you must do it only once. Any bound control that you add to a form inherits the properties you set in the table design. If you wait and add the validations and restrictions to a form, you must do it for every form that refers to that data.

However, there might be times when you want to superimpose more validation in the form. For example, you might want to display different error messages when the data is invalid or prevent entering data in a field altogether. If you want to validate unbound controls, you must do it in the form design. The validation rules for controls in a form are created just the same as for a field in table design.

You can combine property settings to accomplish specific purposes. For example, if you want the form to be read-only, set Allow Edits, Allow Additions, and Allow Deletions to No.

NOTE *If you have set one of these properties in the table design and set the same property to a different value in the form design, the bound control property in the form overrides the field property.*

The Enabled property determines whether a control can have focus. The Locked property determines whether data can be changed in Form view. Combining the two settings for a control can create custom results as shown in Table 10-1.

You can also combine the Enabled and Tab Stop properties. If you set Enabled to Yes and Tab Stop to No, users cannot select the control by pressing TAB but can still select it by clicking the control or its label.

Validate with Events

Attaching macros or event procedures to form and control event properties can give you additional flexibility and power over data entry. For example, you can require that at least two of

Enabled Setting	Locked Setting	Results
Yes	Yes	Control can receive focus. The data is displayed normally and can be copied but not edited.
Yes	No	Control can receive focus. Use this combination to allow editing of objects in unbound object frames. The data is displayed normally and can be copied or edited.
No	Yes	Control cannot receive focus. Data is displayed normally but cannot be copied or edited.
No	No	Control cannot receive focus. Control and data both appear dimmed and are disabled.

TABLE 10-1 Combining Enabled and Locked Properties

three fields must be filled in before you can save the record. You would also use an event procedure if the validation refers to controls on other forms or if the control contains a function.

If you want to validate the data before the whole record is updated, add the procedure to a form event. To validate the data before moving to the next control, add the procedure to a control event. Table 10-2 shows a few of the form and control events that can be used for data validation.

See Chapter 15 for more information about events and their sequence of occurrence. You will also see how to create the macros that will validate the data.

Event	Description
Before Update (form)	Rule enforced before saving new or changed data in a record
On Delete (form)	Rule enforced before deleting a record
Before Update (control)	Rule enforced before saving new or changed data in a control
On Exit (control)	Rule enforced before leaving the control

TABLE 10-2   Data Validation Events

Chapter 11

Create and Customize Reports and Subreports

How to...

- Create and save a new report design
- Preview and print the report
- Modify the report design
- Sort and group records in the report
- Add a subreport
- Design a multiple-column report
- Print mailing labels

This chapter introduces you to the Police Department database, which is used 24 hours a day by a local police department. It is a user-interactive system that tracks incidents and maintains records of all persons who report or who are involved in activities that require police attention. The database consists of four tables:

- **Alpha Card**   Maintains a list of all persons who have filed a report, called in an incident, or might be a suspect in an incident.
- **Alpha Entry**   Contains details of all the reports and is related to records in the Alpha Card table.
- **Explanations**   Contains a more detailed version of the police shorthand Entry descriptions.
- **Penal Codes**   Provides a lookup list and contains the Penal code numbers with their descriptions.

The Police database provides the opportunity to see how to create simple and more complex reports. It is important to the department to be able to summarize crimes and maintain records of the incidents. So let's get right to work creating reports that are useful to the Bayview City Police Department.

Start a New Report

Although you create Access reports using many of the same techniques you use for forms, the design concepts of forms are different from that of reports. Forms deal with data and the processes of data management such as data entry, validation, and retrieval. Reports, on the other hand, deal with information derived from the data and are more widely distributed, often to people who might never have seen a computer. Therefore, reports must be self-explanatory and focus on the purpose of the report in plain language.

The Access Report Wizards help you prepare many types of reports, from simple ones that contain complete information from one or more tables to reports that calculate and summarize information and present it in a variety of visual representations including charts and graphs. You can also create multiple column reports to be used for printing mailing labels of all kinds and use Access tables for mail merge applications.

As with most Access activities, there are several ways to start a new report design; you can begin from anywhere in the Database window. Use one of the following methods to open the New Report dialog box:

- Click New on the Reports page of the Database window.
- Choose Insert | Report from any object page.

- Click the New Object button and choose Report from the list.
- Click Tables or Queries under Objects and select a table or query name, then choose Insert | Report or click the New Object button and choose Report from the list.

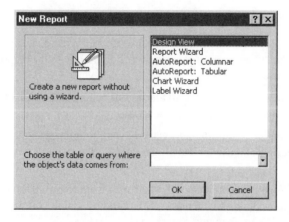

The New Report dialog box offers six ways to create a report, including three wizards and two AutoReport layouts. If you have selected or opened a table or query before starting the new report, that name also appears in the dialog box.

The next step is to choose the method you want to use from the New Report dialog box list and select a table or query as the basis for the report, if desired. You must select a table or query if you want to choose one of the AutoReports. If you choose one of the wizards without first selecting a table or query as the basis, you can select one from the first wizard dialog box. If you choose Design View without naming a table or query, you will not have access to any field names unless you enter a table or query name in the Record Source property; but you can add other non-data-related controls to the design. Click OK after making the selections in the New Report dialog box to move on to the report building process.

Use the Report Wizard

The Report Wizard behaves much like the Form Wizard. It presents you with a series of dialog boxes that guide you through the design process. Most of the dialog boxes present the same kinds of options but the Report Wizard includes a couple of new ones that let you choose the sorting, grouping, and summarizing features.

In our first example, use the Report Wizard to create a report based on the Alpha Entry by Code Query, which limits the data in the Alpha Entry table of the Police database to only those with a numeric incident code. This screens out the employment fingerprint and traffic collision reports that do not involve a crime.

Field:	EntryNo	Index	Entry	DR	Code	Date
Table:	Alpha Entry	Alpha Entry	Alpha Entry	Alpha Entry	Alpha Entry	Alpha Ent
Sort:						
Show:	☑	☑	☑	☑	☑	
Criteria:					<>0	
or:						

To create this new report with the help of the Report Wizard:

1. Open the New Report dialog box and choose Report Wizard. You also can simply double-click the "Create report by using wizard" option on the Reports page of the Database window.

2. Click the down arrow in the Tables/Queries box, choose the Alpha Entry by Code Query as the basis for the report, and then click OK.

3. In the first dialog box, choose the fields you want to include in the report from the tables and queries in the database. Select all the fields in the Alpha Entry by Code Query and click Next.

4. In the second dialog box, the wizard asks if you want to group the records by any of the field values. Select Code as the name of the field by which you want to group and click the right arrow (>), as shown in Figure 11-1.

   ■ If you change your mind, select the field name and click the left arrow (<) to remove the group designation. The up and down arrows near Priority change the grouping order level.

   ■ If you are grouping on a field with numeric values, you can group by an interval such as 50 or 100. Click Grouping Options and choose from the drop-down list in the Grouping Intervals dialog box.

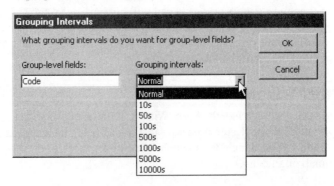

■ If one of the fields you are grouping on is a number or currency field, the Summary Options button becomes available in the next dialog box. You'll learn more about adding summaries in a later section.

5. Click Next to move to the next dialog box, which like the grouping level dialog box is unique to the Report Wizard. This dialog box asks if you want to sort your records within the groups in other than primary key order. The groups are automatically sorted in ascending order by the group field value. Figure 11-2 shows a sort specified by date in ascending order. You can sort on up to four fields by clicking the arrow next to the sort box and choosing the field from the list. If you want the sort in descending order, click the Ascending button to the right of the sort box. When you are done, click Next.

6. In the next dialog box (see Figure 11-3), you select the layout you want for the report and the print orientation. Choose a format and look at the sample in the left pane. For this example, select Align Left 1 and click Next.

TIP   *If you have selected a lot of fields, you might want to change the print orientation to landscape.*

11

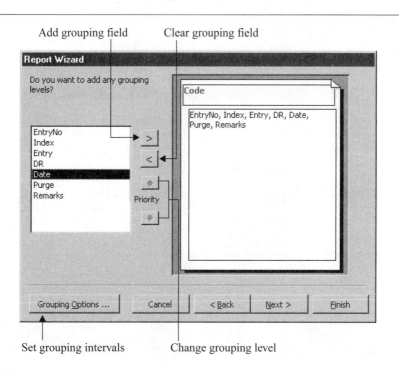

Add grouping field   Clear grouping field

Set grouping intervals   Change grouping level

FIGURE 11-1   Choosing Code as the grouping level

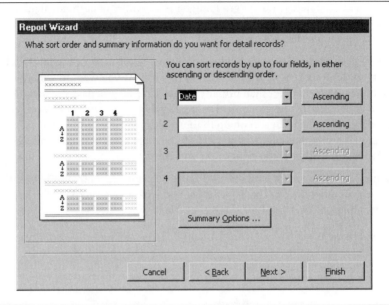

FIGURE 11-2   Specifying the record sort order

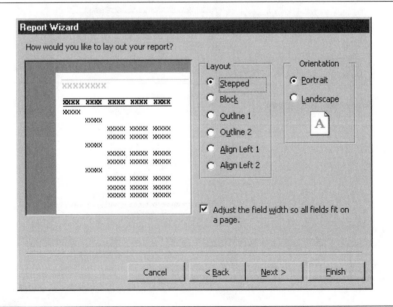

FIGURE 11-3   Choosing the report layout and orientation

7. The next wizard dialog box offers six different styles from which to choose.

8. In the final dialog box, enter **Alpha Entry by Code Report** as the report name and click Finish.

Figure 11-4 shows a Print Preview of the Alpha Entry by Code Report generated by the Report Wizard.

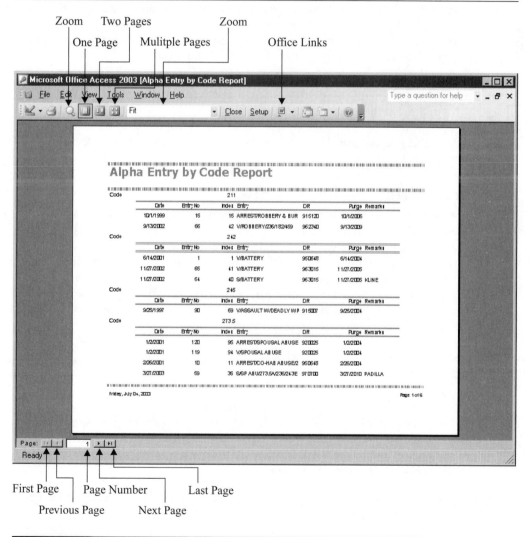

FIGURE 11-4   The Alpha Entry by Code Report in Print Preview

 *If you also want to see an interpretation of the code with the code number in the group header, add the Description field from the Penal Codes table to the query.*

If some of the fields seem incomplete, you can switch to Report Design view and resize them to fit the contents.

Preview and Print the Report

When the Report Wizard has finished creating the report design, you can go directly to the report Design view to make changes or preview the report as it will be printed. If you have not used the Report Wizard or you just want to preview an existing report, select the desired report name in the Reports page of the Database window, then do one of the following:

■ Click the Preview button in the Database window, choose File | Print Preview, or simply press ALT-P.

 ■ Click the Print Preview toolbar button.

■ Right-click the report name in the Reports page and choose Print Preview from the shortcut menu.

Work in the Print Preview Window

The Access Print Preview window (refer to Figure 11-4) offers all kinds of ways to view the report including moving around within and among pages, looking at several pages at once, and changing the magnification so you can see the details more clearly.

The horizontal and vertical scroll bars enable you to move about on the current page. The navigation buttons at the bottom of the Print Preview window let you move among pages in the report. Click one of the buttons to move to the first, previous, next, or last page of the report. You can also enter the page number in the page number box and press ENTER to move to a specific page.

To close the Print Preview window, do one of the following:

■ Click the Close toolbar button

■ Press C or ESC

■ Choose File | Close

 If you open a report in Design view and then switch to Print Preview, clicking the Close toolbar button or pressing CTRL-C or ESC returns to Design view. However, choosing File | Close or clicking the Close button in the upper-right corner of the Print Preview window closes the Design view window too.

When the Preview window closes, you return to the Database window or the report Design view, depending on where you were when you opened the Print Preview.

View Multiple Pages

Previewing several pages at once can help you find pages that have too much white space or another format error. Using the Print Preview toolbar buttons, you can view one or two pages adjusted to fit the screen or up to 20 pages arranged in four rows of five pages each.

To view one complete page at a time, do one of the following:

- Click the One Page toolbar button.
- Right-click and choose One Page from the shortcut menu.
- Choose View | Pages and choose One Page from the list.

To view two or more complete pages adjusted to fit the screen, choose Fit in the Zoom box and use one of the following methods:

- Click the Two Pages toolbar button.
- Click the Multiple Pages toolbar button and drag the mouse pointer over the grid to select the number of pages and the arrangement you want.

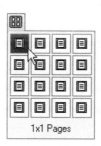

- Choose View | Pages and choose the number of pages from the list. You have a choice of 1, 2, 4, 8, or 12 pages.
- Right-click and choose Multiple Pages from the shortcut menu, then drag the mouse pointer over the grid to select the number of pages and the arrangement you want to see.

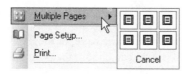

To return to previewing a single page, click the One Page toolbar button.

Change the Magnification

When you first open the Print Preview window, the report is automatically displayed to fit a single page vertically on the screen. You can increase or decrease this degree of magnification to

11

almost any value or ask Access to adjust the report to fit on the screen. Click the Zoom toolbar button to toggle between Fit and the most recent magnification you set. To change the magnification, click the arrow next to the Zoom combo box on the toolbar and choose a percentage between 10 percent and 1000 percent from the list, or enter a value and press ENTER.

Additionally, you can right-click anywhere in the report preview and click Zoom in the shortcut menu, where you have the same choices as with the toolbar Zoom button.

When the mouse pointer passes over the report preview, it changes to a magnifying glass you can click to zoom in and out in the report. This alternates the preview between Fit and the last percentage you have chosen. When the glass shows a minus sign (–), clicking zooms out, making the preview less magnified; clicking the magnifying glass with a plus sign (+) zooms in on the area where the pointer was when you clicked it.

Use the Layout Preview

Layout Preview is another way to preview a report. The window looks like the Print Preview window but shows just enough data to demonstrate every section of the report. This can help you verify that your new design is doing what you want. Layout Preview is available only from the report Design view. To see the Alpha Card with Entries report in Layout Preview:

1. Click View and choose Design View, or choose View | Design View. If you opened the Print Preview window from the Design view, click Close to return to the Design view.

2. Click View and choose Layout Preview, or choose View | Layout Preview. The report is reduced from 15 pages in Print Preview to two pages.

3. To return to Print Preview, close the Layout Preview and switch from Design view to Print Preview.

Print the Report

You can print the report from the preview window, from the Design view, or from the Database window without opening the report. Printing from the Layout Preview does not print the complete report, only the layout pages. Clicking the Print toolbar button or selecting Print from the shortcut menu sends the report directly to the printer without opening the Print dialog box. Choosing File | Print opens the Print dialog box, where you can select other print options.

If you want to change any of the page options such as the margins, the page layout, the printer selection, the number of columns on the page, or the page size, you must run Page Setup. After setting the page specifications, you can choose the print options such as number of copies and the range of pages to print.

Run Page Setup

You can open the Page Setup dialog box from any view of a report or from the Database window without opening the report by choosing File | Page Setup. If you are in the Database window, select the report name before choosing Page Setup. If you are previewing the report in either the Layout or Print Preview, you can also click the Setup toolbar button or right-click in the report and choose Page Setup from the shortcut menu.

The page settings are stored with the report; they must be set only once to be in effect every time you print the report. The Page Setup dialog box has three tabs: Margins, Page, and Columns.

■ Click the Margins tab to set the width of each of the four page margins and choose whether to print only the data, without any of the labels or other unbound objects.

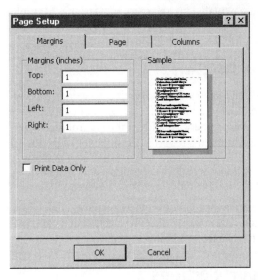

■ Click the Page tab to set the orientation of the print on the page (portrait or landscape), select the paper size and source, and select a different printer if you have more than one in your system. The choice of paper sources depends on the printer you are using.

11

If you want to print using a printer other than the default printer, click Use Specific Printer, then click the Printer button. This opens a dialog box that displays a list of the printers currently installed in the system. Select a different printer and click OK to return to the Page Setup dialog box. After you have made all the desired changes to the page setup, click OK to return to the previous view of the report or the Database window.

The column options are explained in the section "Design a Multiple-Column Report" later in this chapter.

Modify the Report Design

Working in the report Design view is almost identical to working in the form Design view; the controls are the same, although you include fewer types of controls in reports. You use the same toolbox, select the controls the same way, and set the control properties with the same property sheets. The method you use to open a report in Design view depends on where you start:

- From the Database window, select the report name and click Design, or right-click the report name and choose Design View from the shortcut menu.

- From the Print Preview or Layout Preview window, click Close if you previewed the report from Design view, or click the View button and choose Design View if you previewed from the Database window.

Examine the Report Sections

The wizard automatically adds page header and footer sections when it creates a report. The Page Header section contains information that is to be printed at the top of each page, such as the field names used as column headings. The Page Footer section contains information to be printed at the bottom of each page, such as the current date and the page number. To toggle the header and footer sections in and out of the design, choose View | Page Header/Footer.

The Report Header and Footer sections contain information to be printed only once at the beginning or the end of the report. The Detail section contains the bulk of the data in the report. Add report headers and footers the same as page sections: choose View | Report Header/Footer. Choose again to delete both the sections. If there are any controls in one of the sections you try to delete, Access displays a message asking if you want to delete all the controls in the sections. Click Yes to delete them or No to abandon the deletion.

The group header and footer sections, which are optional, contain information to be printed at the top and bottom of each group of records. These sections are used when you group the records by the values in a specific field, such as by Code in the Alpha Entry by Code Report shown earlier.

You select a section in a report design the same way as in a form design by using one of the following methods:

- Click the Object toolbar button and choose the desired section from the list.
- Click the section selector at the left of the section label line.

- Click anywhere in the section label line.
- Click anywhere in the section, outside of any control.

To change the size of a report section, select the section and drag the lower boundary up or down. The report and page sections come in pairs, so if you want to remove one, just reduce its height to zero; the section must be empty before you can do that. When you add a group, you don't need to use both the header and footer. You can choose whether you want a group header or footer, or both, by setting the group properties.

Set Report and Section Properties

Property sheets are opened and used in a report design the same as in a form design; many of the properties are also the same. Some additional properties that relate to the printed report do not apply to forms. Some of the special properties include the following:

- When you create a report with a special title page and you don't want to print the page header or footer information on the same page, set the Page Header and Page Footer report properties to Not With Rpt Hdr. Then, set the report header Force New Page property to After Section to continue printing on a new page.

- If you want the report footer information printed on a separate page at the end of the report, set both the Page Header and Page Footer properties to Not With Rpt Hdr/Ftr and then set the report footer Force New Page property to Before Section.

- When you create a report based on a table or query that was saved with a sort order or a filter, the report inherits both properties. If you look at the report properties, you can see the Filter and Order By expressions that were saved with the table. In addition, the Order By On property is set to Yes and the records are sorted by the inherited sort order. The inherited filter is not applied. To change the report or section filter and sort properties, do the following:

  - To apply the filter, set the Filter On property to Yes.
  - To remove both the filter and the sort, change the Filter On and Sort Order On settings to No.
  - To change the filter or sort order, type a new expression in the Filter or Order By property box and set both the Filter On and Order By On properties to Yes.
  - To suppress printing a section that contains information, set the section's Visible property to No.

Each of the report sections also has a list of properties that you can set to get just the appearance and behavior you want. For example, you can set a different color or add a special effect.

Page headers and footers have no additional properties but the remaining sections—report header and footer, group header and footer, and detail sections—share several other properties. For example, Force New Page specifies whether the section is to be printed on a separate page rather than the current page. To print a complete section all on one page, set the Keep Together

11

property to Yes. To allow a section to expand or shrink to fit the data, set Can Grow and Can Shrink to Yes.

The group header section has one more property that is unique to that section: Repeat Section, which is used to specify whether a group header is repeated on the next page or column when a group spans more than one page or column. The default setting is No. If the group header contains column headings and other relevant information, you might want to change it to Yes so it will print at the top of each page or column.

Change the Report Style

One of the Report Wizard dialog boxes offers a list of styles to choose from. If you find you don't like the style you selected, you can change to one of the other styles in the list by clicking the AutoFormat toolbar button in Design view. Click the report selector if you want to reformat the entire report or one of the sections to reformat only that section. You can also choose Format | AutoFormat to open the same dialog box. Click the Options button to apply the font, color, and border formatting selectively. By default, all three options are checked. If you clear them one at a time, you can see the difference in the displayed sample.

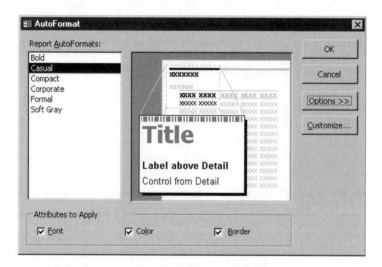

Add Page Numbers and Date/Time Controls

The Report Wizard automatically adds page numbers and the current date/time to the Page Footer section of the Alpha Card with Entries report. The page number is an unbound text box control that you can add to a report design and format in several ways. The date/time field is also an unbound control and is based on your current system's date/time settings.

Add a Page Number

If you have not used the Report Wizard but want to add a page number to your report:

1. Choose Insert | Page Numbers to open the Page Numbers dialog box.

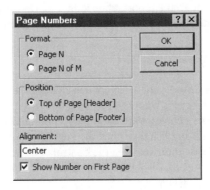

2. Choose Page N of M, where N is the current page number and M is the total number of pages.

3. Choose to see the page number at the top or bottom of the page.

4. Choose the Alignment from the drop-down list: left, center, or right. If the report prints on both sides of the page, you can also choose Inside or Outside.

5. Clear Show Number on First Page box to prevent printing the page number on the title page.

You Can Change the Page Number Format

The Page Numbers dialog box gives you a choice of only two formats for the page number text box; however, you don't have to stick with those. If you want to include characters with the values, you can enter your own custom page format in the Control Source property of the page number text box. Some expressions you might want to use for page numbers are as follows:

Expression	Displays
=[Page]	1, 2, 3
="Entry Report: Page "&[Page]	Entry Report: Page 1, Entry Report: Page 2, Entry Report: Page 3
=[Page]&"/"&[Pages]&" Pages"	1/3 Pages, 2/3 Pages, 3/3 Pages

11

Add a Date/Time Control

To add the current date and time to the report, choose Insert | Date and Time and choose the format you want from the Date and Time dialog box, the same as with forms. See Chapter 10 for more details.

Add Page Breaks

If left to its own devices, Access starts a new page when a page fills up. You can add a page break control within a section to tell Access where you want a new page to begin. For example, a report title and an abstract of the report's contents are all in the Report Header section, but you want them printed on separate pages. To accomplish this, click the Page Break button in the toolbox and place the control in the report header section between the controls you want on the first page and those you want on the second page. Access displays the position of the page break as a short dotted line at the left edge in the report design.

Save the Report Design

When you create a report with the help of the Report Wizard, the report is saved for you with the name you entered in the final wizard dialog box. If you don't use the wizard, you should make a practice of saving the report design frequently as you refine it. This guards against catastrophe and gives you a recent starting point if something goes wrong.

Choose File | Save or click the Save toolbar button or press CTRL-S to save the report without closing the Design window. If this is the first time you have saved the report, you are prompted to enter a name for it in the Save As dialog box.

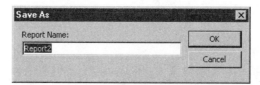

There are two other options on the File menu when saving a report design:

- **Save As**   Opens the same Save As dialog box, where you can choose to save the report design to the current database with the same name or a new name.

- **Export**   Opens the Export Report To dialog box where you locate the folder in which you want to save the report and enter a report name. See Chapter 18 for more information about exporting Access reports and other objects.

To close the report, choose File | Close.

Sort and Group Records in a Report

One of the most useful features of Access reports is the ability to sort and group records based on the value in one or more of the fields. After doing so, you can summarize the information in many ways to illustrate trends and draw conclusions. You can also change the sort order that the report has inherited from the underlying record source. Records can be grouped on Text, Number, Date/Time, Currency, or AutoNumber field types or expressions containing those field values. Access will nest up to ten group levels, each group subordinate to the previous group.

Depending on the data type of the group-on field, there are different ways to group the records. For example, if the field is a Text field, you can group the entire value or the first few characters of the value. Date/Time values can be grouped by each value or any time increment of the value: year, day, hour, minute, and so on.

Change the Sort Order

You can remove or reapply the sort order the report has inherited from the record source by setting the report's Order By On property. Choose No to remove the sort order or Yes to reapply it. If you want to use the inherited sort order, you must also set the Filter On property to No.

To sort the records in the report in a different order than the underlying table or query, set the report's Order By On property to Yes and its Order By property as follows:

- To sort the records by values in one field in ascending order, type the field name enclosed in brackets followed by **ASC**; for example, **[Code] ASC**.

- To sort the records by values in one field in descending order, type the field name enclosed in brackets followed by **DESC**; for example, **[Last Name] DESC**.

- To sort the records by values in more than one field in ascending or descending order, type each field name enclosed in brackets followed by **ASC** or **DESC** and separated by commas. For example, the setting **[Code] ASC, [Last Name] DESC** sorts first by the Code field in ascending order, then by the Last Name field in descending order.

If you don't specify ASC or DESC, Access automatically sorts in ascending order. The new setting overrides the inherited sort order without affecting the data source. Be sure to set the Order By On property to Yes to effect the new sort order.

Add Group Sections

To illustrate grouping records in a report, create a new report based on a query that extracts only those records from the Alpha Entry table with a value in the Code field. This eliminates Alpha Entry records not related to a potentially criminal offense.

The Alpha Entry by Code query contains the expression <>0 in the Criteria row of the Code column in the grid. After dragging the field names from the list to the detail section of the new Entries by Year report, you can proceed to group the records by the year the incident was reported.

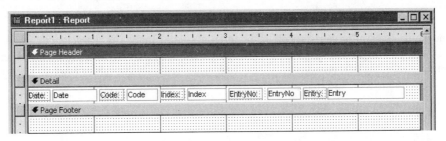

To add a group section to this report:

1. In Design view, click the Sorting and Grouping toolbar button or choose View | Sorting and Grouping.

2. Select the Date field from the drop-down Field/Expression list.

3. Select Ascending as the order in which you want the groups arranged. (The detail records within each group will appear ordered by the value in the primary key field of the parent table or query unless you change the report Order By property.)

4. In the lower pane of the Sorting and Grouping dialog box, set the properties of one or both group sections to Yes to add a group header or footer.

You must choose a group header or footer for Access to group the records. If you don't select Yes in either the Group Header or Footer property, the records are only sorted by the field or expression, not grouped.

5. Select Year from the Group On list and set the Interval to 1.

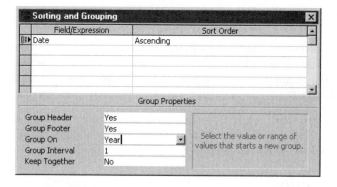

The Sorting and Grouping dialog box settings will group the records by the year value in the Date field. The Date groups will appear in ascending order from the earliest year to the latest, and the report has both a group header and a group footer section. You can see the new Date group header and footer sections in the design behind the dialog box.

The options available in the Group On property list vary with the data type of the field or expression entered in the Field/Expression column. For example, if you are grouping on a date/time field, there are several options for date and time intervals.

The Group Interval property specifies the interval or the number of characters to group on. For example, you might want to group records by values in a currency field in $50 increments. If you set the Group Interval property to 50, the first group will include values from $0 to $49, the second from $50 to $99, and so on.

You can set the Keep Together property to Yes to prevent a group that occupies less than a page from being split over two pages. If the group is larger than one page, this property is ignored.

Customize Group Headers and Footers

You must include one of the group sections to group records in a report; however, that doesn't mean you have to print any information in it. For example, suppose that you want to group records by Code but don't intend to summarize them with a total or an average. Changing the section's Visible property to No suppresses previewing and printing the section. If there is no information in the group section, you can reduce its height to 0 instead, but leave the section in the report design.

To remove a group header or footer, open the Sorting and Grouping dialog box and change the corresponding property to No. If you have placed information in the section you try to delete, Access warns you that you will delete the information with the section.

If you switch the Entries by Year report to Print Preview, you can see that the Alpha Entry records are indeed grouped by year but it is not very obvious. The grouping would stand out better if the year value appeared in the group header section. Moving the field labels to the group header also would allow more room for the field data in the detail section. Unfortunately, attached labels can't be dragged to a different section, so hold down SHIFT and select the labels. Then click Cut (CTRL-X) and move to the group header section. Click Paste (CTRL-V) and the labels are placed above the text box controls. You may have to move them a bit to line them up accurately.

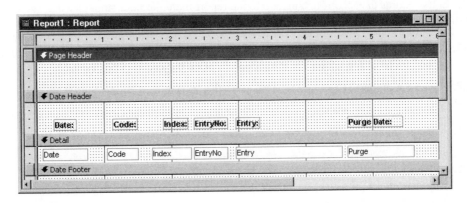

To add a new text box control to the group header that shows the year value for the group:

1. Click the Text Box control tool in the toolbox and place the control in the group header section.

2. Open the property sheet and enter the expression =**Year([Date])** in the Control Source property box. The Year() function extracts the year value from the Date field.

3. Select the attached label, then click in it and replace Text*n* with **Year Reported:** as the label for the year control.

4. Switch to Print Preview to see the year value in the group header.

Add Summaries and Running Totals

In Chapter 9, you saw how to add calculated controls to form designs using expressions. You can also use calculated controls to summarize data in a report. Earlier you saw how the Report Wizard offered to add summaries to a report that contained groupings. You were limited to arithmetic summaries involving number, currency, or AutoNumber fields. When you design your own report with groupings, you can use many more types of group summaries including running totals that accumulate the value throughout the report.

Add a Count Summary

Let's add to the group footer of the Entries by Year report a summary that counts the number of Alpha Entry records in each group and add to the report footer another summary that shows the total number of records in the report.

1. In the report Design view, click the Text Box control tool in the toolbox and click in the group footer at the left end of the section to place the new text box control.

2. Open the property sheet and type **=Count([Entry])** in the Control Source property box.

3. Change the Align property to Left so the number will appear closer to the label.

4. Change the label to **Total This Year:**, then move and resize the text box and label controls to fit.

5. Increase the height of the report footer section to make room for the grand total summary field.

6. Select the calculated control in the group footer and click Copy, then click in the report footer near the left end and click Paste. A copy of the group summary control appears in the report footer.

7. Click in the label and change the caption to **Grand Total:**.

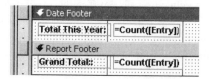

Add a Running Total

When you are dealing with financial data, often it is important to show running totals within groups and overall. You can add a calculated control that sums up the values in a group and accumulates the values from group to group. At the end of the report, you can print the overall total for the whole report.

When you create a calculated control using one of the aggregate functions such as Sum, Avg, Count, and so on, you can set the Running Sum property to Over Group or Over All. The Over Group setting accumulates the values in the group, then resets the value to 0 at the beginning of the next group. The Over All setting accumulates the values to the end of the report, printing subtotals at intermediate points as required.

> **TIP**   *If you are interested only in the summary data in a report, you can avoid printing the details by changing the detail section Visible property to No or by reducing the section height to 0.*

Apply the Finishing Touches

To finish the Entries by Year report, add a title in the report header. Because the information in the report header prints only on the first page of the report, you can add a continuation title and the page number to the page header that will print on every page except the first.

1. Choose View | Page Header/Footer.

2. Shrink the page footer section (nothing will be placed in it).

3. Change the report Page Header property to Not with Rpt Hdr.

4. Draw some lines under the titles to separate the report header and page header from the rest of the report and another line at the bottom of the group footer to separate the groups.

5. Reduce the width of the Year and Count controls to move the values closer to the attached labels.

Figure 11-5 shows the completed report in Design view and Figure 11-6 shows the printed first page of the report. If you move to the next page, you will see the continuation page header title.

Modify and Add Groups

To change the sort order of the records in an ungrouped report or of the groups in a grouped report, open the Sorting and Grouping dialog box and choose from the Sort Order drop-down list. If you want to change the grouping levels of existing groups, click the row selector of the group you want to move. Click it again and drag the row to the desired position in the list of groupings. If the groups you move have headers or footers, Access moves them and all the controls they contain to the new positions in the report design. The controls might need some adjustment after repositioning.

11

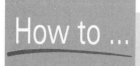

How to ... Number Items in a Report

Sometimes it is handy to have the items in a report numbered so you can reference each one uniquely by number; for example, in a teleconference, you would need to be sure everyone is talking about the same item. To number the items:

1. Add a calculated text box control to the detail section in a prominent position at the left of the record data.

2. Remove the new text box label.

3. Double-click the new control to open its property sheet and change the Control Source property to the expression =1.

4. Set the Running Sum property to Over All, which increments the calculated text box value by 1 for each record in the detail section.

This works for grouped records as well. To number the records in each group separately, add the calculated control to the detail section as above but set the Running Sum property to Over Group instead of Over All.

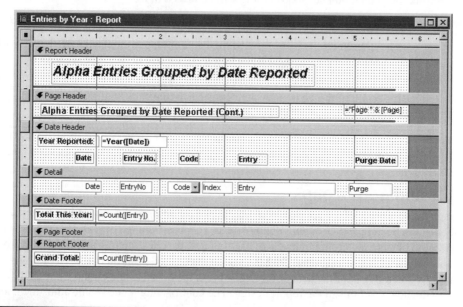

FIGURE 11-5   The Entries by Year report design

Alpha Entries Grouped by Date Reported

Year Reported: 1990

Date	Entry No.	Cod	Inde	Entry	Purge Date
6 /24/90	73	488	50	V/PETTY THEFT	6 /24/02

Total This Year: 1

Year Reported: 1993

Date	Entry No.	Cod	Inde	Entry	Purge Date
12/19/93	118	459	93	V/BURGLARY	12/19/00

Total This Year: 1

Year Reported: 1994

Date	Entry No.	Cod	Inde	Entry	Purge Date
10/26/94	19	20001	16	R/O VEH #1/H&R FELONY	10/26/01
11/5 /94	39	459	21	V/BURGLARY	11/5 /01
4 /16/94	76	459	52	V/BURGLARY	4 /16/01
3 /27/94	75	459	52	V/BURGLARY	3 /17/01
9 /25/94	90	245	69	V/ASSAULT W/DEADLY	9 /25/01
12/18/94	92	459	71	V/BURGLARY	12/18/04

Total This Year: 6

Year Reported: 1995

Date	Entry No.	Cod	Inde	Entry	Purge Date
4 /9 /95	41	459	23	ARREST/BURGLARY & 496.1	4 /9 /02
12/10/95	107	459	84	V/BURGLARY &	12/10/02

Total This Year: 2

Year Reported: 1996

Date	Entry No.	Cod	Inde	Entry	Purge Date
10/15/96	3	459	4	V/BURGLARY	10/15/03
8 /7 /96	7	487	8	V/GRAND THEFT	8 /7 /03
7 /5 /96	26	10851	16	R/O STOL VEH	7 /5 /03
7 /16/96	28	10851	16	R/O/STOL VEH	7 /16/03
7 /18/96	30	10851	16	R/O/STOL VEH	7 /18/03
12/20/96	48	10851	29	R/O STOL TRLR	12/20/03
1 /29/96	51	10851	30	R/O/RCVD VEH	1 /29/03
1 /27/96	50	10851	30	R/O/STOL VEH	1 /27/03
8 /6 /96	61	10851	37	R/O/STOL VEH	8 /6 /03

11

FIGURE 11-6   Printed first page of the Entries by Year report

To change the group-on field or expression, select it and choose another field from the drop-down list or enter a different expression. If you want to add a grouping level, click in the next empty Field/Expression row and choose the field from the drop-down list or enter an expression. For example, you could further group the Entries by Year report by quarter within the year group. You can also insert a grouping level above an existing one by clicking the row selector where you want the new level and pressing INS. To remove a grouping, click the row selector and press DEL.

Create a Summary Report with the Report Wizard

The Report Wizard's summarizing capabilities are very useful when creating reports involving numeric or monetary information. For this example, let's return to the Home Tech Repair database, which has some currency fields that can demonstrate the summary options. When you choose to group the Workorder records by Supervisor, the next dialog box in which you set the sort order now has the Summary Options button available. Clicking this button opens the Summary Options dialog box, which shows the names of all the fields in the report that contain number or currency data.

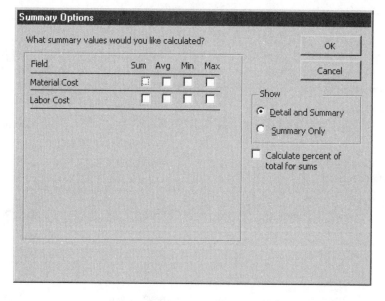

Click the check boxes for all the summary values you want the wizard to calculate for you. In the Show option group, you can choose to include the detail records with the summaries or show only the summary values. The other option, "Calculate percent of total for sums," includes the relative size of each group sum compared to the grand total, which is calculated and printed at the end of the report. Figure 11-7 shows the printed first page of a report that groups the Home Tech Repair work orders by supervisor and computes the sum, average, minimum, and maximum of the Material Costs and Labor Costs for each group of work orders.

Workorder Summary

Supervisor	10		

Start Date	Workorder Number	Material Cost	Labor Cost
2/25/01	001	$472.50	$472.50
6/25/01	009	$1,100.00	$450.00
7/10/01	013	$400.00	$1,100.00
7/23/01	016	$250.00	$125.00

Summary for 'Supervisor' = 10 (4 detail records)

	Material Cost	Labor Cost
Sum	$2,222.50	$2,147.50
Avg	$555.63	$536.88
Min	$250.00	$125.00
Max	$1,100.00	$1,100.00
Percent	23.38%	14.60%

Supervisor	12		

Start Date	Workorder Number	Material Cost	Labor Cost
3/15/01	002	$1,155.00	$840.00
4/15/01	004	$115.50	$315.00
6/15/01	008	$400.00	$750.00
7/12/01	014	$75.00	$300.00
7/15/01	015	$420.00	$100.00

Summary for 'Supervisor' = 12 (5 detail records)

	Material Cost	Labor Cost
Sum	$2,165.50	$2,305.00
Avg	$433.10	$461.00
Min	$75.00	$100.00
Max	$1,155.00	$840.00
Percent	22.78%	15.67%

Supervisor	13		

Start Date	Workorder Number	Material Cost	Labor Cost
6/15/01	007	$2,500.00	$7,200.00

Wednesday, February 28, 2001

FIGURE 11-7	Summarizing work order costs by supervisor

The Report Wizard also automatically counts the number of detail records in each group and displays it at the top of the summary section. A two-point dash-dot line has been added to the group footer to separate one supervisor's work orders from the next visually.

NOTE *You might also want to replace the Supervisor ID field with the LastName field to make the report more understandable to outsiders.*

Print an Alphabetic Index

By combining the Group On and Group Interval settings, you can create an alphabetic list of items grouped by the leading character. For example, to create a list such as that shown in Figure 11-8:

1. Select the Member List table in the Database window and choose Insert | Report.

2. Select Design View in the New Report dialog box and click OK.

3. Place the LastName field in the detail section and delete the attached label.

4. Open the report's Property sheet and set the Sort By property to LastName and the Sort By On property to Yes.

 5. Click the Sorting and Grouping button, choose LastName as the field to group on, and set the following group properties:

   ■ Set Group Header to Yes.

   ■ Set Group Footer to No.

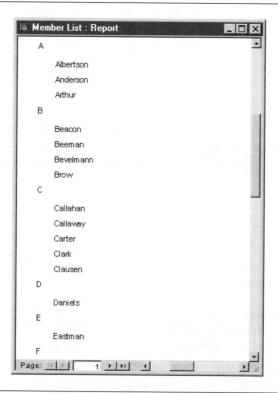

| FIGURE 11-8 | An alphabetic Member List |

- ■ Set Group On to Prefix Characters.
- ■ Set Group Interval to 1.

6. To place the initial character in the group header, add a text box control to the group header and delete the attached label.

7. Set the new text box Control Source property to **=Left([LastName],1)**. Figure 11-9 shows the completed report design and the Sorting and Grouping dialog box.

 Be careful to avoid using the word "Name" as a field name. Access reserves that word as the name of the current object. If you use the expression =Left([Name],1) in the group header, you will see "M" (the first letter of the report name) in every group header. There are many more reserved words in the Access language.

Add a Subreport

A *subreport,* a complete report in its own right, is inserted into another report, called the *main report.* A main report can be either bound or unbound. A bound main report is based on a table or query, and its subreports contain related information. For example, the main report could

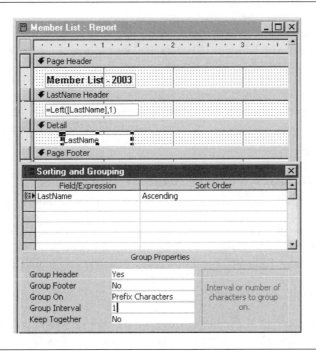

FIGURE 11-9   The Member List report in Design view

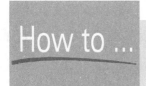

Hide Duplicates and Other Tips

Duplicate values appearing in the detail section can clutter up a report. For example, a report grouping the Alpha Entry records by code would show multiple records with the same code value. There are two ways to solve the problem: Move the Code field to the group header section, where it will be printed only once, or leave it in the detail section and change a control property.

■ To move the control, drag it from the detail section to the desired position in the group header.

■ To leave the control in the detail section and avoid printing duplicate values, open the control property sheet and set the Hide Duplicates format property to Yes.

Two other properties are useful when printing reports containing memo fields that might contain a varying amount of data or possibly none at all. Changing the Can Shrink property to Yes will prevent blank lines when there is no value in the field. Changing Can Grow to Yes lets the field value expand as necessary.

contain details about the year's business; the subreport could show charts and graphs summarizing and illustrating the numbers in the main report.

An unbound main report is not based on a table or query but can serve as a container for one or more subreports. For example, you may produce an annual report with a title page containing some introductory information. This constitutes the unbound main report. The one or more subreports contain parallel information unrelated to each other but nevertheless important to the business during the previous year.

Create a Subreport with the Report Wizard

When you use the Report Wizard to create a report based on two or more tables or queries, you can specify which table contains the main data and which contains the subordinate data. In the example in this section, the Alpha Card table is specified as the parent table and the Alpha Entry table as the related child table. The Entry Explanation table, which is related one-to-one to the Alpha Entry table, also is included. The resulting report will show multiple Alpha Entry records for a single Alpha Card record.

To create the report and subreport:

1. Double-click the "Create report by using wizard" item on the Reports page or open the New Report dialog box and choose Report Wizard, then click OK.

2. In the first dialog box, choose the Index and Name fields from the Alpha Card table; the EntryNo, Entry, Code, and Date fields from the Alpha Entry table; and the Explanation field from the Entry Explanation table. Click Next.

3. In the second dialog box, the wizard asks how you want to view the data. Access assumes that the parent table of the relationship is to appear as the main report. Accept the choice and click Next.

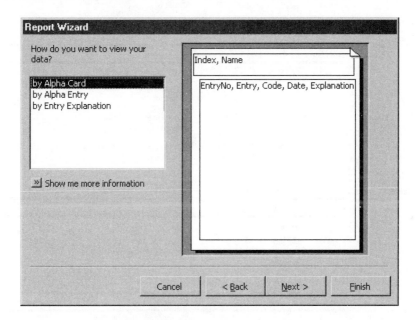

4. Click Next twice to skip this and the Sort Options dialog box to reach the Layout dialog box, in which you select a layout.

5. Choose Outline 1 and click Next twice.

6. In the last dialog box, name the report **Alpha Card with Entries** and click Finish.

Figure 11-10 shows the printed first page of the new Alpha Card with Entries report. As you navigate through the pages, you will see that there are several improvements to be made. For example, you might truncate the title in order to widen the label control. You might also want to add a line to better separate the groups of records.

Create a Subreport Control

As an example of creating a new subreport without the help of the Report Wizard, let's add the Alpha Entry information to the Alpha Card report, relating the two reports by the Index field.

Alpha Card with Entries

Index		1		
Name		ALLEN, FRANK ROGER		

EntryNo	Date	Entry	Explanation	Code
1	6 /14/95	V/BATTERY	Victim of battery	242

Index		3		
Name		AIYER, ROBERT L		

EntryNo	Date	Entry	Explanation	Code
134	7 /11/96	V/BURGLARY	Victim of house burglary	459
133	1 /8 /96	DRIVER #1/NONINJ TC	Driver #1 in a non-injury traffic collision.	
132	10/21/96	TURNED IN FOUND	Turned in jewelry found in store parking lot.	
2	4 /25/94	V/GRAND THEFT BIKE	Victim of grand theft. Bicycle was stolen.	487

Index		4		
Name		AILLEM, PAUL CALVIN		

EntryNo	Date	Entry	Explanation	Code
3	10/15/93	V/BURGLARY	Victim of burglary	459
135	12/3 /96	R/O STOL/RCVD	Registered owner of recovered stolen vehicle.	10851

Index		5		
Name		AIZENBAUM, ESTELA		

EntryNo	Date	Entry	Explanation	Code
4	8 /6 /94	V/ATTEMPT AUTO THEFT	Victim of an attempted auto theft.	10852

Index		6		
Name		AKEN, HAILESILASSIE B		

EntryNo	Date	Entry	Explanation	Code
5	3 /31/96	DRIVER #1/NONINJ TC	Driver #1 in non-injury traffic collision	

Wednesday, February 28, 2001

FIGURE 11-10   Printed Alpha Card with Entries report

Just to be safe, save the Alpha Card report with a different name before adding the subreport as follows:

1. Right-click the Alpha Card report in the Database window and choose Save As from the shortcut menu.

2. Enter the new name, **Alpha Card with Subreport**, in the Save As dialog box and click OK.

3. Open the Alpha Card with Subreport report in Design view and open the toolbox.

4. Increase the height of the detail section and move the line to the bottom to make room for the subreport in between.

 5. Make sure you have pushed in the Control Wizards button on the toolbox, then click the Subform/Subreport tool and click in the report design between the last row of controls and the line at the bottom of the detail section. Access draws a square frame in the report design and opens the first dialog box where you can select an existing report or form as the subreport, or create a new one based on a table or query.

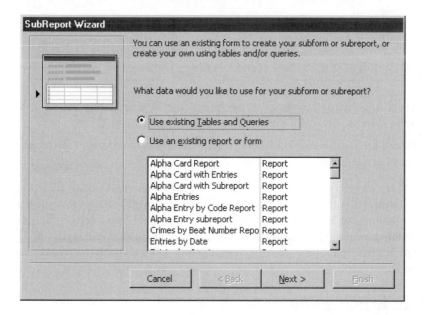

> **NOTE** *You can also draw a custom subreport frame to the desired size before releasing the mouse button and starting the wizard.*

6. Choose "Use existing Tables and Queries" to create the new subreport, then click Next.

7. In the next dialog box, select Alpha Entry from the Tables/Queries drop-down list, then click >> to select all the fields and click Next.

8. Accept the link the wizard suggests, which links the report and subreport by the Index field. Then click Next.

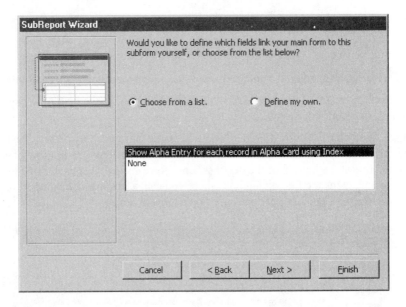

9. Accept Alpha Entry subreport1 as the report name or enter a different name, such as **Alpha Entries**, then click Finish to return to the main report Design view.

10. You can delete the subreport label if it is in the way, then move and resize the subreport control as appropriate.

Figure 11-11 shows a preview of the report with the new subreport. Your subreport's style might be different. As you can see in the preview, there are several refinements you can make in the subreport to improve its appearance. For example, you could hide the Index field and spread out the remaining controls to make room for the Entry information; additionally, the Code field doesn't need so much space because it contains no more than six characters, so you can reduce the width of that control.

Insert an Existing Subreport

To use an existing report as a subreport, make sure the underlying tables or queries are properly related to those used by the main report, then open the Subform/Subreport Wizard as described previously. Instead of choosing "Use existing Tables and Queries" in the first wizard dialog box, choose "Use an existing report or form," then select the desired report or form from the drop-down list of all the reports and forms in the current database. Follow the instructions in the remaining wizard dialog boxes.

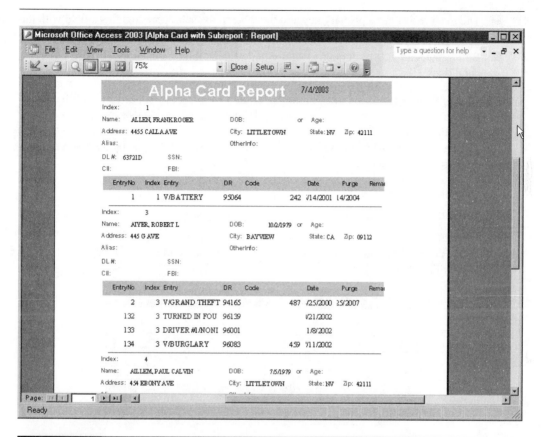

FIGURE 11-11   Previewing the report with the new subreport

TIP   *You can also just drag the name of the report you want to use as a subreport from the Database window onto the Design view of the main report.*

Link the Report and Subreport

If you insert the subreport in a bound report, the underlying tables must be linked so both reports will contain corresponding data. You must set the links in the Relationships window before trying to insert the subreport.

When you use the wizard to create a subreport or drag an existing report or datasheet from the Database window, Access automatically links the main report and subreport if one of the following conditions is met:

■ The reports are based on related tables

■ The main report has a primary key and the table in the subreport contains a field with the same name and of the same or compatible data type

■ Both reports are based on queries whose underlying tables meet either of those same conditions

The linking fields must be included in the underlying record sources, but you don't have to show them in either report. The wizard automatically includes linking fields even if you don't select them with the field picker.

If for some reason the wizard hasn't linked the tables properly, you can set the properties yourself by doing the following:

1. Open the main report in Design view.

2. Select the subreport control and open the property sheet.

3. Enter the name of the linking field (not the control) in the subreport in the Link Child Fields property box and enter the name of the linking field in the main report in the Link Master Fields property box.

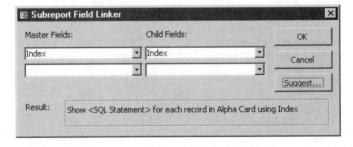

 *If you aren't sure about the field names, select the Build button (...) next to one of the Link properties and choose them with the help of the Subreport Field Linker dialog box.*

You can link on more than one field by entering the field names in the property sheet, separated by semicolons, or by selecting them in the Subreport Field Linker dialog box.

Modify a Subreport Control

The first thing you might want to do with a new subreport control is to edit or delete the attached control label in the main report Design view. Make changes in the subreport design to match the style and arrangement of the controls in the main report. Subreport controls share many of the properties with other types of controls, for example, the position and size properties as well as the Special Effect and border properties. By default, the Can Grow property is set to Yes and the Can Shrink property to No. In addition to the link field properties, the subreport has a Name property which is set to the name you saved the file with or the name you entered in the Subform/ Subreport Wizard dialog box.

Design a Multiple-Column Report

Another way to arrange information in a report is in columns. When information is arranged in a tabular layout, it is easy to scan down a column of data and compare values in different records. Arranging the information in columns makes it easier to focus on individual records because all the data for one record is grouped together.

The Report Wizard gives you a choice of tabular or columnar layout in one of the dialog boxes. Choosing Columnar creates a report with the fields arranged in a single column on the page. Using Page Setup, you can change the layout to include as many columns as will fit across the page. Figure 11-12 compares the columnar report created by the Report Wizard with the same data in a newspaper column report.

To create this three-column report:

1. Select the Name List table in the Database window and choose Insert | Report.

2. Choose AutoReport: Columnar from the New Report dialog box.

3. In Design view or Print Preview, choose File | Page Setup. The three-tab Page Setup dialog box opens.

4. Click the Columns tab and change the Number of Columns to **3**.

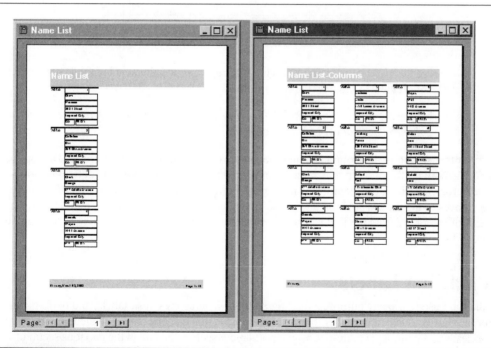

FIGURE 11-12   Comparing a columnar and a three-column report

5. Leave the Column Spacing at the default, **.25"**. If you have left some space between the bottom control in the detail section and the lower boundary of the section, you can also leave the Row Spacing at **0**.

6. In the Column Size group, set the Width to **2"**. You can also set the Height here or use the height drawn in Design view.

7. Choose OK. If you are in Print Preview, the report shows the new layout. If not, switch to Print Preview to see how the report looks.

Make sure the total of the width of the columns and the margins plus the spaces between the columns does not exceed the page width.

Another setting in the Columns dialog box is the Column Layout option group. This option group determines the order in which the records are laid out on the page. The default is Down, then Across, which places records down the page in the first column to the bottom of the page, then moves to the second column, and so on. The alternative choice is Across, then Down, which places the records across the first row to the right margin of the page, then moves to the second row, and so on.

Print Mailing Labels

Labels are used for many purposes: mailing addresses, name tags, disk labels, and book-plates. Because labels usually are smaller than a sheet of paper, you can print many of them on one page. This leads to a multiple-column-per-page report layout such as the one in the previous section.

Label printing is so common that Access has provided a special Label Wizard to help with the layout. After you create the label design, you can use it to print addresses on envelopes as well with a few changes to the page layout. Through the Label Wizard, you can create your own custom label size and layout and save it to use again.

Use the Label Wizard

The Label Wizard helps with every stage of the label design, including choosing the layout, changing the text appearance, adding field data to a prototype label, and even offering to sort the labels for you before printing. As an example of printing mailing labels, the local police department keeps the names and addresses of the Retired Senior Volunteer Program (RSVP) members in the Name List table in the department's Access database so that the program can mail monthly notices to the members.

To create mailing labels for the volunteers:

1. Open the New Report dialog box and choose Label Wizard. If you have not already selected the table or query that contains the label data, select Name List from the drop-down list and click OK.

2. In the first dialog box, set the following options:

 - Select the desired Unit of Measure: English or Metric.

 - Select the Label Type: Sheet feed or Continuous.

 - Choose the brand of label from the "Filter by manufacturer" drop-down list.

 - Choose the desired label size from the Product Number list. The dimensions are specified as height times width.

 - If you want to create a custom label size, click the Customize button.

 - If you have already created some custom label sizes, you can choose "Show custom label sizes" to see that list.

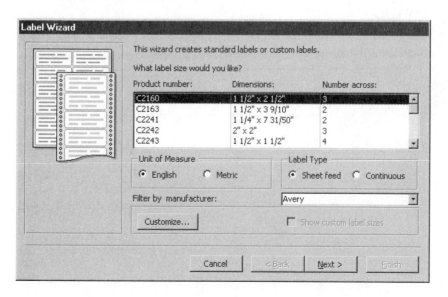

11

3. Click Next to open the second dialog box, where you can select the font name, size, and weight, and text colors. Italics and underlining also are options here.

4. Click Next to continue. The next Label Wizard dialog box displays a blank label prototype where you arrange the data. Double-click the field name to move it to the prototype label. Be sure to enter a space between fields. Press ENTER to move to the next line in the label.

5. Access automatically concatenates the values in the fields and trims the spaces from the names and addresses. Notice the spaces entered between the field names and the comma entered between the City and State fields.

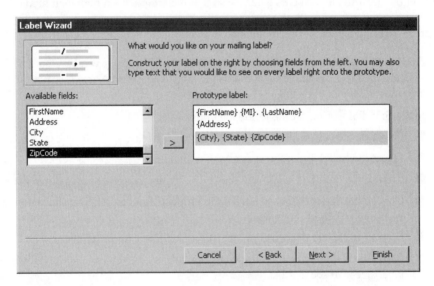

6. Click Next to move to the next dialog box, where you can choose to sort the records before printing the labels. Click Next to move to the last Label Wizard dialog box, where you enter a name for the label design.

It is a good idea to print one page of the new labels on plain paper and compare it with your label stock before committing to print many pages of labels on expensive label sheets.

Figure 11-13 shows a preview of the new labels for the Name List, using the Avery 5160 label size. The labels are sorted by Last Name.

TIP *You can use the same report design you created for printing the labels to print the addresses on envelopes. All you need to do is change the Page Setup options to reflect the different size and arrangement of the controls.*

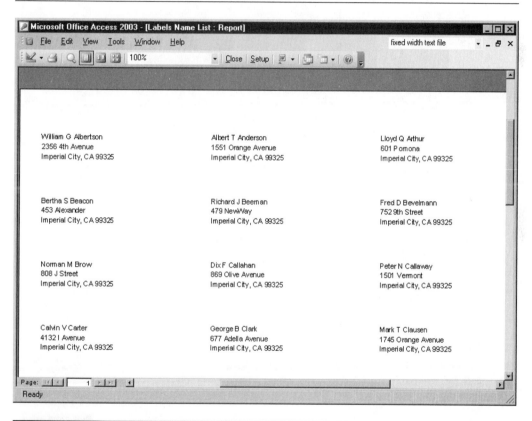

FIGURE 11-13   Previewing the first page of new labels

Chapter 12

Create Charts and Graphs

How to...

- Choose the appropriate type of chart
- Create a new chart with the Chart Wizard
- Create a new chart without the Chart Wizard
- Add an existing chart to a form or report
- Modify the chart

Charts and graphs enhance data presented in forms and reports by summarizing and illustrating information in easily understood ways. With these tools, the reader can analyze trends and make comparisons. Access offers a wide variety of chart types including column, bar, line, pie, XY scatter, area, and many others. If you want the chart to reflect the values in the currently displayed record, you can also link the chart to a field in the underlying table or query.

Choose a Chart Type

When you decide to add a chart to a form or report, you must first understand the purpose of the chart. Do you want to point out trends over a period of time or compare the relative values summarized by groups? Figure 12-1 shows a typical column chart based on data from the Northwind sample database that came with Access. This chart compares the sales of eight product categories during 1997.

Many other types of charts can show comparisons among data groups. For example, Figure 12-2 shows the same Northwind sales data displayed in an exploding pie chart. Each slice of the pie represents a product category.

Another reason to include charts in a form or report is to show trends over a period of time. Figure 12-3, which uses data from the Police database, shows a line chart that tracks the number of crimes that were reported over a four-year period. The crimes are grouped as violent or non-violent and a legend is included, which identifies the lines.

Create a New Chart with the Chart Wizard

The way you create a new chart depends on the type of chart you want. Do you want a stand-alone chart in its own form or report design, or a chart embedded in an existing form or report? In either case, you'll use the Chart Wizard to create it. The chart exists in a chart control in the form or report.

Select the Data for the Chart

Once you decide on what the chart is intended to accomplish, you can locate the data the chart will require. If the data is all contained in one table, you can use the table as the basis for the chart. If not, you can create a select or crosstab query that will group and summarize the data

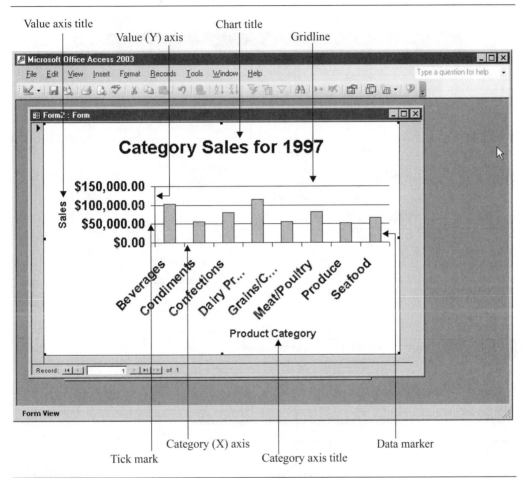

FIGURE 12-1 A typical Access column chart

for the chart. With a select query, you can combine data and add calculated fields such as an extended price, and add totals that summarize field values.

You can use up to six fields of any data type except OLE and Memo. There are only two requirements:

- You must include at least one field for categorizing data, such as the year the crime was reported or the area of the city where it occurred.

- You must include a field or a calculated field that you can add up, average, or count, such as the number of violent crimes or the sales during the third quarter of 2002.

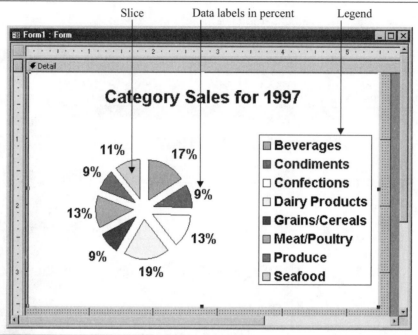

FIGURE 12-2   A pie chart with data labels in percent

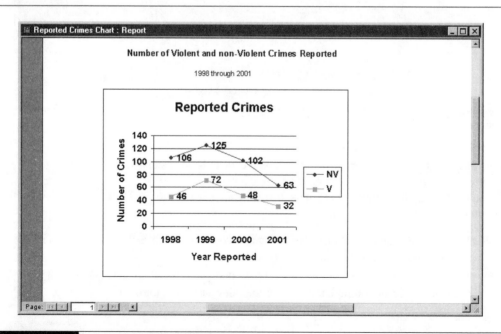

FIGURE 12-3   A line chart showing a trend over time

A simple chart can contain only two fields: one as the category and the other as the data or value that corresponds to the category. For example, in Figure 12-1 there are only two fields: Product Category, which is used as the category, and Sales, which was summed to form the value.

Use the Access Chart Wizard

The easiest way to create a new chart is to invoke the Chart Wizard. You can start the Chart Wizard in one of the following ways:

■   If you are creating a free-standing chart, start a new form or report and choose Chart Wizard in the New Form (or Report) dialog box. Select the table or query you want to use as the basis for the chart and click OK.

■   If you want to insert a new chart in an existing form or report, open the form or report in Design view and choose Insert | Chart. Click in the design where you want to place the chart. The Chart Wizard opens and the first dialog box asks you to select the table or query to use as the basis for the chart.

Once you have specified the underlying record source, follow the instructions in the wizard dialog boxes as follows (this example uses the Crimes by Beat Number table in the Police database):

1.   Choose the fields you want to use in the chart; for example, Year, Crime Type, and Number of Crimes. Click Next.

2.   Select the type of chart you want to create (see Figure 12-4) and click Next. You can click each type of chart and read a description in the right pane.

12

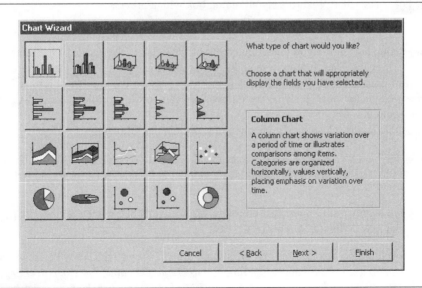

Selecting the type of chart

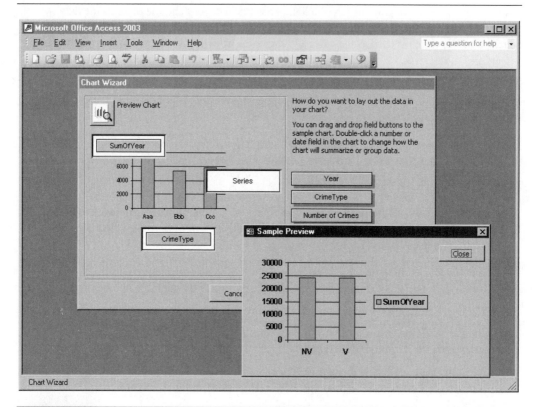

FIGURE 12-5   The Chart Wizard's layout dialog box with a preview

The next dialog box shows you the arrangement of the fields in the layout of the sample chart. Click the Preview Chart button to see how this arrangement would look (see Figure 12-5).

The preview does not show what the chart is meant to present: the number of crimes by type that were reported in each year. It shows the number of years in which violent and non-violent crimes were reported.

To change this layout, close the Preview window and do the following:

1. Drag the SumOfYear label to the area below the chart to replace Crime Type. The label changes to Year because it represents a category on the X axis rather than a numeric value on the Y axis.

2. Drag the Number of Crimes field button to the Data area below the Preview Chart. The label changes to SumOfNumber of Crimes.

NOTE   *When you drag a field to the Data area in the sample chart, the Chart Wizard assumes you want to use the Sum aggregate function to create the value, but you can change to another function by double-clicking a number field, choosing the function from the Summarize dialog box, and clicking OK.*

3. Drag the Crime Type field button to the Series area.

4. To remove a field from the Preview Chart, drag it off the chart. The field name is replaced by Series, Data, or Axis, depending on the chart area.

5. Click the Preview Chart button again to see the effects of the changes. Figure 12-6 shows the new layout with a preview.

6. Close the Preview window and click Next.

7. In the final Chart Wizard dialog box, enter a name for the chart, such as "Crimes by Year Chart," or accept the name of the table or query you used as the basis.

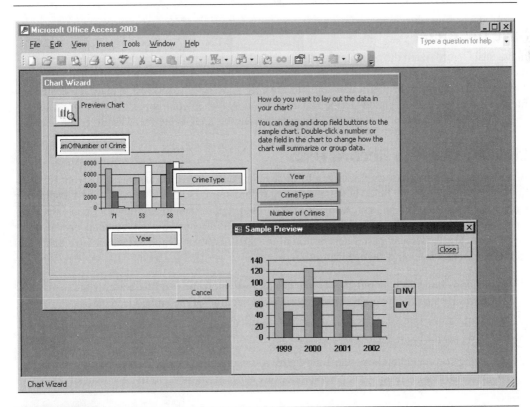

FIGURE 12-6   Chart layout with the preview after modification

8. Choose to display a legend explaining the series data.

9. Click Finish. The chart appears in the new form. You might have to resize the form or the chart to get the appearance you want.

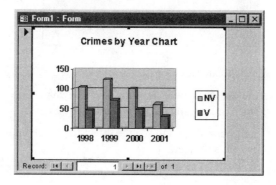

When you first create a chart, it shows sample data rather than the data you asked it to process. Don't worry, the chart will show the real data the first time you view the form in Form view or the report in Print Preview.

Save the Chart

In the final Chart Wizard dialog box, you assigned a title to the new chart, but have not yet named the host form or report, as you can see from the "Form1: Form" name still in the title bar. To name and save the form or report that contains the chart, choose File | Save and enter the desired filename. The new name is added to the Database window. When you reopen the form or report containing the chart, it will contain the current data from the underlying record source.

Link the Chart to Record Data

When you start a new chart from within a form or report design, Access assumes you want to link the chart to one of the fields in the underlying record source so that a different chart displays with each record. To do this, first create the host form or report, then insert the new or an existing chart. For example, create a columnar form based on the City Beats table that contains only two fields: the beat number and a brief description of the territory, then switch to Design view and create a new chart by doing the following:

1. Choose Insert | Chart and click in the design just below the text box controls in the form. Be sure that you have made room in the section for the embedded chart.

2. In the first Chart Wizard dialog box, choose the Crimes by Beat Number table as the basis for the chart and click Next.

3. In the second dialog box, select the fields you want in the chart. For this chart, choose Year, BeatNo, Crime Type, and Number of Crimes from the field list, then click Next.

4. In the next dialog box, choose a simple column chart and click Next.

5. In the layout dialog box, drag the Year field to the Axis area, the Number of Crimes to the Data area, and the Crime Type to the Series area. Click Next.

6. In the next dialog box, the wizard suggests BeatNo as the linking fields in both the form and chart because they have the same name. If there are no matching names between the tables, the wizard makes no suggestion. You can change the linking field names or choose not to link the chart to the form by choosing <No Field>. Click Next to move to the final dialog box and name the form "City Beats Crimes."

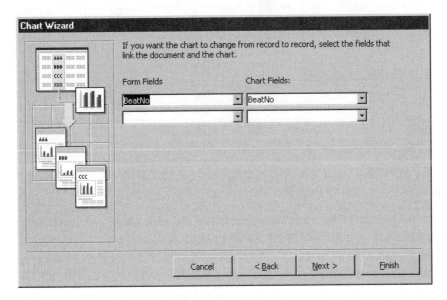

The linking fields need not have the same names, but they must have the same kind of data and be of the same or compatible data types.

Figure 12-7 shows the finished form with the linked chart. As you move through the records, the heights of the data column markers change to reflect the number of crimes that were reported in that beat area.

It might take a few seconds to reconstruct the chart when you move to the next record— be patient.

Add an Existing Chart to a Form or Report

You can insert an existing chart into a form or report whether it is created within the current database or in another Access database. You can drag or copy the chart from one form or report to the other. To use drag-and-drop to insert the chart from another database, you must have two instances of Access running: one as the source and one as the destination.

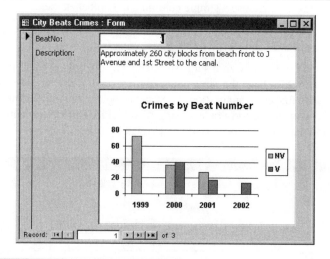

FIGURE 12-7 Viewing the new form with a linked chart

To insert a new chart created with Microsoft Graph in another Office program, open the form or report in Design view and do the following:

1. Click the Unbound Object Frame toolbox button and click where you want the chart. You can also draw the frame in the design.

2. In the Insert Object dialog box, click Create from File, then enter the path to the file or click Browse to locate the file if you don't know the path.

3. If you want to link the chart to the form or report, select Link. If you want the chart to appear as an icon instead of the full chart, select Display as Icon. Click OK.

Modify the Chart

The tools you use to modify a chart depend on what kind of changes you want to make. Some changes you can make within Access, others must be made in Microsoft Graph. If you want to change any of the properties or the position of the control, do so in Access. If you want to change the underlying data, you can create a new query and change the Row Source property of the chart within Access. You can also edit the SQL statement in the Row Source property rather than create a new query. However, if you want to change any of the chart's elements, such as the axis titles or the chart type, or change the appearance of the chart, you must activate Microsoft Graph for in-place editing.

Modify with Access

To modify the chart with Access, open the host form or report in Design view and select the chart control frame. With the frame selected, you can do the following:

- Drag the frame to a different position in the form or report.
- Drag the sizing handles to change the frame size. This resizes only the frame. Double-click the chart object to activate Graph and change the size of the chart itself. By default, the frame's Size Mode property is set to Clip. Change it to Stretch or Zoom if you need to resize the frame.
- Use the Formatting (Form/Report) toolbar to change the frame's fill color, border color and width, and special effects.
- Open the property sheet and change any of the control properties including the Row Source, Link Master Fields, and Link Child Fields.

For example, to unlink the Crimes by Beat Number chart from the form:

1. Open the City Beats Crimes form in Design view.
2. Select the chart control and open the property sheet.
3. Delete the BeatNo field names from the Link Master Fields and Link Child Fields properties.

When you return to Form view and move through the records, you can see that the chart no longer changes with each record. Instead, it always shows the total crimes for all beats when you navigate through the records.

12

How to ... Save Disk Space

If disk space is a concern, you can save space by converting the unbound object control to an image control. Select the chart in form or report Design view and choose Format | Change To. Then select Image, the only option available to an unbound OLE Object control. The data shown in the chart will not be updated with changes in the underlying record source. Use caution with the transformation because it can't be undone.

Edit the Row Source Property

If you created the chart in Access with the Chart Wizard, it creates a query whose SQL statement becomes the row source for the chart. You can modify the row source by using the query grid or by editing the SQL statement itself.

To change the row source:

1. Open the Sum Crimes report in Design view and open the property sheet for the chart control.

2. Click the Build button (…) next to the Row Source property to open the SQL Statement: Query Builder dialog box, which shows the Sum Crimes Chart created from the Sum Crimes query along with the Query Builder dialog box.

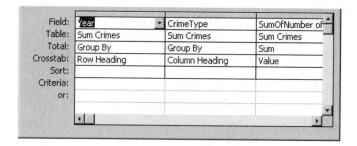

Field:	Year	CrimeType	SumOfNumber of
Table:	Sum Crimes	Sum Crimes	Sum Crimes
Total:	Group By	Group By	Sum
Crosstab:	Row Heading	Column Heading	Value
Sort:			
Criteria:			
or:			

3. To limit the chart to crimes occurring in specific years, enter **Between 1999 And 2002** in the Criteria row of the Year column.

4. Close the Query Builder dialog box and respond Yes to save the changes, then switch to Print Preview. You now see only three sets of columns.

Edit the Chart Legend

When you add a series to the chart layout that summarizes data within the category, as shown in Figure 12-8, the legend is not always as informative as it should be. The two charts illustrate the same data and are based on tables that contain the same data but use different table structures.

The chart on the left is based on the Crimes by Beat Number table. From this table, the Chart Wizard created a crosstab query that totals the number of both types of crimes reported for each beat.

Field:	Year	BeatNo	Number of Crimes
Table:	Crimes by Beat Number	Crimes by Beat Number	Crimes by Beat Number
Total:	Group By	Group By	Sum
Crosstab:	Row Heading	Column Heading	Value
Sort:			
Criteria:			
or:			

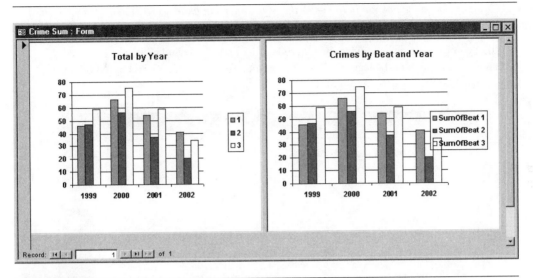

FIGURE 12-8 Two charts illustrating the same data

The legend in the chart on the left takes its values from the field whose Crosstab row shows Column Heading, which is BeatNo (1, 2, and 3). The legend would be more informative if you edited it to read Beat 1, Beat 2, and Beat 3. There are two ways to do this after opening the Query Builder for the Row Source property:

- Open the Query Builder and change the BeatNo field in the query grid to the expression **"Beat "&[BeatNo]**. Be sure to include a space after **Beat** within the quotation marks to separate it from the number in the result.

Field:	Year	Expr1: "Beat " & BeatNo	Number of Crimes	
Table:	Crimes by Beat Numl		Crimes by Beat Numl	
Total:	Group By	Group By	Sum	
Crosstab:	Row Heading	Column Heading	Value	
Sort:				
Criteria:				
or:				

- Choose View | SQL View (or click the View button and choose SQL View) and change the PIVOT clause from

```
PIVOT [BeatNo];
```

to

```
PIVOT "Beat "&[BeatNo];
```

12

If you make the change in the grid, the SQL statement changes to match, and vice versa.

When you save the design, close the Query Builder dialog box and switch to Form view. You can see the change in the legend. The chart on the right in Figure 12-8 is based on the more compact Crimes by Beat and Year table.

LineNo	Year	Type	Beat 1	Beat 2	Beat 3
1	1999	V	16	12	18
2	1999	NV	30	35	41
3	2000	V	24	18	30
4	2000	NV	42	38	45
5	2001	V	18	10	20
6	2001	NV	36	27	39
7	2002	V	14	8	10
8	2002	NV	27	12	24
(AutoNumber)					

Record: 1 of 8

For this chart, the Chart Wizard has created a select query that sums the value in each of the Beat*n* fields by year. The legend shows SumOfBeat 1, SumOfBeat 2, and SumOfBeat 3. You can use one of two methods to change the legend text: add expressions to the Field row of the query grid or edit the SQL statement.

Open the form in Design view and start the Query Builder as before. This time edit the SQL statement. Switch to SQL view and edit the AS clauses by deleting SumOf from each clause.

TIP
Be sure to leave the brackets around the field names because they contain spaces.

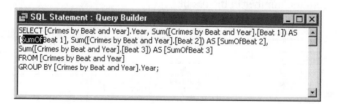

SQL Statement : Query Builder

```
SELECT [Crimes by Beat and Year].Year, Sum([Crimes by Beat and Year].[Beat 1]) AS
[SumOfBeat 1], Sum([Crimes by Beat and Year].[Beat 2]) AS [SumOfBeat 2],
Sum([Crimes by Beat and Year].[Beat 3]) AS [SumOfBeat 3]
FROM [Crimes by Beat and Year]
GROUP BY [Crimes by Beat and Year].Year;
```

Save the changes and switch to Form view. Figure 12-9 shows the two charts with their new legends.

Edit with Microsoft Graph

Microsoft Graph is an applet you can use within Access to edit the charts you have created with the Chart Wizard. When you activate Graph, use the special toolbars that appear in the Access window to edit the chart in place.

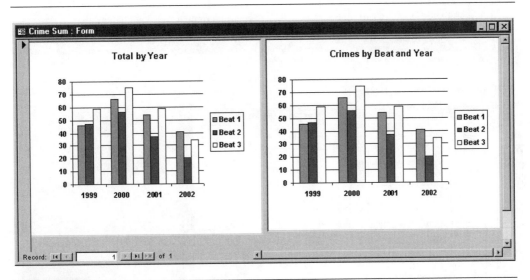

FIGURE 12-9   The charts with legends edited in Access

To activate Microsoft Graph, double-click the chart control in the form or report Design view. Figure 12-10 shows the Entries by Quarter form when Microsoft Graph is active. In addition to the form window containing the chart, a Datasheet window appears containing unrelated sample data. Notice the cross-hatched border around the chart, which indicates that Microsoft Graph is currently running. The title you entered in the Chart Wizard dialog box appears as the chart title in Graph but the data shown in the datasheet is sample data used for illustration only.

To show or hide the datasheet, choose View | Datasheet, which toggles the Datasheet window in and out of focus, or right-click the Chart window and choose Datasheet from the shortcut menu. To close the Datasheet, click the Close button. To leave the Microsoft Graph window and return to the Access form or report Design view, click anywhere outside the chart object. The changes you made to the chart in Microsoft Graph are shown in the Access chart. You must save the form or report design to save the changes.

Look at the Graph Toolbars

The Microsoft Graph window normally has two toolbars: Standard and Formatting. The Drawing, Picture, and WordArt toolbars, which can be used to add special objects to the chart, are available upon demand. To add a toolbar, right-click in any toolbar and select the one you want to add. You can also choose from the View | Toolbars menu. To see what the toolbar button does, rest the mouse pointer on the button and read the ScreenTip. All the buttons have menu equivalents.

12

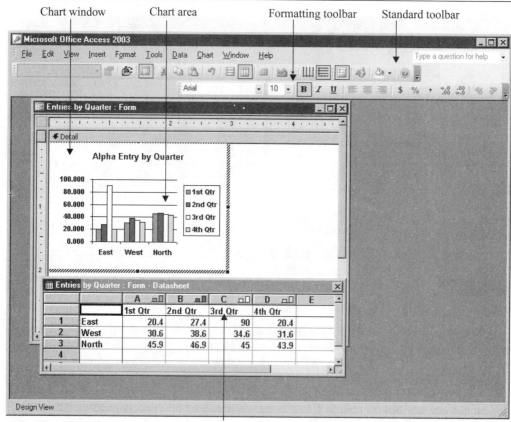

FIGURE 12-10 A typical Microsoft Graph window

Change the Chart Appearance

You have a lot of ways to change the appearance of the chart. For example, you can change the size of the chart itself or change any of the text elements in the chart. To change the size of the chart, select the chart area and drag the sizing handles until it reaches the proper size.

Format Text Elements The same options are available to you when you format most of the text elements in the chart. Select the element and choose Format | Selected *object* to open the Format dialog box or press CTRL-1. The dialog box has three tabs: Patterns, Font, and Alignment.

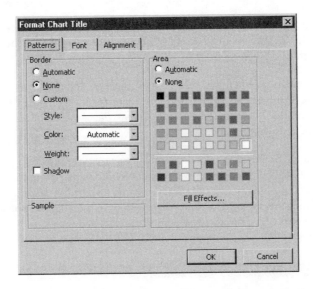

Select Fill Effects in the Format dialog box to open another dialog box where you can choose gradients, fill textures, or patterns and even select a picture to use as a background.

The Font tab contains the standard font name, size, weight, colors, and effects such as underline, strikethrough, superscript, and subscript. When you select the chart title or one of the axis titles and choose Format | Selected, the Alignment tab appears, in which you can choose the text alignment plus the orientation. You can display the text vertically or at a specific angle by clicking on the arc in the Orientation area.

12

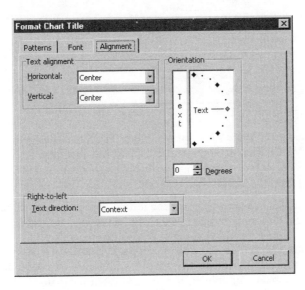

If you select the legend and choose Format | Selected Legend, the Alignment tab is replaced by the Placement tab. In the Placement tab you can choose to display the legend at the bottom, corner, top, right, or left of the plot area.

Format Other Chart Elements   When you select one of the axes and choose Format | Selected, the Format Axis dialog box shows five tabs: Patterns, Scale, Font, Number, and Alignment. The Patterns, Font, and Alignment tabs are the same as for text elements. The other tabs offer the following options:

■ The options in the Scale tab depend on which axis you have selected. If you select the Value (Y) axis, you can choose to set manually the minimum and maximum values for the axis as well as the major and minor units for the gridlines and tick marks. The alternative is to let Microsoft Graph set these values automatically. You can also specify where the Category (X) axis is to cross the Value axis and whether to arrange the values in reverse order.

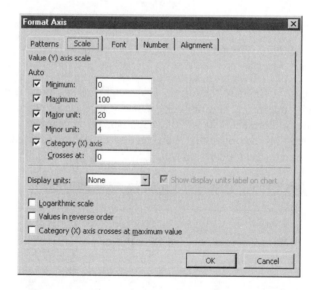

■ The Number tab gives you a selection of number categories and specific formats for the values on the Value (Y) axis. There is also a check box that links the values to the source data. Clear this check box to create a snapshot chart that does not update with changes to the underlying data.

■ When you select the Category (X) axis, the formatting options are slightly different. The Scale tab contains options that relate to data categories instead of values.

When you format the data series by clicking one of the columns, bars, or other representations of the data, the Format (data series) dialog box appears with four or five tabs, depending on the type of data series. For example, the column and line series Format dialog box contains five tabs:

Patterns, Axis, Y Error Bars, Data Labels, and Options. The 3-D and pie series Format dialog boxes show four tabs.

The Patterns tab offers the same color, border, and fill options as before. The other tabs offer the following options:

- **Axis tab**   Specifies whether to plot the series on the primary or secondary axis. A sample chart illustrates the current choice.

- **Y Error Bars tab**   Offers the option of displaying the statistical error estimation or the standard deviation in the values either as values or percentages. This option is handy for presenting the results of a statistical survey for which you need to express the validity.

- **Data Labels tab**   Enables you to display the data values and labels with the data series. You can display the values as percentages or in the unit of the value itself.

- **Options tab**   For a column data series, this tab enables you to overlap the series and set the amount of overlap, and also specify the amount of space between the sets of data series. Options vary with different types of data series.

A 3-D column data series Format dialog box includes the Shape tab that offers different configurations including cones, pyramids, and cylinders.

When you choose to format the data table that you have added below the chart, you see only two tabs in the Format dialog box: Patterns and Font. To format the plot area or the walls of a chart, you have only the Patterns options.

Change Chart Type   When you are creating charts to analyze the data in your database, you may want to try out different representations. You may want to show trends with a line chart or comparative values with a pie chart. There are two ways to change the chart type:

- Click the Chart Type toolbar button and choose from the palette containing 18 chart types.

12

■ Choose Chart | Chart Type and choose from the Chart Type dialog box. The Standard Types include 14 types with many sub-types for each. In the Standard Types tab, press and hold the button below the Chart sub-type pane to see a sample of the selected chart. The Custom Types tab shows an additional 20 chart types from the built-in list of charts; if you have created any custom chart types, they are displayed when you choose Select from User-Defined.

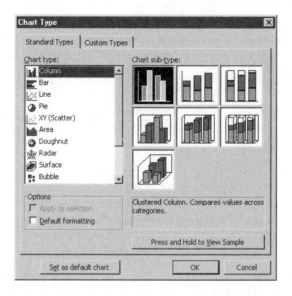

After making your selection, click OK to apply it to the current chart. You can also specify a chart type as the default chart.

Set Chart Options   You can adjust many additional chart features to achieve the appearance you want. When you choose Chart | Chart Options, the Chart Options dialog box opens with six tabs: Titles, Axes, Gridlines, Legend, Data Labels, and Data Table.

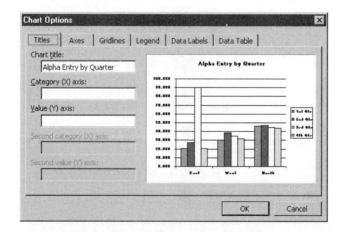

The tabs offer the following options:

- In the Titles tab, you enter the text you want to display as the chart title and the axes titles. You can specify a primary and secondary title for each axis but only one for the chart itself.

- In the Axes tab, you specify whether to display the axes and choose the method by which to display the Category (X) axis.

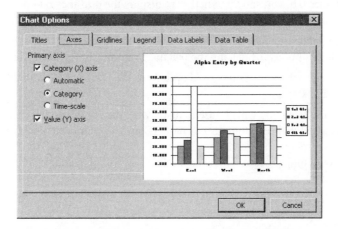

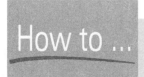 **Troubleshoot Charts**

Sometimes the changes you make in Microsoft Graph fail to show up in the chart when you switch to Form view or Print Preview even though they appear in Design view. For example, you can change the column headings in the Microsoft Graph datasheet to display the text you want in the legend. When you return to Access, the new labels appear in the design but not in Form view or Print Preview.

The reason for this seeming inconsistency is that you have several places in which to specify the chart information and Access must set an order of precedence to decide which values to use. The order is as follows:

- First, the data in the underlying table or query; for example, the field names or the expressions in the Field row of the query grid.

- Second, the contents of the Row Source property.

- Last, the data entered in Microsoft Graph.

If you set the legend text in Microsoft Graph but the underlying query column headings are different, they will override the Microsoft Graph settings. If the columns don't appear in the order you want in the chart, open the Query Builder and rearrange the fields, left to right; then choose the sort order for each.

- In the Gridlines tab, you specify whether to display the gridlines on one or both of the axes. You can choose to display both major and minor gridlines on each axis.

- In the Legend tab, you choose whether to display the legend with the chart. The Legend tab offers these options for placing the legend: Bottom, Corner, Top, Right, or Left.

- The Data Labels tab includes the same options as the Data Labels tab in the Format Data Series dialog box.

- In the Data Table tab you can choose to display the data in the underlying data source in a grid attached to the bottom of the chart. When you choose to display the data table, you can also display the legend keys. Figure 12-11 shows the Total by Year chart with the corresponding data table. The Data Table option is not available for some of the chart types.

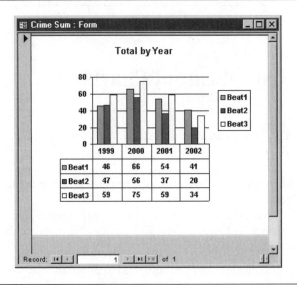

FIGURE 12-11   The data table added to the chart

Part III

Improve the Access 2003 Workplace

Chapter 13

Customize the Workplace

How to...

- ■ Personalize your workplace
- ■ Create custom groups
- ■ Change Access startup options
- ■ Excuse or modify the Office Assistant

Some of the features discussed in this chapter have been briefly mentioned in previous chapters; some are covered in detail later. However, we have brought them all together in one place for easy reference. Using the many Access and Windows options, you can change the default appearance and behavior of many aspects of your workplace. In addition to making changes that affect the current Access database, you can change many Access startup options such as displaying a startup form; opening a specific database; and displaying custom icons, menus, and toolbars.

Personalize the Workplace

You don't have to bow down to the layout and behavior of the Access environment as it is when first installed. The Access developers have designed a workplace that is appropriate for most users, but if there are some aspects you would like to change, it is easy to change them. For example, if you have a large screen, you might want to see a larger font size. Of course, you can change each of these factors every time you work with Access, but you also can change the default settings once and for all.

Rearrange Icons

In the Database window, each page displays icons representing objects of that type in the current database. You can change the icon size and amount of detail shown with the icons and arrange them in a specific order, such as by name or date last modified. The changes you make on one page are applied to all the object pages.

The buttons at the top of the Database window and the commands in the View menu contain ways to display the object icons as follows:

- ■ Choose Large Icons to show expanded object icons in rows with the name appearing below each one.

- ■ Choose Small Icons to show smaller object icons in rows but with the name beside each one.

- ■ Choose List to show the object icons in columns with the name beside each one.

- ■ Choose Details to show each object icon in a single row with its name and four additional columns containing other information about the object: the description you entered in the object property sheet, the time/date the object was last modified, the time/date the object was created, and the type of object.

When you show the object icons with the details, you can make other adjustments to the display. For example, you can resize the column width by dragging the vertical column separator in the column heading or resize it to fit the widest information in it by double-clicking the column separator. If you want to sort the icons by one of the detail categories, just click once in the column heading to sort in ascending order. Click in the column heading again to change the order to descending.

TIP   *The View | Arrange Icons commands sort the icons in ascending order by name, type, date/time created, or date/time modified. These commands accomplish the same arrangements as clicking once in the column headings of the details. The Auto Arrange command, which is available only if you have selected Large Icons or Small Icons, moves the icons back into the specified arrangement.*

Create a Shortcut

If you use an Access object regularly, you can create a shortcut that launches Access and opens the database object directly from the Windows desktop. The easiest way is to drag the object from the Access Database window to the Windows desktop. You must first resize the Access window so you can see the area on the desktop where you want to place the shortcut icon. When you double-click the shortcut, Access opens the database that contains the object and displays the object.

NOTE   *To delete a shortcut, click it and press DEL. This does not delete the object itself; only the shortcut.*

Another way to create a shortcut is to use the Create Shortcut command on the object shortcut menu. With this method, you can create a shortcut in a location other than the desktop by entering a path in the Create Shortcut dialog box. Type a new path in the Location box or click Browse to search for the desired location and let Access fill in the path for you. If the database is on a network, Access automatically selects the This Database is on the Network check box and fills in the path in the Full Network Path box.

13

 *If you have moved the database that is the destination of a shortcut, remove the shortcut and create a new one with the new path.*

Set Workplace Options

Access is installed with certain characteristics set as defaults. For example, the width of the print margins, default database folder, color of hyperlinks, gridlines, and font styles in a datasheet are set by default. If you find yourself changing specific default values when you work with a database, you can reset the default value to the one you use the most. All default values can be overridden later, if necessary.

 Access stores most option settings in the workgroup information file instead of your database file. Changes you make to those settings in the Options dialog box apply to any database opened or created by anyone who uses the same workgroup information file. If you don't check with the others in your workgroup, you might surprise them with your changes. See Chapter 20 for information about workgroups and the workgroup information file.

To change default values, choose Tools | Options and click the tab that contains the values you want to change. To change values on more than one tab, keep the Options dialog box open and click another tab. When you are finished setting the default values, click OK to close the dialog box.

This chapter won't cover every option on every tab of the Options dialog box, so if you want to know more about any of the settings, close the Options dialog box, type the option name in the Ask a Question box, and press ENTER to view the Help topic.

The Options dialog box has 12 tabs, as shown in Figure 13-1. The following sections describe the most commonly used options.

The tab that is visible when you open the Options dialog box is the one you last accessed.

View Options

The options on the View tab relate to what you see on the screen during specific activities. For example, some of the options determine what you see at startup, others while you are working in the Database window or when you are creating a macro.

For example, if you don't want to see the Startup task pane, clear the Startup Task Pane check box. The "New object shortcuts" option in the Show group refers to items such as "Create form by using wizards" that appear in the object pages of the database window. If you are building an application for an end user who won't be creating or editing any Access objects, you can clear this check box and have more room in the Database window for the object icons.

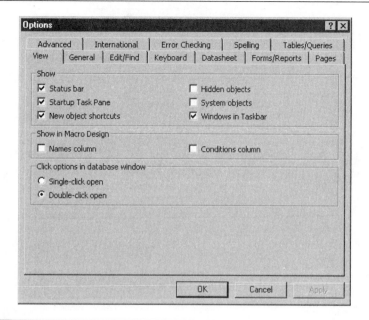

FIGURE 13-1   Setting View default options in the Options dialog box

When you start a new macro, by default the Macro Name and Condition columns are not displayed. If you need them most of the time, check these options to save a little time in macro building. If you don't need them, you can clear them after opening the macro design window.

General Options

The General tab (see Figure 13-2) shows options that don't fit comfortably into any of the other categories of settings. In the "Print margins" group, you can enter any number that is compatible with your printer and paper size, ranging from 0 to the height or width of the printed page. If you want to print a document using other margin sizes, override these default settings by running Page Setup before you print a form or report.

With the "Recently used file list" option on the General tab, you can specify the number of filenames to display in the Getting Started task pane or at the bottom of the list when you choose File. The default setting is 4 but you can change that to any number from 0 to 9. If you don't want to use the default My Documents folder, enter a different path in the Default database folder box.

The Name AutoCorrect group helps Access propagate name changes to objects that refer to the renamed object. The group offers three options that help fix common side effects that occur when you make changes in an object through a user interface. Access stores an identifier for each object and tracks naming information. When Access notices that an object has been changed since the last Name AutoCorrect event, it runs the process again for all items in that object. For

13

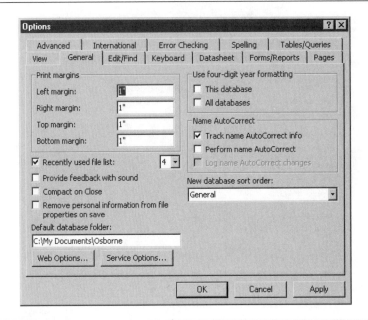

FIGURE 13-2   Setting General default options

example, if you have added a text box to a form that is bound to the Alpha Card table and you change the Alpha Card table name to Alpha Card Plus, Access can track down all the items from the original Alpha Card and change their names to match the new table name.

Edit/Find Options

The Edit/Find tab (see Figure 13-3) default settings are meant to speed up finding, replacing, and filtering processes as much as possible. For example, Fast search searches the current field only and matches the entire field. Other settings require confirmation before changing data, deleting documents or running an action query.

The Confirm group is the one that always asks you if you really want to do what you just did. It's a good idea to leave all these checked as a precaution against any unintended changes or deletions.

The "Filter by form defaults for…" group contains options that limit or extend the size of the value list displayed in the Filter by Form window and sets the maximum number of records to read when building a list of unique values for a given field. The more fields you include in the filter operation, the longer it takes. These settings apply only to the current database.

■ **Local indexed fields** limits the value list to the indexed fields in the current database.

■ **Local nonindexed fields** includes the fields in the current database that are not indexed.

Customize Your Hyperlinks

If you are fussy about the looks of the hyperlinks in your Access documents, click the Web Options button. Choose the colors you want for the hyperlinks before and after jumping to them. You can also remove the underline that shows up when you move the mouse pointer to the hyperlink.

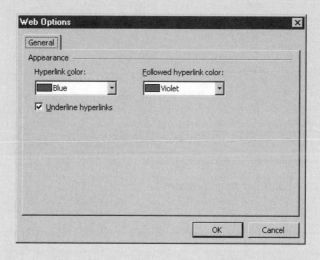

- **ODBC fields** includes fields in a linked table in an external source.

- Enter a number in the **Don't display lists where more than this number of records read:** box. This will set the maximum number of records you want to read to build the list of unique values for the field. If the number of records exceeds this amount, no values will be displayed for the field in the Filter by Form window.

Keyboard Options

The settings in the Keyboard tab (see Figure 13-4) determine the consequences of pressing certain keys such as ENTER, TAB, RIGHT ARROW, and LEFT ARROW.

The selection you choose in the "Move after enter" group of options determines the behavior of the insertion point (cursor) after you press ENTER. It can either stay put, move to the next field, or to the next record.

- The "Arrow key behavior" settings specify what happens when you press RIGHT ARROW and LEFT ARROW. Choosing Next field moves the insertion point to the next or previous field when you press RIGHT ARROW or LEFT ARROW whereas Next character moves the insertion point to the next or previous character in the current field instead.

13

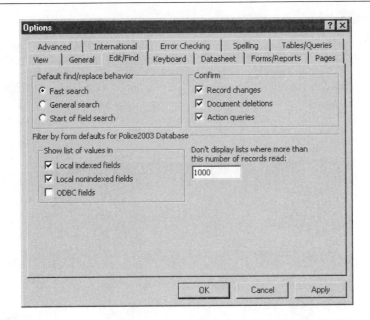

FIGURE 13-3 Setting Edit/Find default options

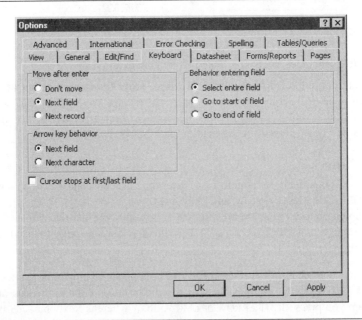

FIGURE 13-4 Setting Keyboard default options

- The "Behavior entering field" group determines what happens when the insertion point enters a field.

- The "Cursor stops at first/last field" setting locks the insertion point within the current record and prevents the RIGHT ARROW and LEFT ARROW keys from moving the insertion point to the next or previous record in a form or datasheet.

Datasheet Options

The Datasheet tab (see Figure 13-5) includes settings for the visual properties of a datasheet. The default colors, fonts, gridlines, and cell special effects are established in this tab. The Show animations option is the one that shows columns sliding over when you insert or delete a column.

Form and Report Options

The settings in the Forms/Reports tab of the Options dialog box (see Figure 13-6) all relate to designing a form or report.

- The Selection behavior group specifies the result of dragging a rectangle in the design to select controls. Partially enclosed is easier to use because it selects all controls that have any part within the drawn rectangle, whereas Fully enclosed selects only those controls that are totally within the drawn rectangle.

13

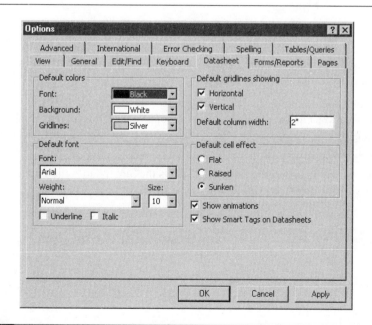

FIGURE 13-5   Setting Datasheet default options

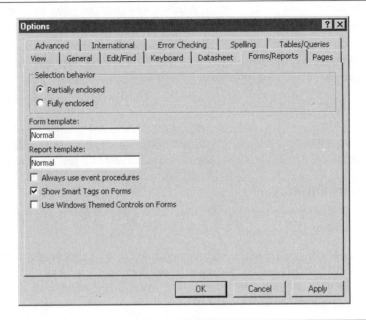

FIGURE 13-6 Setting form and report default options

■ The Form template and Report template settings allow you to specify an existing form or report as the default template for new designs. Type the name of the form or report you want to use as the default template.

■ The "Always use event procedures" setting takes you directly to the VB Editor window when you click the Build button in a property sheet, bypassing the Choose Builder dialog box, which usually offers the choice of Expression Builder, Macro Builder, or Code Builder.

■ The Show Smart Tags on Forms setting displays the Smart Tab Action button when you move to a control that has a Smart Tag attached.

■ The Use Windows Themed Controls on Forms applies to Access forms the Windows theme (or scheme, depending on your version of Windows) sets in the Display Properties dialog box.

Advanced Options

The Advanced tab (see Figure 13-7) contains five groups of options, including a list of timing settings plus a couple of individual options. Many of the settings in this tab relate to a multiple-user environment or interfacing with external applications. For example, the DDE operations options either ignore requests from external sources or allow updating of DDE links.

The next group of selections in the Advanced tab deals with shared databases and interactions with external sources. For example, enter a number between 0 and 300 seconds in the OLE/DDE Timeout (sec) option to set the period of time Access should wait to re-attempt a failed OLE or DDE operation. The "Number of update retries" option refers to the number of times Access tries to save a changed record that is locked by another user. You can enter a number between 0 and 10.

In the Default File Format option, you can choose between Access 2000 and Access 2002-2003 as the default format for new databases.

In the "Default open mode" group, you have a choice between Shared, which allows others to open the database at the same time you have it open, and Exclusive, which gives you sole access to the database. See Chapter 20 for more information about running Access in a shared environment.

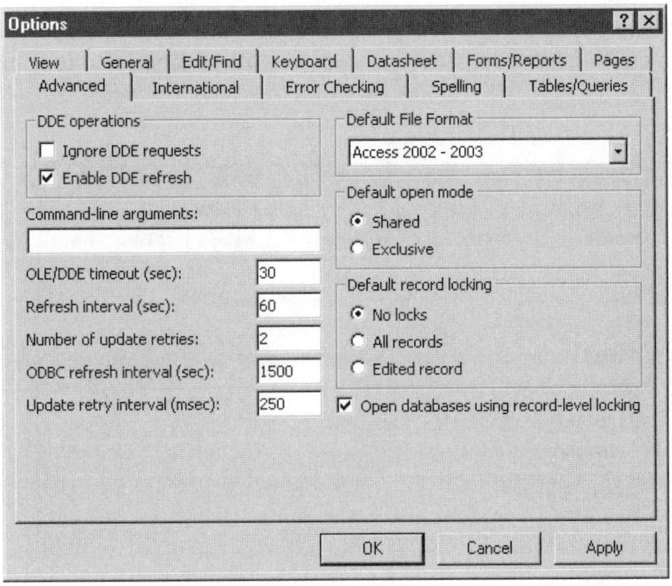

FIGURE 13-7   Setting the Advanced default options

You can set the Default record locking option to No locks, which does not lock records while they are being edited; All records, which locks all the records in a form or datasheet (and the underlying tables) as long as the form or datasheet is open; or Edited record, which locks only the record currently being edited.

The last option in the Advanced tab is Open databases using record-level locking, which minimizes the page size required by the Unicode format representation. When you check this option, instead of locking an entire page that might include several records, only one row or record is locked at a time.

International Options

The International tab (see Figure 13-8) contains options that deal with the direction and alignment of the text and the movement of the cursor through data. If you are building a database for Middle Eastern language users, change the Default direction to right-to-left and set the General alignment to Interface mode, which sets the text alignment consistent with the user interface language. For example, if the language reads right to left, the text is aligned to the right.

If you have date fields in the database, you also might want to check Use Hijri Calendar to change to the Middle Eastern calendar.

Error Checking Options

Automatic error checking is a new option with Access 2003 and a most welcome addition. The feature detects errors in form and report designs and even offers ways to correct them. You can

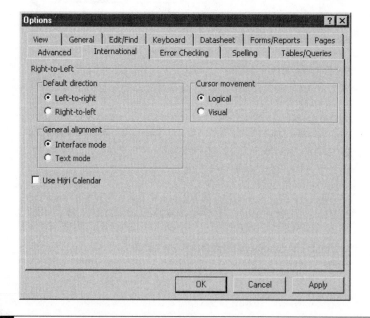

FIGURE 13-8   Setting International default options

How to ... Design for Multiple Languages

When you have a database that involves two languages, one left-to-right and the other right-to-left, you can specify how the cursor decides which way to move as you enter text or when to click the RIGHT ARROW or LEFT ARROW keys. In the Cursor movement group, you have a choice between Logical and Visual.

- If you choose Logical, the cursor moves within bidirectional text according to the direction of the language it is encountering. For example, if the same sentence includes both English and Arabic words, the insertion point moves left to right in the English text, then starts at the rightmost character of the Arabic word and continues to move in a right-to-left direction.

- If you choose Visual, the cursor moves within bidirectional text by moving to the next adjacent character. For example, if the same sentence includes both English and Arabic text, the insertion point moves left to right through the English text and continues at the leftmost character of the Arabic word in the left-to-right direction.

apply automatic error detection to five types of common errors. You set the error checking rules on the Error Checking tab of the Options dialog box, as shown in Figure 13-9.

To request any error checking, check the "Enable error checking" check box. Then choose a color for the error indicator, the small triangle that appears in the upper-left corner of the control that caused the error. The types of errors you can monitor include:

- An "Unassociated label and control" error occurs when you select a label and a control that are not associated with each other.

- The "New unassociated labels" error occurs when you add a label to a form or report that is not associated with another control.

- "Keyboard shortcut" errors occur when you select a control on a form that shows an invalid shortcut key. Examples include duplicate shortcut keys, an unassociated label, or an underlined space.

- The "Invalid control properties" error occurs when you select a control that has an invalid value in one or more properties.

- "Common report" errors occur when the report has an invalid sorting and grouping definition or when the report width exceeds the paper width.

Spelling Options

The Spelling options tab contains options for adjusting the AutoCorrect feature, changing the dictionary, and setting exceptions to correcting apparent misspellings. The spelling option settings are shared with other Office users.

13

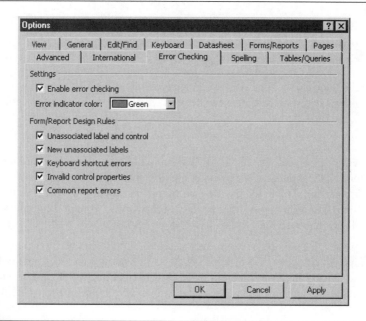

Setting automatic Error Checking default options

Table and Query Options

The Tables/Queries tab of the Options dialog box is divided into two sections: one for table design and the other for query design (see Figure 13-10).

The Table design group includes default field size and type choices that you can select to match your most frequent data entries.

The AutoIndex on Import/Create setting is very useful when you import a table from an external source or create a new table in Design view. This setting tells Access to automatically index on all fields in the imported table that begin or end with the characters you type in the box. For example, the entries in the AutoIndex box instruct Access to create an index on all fields whose names begin or end with the characters ID, key, code, or num. Separate multiple entries by semicolons.

The new Show Property Update Options buttons option gives you the option of propagating property changes made to fields in a table or query to controls in a form or report that are bound to those fields.

In the Query design default settings, you can display the table names in the Table row of the query grid. This helps to keep track of the field source when multiple tables are used in a query. If you want all the fields in the design returned when you run the query but don't want to bother adding them to the grid, check "Output all fields." When you select this option, only new queries are affected.

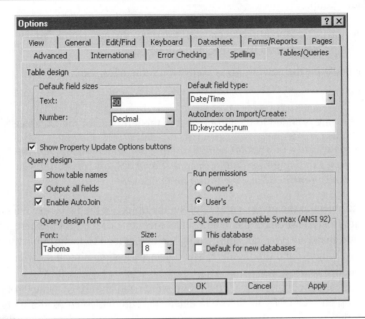

FIGURE 13-10 Setting table and query default options

The Enable AutoJoin option automatically creates an inner join between two tables in the query grid if they have fields with the same name and of the same data type. One of the fields must be the primary key field for that table. If you want to define the relationships yourself, clear the option.

You can also change the Run permissions setting to Owner's to keep others from saving any changes to a new query. In the SQL Server Compatible Syntax (ANSI 92) option group, you can choose options that help ensure that current or new databases are SQL server compatible.

13

TIP   *You also can set some of the default features on menu bars and toolbars. For details of the options at your disposal, refer to Chapter 16.*

Create Custom Groups

Groups help you organize different database objects by placing shortcuts to the objects in a custom group. For example, you can group all the pieces that you use to create and print your company's annual report. You can always place an object in the Favorites group but if you want to begin grouping objects from your Access database in a different group, you can create a new custom group. You can also add objects from other applications to the group.

To create a new group:

1. Right-click on one of the objects you want to add to the group and choose Add to Group | New Group from the shortcut menu.

2. Enter the name for the new group in the New Group dialog box.

3. Click OK.

The new group name is added to the Groups list in the left pane of the Database window.

 You also can create a new group without adding an object to it right away by right-clicking on an existing group button, such as Favorites, and choosing New Group from the shortcut menu. Name the group and click OK.

To add another object to the group, right-click on the object in the Database window, then point to Add to Group in the shortcut menu and select the name of the group where you want to place the object. Alternatively, you can simply drag the object icon to the group name in the left pane of the Database window and drop it there. The object always remains in its original location; only a shortcut is added to the group.

To rename or delete a group, right-click the group button and choose Rename Group or Delete Group from the shortcut menu. If you choose to delete a group that contains shortcuts, Access warns you that all the shortcuts will also be permanently deleted. When you delete the shortcut from the group, the original object remains unaffected. If you choose to rename the group, a Rename Group dialog box opens where you can type a new name, then click OK.

Change the Way Access Starts

Access receives information from several sources that tell it how to start and what to show when it does start. Some startup settings affect only the current Access database; others affect the way Access itself appears and behaves. The easiest way to control Access at startup is to set options in the Startup dialog box.

The startup options you set in the Startup dialog box apply only to the current database so you can choose different options for each of your databases or applications. When you set a startup option such as a title bar with a custom name and icon, Access automatically sets the corresponding database property for you. To set startup options, choose Tools | Startup to open the Startup dialog box.

Most of the changes in the startup options take effect the next time you open the database. Only the Application Title and Application Icon options take effect as soon as you close the dialog box.

> **TIP** *After you have set startup options, you can bypass them by pressing SHIFT when you open the database.*

- ■ **Application Title** To display a custom title in the Database window title bar, enter the text you want displayed in the Application Title box.

- ■ **Application Icon** To add a custom icon to the title bar in place of the default Access icon in the Windows title bar, type the name of the bitmap (.bmp) or icon (.ico) file in the Application Icon box. If you don't know the name of the file you want to use, click the Browse button next to the box and use the Icon Browser to locate the file. You can also choose to display the icon on form and report title bars.

> **TIP** *If you are creating an application that is to be distributed to multiple users, you should place the icon file in the same folder as the host application.*

- ■ **Menu Bar** When you create a custom global menu bar that offers limited commands, you can control what your users can do with the database. Use this option to replace the default menu bar with your custom menu bar by choosing the name of the menu from the drop-down list. This choice has no effect on the custom menu bars you have created for a form or report. See Chapter 20 for information about creating custom startup menu bars.

> **NOTE** *The user might still have access to the built-in global menu if the Allow Full Menus option is checked.*

- ■ **Allow Full Menus** When this option is checked, the user has access to all the built-in menus. If you clear this option, Access hides certain menus such as View and Insert that give the user the power to open an object in Design view and make changes.

13

- **Allow Default Shortcut Menus**   Leave this option checked to allow access to the built-in shortcut menus that appear when you right-click an object, a toolbar, or a menu bar. Clear the option to disable all shortcut menus. If you want the user to be able to use the shortcut menus but not to customize toolbars and menu bars, leave the option checked but clear the Allow Toolbar/Menu Changes check box.

- **Display Form/Page**   Many applications display a special form or data access page when opening, either as a welcoming screen or as a switchboard with a list of actions you can take next, such as enter/edit data or preview a report. After you create the special form and save it in the current database, you can use it as the startup form. To choose a form for display at startup, click the drop-down arrow in the Display Form box and choose the form from the list of forms in the current database.

- **Display Database Window**   If you don't want the user to see the Database window behind the opening form, clear the Display Database Window check box. The user might still be able to access the Database window by pressing F11. If you hide the Database window, the startup form must be a switchboard with navigation tools for using the database. See Chapter 17 for more information about creating and using switchboard forms.

- **Display Status Bar**   Clear this option to prevent the status bar from appearing at the bottom of the window.

TIP   *This option applies only to the current database, but you can keep from displaying the status bar in all databases by clearing the Status Bar option in the View tab of the Options dialog box.*

- **Shortcut Menu Bar**   Select the name of a custom shortcut menu to replace the built-in shortcut menus for forms and reports in the current database. Choose Default to use the built-in shortcut menus.

- **Allow Built-in Toolbars**   Check this option to give the user access to all the built-in toolbars in the current database or clear the option to prevent user access. If you want the user to be able to use but not modify the built-in toolbars, select this option and clear the Allow Toolbar/Menu Changes option. If you want the user to be able to use and modify the toolbars, select both options.

- **Allow Toolbar/Menu Changes**   Check this option to permit the user to modify any of the built-in or custom toolbars and menu bars in the database. Clear the option to lock the toolbars by preventing access to the Customize dialog box. This option disables the right mouse button click on a toolbar and the Tools | Customize command.

TIP   *If this option is cleared, the user can still move, size, and dock toolbars and menu bars unless specifically denied in the Customize dialog box for the toolbar or menu bar.*

■ **Use Access Special Keys**   You can use the special key combinations that display the Database or Immediate window, menu bars, or modules in the Module window. If you have cleared this option and specified a custom menu bar, the built-in menu bar is not accessible. The special keys are

■ **F11**   Brings the Database window to the front if you are in the Access window

■ **CTRL-G**   Displays the Immediate window

■ **CTRL-BREAK**   Stops retrieving records from the server

■ **ALT-F11**   Starts the Visual Basic Editor

You can use the selections in the Startup dialog box instead of or in conjunction with the actions contained in the AutoExec macro. An AutoExec macro is a series of actions that take place when you open the database (after the Startup options have taken effect). Because of the sequence of events, it is important to avoid conflicts between the two. For example, the AutoExec macro could undo the options you set in the Startup dialog box. See Chapter 15 for more information about AutoExec macros and how they are used.

Modify the Office Assistant

The Office Assistant can offer help and tips and answer questions relating to the Office program you are currently using. Just like the list of relevant topics you see when you type a question in the question box, the Assistant can display that list, specific tips about using the features or keyboard shortcuts more effectively, and a variety of messages.

The Assistant is an animated character with sound that you can change to any one of the seven characters that come with Office. If you get tired of the paper clip, you can change to a cat or a dog or even an Einstein character. There are also many options that you can set to customize the Assistant to match your needs.

Show and Hide

To open the Office Assistant, choose Help | Show the Office Assistant. If the Office Assistant has not been installed, Access asks whether you want to install it now. Click Yes. Access may prompt you to insert the Microsoft Office CD. To hide the Assistant, right-click the character and choose Hide from the shortcut menu. You can also choose Help | Hide Office Assistant to close the assistant. To close the Office Assistant balloon, click the character.

Set Office Assistant Options

To customize the help offered by the Assistant, you can change some of the options. If the Assistant balloon is visible, click Options to display the Options tab of the Office Assistant dialog box (see Figure 13-11). If the balloon is not visible, right-click the character and choose Options from the shortcut menu.

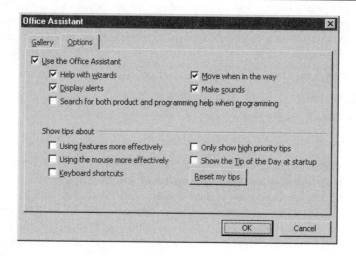

FIGURE 13-11 Setting the Office Assistant options

To prevent the Office Assistant from appearing at all, clear the Use the Office Assistant option. The other options in the Office Assistant Options dialog box (except the "Reset my tips" button) then become unavailable. The remaining options in the upper group specify the Assistant's behavior.

The selections in the "Show tips about" group tell the Assistant what types of tips to display. For example, you can see tips about using the mouse and other features more effectively or display the shortcut keys that will accomplish the same job you are undertaking.

"Show the Tip of the Day at startup" displays a randomly selected tip each time you start an Office program. Once the tip was, "Did you know you can get hurt if you run with scissors?"

Choose a Different Assistant

To change the character used by the Office Assistant, click Options in the Assistant balloon, then click the Gallery tab (see Figure 13-12). Use the Next and Back buttons to preview each of the alternative characters, watch their actions, and hear the accompanying sounds.

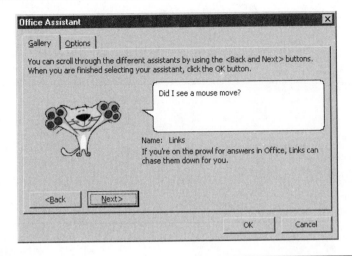

FIGURE 13-12 Choosing a different Office Assistant character

When you find the one you want, click OK. Access asks whether you want to install the new Assistant. Click Yes to install it. After the change of character, the Office Assistant dialog box closes and you can get back to work.

13

Chapter 14

Speed Up Your Database

How to...

- Optimize your database
- Optimize the tables and queries
- Optimize the forms, reports, and their controls
- Back up and restore the database
- Compact and repair the database

Unless you have a system that runs at 15 gazillion megahertz, you probably are interested in improving your database performance and speeding things up. Optimization is the ultimate goal, and stacking up performance improvements can help you get there. Access offers many ways to create an efficient database, including the Analyzer tools, which can examine the organization of your database, suggest ways to improve the distribution of information among the tables, and speed up overall database performance. For the purpose of security and reliability, there also are tools to back up and restore databases in case of emergency. Other tools compact the database to consume less disk space and repair databases that have become damaged.

Optimize a Database

Access provides two analytical tools that can save you a lot of time and help you optimize the structure of a new database. You can optimize the performance of a database without using the Analyzers by focusing on each of the elements that comprise the database—for example, the efficient distribution of data among the tables, the features of the database including the filters and indexes, and the objects themselves.

Use the Analyzer Wizards

The Table Analyzer examines the distribution of data among the tables and presents suggestions and ideas for further improvement. Another tool, the Performance Analyzer, looks at any or all of the objects in the database and makes suggestions to improve their performance. It also can examine the relationships you have established in the database and the set of Visual Basic code modules in the database, including both class and standard modules.

Table Analyzer

When you design a new database, you try to reduce the redundancy of data by creating a set of related tables. The Access Table Analyzer can look at the data distribution and make suggestions for additional optimization, including adding more indexes and further normalization to reduce data redundancy.

To start the Table Analyzer:

1. With the database open, choose Tools | Analyze | Table (see Figure 14-1).

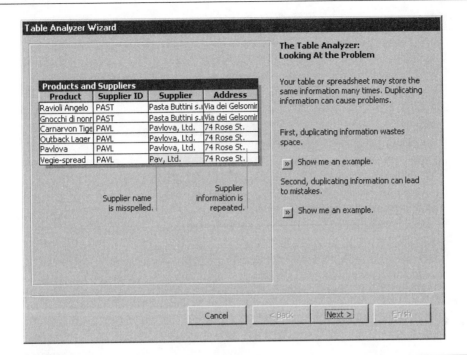

FIGURE 14-1   Optimizing with the Table Analyzer

NOTE   *The first two dialog boxes offer a good description of the process of table optimization by first describing the problem, then showing possible solutions to the problem. Each dialog box also offers a look at examples of the problems and the solutions.*

2. Click Next. The second Table Analyzer dialog box shows how it plans to solve the problem by splitting tables so that each piece of data is stored only once.

3. Click Next. The third Table Analyzer dialog box shows a list of tables in the current database (see Figure 14-2).

TIP   *If you expect to use the Table Analyzer often and don't want to see the two introductory dialog boxes each time, clear the check mark next to "Show introductory pages?" in the dialog box showing the list of tables.*

4. Select the table that contains repeated data and click Next.

5. The wizard presents a diagram of the suggested redistribution of information (see Figure 14-3).

14

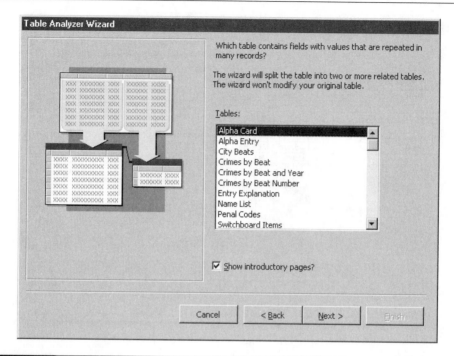

FIGURE 14-2 Selecting a table to analyze

The Table Analyzer has found that the values in the ZipCode and City fields are repeated many times in the Police database Name List table. It has suggested that you create a lookup table for each field with a link from the new Table2 to the original Name List table (now called Table1) and an additional link from the new Table3 back to Table2. Notice that the wizard has not changed any table names; changing table names is only a suggestion.

> TIP *Click the Tips button (the light bulb icon) to get instructions about how to handle the wizard's suggestions.*

To change the Table3 name:

1. Select Table3 and click the Rename Table button in the upper-right corner of the dialog box.

2. Enter a new name in the Table Name text box. When you change the name of the related table, the wizard changes the table name in the linked field in the primary table (Table2,

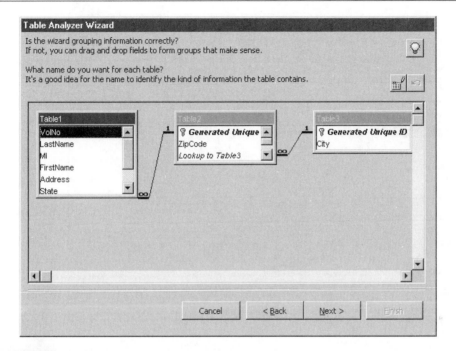

FIGURE 14-3   The Table Analyzer makes suggestions.

in this case) to match. If you change your mind about the new name you entered for a table, click the Undo button next to the Rename Table button.

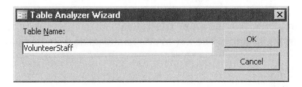

TIP   *You can also drag the field names from one table to the other to change the way the fields are grouped if it doesn't make sense to you.*

3. Click Next to move to the dialog box in which you verify that the primary key fields are correct (see Figure 14-4). The wizard has, by default, added a unique field to each new table and created the corresponding linking fields.

14

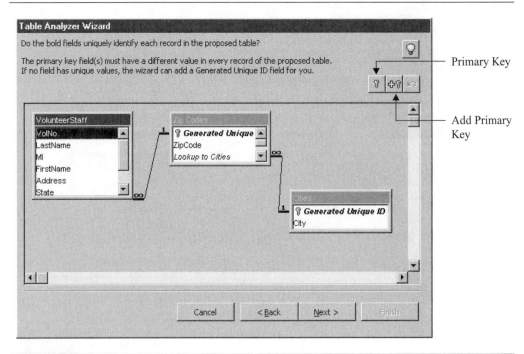

Each of the new tables has been renamed and assigned a designated primary key field, but Table1 (VolunteerStaff) has no primary key field. Access always recommends that tables have primary key fields assigned. You can specify a primary key for Table1 in one of two ways:

- Select an existing field that you know has unique values—for example, VolNo—and click the Primary Key button. The key symbol appears next to the field name.

- Select the table and click the Add Primary Key button. A new Generated Unique ID field is added to Table1.

After adding key fields, click Next. In the final dialog box, the wizard offers to create a query that uses the same name and looks like the original table. Allowing the wizard to do this enables you to work with the data all in one place and guarantees that all the forms and reports you have created using the original table as a basis will continue to work properly. You can also choose to create this query yourself.

If you chose to decide which fields to place in which tables (refer to Figure 14-3), the next dialog box shows only the original table without the new, intermediate Table2. You can create the new table by dragging a field name from the list in Table1. You can also rename the tables and define the primary key field for the new table using the buttons in the dialog box. After you click Next, the wizard offers to create a query for you as before.

Using the Performance Analyzer

The Performance Analyzer looks at the objects in the database and suggests ways to improve the application's performance. When you finish with the Performance Analyzer, many of the suggestions can be implemented automatically.

To start the Performance Analyzer:

1. Choose Tools | Analyze | Performance. The first dialog box includes a tab for each type of database object. Each tab contains the names of all those objects in the current database. The Current Database tab contains the Relationships and VBA Project options. If you click the All Object Types tab, you can see all the names in one place.

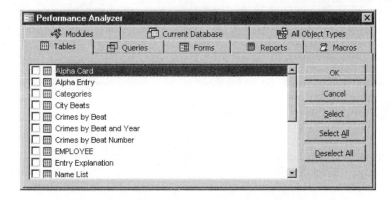

2. Select the appropriate tab and select the names individually or click Select All to choose all the objects.

3. If you want to analyze the entire database, click the All Object Types tab and choose Select All.

4. After selecting the items you want analyzed, click OK.

A message box informs you about the progress of the analysis and when all the objects have been inspected; the wizard displays a dialog box with a list of recommendations, suggestions, and ideas (see Figure 14-5). Any problems that have been fixed are also denoted. The Analysis Notes pane describes the general overall findings. When you select one of the items in the list, additional explanations are displayed in the Analysis Notes pane.

TIP   *If you include queries in the objects to analyze, be sure to have enough data in the tables to give the query a good workout.*

14

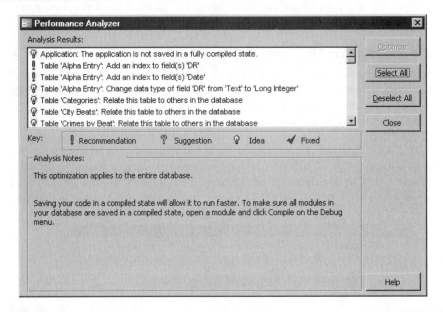

FIGURE 14-5 The findings of the Performance Analyzer

The Analyzer has recommended that you add an index to the Date and DR fields of the Alpha Entry table. When you select one of these recommendations, the Analysis Notes show that if you index on this field, it will benefit the Alpha Entry table and your queries will run faster. To implement a recommendation, select it and click Optimize. After considering all the items in the list, click Close to close the Performance Analyzer.

 *The Performance Analyzer doesn't always have the whole picture. Accept its recommendations and suggestions carefully. For example, adding indexes might improve query performance but it also increases the disk space needed for the database and could slow down entering and editing data.*

Optimize Tables and Queries

After you have done all you can to normalize the database and distribute data efficiently among the tables, there are a few other things you can do to speed up data processing. Some examples are

- Choose the appropriate data type for each field to save space and improve join operations. Also, if you know the range of values that will be stored in the field, choose the smallest field size that the data type will accept. You have no choice with date/time fields, but you can reduce the default 50-character field size for text fields if the data is, for example, a ZIP code.

■ Make sure the fields on either side of a relationship are of the same or a compatible data type.

Optimize with Indexes

In addition to the primary key, which is automatically indexed, you can create indexes on one or more fields to find and sort records faster. Indexes can speed up queries if the fields on both sides of the join are indexed. In a one-to-many relationship, the primary table is already indexed on the primary key field; creating an index for the foreign key field in the related table helps when the query is run. Also, indexing any field used in a criteria rule in the query reduces processing time for the query.

Multiple-field indexes help distinguish between records that might have more than one record with the same value in the first field. If you are creating a multiple-field index, use only as many fields as necessary.

NOTE   *Although indexes can speed up searches and sorts, and queries of related tables, they can also add to the database size. Each index represents a condensed lookup table. Additional problems can occur in a multiple-user environment because indexes can reduce the concurrency of the database, thereby limiting the ability of more than one user to modify data at the same time.*

Optimize Queries

Queries are key to retrieving the right data from your database. There are many things you can do to help speed up running queries. Among the guidelines for optimizing queries are the following:

■ Include only the fields you need in the query. If a field is not needed in the result set but you are using it as a criterion, clear the Show check box in the query grid.

■ Avoid calculated fields in a query as much as possible. If you need an expression in the result of the query, add a control to the form or report instead and use the expression as the control source.

■ Use Between…And… in a criteria expression rather than the > and < operators.

■ If you want to count all the records in the recordset, use Count(*) instead of Count([*fieldname*]).

■ When grouping records by values in one of the joined fields, be sure to place the Group By aggregate function in the field on the side of the join containing the values you want to summarize. If you place Group By in the joined field, Access must join all the records and calculate the aggregate using only the necessary fields.

■ Use as few Group By aggregates as possible. You might be able to use the First function instead in some cases.

■ Try not to use restrictive criteria on non-indexed or calculated fields.

■ If you need to place criteria on one of the fields used to join two tables in a one-to-many relationship, you can place it on either field in the grid. Run some tests to see which placement results in a faster query.

14

■ If you are working with fairly static data, consider running a make-table query and using the resulting table instead of the query as the basis for forms and reports. You can always run the make-table query again if the data changes. Be sure to add indexes to the resulting table.

■ When you create a crosstab query, try to use fixed column headings to save the time it takes to update them.

Optimize Filter By Form

The Filter By Form defaults for *databasename* settings in the Edit/Find tab of the Options dialog box can improve the performance of all tables and queries, and all text box controls that use the Database Default setting in the Filter Lookup property. As discussed in Chapter 13, the Filter By Form Defaults group of options can limit the displayed list of values to indexed fields only or include local indexed and non-indexed fields. You can also set a limit on the number of records that must be read to come up with the list of unique values to display in the drop-down list in the grid.

If the list of field values takes too long to display, you can optimize the Filter By Form for a single text box control on a form by setting the control's Filter Lookup property (on the Data tab) to Never. This suppresses displaying the field values on the drop-down list in the Filter By Form window.

Optimize Forms and Reports

Most of the optimization strategies can be used on forms, reports, subforms, and subreports. There are also techniques that you can apply to individual text box and combo box controls to improve their performance in forms and reports.

The following tips apply to both forms and reports:

■ Base the subform or subreport on a saved query that includes only the required fields and that has a filter that results in only the required set of records.

■ If the record order is not important, you can save time by not sorting records in an underlying query, especially if the query uses fields from multiple tables.

■ Try not to sort or group on expressions.

■ Make sure the underlying query is optimized before loading the form or report.

■ Index on the fields you use for sorting or grouping.

■ Don't overdo the design with bitmaps and graphic objects. However, when you need to add graphics, convert the unbound object frame controls to image controls, which take less time to load.

■ You can save a lot of disk space by using black-and-white bitmaps rather than color.

■ Don't overlap controls unless absolutely necessary. Access must draw the controls in the form or report window twice to place overlapping controls.

■ Use subforms and subreports sparingly; they occupy as much space as the main form or report. Base all subforms and subreports on queries instead of tables and include only the necessary fields.

■ Index all fields in a subform or subreport that are linked to the main form or report. In addition, index all fields used in the criteria.

■ If the form or report has no event procedures associated with it, make sure the form or report Has Module property is set to No. The form or report will load faster and take less disk space without taking up the reserved class module space.

A few more strategies apply only to forms:

■ Don't leave a form open if you aren't using it. Access still must take time to refresh the window whether you are working in it or not.

■ Design a form with as few controls as possible. Having a large number of controls reduces the efficiency of the form. If you need a lot of controls, consider adding a tab control to create a multiple-page form with controls grouped logically on the pages.

■ If the underlying record source contains a lot of records and you are planning to use the form primarily for data entry, change the form's Data Entry property to Yes. When the form opens, it automatically moves to the end of the recordset and displays a blank record in the form. If you open the form with records showing, Access must read every record before it can display a blank new record.

■ If you don't expect to edit the records in a subform, you can save time by setting the subform's Allow Edits, Allow Additions, and Allow Deletions properties all to No. An alternative is to set the Recordset Type to Snapshot instead of to the default Dynaset. These are all properties of the subform object itself, not the subform control on the main form.

■ Use a hyperlink instead of a command button to open a form. Command buttons added with the help of the Command Button Wizard result in an event procedure written in Visual Basic code; avoiding the use of such command buttons will eliminate the class module and save space and time.

Optimize Controls

List box, combo box, and drop-down list box (the data access page version) controls all show field values from which you can choose. They are bound to a field in the underlying record source. When you use a wizard to create the list box or combo box control, it automatically constructs a SQL statement and assigns it to the control's Record Source property. You can save time by basing the control on a saved query instead of the SQL statement, which must be evaluated each time you activate the control.

14

To convert the wizard's SQL statement to a saved query:

1. Open the control's property sheet and click the Build button next to the Row Source property. The SQL statement appears in the Query Builder window.

2. Choose File | Save and enter a name for the query.

3. When you close the Query Builder window, Access asks if you want to save the query with that name and update the property with the query name. Respond Yes.

There are several more ways to optimize the behavior of these controls:

■ Be sure to index on the first field displayed in the combo box or list box and on the bound field in the underlying table, if they are different fields.

■ Set the AutoExpand property of the combo box control to No if you don't require the fill-in-as-you-type feature.

■ If you do use the fill-in-as-you-type feature by setting the AutoExpand property to Yes, be sure the first field in the displayed list is a Text data type rather than a Number data type. Access converts the numeric value to text to find a match for completing the entry. Using text in the first field eliminates the need for this conversion.

■ Use the default format and property settings for the controls. Access saves only the exceptions to the default settings with the form. If you find you are changing the same property frequently, you can change the default setting for the control and avoid having to store both.

Back Up and Restore a Database

To reduce the risk of losing data, it is a good idea to have a backup copy of your database. The database must be closed before you can back it up. If you are working in a multiple-user environment, make sure all the users have closed the database before you start the backup process. There are several ways to make a backup copy:

■ Double-click the My Computer shortcut and open successive folders until you locate the folder that contains your database. Drag the filename in the Windows Explorer list from the hard disk to another disk drive.

■ Right-click the filename or database shortcut in Windows Explorer and point to Send To in the shortcut menu, then click the drive to which you want to copy.

■ Use the Microsoft Windows 2000 or later Backup and Recovery Tools, the MS-DOS Copy command, or other third-party backup software. Some programs also offer the option of compressing the files.

If you are working in a multiple-user environment with user-level security, be sure to make a backup copy of the workgroup information file as well. You will not be able to start Access if the file is damaged or missing. See Chapter 20 for more information about workgroups and shared databases.

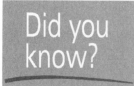

You Can Back Up Just Part of Your Database

You can back up individual objects of your database without copying the entire file. To do this, create a new, blank database and import the objects into it from the original database. See Chapter 18 for information about importing database objects.

To restore the database from a copy, use the recover feature of the same method you used to make the backup copy. If you used Windows Explorer, drag the filename from the floppy disk list to the database folder on the hard drive.

CAUTION *If the backup copy and the existing database in the database folder have the same name, you can replace the existing database when you restore the backup copy. If you want to save the original database, rename it before restoring from the backup copy.*

Compact and Repair a Database

Access provides some other useful tools for managing databases. One of them converts databases to or from previous versions of Access. Another creates an MDE file from the current database. An MDE file contains compiled versions of all the code in the database with none of the original source code. MDE databases run faster but the user cannot access the source code for viewing or editing.

NOTE *See Appendix A for information about converting databases to and from Access 2003.*

Another utility repairs and compacts a database. As you delete tables and queries and create new ones, your database can become scattered about on the disk with useless small blocks of space between. Compacting the database makes a copy of the database and rearranges the file so that the disk space is used more efficiently. You can compact an open database in place by choosing Tools | Database Utilities | Compact and Repair Database. Access takes only a few moments to compact the database, showing progress in the status bar.

If a database becomes damaged in some way, Access usually detects this when you try to open the database or if you try to compact, encrypt, or decrypt it. When damage is found, Access offers the option to repair the database at once. However, if your database begins to act strangely but Access has not noticed any damage, you can use the Compact and Repair Database utility manually.

Click Start to begin the rather lengthy process. Access runs the Office 2003 Installer and probably will ask you to insert the installation disk. It might also ask you to close certain open applications. Be aware that repairs can take a long time and you can click Cancel at any time to abort the process.

14

To compact and repair a closed database:

1. Close all databases. Then, from the empty Access window, choose Tools | Database Utilities | Compact and Repair Database.

2. In the Database to Compact From dialog box which looks just like the Open dialog box, select the name of the database you want to compact and click Compact.

3. In the Compact Database Into dialog box, specify the drive and folder for the compacted database and enter a name for the copy or choose a name from the list.

4. Click Save. If you choose the same name as the original database, Access asks for confirmation before replacing the file.

You can stop the process at any time by pressing ESC or CTRL-BREAK.

If the compaction is successful and you choose to use the same name and path for the compacted file, Access replaces the original database file with the compacted version. If Access is not successful in compacting a database, one of the following reasons might be to blame:

- Another user has the database open.

- Your disk does not have enough free space for both the original copy and the compacted copy of the database. To remedy this, delete as many unnecessary files as you can and try compacting the database again.

- You do not have permission to copy all the tables in the database. You need both Open/Run and Open Exclusive permissions in order to make copies of the data. If you are not the owner of this database, find the owner and try to obtain permission. If you are the owner, update the permissions for all the tables.

- The database is on a read-only network or the file attribute is set to read-only.

NOTE   *You can save time by specifying that the database is automatically compacted when you close it, if the file size would be reduced by more than 256KB. Check the Compact on Close option on the General tab of the Options dialog box. If another user has the database open, Access will not compact it until the last user closes it.*

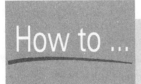 **Document a Database**

One of the most important tasks in a database management system is documentation, especially if many people are involved with its development and use. One of the Access analysis tools is the Documenter, which analyzes the current database and prints a report of the details of the entire database or only specified parts.

To run the Documenter:

1. Choose Tools | Analyze | Documenter.

2. Select the items on each tab that you want documented or choose Select All on the All Object Types tab to select everything in the database, including the relationships and the database properties.

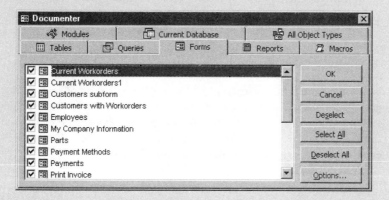

3. To limit the amount of information to print in the table definitions, click Options and check the desired options in the Print Table Definition dialog box.

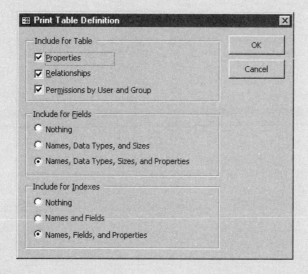

4. To limit the information in another object type, select one of the objects and click Options. Each object has a list of details from which to select.

14

5. After making all your selections, click OK twice to start the Documenter.

 *You can stop the Documenter any time by pressing CTRL-BREAK.*

The status bar shows the progress of the analysis with messages and odometers. When the Documenter is finished, the report is opened in Print Preview.

 *You might want to look at how many pages the definition report contains before starting to print it. Some definitions, even with small databases, are quite lengthy.*

If you want to save the report, you can output the definitions to one of several file formats. You can output them in HTML format or into an Excel worksheet, a Rich Text Format file, a DOS text file, or a file in report snapshot format. Choose File | Export to open the Export Report To dialog box, select the desired file format from the Save as type box, enter a name for the report, and click Export.

Chapter 15

Automate with Macros

How to...

- Create a simple macro
- Test and debug a macro
- Assign a macro to an event property
- Add conditions to the macro
- Create an AutoExec macro that runs when you launch Access
- Create a macro group

Macros are individual Access objects that are listed in the Macros tab in the Database window. Once you have created and saved a macro, you can attach it to an event property of any object in your database. Macros provide a quick and easy way to program your Access application to do what you want. With macros, you can specify customized responses to user actions such as clicking a button, opening a form, or selecting an option in an options group. Macros can also respond to system conditions such as an empty recordset.

A macro is a list of one or more actions that work together to carry out a particular task in response to an event. Each *action* carries out one particular operation. You create the list of actions in the order in which you want them to execute. In addition to selecting the action to be taken, you specify other details of the action, called *arguments.* These arguments provide additional information such as which form to open or how to filter the records to be displayed.

You can also set conditions under which the macro action is to be performed, such as to display a message box if a field contains a certain value or is blank. The macro runs only if the condition evaluates to True. If the condition is False, the action is skipped. If there is another action in the macro, it is executed; if not, the macro stops.

Create a Simple Macro

The first step in creating a macro is to list the actions you want performed when an event occurs. Each action might require specific arguments or need to be performed only under certain conditions. Make sure you choose the right event to which the macro should respond.

To start your new macro, click New in the Macros tab of the Database window. The Macro window opens showing a blank macro (see Figure 15-1). The drop-down list in the Action column contains a list of actions from which to choose. Entries in the Comment column are optional but highly recommended as a reminder of what the macro is meant to accomplish.

Comments are especially useful because macros are stored as separate objects, not linked with a particular form or report. The comments can explain how the macro is used and to which events it is attached. This can be especially important if you rename the macro. You will need to find all the references to it and change the name there, too.

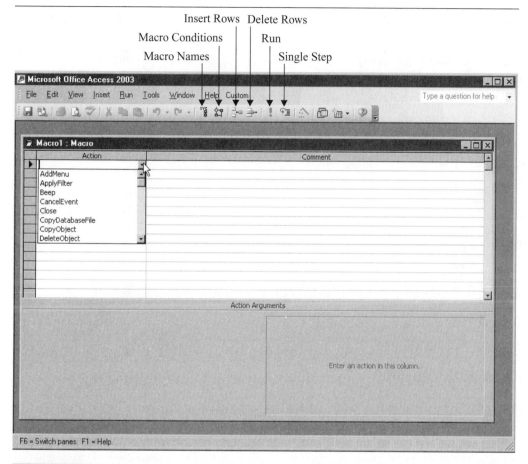

FIGURE 15-1   Working in the Macro window

Choose Macro Actions

Access offers actions that cover data management activities such as opening forms and reports, printing reports, filtering data, validating data, moving among records in a form, playing sounds, displaying message boxes, and even exchanging data with other programs. To add an action to a macro, you can either choose from the drop-down list or type the name yourself. Once you select an action from the list, the lower pane displays the associated arguments, some of which are required; others are optional, depending on the action.

As an example, create a macro in the Police database that opens the Alpha Card form in read-only mode by doing the following:

1. Click New in the Macros tab of the Database window to open the blank macro.

2. Click the Action drop-down arrow, scroll down the list, and choose OpenForm from the list.

The Action Arguments pane now contains the arguments for the OpenForm action, and the information pane describes the selected OpenForm action. The Form Name argument is required. Other required arguments show selections whereas the optional arguments are blank.

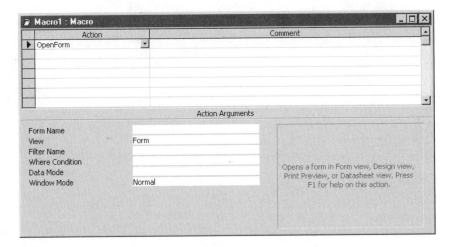

Set Action Arguments

Most macro actions have a list of associated arguments that give Access more information about how you want the action carried out. Some arguments are required, others are optional. When you add an action to a macro, the argument list appears in the lower pane.

You can usually type the value you want in the argument box but many offer drop-down lists. Some require that if you enter a value it must be one that is in the list. A description of the current argument is displayed in a pane to the right of the argument list. If you need more help, press F1 with the insertion point in the argument box.

To continue with the Alpha Card form example:

1. Click in the Form Name box in the Action Arguments pane and select Alpha Card from the drop-down list of all the forms in the current database.

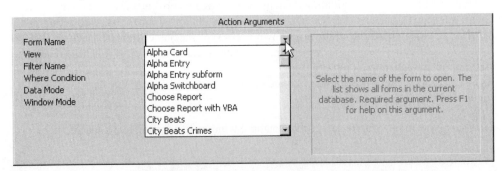

2. Set the other arguments as follows:

   ■ Accept the default Form as the View argument.

   ■ Leave the Filter Name argument blank because we want to see all the records.

   ■ Again, we want all the records so do not add a SQL WHERE clause in the Where Condition argument.

   ■ Choose Read Only from the Data Mode list.

   ■ Leave Window Mode with the default Normal setting.

3. Close the Macro window and enter **Open Alpha Card** as the name for the macro in the Save As dialog box.

4. Click OK. If you return to the Macros tab of the Database window, you will see the name of the new macro.

> TIP *In some cases, choices for one argument can determine which choices are available for an argument farther down in the list. For this reason, it is best to set the arguments in the order they are listed in the Action Arguments pane.*

Instead of selecting from a list or entering a value, you can enter an expression that evaluates to the argument value you want to use. Always precede the expression with an equal sign so Access recognizes it as an expression instead of an identifier. For example, the expression =*[EntryNo]* sets the argument to the value in the EntryNo control. If you would like help from the Expression Builder, click the Build button, which appears at the right of the argument box when you click in an argument that will accept an expression.

Test and Debug a Macro

Once you complete the macro, you can run it to see if it behaves as planned. You have a choice of running the complete macro at once or stepping through each action one at a time. If an error occurs in the macro or you don't get the results you expect, use the step-through method of running the macro to locate the action that causes the error.

Start the Macro

There are several ways to run a macro after you have finished adding the actions and setting the arguments. While still in the Macro window, you can click the Run button or choose Run | Run to run the macro in place. After you have named and saved the macro, you can run it from the Database window using one of the following methods:

■ Select the macro name and click Run.

■ Double-click the macro name.

■ Right-click the macro name and choose Run from the shortcut menu.

■ Choose Tools | Macro | Run Macro and then enter the macro name in the Run Macro dialog box.

15

If your macro depends on a particular form or report being open before it can run, be sure to open the form or report first.

If an error occurs during the operation, Access displays an error message. Read the message and click OK to open the Action Failed dialog box, which tells you which action in the macro failed and the arguments that were being used at the time. The Arguments box shows that the second argument, Object Name, is required but missing from the GoToRecord action. It also shows any conditions that were in effect. Your only option in this dialog box is to click Halt to stop the macro. Before closing the dialog box, note the action name and other data about where the fault occurred. It is up to you to switch to the Macro window to correct the problem.

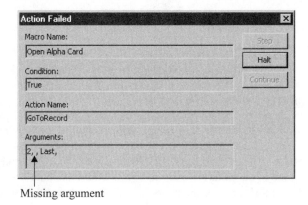

Missing argument

Step Through a Macro

If you have created a macro with many actions and it contains an error, you can use the Single Step method to move through the macro one action at a time. You must be in the Macro window to step through the macro actions.

To start stepping through the macro:

1. Click Single Step or choose Run | Single Step.

2. Click Run or choose Run | Run to carry out the first action. A Macro Single Step dialog box opens showing the details of the first step in your macro.

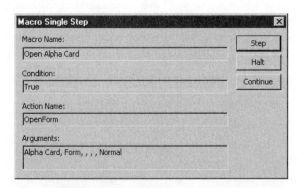

3. Your options in this dialog box are as follows:

- **Step**   Moves to the next action (default).
- **Halt**   Stops macro execution.
- **Continue**   Quits single stepping and runs the rest of the macro without stopping. If another error occurs, the macro stops and another Action Failed dialog box appears.

4. After the macro finishes, click the Single Step button again to turn it off; otherwise, the next macro you run will single step, too.

Modify a Macro

After you see how a macro runs, you might decide to make some changes to it such as adding an action, changing the order of the actions, adding a condition to the action, adding a Where Condition argument to limit the records, or creating additional macros to include in a macro group.

  To open a macro for modification, select the macro name in the Database window and click Design. Use the Insert Rows and Delete Rows toolbar buttons or the Insert and Edit menu commands to add or delete actions. You can also use the standard Cut, Copy, and Paste operations to edit a macro. The Undo button is also available to reject any changes. After making the changes to the macro, save it again. If you save it with a different name, be sure to change all references to the macro accordingly.

 If the macro operates on important data, make a temporary copy of the data to use during the modification process. This way, if anything goes wrong, you have not destroyed valuable information.

Assign a Macro to an Event Property

Once you have created the macro that will carry out the action you want, you must decide when you want it to happen. Access responds to all kinds of events that occur when you are working with a form or report including mouse clicks, changes in data, changes in focus, and opening or closing of a form or report. After you decide when you want the macro to run, set the corresponding event property of the form, report, or control to the name of the macro. For example, if you want to run a macro that sounds a beep when a form opens, assign the macro to the On Open property of the form.

See the sidebar "About Events and Event Properties" in Chapter 10 for a brief orientation.

To attach a macro to an event property:

1. Open the form or report in Design view and select the form, report, or section or control to which you want to attach the macro.

2. Open the property sheet and click the Event tab to see a list of events that can occur for the selected object.

15

3. Click the property whose event you want to run the macro and choose the macro name from the drop-down list.

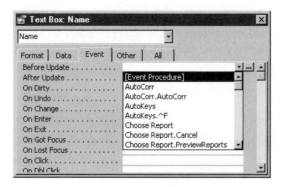

4. Save and close the form or report design.

When the event occurs, the built-in response occurs first, then the macro runs. For example, when you click a button, the built-in response occurs and the button appears pressed. If you have attached a macro to the On Click event property, the macro runs next.

Decide Which Event to Use

Although the property sheet shows quite a long list of event properties for forms and controls, there are a few that you will use more often, for example, when a form opens or the data in a control changes. Table 15-1 lists some of the commonly used form and control event properties.

Property	Occurs When	Use To
On Open	The form opens before the first record is displayed.	Open, close, or minimize other forms or maximize this form.
On Current	The form is opened and focus moves to a record, or the form is refreshed or requeried.	Synchronize data among forms or move focus to a specific control.
Before Update	After the focus leaves a record but before the data is saved in the database. Also occurs after a control loses focus but before the control is changed.	Display a message to confirm the change. Validate data entered in a control.
After Update	After the record changes have been saved in the database. Also occurs after a control loses focus and after the control is changed.	Update the data in other controls, forms, or reports. Move focus to a different page, control, or record in the form. Also transmit new data to other applications.

TABLE 15-1 Commonly Used Form and Control Event Properties

Property	Occurs When	Use To
On Click	Press and release the left mouse button over a control.	Carry out commands and commandlike actions.
On Enter	Move to a control before it gets focus.	Display information about data to enter in the control or a request for a user password.

TABLE 15-1   Commonly Used Form and Control Event Properties *(continued)*

Reports and report sections have fewer event properties because there is little user interaction with a report. Some of the more common event properties used to attach macros and event procedures to reports are

- ■ **On No Data**   Runs a macro when the report has an empty underlying recordset. Use to cancel the print event.

- ■ **On Open**   Runs a macro when the report opens but before printing begins. Use to prompt for a filter for the records to be included in the report.

- ■ **On Page**   Runs a macro after the page has been formatted but before printing begins. Use to add a graphic or border design to the report.

Add Conditions to a Macro

When you want a macro to run only under specific circumstances, you can add a condition to any of the macro actions. The macro condition effectively states, "If this condition is true, run this action. If it is not true, go to the next action, if any." You can use conditions to set control values or control properties and even run additional macros. Such test comparisons are not case sensitive.

Some examples of using conditions are

- ■ If the balance of an account is negative, change the color of the number to red.

- ■ If a student's grades are exemplary, print a congratulatory message.

- ■ If the inventory level of an item is low, display a message to remind the user to reorder.

- ■ If the order exceeds a specific total, calculate the amount due with a volume discount.

NOTE   *Do not confuse the macro condition, which determines whether the action takes place, with the Where Condition, which limits the records in the form or report. The macro condition is entered in the Condition column of the macro sheet; the Where Condition is an argument of many macro actions.*

Normally, a condition applies only to the action on the same row in the macro sheet. If the condition is not met, the next action is executed. To continue the condition to the next action,

15

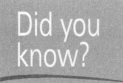

About Default Events

Most of the macros used in an application are attached to the default events for the object. A *default event* is not one that occurs automatically; it is the event that is most often associated with a particular object. For example, the Click event is the most common event associated with command buttons and check boxes; Open is the most common event for forms. When you use the Macro Builder to create a macro for an object, the macro is automatically attached to the default event.

When you open the form or report in Design view and look at the property sheet for the text box control, you will see the name of the macro in the Before Update event property.

enter an ellipsis (…) in the Condition column of the next row. You can apply the condition to several sequential actions.

You can also use conditions to create an If…Then…Else structure in a macro. This conditional logic runs one or more actions if the condition is met and a different set if the condition evaluates to False. This structure is very useful for changing the order of execution based on the outcome of the condition. For example, you might want to carry out a calculation if a field has a value but to move to another record if the field is blank. Use the ISNULL function to test for blanks and NOT ISNULL to test for a value.

Create a Macro to Display a Warning

The MsgBox action is one of the most useful macro actions when interacting with the user. You can use it to display warnings, alerts, and other information. The MsgBox action has four arguments: Message, Beep, Type, and Title. One example of using a macro with a condition is the PurgeValid macro, which ensures that certain reports of serious criminal activity in the Police Alpha Entry table are not purged from the database by accident.

The macro is based on a condition that compares the Code value, which identifies the crime, with the value in the Purge field. The Purge field contains the date when the record might be erased from the file. The report of certain crimes is never to be erased. If the Code is in a certain range, there should be no date entered in the Purge field.

An additional condition is combined with the test for the Code value. This condition skips records with blank Purge fields. The reason for this added test is that when the user tabs through the form, the Purge control can focus on whether it has a value or not; you don't want to see the message if you have just skipped through the control. Figure 15-2 shows a macro that checks the code value; if the value is within the danger range, the macro displays a message when the user tries to enter a date in the Purge field.

To create the PurgeValid macro:

1. Start a new macro and choose the MsgBox action.

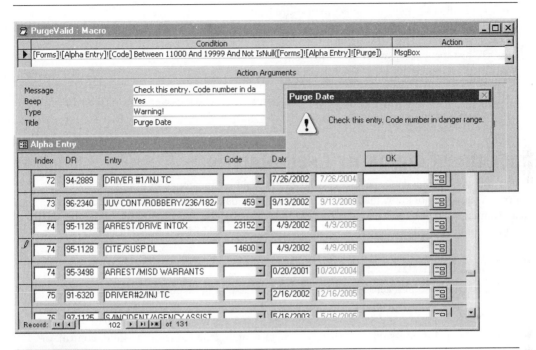

FIGURE 15-2 A macro designed for data validation

2. Click the Conditions button or choose View | Conditions.

3. Enter the expression **[Forms]![Alpha Entry]![Code] Between 11000 And 19999 And Not IsNull([Forms]![Alpha Entry]![Purge])** in the condition row of the MsgBox action.

4. In the Message argument, enter **Check this entry. Code number in danger range.**

TIP
Do not enclose the message in quotations marks unless you also want to display the marks.

5. Set the Beep argument to Yes.

6. Select Warning! as the Type.

7. Enter Purge Date as the message box Title.

Now, attach the macro to the Before Update event property of the Purge control. To do this:

1. Save the macro with the name **PurgeValid.**

2. Open the Alpha Entry form in Design view.

3. Click the Purge text box control and open the property sheet.

15

4. Click the Event tab and select the Before Update property.

5. Choose PurgeValid from the drop-down list of macros.

6. To test the macro, switch to Form view.

7. Move to a record with a code number in the danger range.

8. Click in the Purge field, enter a date, and press TAB. The message appears warning you not to enter a date in this record.

Create Other Commonly Used Macros

When you work with a database, Access causes many things to happen in response to your actions. You might not know that you can customize the database with macros to accomplish many similar operations according to your designs. This section discusses some of the more common applications for macros.

Set Control Values and Properties

SetValue is a very useful macro action that sets the value of a field, control, or property of a form, a form datasheet, or a report. You can set a value for almost any control, form, and report property in any view with the SetValue action. The action has two arguments, both of which are required: Item and Expression. The Item argument contains the name of the field, control, or property whose value you want to set. The Expression argument contains the value you want to set for the item. Do not precede the expression with an equal sign. Use full syntax complete with all the identifiers when referring to any Access objects in the Item or the Expression argument.

Set Control Values

In addition to entering the value itself, you can set the value of a control based on the value of another control in the same or a different form or report. You can also use the result of a calculation or the value returned by an option group to set the value of a control. For example, when you are adding new records to the Alpha Entry recordset in the subform of the Alpha Card form, you can compute the value of the Purge field. Depending on the Code value, the entry can be purged from the person's file after a certain length of time, usually three or seven years. To save data entry time, you can write a macro that examines the Code value and uses the DateAdd function to set the Purge date by adding a specified number of years to the Date field value.

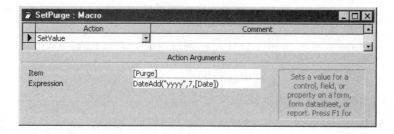

 *The first argument in the DateAdd function, "yyyy," indicates that the interval you want to increment is the year part of the date value. The second argument is the number to add; the third names the control that contains the original date.*

Set Control Properties

You can set many of the properties of forms, reports, and controls by running a macro. For example, you can hide a control from view on the form or disable it so the user can't enter data in it. You can also change colors, fonts, and other appearance properties.

As an example of setting a property with a macro, disable the Drivers License control if the subject of the Alpha Card report is younger than 16. To do this, set the Enabled property to No. When a control is disabled, it still appears on the screen but is dimmed; you can't reach it by pressing TAB or by clicking it.

To ensure that you enter the correct identifier, you can use the Expression Builder. After adding the SetValue action to the macro, click Build (…) next to the Item argument to open the Expression Builder, then do the following:

1. Double-click on the Forms folder, then double-click on the All Forms folder in the left panel to open the list of forms in the current database.

2. Choose the Alpha Card form. A list of all controls and labels in the form appears in the center panel.

3. Choose Drivers License. A list of all the properties that apply to the Drivers License text box control appears in the right panel.

4. Choose Enabled and click Paste. When you click OK, the expression is placed in the Item argument box.

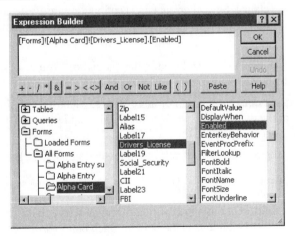

To complete the macro:

1. Enter No in the Expression argument.

2. Add a condition to the Action row that runs the macro only if the Age value is less than 16.

3. Attach the macro to the Age control's After Update event property.

You probably will want to add another macro to reenable the Drivers License when you move to the next record.

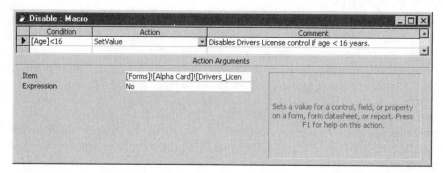

If you want to hide a control, set its Visible property to No. If the property value is a string expression, enclose it in quotation marks in the Expression argument box.

Change the Flow of Operations

Adding conditions that determine whether a macro action is carried out is one way to control the flow of operations. You can add the MsgBox function to a macro condition to let the user decide which action to carry out. The MsgBox function is similar to the MsgBox action with the exception that the function returns a value, depending on which button the user clicks in the message box. The MsgBox function displays a dialog box containing the message and waits for the user to click a button indicating the user's choice. Several arrangements of buttons are available in the dialog box.

The MsgBox function has three main arguments and two additional arguments; only the first one is required:

- **Prompt**   A string expression displayed in the dialog box. You can display up to 1,024 characters, depending on the font size.

- **Button**   A number equal to the sum of three values, which specify the visual characteristics of the message box such as the number and type of buttons, the default button, the icon style, and the modality of the message box.

- **Title**   A string expression that is displayed in the dialog box title bar.

Two additional arguments can specify a Help file and context number in the file where you can find context sensitive help.

You can display seven different buttons in various arrangements, plus a choice of four icons. You also can specify which of the buttons is the default. Each button arrangement and dialog box feature has a numeric value. These values are totaled and placed in the Button argument. The six arrangements of the seven buttons and their values are:

- 0 displays only OK

- 1 displays OK with Cancel

- 2 displays Abort, Retry, and Ignore

- 3 displays Yes, No, and Cancel

- 4 displays Yes and No

- 5 displays Retry and Cancel

Add 16 to the button sum to show the Critical Message icon or 32 for the Warning Query, 48 for the Warning Message, or 64 for the Information Message. Finally, you can add to the sum to specify which button is the default. The default button activates if you press ENTER.

For example, to display the Yes, No, and Cancel buttons in that order, add 3 to the Button sum. If you want to display the Critical Message icon, add 16 to the sum. To set the No button as the default, add 256 to the sum. For these features, enter 275 as the Button argument in the MsgBox function. See the Help topic "MsgBox Function" for a complete list of all the button arrangements and dialog box features.

When you use the MsgBox function in a macro condition, you can compare the returned value to a specific number and carry out the action if the comparison is True. For example, you can use the MsgBox function to display a confirmation message before deleting a record. The box contains three buttons: Yes, No, and Cancel.

When the user clicks one of the buttons, the MsgBox function returns a value depending on which button was clicked: 1 for OK, 2 for Cancel, 3 for Abort, 4 for Retry, 5 for Ignore, 6 for Yes, and 7 for No.

For example, if the user clicks the Yes button, the function returns 6; so if any other value is returned, the user did not click Yes. Figure 15-3 shows a macro using the MsgBox function in a condition that evaluates to True if the function returned any value except 6 (Yes). If the value is

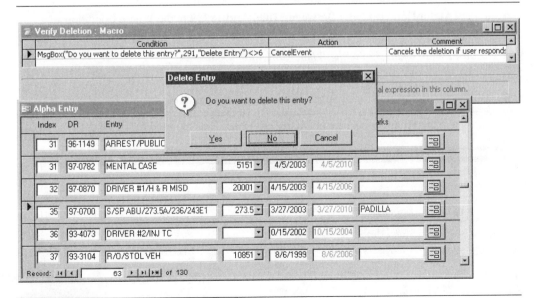

FIGURE 15-3   Using the MsgBox function in a macro condition

15

not 6, the deletion event is canceled. You could add other conditions that carry out actions as a result of the other button selections.

The Button argument in the MsgBox function in Figure 15-3 is 291, which is the sum of the Yes, No, and Cancel button arrangement (3), the Warning Query icon (32), and setting the second button (No) as the default (256).

After you save the Verify Deletion macro, attach it to the form's Before Del Confirm event property. The message box displays when you select a record and press DEL. In Figure 15-3, the user selected the Alpha Entry record for Index 24 before pressing DEL. You can see that it has been deleted from the Form view but has not yet been confirmed. If you click No in the box, the record is returned. If you respond by clicking Yes, Access deletes the record.

If the deletion will result in cascade deletions of other records or interfere in some other way with the relationships in the database, Access displays another confirmation message.

Filter Records

You can create a macro to limit the records you want to print by adding a Where Condition to the OpenReport action. For example, suppose that you want to preview the Alpha Entry records for all incidents with a Code in the danger range, 11000 to 19999. Start a new macro in the macro design window and do the following:

1. Choose OpenReport in the Action column.

2. In the Report Name argument, select Alpha Entries from the list of available reports.

3. Choose Print Preview as the View argument.

4. Enter **[Alpha Entry]![Code] Between 11000 And 19999** in the Where Condition argument or click the Build button to get help from the Expression Builder.

Don't use an equal sign in the Where Condition argument.

5. Click Run.

You can see in the Print Preview that only three of the incidents reported fall in the danger range.

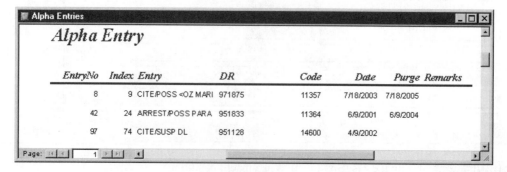

If you want to see a fancy example of filtering records by using macro conditions, open the Northwind sample database's Customer Phone List macro.

Create an AutoExec Macro

You can create a special macro that runs when you first open a database. The AutoExec macro can carry out such actions as opening a form for data entry, displaying a message box prompting the user to enter his or her name, or playing a sound greeting. All you need to do is create the macro with the actions you want carried out at startup and save it with the name AutoExec. A database can have only one macro named AutoExec.

When you open a database, all the startup options you have set in the Startup dialog box take place first. You can see these by choosing Tools | Startup. Access looks for a macro named AutoExec and executes the actions in it. You can bypass both the startup options and the AutoExec macro by pressing SHIFT when you open the database.

 Many of the same options can be set in the AutoExec macro as in the Startup dialog box. Be careful not to include conflicting settings in the macro. See Chapter 13 for information about the startup settings.

Create a Macro Group

If you have created several macros that apply to controls on the same form or report, you can group them together as one file. There are two advantages to using macro groups:

- It reduces the number of macro names in the Database window.

- You can find all the macros for a single form or report in one place where they are easy to edit.

An example of using grouped macros is the Choose Report dialog box that asks you to select the report you are interested in and then decide to print or preview the report. See Chapter 17 for details of this form.

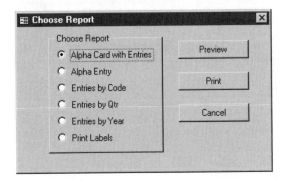

15

To create a macro group:

1. Open the macro sheet as usual.

2. Click the Macro Names button or choose View | Macro Names.

3. Add a macro to the sheet and enter a name for it in the Macro Name column of the first row of the macro.

4. Add the rest of the actions to the macro.

5. To add another macro, enter the name in the Macro Name column and add the actions you want to occur. Figure 15-4 shows the completed Choose Report macro group.

6. Save and close the macro window.

When Access runs a macro in a group, it begins with the action in the row that contains the macro name and continues until it finds no more actions or encounters another macro name. After adding all the macros to the group, close and save it as usual with the group name.

TIP   *You will find the macros in a group will be much easier to read if you leave at least one blank row between the macros.*

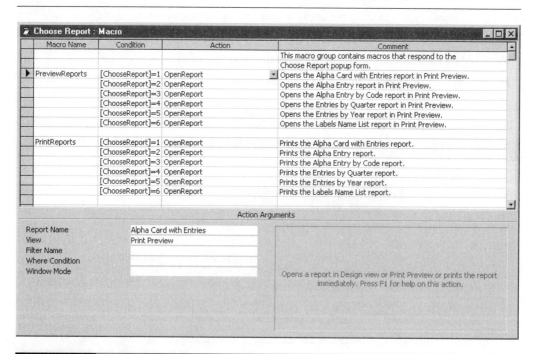

FIGURE 15-4   Grouping macros

When you assign macros from a group to an event property, you must use the group name as well as the macro name. In the property sheet for a control, the drop-down list in an event property shows compound names for all the macros in a group and the names of all the single macros. The group name and the macro name both appear separated by a period: *macrogroupname.macroname*.

Assign AutoKeys

Access offers a special macro group named AutoKeys in which you can assign an action or set of actions to a specific key or key combination. Pressing the key or combination of keys carries out the action you specify. You can add as many individual macros to the group as you need, each one named with the key or key combination that will run it.

For example, the following macro opens the Alpha Card form when the user presses CTRL-F. The SendKey syntax form is used as the macro name. The carat symbol (^) represents CTRL and the plus sign (+) represents SHIFT. Function keys and other key names are enclosed in curly brackets. See the Help topic "AutoKey Combinations" for a list of key combinations and their SendKey syntax for the macro name.

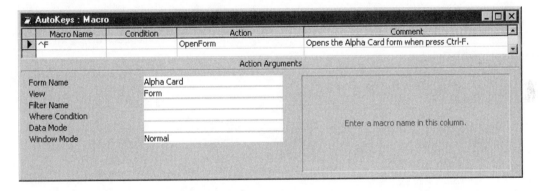

 If you assign a key combination that is already used by Access (for example, CTRL-C), the Access assignment will no longer work unless you change it manually or reset to default. Be warned, though, that resetting to the default will remove all custom assignments.

15

Chapter 16

Customize Menus and Toolbars

How to...

- Customize Access command bars
- Build custom command bars
- Attach a customized command bar to an object
- Modify and delete custom command bars
- Restore built-in command bars

In Access 97, Microsoft blended the three types of user interaction tools into a single global concept: the command bar. Although the terms *toolbars, menu bars,* and *shortcut menus* are still valid in Access 2003 and do describe differing implementations, the methods used to create and modify custom command bars are the same for all types. The purpose is to make them more consistent and easier to use and customize.

You have worked extensively with all of these interaction tools in the previous chapters of this book and when running other Office programs. In this chapter, you will see how to work with and customize built-in command bars and create custom command bars for an application.

Use Access Command Bars

The basic element of toolbars, menu bars, and shortcut menus is the command the user chooses to cause an action such as printing a report or running a query. You reach a command by clicking a toolbar button or choosing from a hierarchy of menus and submenus.

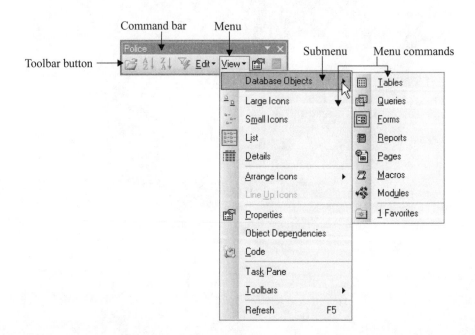

The command can appear as a button with an image or a menu command showing text. Menu commands with equivalent toolbar buttons often also display the icon that appears on the button. You can set options so that menu commands and buttons can show both text and images. You can also group a set of related items in a menu, toolbar, or shortcut menu.

Some command bars are classified as *global* and are available to any database or application. *Built-in command bars* are predefined and are automatically displayed in specific views in any database. *Custom command bars* are user-defined and are limited to the database in which they were created. Custom command bars can also be attached to specific forms or reports.

Show and Hide Built-in Toolbars

The built-in Access toolbars appear automatically in certain contexts. For example, when you are in form Design view, the default toolbars are Form Design and Formatting (Form/Report). If you right-click in one of the toolbars, you will see that you can also display several other toolbars; the list varies depending on the current view.

To add to the window any toolbars not in the list, open the Customize dialog box using one of the following methods:

- Right-click in a toolbar and choose Customize at the bottom of the shortcut menu
- Choose View | Toolbars | Customize
- Choose Tools | Customize

The Toolbars tab of the Customize dialog box contains a list of all three types of available toolbars. Click the check box of any toolbar you want to add to the display and click Close. Clear the check mark to remove the toolbar from the screen.

You can also remove a toolbar from the display by right-clicking in any toolbar and removing the check mark from the name in the drop-down list. If the toolbar is not the default for this view, the name will also be removed from the drop-down list. Default toolbar names remain on that list even though they are not showing.

Three additional toolbars, which are not defaults for any view, appear in the Toolbars list in the Customize dialog box:

■ The Source Code Control toolbar displays buttons you can use to control changes while creating Visual Basic code in a multiple-developer environment.

■ The Utility 1 and Utility 2 toolbars are empty, built-in toolbars you can use to create custom global toolbars as described in the section "Create a Global Toolbar" later in this chapter.

Two other items on the Toolbars list that are not really toolbars are Menu Bar and Shortcut Menus. Menu Bar displays the default menu bar for the current view. The names of any new custom command bars you create will appear in alphabetic order at the end of the list.

When you check Shortcut Menus in the Toolbars list, a menu bar is displayed containing all the built-in shortcut menus. As shown in Figure 16-1, clicking Report on the Shortcut Menus menu

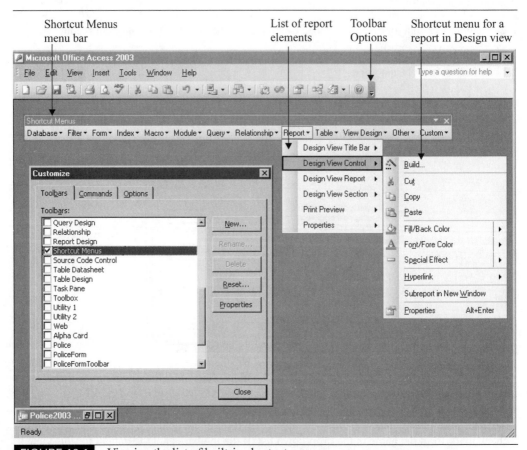

FIGURE 16-1   Viewing the list of built-in shortcut menus

bar displays a list of elements in the report that have associated shortcut menus, such as Design View Title Bar or Design View Control. When you click on one of the elements in the list, you see the shortcut menu that appears when you right-click on that part of the report in either Design View or Print Preview.

NOTE *If you create custom shortcut menus, the names are not displayed separately in the Toolbars list. Instead, they are listed as menu items in the Custom category on the Shortcut Menus menu bar.*

Show and Hide Toolbar Buttons

You don't have to display all the default toolbar buttons on a toolbar. Using the Toolbar Options button, you can choose which buttons to display. Click the Toolbar Options button (actually a gray area rather than a conventional button) on the right end of the toolbar (or at the right end of the title bar next to the Close button if the toolbar is floating) to display the list of available buttons. Click the Add or Remove Buttons drop-down arrow and point to the toolbar name in the list of buttons. Figure 16-2 shows the list of buttons normally displayed on the Table Datasheet toolbar. The arrow at the end of the list indicates there are additional buttons not in view.

To hide a button, clear the check mark next to the button name. To restore the button to the toolbar, check it in the list again. The last item in the list is Reset Toolbar, which restores the toolbar to its original default button set.

Move and Resize Command Bars

A command bar is *docked* if it is fixed to one edge of the window. Menu bars and toolbars normally appear docked at the top of the window. You can drag them away from the edge and turn them into *floating* command bars, which can be moved about on the screen. A docked command bar has no title bar, whereas a floating command bar has an identifying title bar. The Design Toolbox that you use to work with a form or report design is an example of a toolbar that is by default a floating toolbar.

To move a toolbar or menu bar from its docked position, click and drag its moving handle (the stack of small dots at the left end of the bar). You can also click on an empty space, on any separator bar in the menu bar, or on a toolbar to drag it away from the dock. To dock the command bar to an edge of the window, drag it to the side until it spreads out to the full height or width of the window.

After moving the command bar away from the edge of the window, you can drag the toolbar borders to change the height and width of the bar. To close a floating toolbar, click the Close button in the title bar. You cannot close a floating menu bar because it does not include a Close button.

You can also change the arrangement of the menu bar and the toolbars when they are docked. For example, if you want the toolbar to appear above the menu bar, click the toolbar moving handle and drag it over the menu bar.

Change Menu and Toolbar Options

In addition to repositioning and resizing a built-in menu or toolbar, you can use the Options tab of the Customize dialog box to set other features. The upper pane sets options for the menus and

16

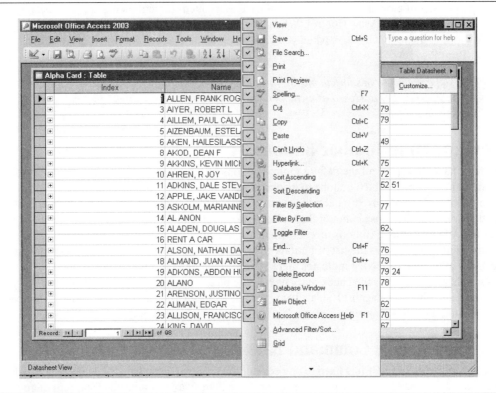

FIGURE 16-2 Toolbar Options list for the Table Datasheet toolbar

toolbars as personalized by Access. The lower pane contains options that change the way command bars look and behave. These option settings all remain in effect until you change them.

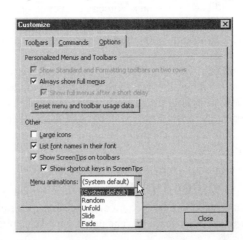

The toolbar shown below has large icons with both ScreenTips and shortcut keys displaying. Notice the double arrows at the right end of the toolbar, indicating that additional buttons are out of view offscreen.

Customize Command Bars

Access provides so many useful menu bars and toolbars; why would anyone want to create custom command bars? One reason could be that you do not want the user to be able to make changes in a form or report design. You can remove the View button from the toolbar to keep the user from switching to Design view.

Other possible customizations are:

- Adding a Save Record button to the toolbar so the user can quickly test the validity of the data just entered without leaving the record

- Removing the New Object button from the toolbar to keep the user from designing new forms, reports, or other Access objects

- Tailoring the commands and button options to match the terminology and practice of a specific application

You use the Customize dialog box to create and customize all three types of command bars. You use the same techniques and tools to modify built-in command bars to create new custom command bars. The difference between them is that the modified command bar is available to all Access databases, whereas the custom bar is available only to the database where it was created.

Create a Global Toolbar

There are two ways to create a custom toolbar that will be available to all your databases: modify a built-in toolbar or create a new global toolbar. The list of available toolbars in the Customize dialog box includes the blank Utility 1 and Utility 2 built-in toolbars. When you add buttons and menu commands to them, they become custom global toolbars and are available to all the databases and Access client projects. They actually are treated as modified built-in toolbars, not custom toolbars. You can't rename these toolbars.

Create Custom Toolbars and Menu Bars

Whether you're creating a new custom toolbar, menu bar, or shortcut menu, it all begins the same way:

1. Open the Customize dialog box using one of the methods described earlier.

16

2. Click the Toolbars tab and click New, then type a name for the new toolbar in the New Toolbar dialog box.

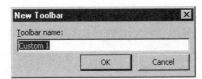

3. Click OK. A tiny, empty toolbar appears in front of the Customize dialog box and the toolbar name, Alpha Card, appears at the bottom of the list in the Toolbars box.

4. On the Toolbars tab, click Properties. The Toolbar Properties dialog box opens.

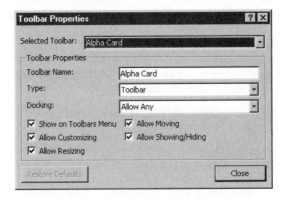

5. Here is where the processes diverge. Do one of the following:

- To continue with a custom toolbar, set the toolbar properties, as described next.
- If you want to create a new menu bar, choose Menu Bar from the Type list, then set the properties.
- If you want to create a new shortcut menu, choose Popup from the Type list and set the properties.

6. Choose Close when you have finished setting the properties.

The Selected Toolbar box in the Toolbar Properties dialog box shows the name of the toolbar. Click the down arrow to see the list of all toolbars, menu bars, and shortcut menus in the current database. Although the properties are called Toolbar Properties, they apply equally to menu bars. Shortcut menus have fewer properties available.

If you change the toolbar type to Popup to create a shortcut menu, the only property available is Allow Customizing; all others are dimmed. Access displays a warning if you try to change a toolbar or menu to a popup.

If you are modifying a built-in toolbar, some of the properties are not available. For example, the Toolbar Name and Type properties are dimmed because you can't rename a built-in toolbar or change its type. Also the Show on Toolbars Menu option is dimmed because the built-in toolbars that are in context with the current view are always shown when you right-click the toolbar or choose View | Toolbars. However, the Restore Defaults button, which you can click to restore a built-in toolbar to its original condition, does become available.

After setting the desired properties for the new toolbar, menu bar, or shortcut menu, you can add buttons and menus.

Add and Delete Toolbar Buttons

Once you create a new toolbar, you can add buttons to it in two ways:

- Copy or move a built-in or previously created custom button from another toolbar.
- Select the button from the list of commands in the Commands tab of the Customize dialog box.

Figure 16-3 shows the commands in the Query Design toolbar. Commands in the list that show an ellipsis (...) after the text (for example, Show Table) open a dialog box. Those with a vertical bar and a black triangle, such as Query Type, open a submenu.

Many commands are available in the Commands box, including the built-in buttons that appear in built-in toolbars. The commands are grouped into categories. Click the desired

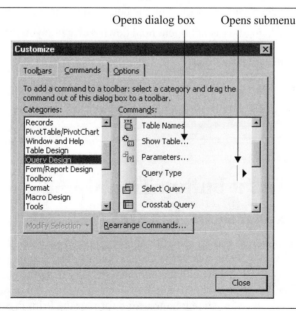

Opens dialog box   Opens submenu

FIGURE 16-3   The Commands tab of the Customize dialog box

16

category to see the commands that are available in that category. You might have to examine more than one category to find the button you want—some are stored in unusual categories.

To add a button from the Customize dialog box:

1. Choose the type of command you want in the Categories list. The Commands list shows images and text of commands in that category.

2. When you find the button you want, drag it to the toolbar. When you see a dark I-beam, drop the button on the toolbar.

3. Continue to add other buttons to the toolbar. You can drop a button between two buttons already in the toolbar. The bar will expand as you add buttons. To move a button already in place, drag it to the desired position.

If another toolbar has a button you can use, you can move or copy it to the new toolbar. Often it is easier to use an existing button than to start from scratch. An additional advantage is that when you copy or move a command from a built-in toolbar, the command keeps all the pointers to Access Help topics.

CAUTION *Moving a button from one toolbar to another removes it from the source toolbar.*

You must have both toolbars showing to move or copy a button. The Customize dialog box can be open or closed. To move a button from another toolbar:

- ■ If the Customize dialog box is open, drag the button to the new toolbar.
- ■ If the Customize dialog box is not open, hold down ALT while you drag the button.

To copy a button from another toolbar:

- ■ If the Customize dialog box is open, hold down CTRL while you drag the button.
- ■ If the Customize dialog box is not open, hold down CTRL-ALT while you drag the button.

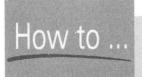

How to ... Add a Button That Opens a Form or Report

If you want to use the button to open a specific form or report or want to run a query, choose All Forms, All Reports, or All Queries in the Categories list. The Commands box shows the names of all the objects of that type in the current database. Drag the name of the object from the Commands box to the toolbar. The default button for that type of object appears on the toolbar—for example, the Form View button for a form or the Print Preview button for a report. There also are button categories that open a table or run a macro.

CAUTION *If you copy a built-in button, the copy is not independent of the original button. If you make changes to the copy of the button, the same changes also affect the built-in button. If you intend to make changes to the button, it is better to create a new custom toolbar and drag the buttons from the Commands box.*

TIP *If you want to add a button that opens a database object in its default view, you can simply drag the object from the Database window to the toolbar. The Customize dialog box must be closed to do this. The button ScreenTip displays the name of the object it will open.*

To remove a button with the Customize dialog box open, drag it off the toolbar or right-click the button and choose Delete from the shortcut menu. When you delete a built-in button, it is still available from the Commands box, but deleting a custom button removes it permanently. If the Customize dialog box is not open, hold down ALT while you drag the button off the toolbar.

TIP *If you want to keep custom buttons for later use instead of deleting them completely, create a new toolbar for storing them until you need them. Move the buttons from one toolbar to the other, then hide the new toolbar by clearing the check mark in the Toolbars box of the Customize dialog box.*

Add Built-in Menus

You can add built-in menus to a toolbar or a menu bar using the same two methods: drag from the Commands box of the Customize dialog box, or move or copy from an existing toolbar or menu bar. The only difference between adding toolbar buttons and menus is that by default the menus show only text whereas the buttons show only an image. These properties can be changed and customized.

With the new menu bar or toolbar showing, open the Customize dialog box and click the Commands tab. Scroll down the Categories list and select Built-in Menus. Figure 16-4 shows some of the built-in menus that are available.

Drag the menu from the Commands box to the menu bar or toolbar and drop the menu when you see the dark I-beam. Most of the commands in the built-in menu are carried over, depending on the context of the new menu bar or toolbar.

Add Custom Menus

If you want to build a new menu that is not a copy of one that Access offers, you can use the New Menu tool and customize it to fit your needs. To add a custom menu to a toolbar or menu bar, create it in place on the bar. To add a new custom menu:

1. With the toolbar or menu bar showing, open the Customize dialog box and click the Commands tab.

16

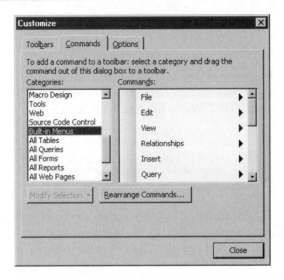

FIGURE 16-4 Selecting a built-in menu

2. Scroll down the list of Categories and select New Menu.

3. Drag New Menu from the Commands box to the menu bar or toolbar.

4. Right-click the new menu and enter a name in the Name box of the shortcut menu and press ENTER (see Figure 16-5).

Adding Menu Commands to a Toolbar or Menu Bar

Menu commands can be added to toolbars and menu bars using the same procedure. The menu commands are placed in a column under the menu name.

To add a menu command:

1. With the menu bar, toolbar, or shortcut menu showing, open the Customize dialog box and click the Commands tab.

2. Click the appropriate menu or view category in the Categories box.

3. Drag the command from the Commands box and rest it on the menu in the menu bar or toolbar. You will see the list of commands already in the menu (or an empty box if the menu is new); drag the command to the position in which you want it to appear. A horizontal bar appears in the drop-down menu just above the position where the command will be inserted. When the bar is in the right place, release the mouse. If the menu is new, release the mouse button over the empty box.

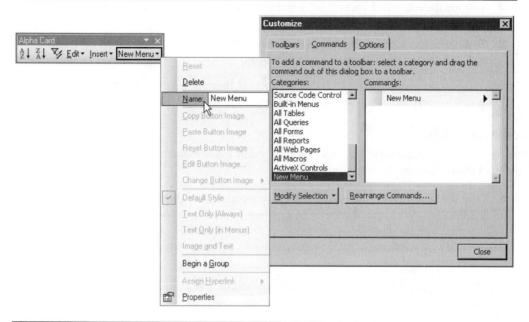

FIGURE 16-5   Adding a new menu to a toolbar

In the following example, the Print Preview command is added as the first command in the new custom menu, named Forms/Reports.

NOTE *If you add a menu command to a built-in menu that appears in more than one view, such as the File menu, that command appears in the menu in all the views where the menu appears.*

You can also move or copy a menu command from another menu bar, toolbar, or shortcut menu. If you are moving or copying a menu command to a menu in a different menu bar or toolbar, both the source and destination bars must be showing and the Customize dialog box also must be open.

■ To move the command, drag it over the menu where you want it to appear; when you see the list of the commands in the menu, release the mouse at the desired position.

16

- To copy the command, press CTRL while you drag the command to the new menu or toolbar.

- To delete a menu command from a menu or toolbar, drag the command off the menu and away from the other menu bars or toolbars.

 If you remove a command from a built-in menu, the command is removed from that menu in every menu bar in which it appears.

Add a Submenu

A submenu is created the same way as a menu. You start a new menu and add commands to it. To add a custom submenu to an existing menu:

1. Drag the New Menu command from the Commands box to the menu you want to contain the submenu. When you see the horizontal line, release the mouse; the New Menu control is placed with the other menu commands. The only difference between adding a command and adding a submenu is that the submenu shows a pointer indicating that it opens another list of menu commands.

NOTE *You can also add one of the built-in menus or toolbar buttons that opens a submenu and customize its commands.*

2. Right-click New Menu and type a name for the submenu, such as **Run Queries**, then press ENTER.

3. Slowly click the new submenu to display a small, empty box to the right of the submenu where the menu commands will be placed. If you click too fast, the box does not appear.

4. Select and drag a command, such as a query name from the All Queries category, to the empty box. When the I-beam appears, release the mouse. The Forms/Reports menu has two submenus: the built-in View menu and a custom submenu for running queries.

5. Drag the names of the other queries you want in the submenu from the All Queries list to the submenu.

Add Commands to a Shortcut Menu

When you close the Toolbar Properties dialog box after choosing Popup as the toolbar type, the new shortcut menu is added to the Custom category on the Shortcut Menus toolbar. The Shortcut

Menus toolbar is the group designation for all shortcut menus in the application. When you are ready to complete the shortcut menu, do the following:

1. Open the Customize dialog box and click Shortcut Menus in the Toolbars box on the Toolbars tab. The Shortcut Menu toolbar appears at the top of the screen.

2. Click the Custom category on the Shortcut Menus toolbar.

3. Add menu commands from the Customize dialog box the same way as for menu bars and toolbars.

> **NOTE** *A shortcut menu can be global or context sensitive. To specify a shortcut menu as global, set the option in the Startup dialog box as described shortly in this chapter in the section "Specify Global Command Bars." A context-sensitive shortcut menu contains commands that relate to the object to which it is attached.*

Attach a Custom Command Bar to an Object

Reports, forms, and controls have properties that specify which command bar is to be displayed when the object is in view. The following properties apply mostly to forms and reports but you can also attach a shortcut menu to controls on a form.

- The Menu Bar property specifies the menu bar to display when a form or report has focus. If the property is left blank, Access displays the built-in menu bar for the report or the global menu bar as defined in the Startup dialog box.

- The Toolbar property specifies the toolbar to use with a form or report when it is opened. If the property is left blank, Access displays the default toolbar for the form or report.

- The Shortcut Menu Bar property specifies the shortcut menu to display when you right-click a form, a report, or a control on a form (but not a control on a report). If the property is left blank, Access displays the default shortcut menu or the global shortcut menu as defined in the Startup dialog box. To display the shortcut menu when you right-click in the form, set the Shortcut Menu property to Yes.

To set one of these properties, open the object's property sheet and click the Other tab. Select the name of the command bar from the drop-down list next to the appropriate property box. Repeat the process for each form, report, or control to which you want to attach a command bar.

> **NOTE** *When you attach a custom command bar to a form, the bar appears only when the form is in Form view. Similarly, a custom command bar attached to a report appears only in Print Preview.*

Specify Global Command Bars

A global menu bar replaces the built-in menu bar in all the windows in an application except where you have specified a custom menu bar for a form or report. A global shortcut menu replaces the shortcut menus for datasheets, forms, form controls, and reports.

16

To specify a custom menu bar or custom shortcut menu as the default for the entire database or application, you must change the settings in the Startup dialog box. To set global command bars to replace the defaults:

1. Choose Tools | Startup to open the Startup dialog box.

2. Click the arrow next to the Menu Bar box and select the name of the menu bar to use instead of default. The list includes only the custom menu bars.

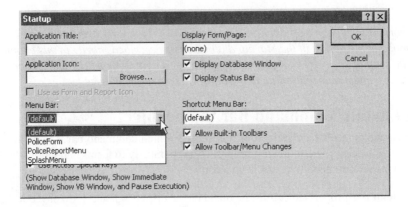

3. Click the arrow next to the Shortcut Menu Bar box and select the shortcut menu to use instead of the default.

4. Click OK to close the dialog box.

The changes will take effect the next time you open the database. To bypass the startup options, press SHIFT while the database is opening.

Delete a Custom Command Bar

To delete a custom toolbar, menu bar, or shortcut menu, open the Customize dialog box as usual and click the Toolbars tab. Select the item you want to delete and click Delete. If the toolbar or menu bar is a built-in one that you have modified, the Delete button is not available. Instead, click Reset to remove the custom features and restore the built-in command bar to its original default state.

Deleting a shortcut menu is a little different. You must convert it to a toolbar before you can delete it. Perform the following steps to delete a custom shortcut menu:

1. Open the Customize dialog box and click the Toolbars tab, then select any toolbar. Since the shortcut menus are not in the list of toolbars, you need to select an available toolbar to get started.

2. Click Properties to open the Toolbar Properties dialog box.

3. In the Selected Toolbar box, choose the name of the shortcut menu you want to delete.

4. Choose Toolbar in the Type list to change it to a toolbar, then click Close to return to the Customize dialog box. The shortcut menu name is added to the list of toolbars.

5. Select the name of the shortcut menu in the list of toolbars and click Delete. Click OK to confirm the deletion.

Modify Command Bars

All changes to command bars are made with the Customize dialog box open. You can add more buttons, menus, and menu commands and rearrange them on the bar. The Rearrange Commands feature is new with Access 2003 and it provides a single platform for modifying command bars. The Rearrange Commands dialog box also gives you access to a shortcut menu where you can specify other settings and properties for individual commands.

You can modify a command bar only if it is visible when the Customize dialog box is displayed. Open the Customize dialog box and select all the toolbars you want to work on. Then select the Commands tab and click the Rearrange Commands button. The Menu Bar box in the Rearrange Commands dialog box contains a complete list of all the menus and submenus in the Menu Bar. In Figure 16-6, the File menu from the built-in Menu Bar is selected in the Menu Bar box and the menu items and submenus are displayed in the Controls box below.

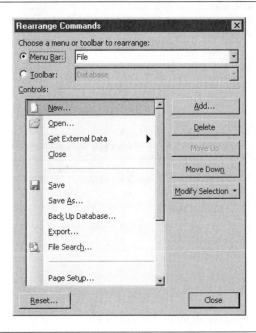

FIGURE 16-6   Opening the Rearrange Commands dialog box

16

You can select any of the menus in the Menu Bar and work with the menu commands and submenus contained in the menu. Figure 16-7 shows the Tools menu selected in the Menu Bar box with the list of commands and submenus it contains. If you want to work with the menu commands in one of the submenus, select it in the Menu Bar box. Then you will see the menu commands from that submenu in the Controls box.

To work with toolbars, click the Toolbar radio button. The Toolbar box displays a list of all the toolbars that are currently visible. Scroll down the list to select the one you want to work with.

Move Controls

To rearrange the controls in a toolbar, select the toolbar from the list of toolbars, then select the control you want to move. Clicking the Move Up button moves the control up one position. Clicking Move Down moves it down one position.

You can move individual commands in the Menu Bar from the Menu Bar box this way but you can't move the menus themselves. For example, suppose that you want to see the View menu first in the bar instead of the File menu. To move a menu in the Menu Bar, select Menu Bar from the list of toolbars. Then you see the list of the menus in the Controls pane. Select one and click Move Up or Move Down as before.

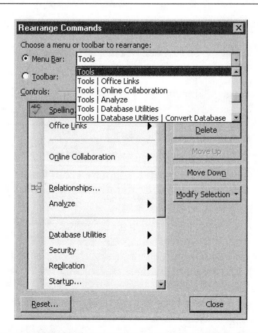

FIGURE 16-7   Selecting a submenu in the Menu Bar box

Add and Delete Controls

To add a new control to the Menu Bar or one of the toolbars, first select the control in the Controls list where you want to place the new control. It will be added before the selected control. Then click the Add button. The Add Command dialog box opens with the same collection of categories and commands you can see in the Commands tab of the Customize dialog box. Pick the category and select the command you want, then click the OK button.

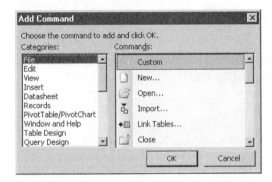

To delete a command from a toolbar, select the command in the Controls box and click the Delete button. You are not asked to confirm the deletion.

Edit Buttons and Menu Commands

If you want to make changes to an individual control's appearance or behavior, you can select the control and click the Modify Selection button. This opens the same shortcut menu that you may remember from previous versions of Access (see Figure 16-8).

Group Controls

When you have a set of buttons, commands, or menus that relate to similar operations, you can group them in a command bar by adding separator bars between controls. For example, the Print, Print Preview, and Spelling buttons appear in a group on the Database toolbar with a bar before Print and another after Spelling.

Use the Move Up or Move Down buttons to place the controls together. Then add a bar at the left of a button or menu, or above a menu command, by selecting the control and clicking the Modify Selection button. Choose Begin a Group from the menu. The Begin a Group option isn't available for a leftmost or top control in the command bar.

To remove the separator bar, repeat the process and clear the Begin a Group check mark.

Add and Edit Images

Built-in toolbar buttons and many of the built-in menu commands show icon images, which you can customize for your application. You can copy images from one button or command to

16

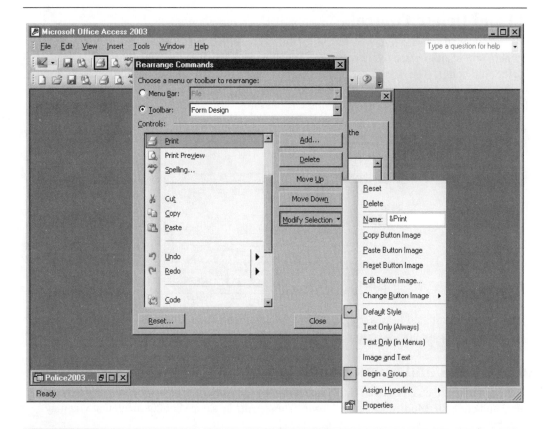

FIGURE 16-8   Editing buttons and menu commands

another, copy a graphics image from another program, choose from a palette of existing images, or even design your own image with the Image Editor.

Assign a Hyperlink

You can add a custom button or menu command to a command bar that jumps to a specified hyperlink in the current database, to another location on your hard drive or local network, or to a Web page. To add a hyperlink command, select the button or command in the Rearrange Commands dialog box and click the Modify Selection button. Select Assign Hyperlink from the shortcut menu. Select the hyperlink address you want to jump to in the Assign Hyperlink dialog box.

Change Control Properties

The last command on the Modify Selection shortcut menu opens the Control Properties dialog box, where you can make further modifications to the buttons, menus, and menu commands on a menu bar or toolbar. For example, set the Control Properties dialog box for the Filter By Selection button.

To change the properties of other controls on the current toolbar or menu bar without closing the dialog box, click the drop-down arrow next to the Selected Control box and choose from the list of controls.

Restore Built-in Command Bars

You can restore all or any part of a modified built-in command bar to the original default settings. Likewise, you can restore the entire toolbar or menu bar to show the original buttons and menus with or without restoring the original default properties. You can also choose to restore only certain individual menus, buttons, or commands.

When you restore an entire built-in toolbar or menu bar, Access displays all the buttons and commands in their original appearance and arrangement. The property settings for the toolbar or menu bar are also restored, including the screen location and size, and showing or hiding the bar, whichever was the toolbar or menu bar's original state.

To restore a toolbar or menu bar:

1. Open the Customize dialog box and click the Toolbars tab.

16

2. Click Properties to open the Properties dialog box. In the Selected Toolbar box, select the name of the toolbar or menu bar you want restored. Notice that the Toolbar Name and Type property boxes are dimmed because it is a built-in toolbar.

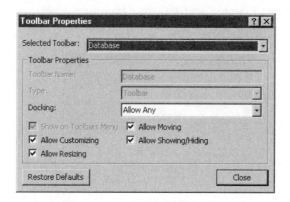

3. Click Restore Defaults and click Close.

   If you want to reset only the buttons and menus on a built-in toolbar, menu bar, or shortcut menu, you can do so from the Customize dialog box. On the Toolbars tab, choose the name of the toolbar or menu bar you want to restore and click Reset. If you want to reset a shortcut menu, select Shortcut Menus in the list of toolbars and click Reset. This resets all the shortcut menus you have modified.

   ■ You can restore the original settings of a single toolbar button or menu command in a toolbar, menu bar, or shortcut menu. To restore the settings, open the Customize dialog box and click the menu bar or toolbar that contains the settings you want to restore. The menu bar or toolbar appears on the screen behind the dialog box. Then right-click the object and choose Reset in the shortcut menu.

 If you restore a menu that appears in more than one menu bar, such as File or Edit, you also restore the menu in the menu bars for all other views that use that menu.

   If the button you want to restore opens a list of options, you cannot use the Reset command to change back to the default image. Instead, if you have changed the image on the built-in button or menu command and you want to restore it to the original image, right-click and choose Reset Button Image in the shortcut menu.

Chapter 17

Create Custom Switchboards and Dialog Boxes

How to...

- Create a switchboard with the help of the Switchboard Manager
- Modify a switchboard
- Create a custom dialog box
- Create a dialog box for user input

When creating an application for a user who wants to concentrate on its purpose and the special tasks it requires, you can add custom user interfaces. Two special-purpose forms can be added to an application to be used as switchboards for choosing activities or as dialog boxes for acquiring user input. A switchboard can offer the user a single point of entry into the application that displays a list of custom activities from which to choose. With a mere click on a switchboard item, the user branches to the operation. In this chapter, we will be working with the Bayview Police Department database that was introduced in Chapter 11.

Working with Windows applications, no doubt you are very familiar with dialog boxes and their many uses. A dialog box offers a set of options from which to choose such as which form or report to open, which filter to apply, or what action to take next. Custom dialog boxes can also prompt the user for data. You can create custom dialog boxes that contain options relevant to the application in easily understood text.

Create Switchboards

Switchboard is a term borrowed from the telephone industry that is used to indicate a single point of entry into an application. The switchboard offers a list of connections to activate next. When the Access Database Wizard creates a new database, it always adds at least one switchboard as the user interface. Figure 17-1 shows the main switchboard for the Order Entry database as created by the Database Wizard.

In addition to the main switchboard, two other switchboard pages are included in the user interface within the Order Entry database:

- The Forms Switchboard, reached by clicking Enter/View Other Information item.
- The Reports Switchboard, reached by clicking Preview Reports.

The ellipses (...) following each of those items tell the user that the choice opens secondary switchboard pages.

Access includes the Switchboard Manager to help make changes to wizard-built switchboards and create your own from scratch. Notice that one of the items on the Main Switchboard in Figure 17-1 is Change Switchboard Items, which launches the Switchboard Manager. Editing a switchboard created by the Database Wizard is the same as editing one you created with the Switchboard Manager.

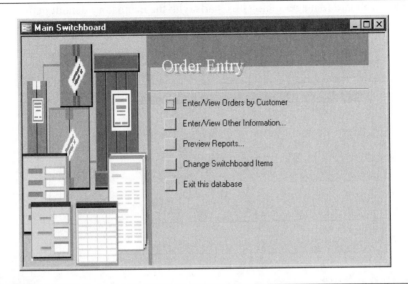

FIGURE 17-1 The Order Entry database main switchboard

Use the Switchboard Manager to Create Switchboards

The last piece of an application that is designed and created after all the forms, reports, and queries have been completed is the switchboard system. The switchboard system for a database consists of a hierarchical arrangement of switchboard *pages* beginning with the main switchboard and usually branching out to two or more subordinate pages. Each page contains a set of items with commands that carry out a specified activity. Most items also include an *argument* that specifies which form to open, which report to preview, which macro or procedure to run, and so on.

To start the Switchboard Manager, choose Tools | Database Utilities | Switchboard Manager. If your database already has a switchboard system, the Switchboard Manager window lists all the switchboard pages when it starts. If your database does not already have a valid switchboard, the Switchboard Manager displays a message asking if you want to create a new one. Click Yes.

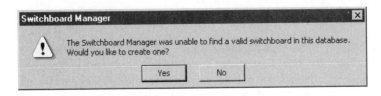

The first Switchboard Manager dialog box starts with the mandatory default main switchboard page.

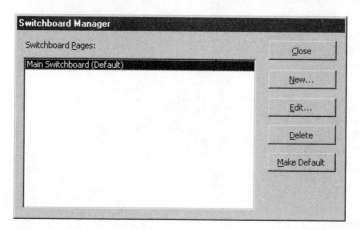

Add Items to the Page

If you are creating a new switchboard system, the first step is to add items to the main switchboard by selecting the page in the Switchboard Manager dialog box and clicking Edit. This opens the Edit Switchboard Page dialog box, which has only one available option at this time: New.

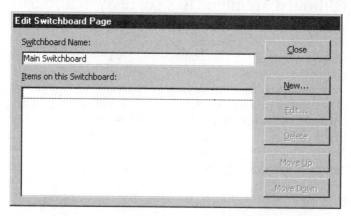

There are no items in the main switchboard for the Police database yet. Before adding them to the switchboard, enter **Bayview City Police** as the switchboard name in place of Main Switchboard. Add the list of items that you have decided should appear when the database starts up and click New to open the Edit Switchboard Item dialog box.

To be able to return to the main switchboard, always add an item at the end of the list on all switchboard pages except the opening switchboard. The item moves control back up the switchboard tree to the main switchboard. The opening switchboard should have an item that closes the database.

Three entries define a switchboard item; they are created by doing the following:

1. Enter the text you want to appear in the list of items in the Text box.

2. Choose the command you want from the drop-down list next to the Command box.

3. Depending on which command you choose, enter the command argument in the third box. The title of the box and the arguments vary with the command chosen.

To create an efficient switchboard system, place the buttons for the most commonly performed tasks on the main switchboard, then buttons for the secondary or subordinate activities on other pages. The activity most often carried out in the Police application is to look up or enter Alpha Card information in the Alpha Card form. This form also displays the Alpha Entry information in a subform. To begin the Police switchboard system:

1. Type **Enter/Edit Alpha Card Data** in the Text box in the Edit Switchboard Item dialog box.

You can use the ampersand (&) character in the item's text box to specify access keys for the items in the switchboard. For example, with Enter/Edit &Alpha Card Data, the user can either click the item or press ALT-A.

2. Click the drop-down arrow next to Command and choose Open Form in Edit Mode from the list of eight commands.

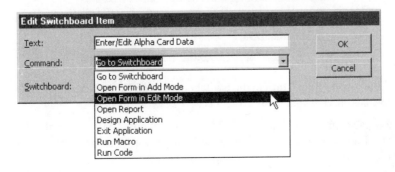

17

3. Click the drop-down arrow next to the Form (formerly Switchboard) box.

4. Choose Alpha Card from the list and click OK.

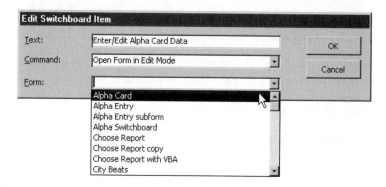

5. You return to the Edit Switchboard Page dialog box, where you now see the new item in the Items on This Switchboard list. Repeat the same steps to add the following two items to the main switchboard:

■ Enter/Edit Alpha Entry Data, which opens the Alpha Entry form in Edit mode.

■ Preview Alpha Card with Entries, which opens the Alpha Card with Entries report.

Add a New Switchboard Page

There are several more forms and reports that the Police database user might want to open but less frequently than those already added to the main switchboard. The less frequently used forms and reports can be grouped on secondary switchboard pages. To add a new page to the switchboard system:

1. Click Close to close the Edit Switchboard Page dialog box and return to the Switchboard Manager dialog box.

2. Click New. The Create New dialog box opens, in which you can start a new page.

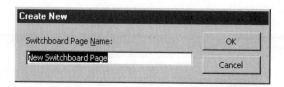

3. Type **Enter/Edit Other Data** in the Switchboard Page Name box and click OK. Include an ampersand if you want to specify an access key for this item.

4. The new page name is added to the list in the Switchboard Manager dialog box. Select the Enter/Edit Other Data switchboard page and click Edit to open the Edit Switchboard Page dialog box as before.

5. Click New to open the Create New dialog box as before and type **Enter/Edit City Beats**. Choose Open Form in Edit Mode from the Command list and City Beats from the Form list.

6. Repeat step 5 to add the following items to the list:

- Enter/Edit Name List, which opens the Name List form in Edit mode.
- Enter/Edit Entry Description, which opens the Explanation form in Edit mode.

7. Finally, add the item that returns to the main switchboard by typing **Return to Main Switchboard.** Choose Go to Switchboard from the Command list and choose Bayview City Police from the Switchboard list. Figure 17-2 shows the completed Edit/Enter Other Data page.

NOTE *As you add pages to the switchboard tree (the logical arrangement of switchboard branches), remember to add items to the main switchboard to branch to the page and add the item to the page that moves back up the tree. Otherwise, the user has no way to move from one page to another in the switchboard.*

The items are added to the page in the order in which you define them. If you need to rearrange them, select an item in the Edit Switchboard Page dialog box and click Move Up or Move Down to change its position in the list. Each click moves the item up or down one position.

To complete the Police switchboard system, create another page titled Preview Other Reports and add the items to it that will open other reports as specified in the item text:

- Alpha Entry
- Entries by Code

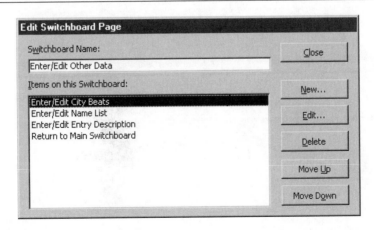

FIGURE 17-2 Items added to the Edit/Enter Other Data switchboard page

17

- Entries by Qtr
- Entries by Year
- Print Labels
- Return to Main Switchboard

When all the pages have been completed for the switchboard system, close the Switchboard Manager. The Switchboard form now appears in the Forms page of the Database window. Double-click the form name (Switchboard) to open the main switchboard form in Form view. Figure 17-3 shows the completed main switchboard for the Police database.

The Switchboard Manager has used the same colors and arrangement for your switchboard as the Database Wizard used for the Asset Tracking database. All it lacks is a picture to make it complete.

Add a Picture

The blank area at the left of the switchboard items in the Access template is intended for a company logo or other image. You can add a picture to the switchboard form just as with any other form. When you add a picture to one switchboard page, the same picture appears on all the pages.

When you open the switchboard form in Design view, you don't see any of the switchboard items you added to it. What you see is more of a template of how all switchboards look with blank command buttons and text boxes. The actual items are stored in a separate table, Switchboard

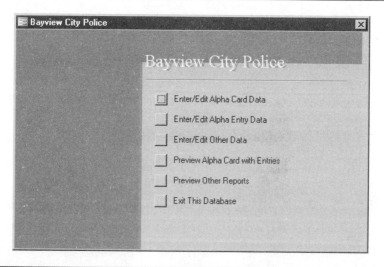

FIGURE 17-3   The new Police main switchboard

Items, which we discuss in the section "View the Switchboard Items Table." To add a picture to the switchboard, open the Switchboard form in Design view and do the following:

1. Choose Insert | Picture.

2. In the Insert Picture dialog box, locate the picture you want to use and click OK. Access places the picture in the upper-left corner of the form. It most likely covers up some of the switchboard.

3. Resize the picture to fit within the solid background.

4. Click the Properties toolbar button to open the property sheet for the picture and change the Size Mode property to Stretch. If the image is distorted, change the property to Zoom and resize the frame to fit the picture dimensions.

5. Switch to Form view and choose the Preview Other Reports item. Figure 17-4 shows the Preview Other Reports page of the completed switchboard.

NOTE *The picture used here is the contacts.gif file found in the Dbwiz subfolder in the Office\Bitmaps folder. It is one of the pictures used by the Database Wizard.*

Display the Switchboard at Startup

When you select a switchboard in the Switchboard Manager dialog box and click Make Default, you designate that page as the one to display when the Switchboard form opens. You still have to tell Access to display the default switchboard by setting the Display Form/Page option in the Startup dialog box to the Switchboard form.

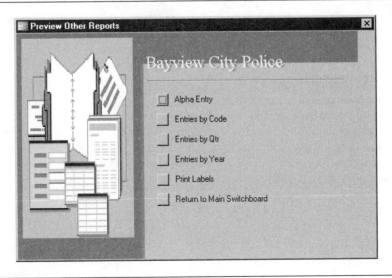

FIGURE 17-4 The completed Preview Other Reports switchboard page

Choose Tools | Startup, click the arrow next to the Display Form/Page box, and choose Switchboard from the list. The change takes effect the next time you start the database. To bypass the switchboard display after setting it as the default startup form, hold down SHIFT while the database opens.

Modify the Switchboard

To edit any item on a switchboard page, open the Switchboard Manager and use the Edit buttons. If the Database Wizard created the switchboard, open the Switchboard Manager by clicking Change Switchboard Items in the main switchboard. If you used the Switchboard Manager at first to create the switchboards, start the Switchboard Manager by choosing Tools | Database Utilities | Switchboard Manager and do the following:

1. Choose the switchboard you want to change and click Edit.

2. To add an item, click New and enter the text, then choose a command and an argument.

3. To change an item, select it and do one of the following:

   ■ To change the displayed text, the command, or the argument, click Edit.

   ■ To delete the item, click Delete.

   ■ To move the item in the list, click Move Up or Move Down.

4. Close the Switchboard Manager.

You can also delete an entire switchboard by selecting it in the Switchboard Pages dialog box and clicking Delete. The page and all its items are deleted.

To change the switchboard that displays when you start the database, select the switchboard you want to display instead and click Make Default. The startup option is still set to display the Switchboard form, but the Switchboard Manager has designated a different screen as the default switchboard. This will take effect the next time you open the database.

View the Switchboard Items Table

When you use the Switchboard Manager to create a switchboard, Access creates a new table named Switchboard Items. Each record in the table represents an item in one of the switchboard pages, and each field in the record describes what command the button carries out and the argument it uses. Figure 17-5 shows the table created for the Police database switchboards.

Table 17-1 describes the contents of the Switchboard Items table. You can widen the columns in the table, but don't make any other changes in the table design.

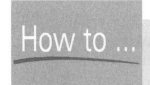

Change the Picture

Whether the Database Wizard added a picture to the switchboard or you inserted it in the one you created with the Switchboard Manager, you can swap it for another picture. The pictures the wizard uses are specially designed and sized for use in switchboards.

To change the picture to another special switchboard bitmap:

1. Open the Switchboard form in Design view.

2. Double-click the picture control to open its property sheet.

3. Click the Format tab, then click the Build (...) button next to the Picture property.

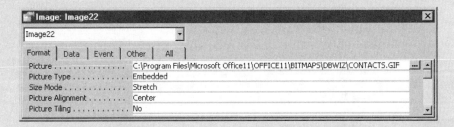

4. The Insert Picture dialog box opens where you can locate the image you want. The special images used by the Database Wizard usually are located in the Bitmaps\Dbwiz folder where you installed Office.

If you have selected a different type of image, you can replace it this way or delete the picture control and insert another as before by choosing Insert | Picture.

The first row of each switchboard contains 0 in both the ItemNumber and the Command field, indicating that the ItemText is the switchboard caption and is to be displayed in the title bar.

The Argument field needs a little explanation. The first row contains Default in the Argument field, indicating the Bayview City Police switchboard has been specified as the default switchboard

SwitchboardID	ItemNumber	ItemText	Command	Argument
1	0	Bayview City Police	0	Default
1	1	Enter/Edit Alpha Card Data	3	Alpha Card
1	2	Enter/Edit Alpha Entry Data	3	Alpha Entry
1	3	Enter/Edit Other Data	1	2
1	4	Preview Alpha Card with Entries	4	Alpha Card with Entries
1	5	Preview Other Reports	1	3
1	6	Exit This Database	6	
2	0	Enter/Edit Other Data	0	
2	1	Enter/Edit City Beats	3	City Beats
2	2	Enter/Edit Name List	3	Name List
2	3	Enter/Edit Entry Description	3	Explanation
2	4	Return to Main Switchboard	1	1
3	0	Preview Other Reports	0	
3	1	Alpha Entry	4	Alpha Entries
3	2	Entries by Code	4	Alpha Entry by Code Report
3	3	Entries by Qtr	4	Entries by Quarter
3	4	Entries by Year	4	Entries by Year
3	5	Print Labels	4	Labels Name List
3	6	Return to Main Switchboard	1	1
*	0			

Record: |◄| |◄| 1 |►| |►I| |►*| of 19

FIGURE 17-5   The Switchboard Items table

to be displayed at startup if the Display Form/Page option is set to Switchboard. A number in the Argument field represents the ID number of the switchboard as the goal of the command, Go to Switchboard. For example, the fourth row shows 2 in the Argument field, indicating that the command is to display switchboard number 2, Enter/Edit Other Data.

Field	Contents
SwitchboardID	A sequential number assigned to the switchboard page.
ItemNumber	A sequential number assigned to each item on a page, beginning with 1. Together with the SwitchboardID, forms the primary key that uniquely identifies the item and switchboard page. Switchboards have ItemNumber 0.
ItemText	Text entered in the Text box of the Edit Switchboard Item dialog box.
Command	Number representing the command selected from the Command list in the Edit Switchboard Item dialog box. Commands are numbered sequentially in the order they appear in the list. For a switchboard page itself, the Command value is 0.
Argument	Number of the switchboard; the name of form, report, macro, or procedure to be used by the command in the Command list in the Edit Switchboard Item dialog box.

TABLE 17-1   The Fields in the Switchboard Items Table

You Can Create a Switchboard
Without the Switchboard Manager

To create a switchboard from scratch, start with a blank form not bound to an underlying table or query; then add command buttons that trigger macros or event procedures to carry out the actions you want. The properties of a switchboard form are quite different from the normal data entry form, which shows record navigation buttons, scroll bars, and other data-related features. You are not creating a "real" switchboard with a corresponding table or that you can modify with the Switchboard Manager; you are instead creating a form that works like a switchboard but one over which you have a lot more control.

Before you place command buttons on the form, change some of the form properties so it will appear more like a switchboard:

- Enter the text you want to see in the switchboard title bar in the Caption property box.
- Make sure the Default View property is Single Form.
- Leave the Allow Form View property as Yes and change the other three Allow... properties to No.
- Change Scroll Bars to Neither to remove both the horizontal and vertical scroll bars.
- Change Record Selectors to No because there will be no data on the form.
- Change Navigation Buttons to No because the user will not be moving among records.
- Change Dividing Lines to No because the form won't display records.
- Set Auto Resize to Yes so the form will always appear the same size in Form view.
- Set Auto Center to Yes to ensure the form opens in the middle of the window; and thus will be easier to view and use.

The next step is to add to the form the command buttons and labels that will carry out the desired actions:

- If the switchboard item is designed to carry out a single action, such as open a form in Form view, you can use the Command Button Wizard to add a command button.
- If the item must carry out two or more actions, you must add the button without the Command Button Wizard and create a macro or Visual Basic event procedure to attach to the button's On Click event property.

By attaching a macro or procedure to the label and the button, and including access keys in the switchboard item labels, there are four ways to trigger the action: click the button, click the label, press ALT with the access key, or press TAB to move focus to the button and press ENTER. To attach the macro to both the button and the label, select them both; then open the Event tab of the Properties sheet and select the macro from the On Click property list.

17

Create a Custom Dialog Box

A dialog box is a special type of window that pops up and stays on the screen until you make a selection, even if it is only to cancel the box. Creating custom dialog boxes for an application is much like creating switchboards. You start with a blank, unbound form and add controls that you can select to carry out specific actions. After completing the form, you create macros or event procedures and attach them to the corresponding controls on the form.

Design the Form

In this section, we will create a dialog box that offers a choice of police reports when the user clicks the Print button on the Alpha Card form. There are four major steps in creating this custom dialog box. To create the Choose Report dialog box for the Police database:

1. Start a new form without choosing a table or query as a basis.

2. In form Design view, click the Toolbox button if the toolbox is not showing and make sure the Control Wizards button is pressed.

3. Click the Option Group control tool and draw a frame in the empty form design to start the Option Group Wizard.

4. In the first wizard dialog box (shown next), enter the label names for the options in the group. After entering a name, press the down arrow or TAB to move to the next line. If you press ENTER, you move to the next dialog box and have to check BACK to continue. After entering all the option labels, click Next.

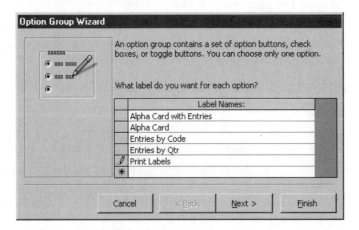

5. In the next wizard dialog box, accept the first option as the default returned value and click Next.

6. In the next dialog box, accept the default and click Next.

7. The next wizard dialog box (shown next) shows a variety of styles for the option group and the options in it. Choose Option Buttons as the type of control and Raised as the style, then click Next.

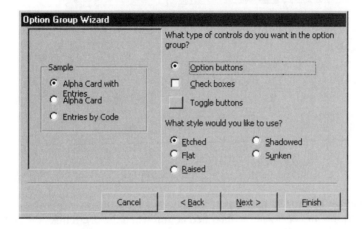

8. In the final wizard dialog box, enter **Choose Report** as the caption for the group that will be displayed at the top of the group frame, then click Finish.

9. Select the option group frame and open the property sheet. Choose the Name property on the Other tab and enter **Choose Report** as the name for the option group.

10. Click Finish.

11. Save and name the new form.

The next step is to add the command buttons to display the selected report in Print Preview, print the selected report, and close the form. Do this without the help of the Command Button Wizard because you want to attach macros to the buttons instead of using the default operations offered by the wizard. To add the three command buttons, make sure the Control Wizards button on the toolbox is not pressed, then do the following:

1. Click the Command Button tool and click in the form design. Repeat twice more, spacing the buttons as desired. The buttons will show the default captions as follows: Command*n*.

2. Select the first button, then click in it and type **Preview**. Press ENTER to save the new caption.

3. Repeat step 2 to change the default captions on the other two buttons to **Print** and **Cancel**.

4. If the buttons are not evenly spaced or accurately aligned, select all three and use the Format | Align or Format | Vertical Spacing command to adjust the buttons.

5. If the buttons are not the same size, choose Format | Size to adjust them.

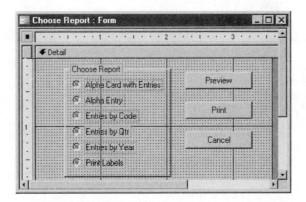

So far, the controls on the Choose Report form do not carry out an action. You must create the macros that will run and perform the intended action when the user clicks the control.

Create and Attach the Macros

You need a macro for each of the command buttons in the form. In addition, you must convey to the Print and Preview macros which report to open. The macros that you attach to the Preview and Print buttons must distinguish among the reports and open the one chosen in the option group.

The option group returns a value depending on which item in the group was selected. As you saw, the Option Group Wizard set default return values so that if you click the first item the group value is 1, if you click the second item the value is 2, and so on. You can use this value in the macro condition to choose the specific report to preview or print.

Create the Macro Group

The best way to respond to a selection from an option group is to build a set of macros that you can attach to each option in the group. To build a macro for the Preview button:

1. Click New in the Macros tab of the Database window and click the Macro Names and Conditions toolbar buttons to show the two optional columns.

2. Type **PreviewReports** as the name of the first macro and choose OpenReport as the Action.

3. In the Action Arguments pane, choose Alpha Card with Entries from the drop-down list of Report Names and choose Print Preview as the View argument.

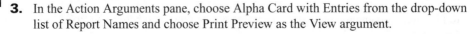

4. In the Condition column, enter the condition under which to preview the report: **[ChooseReport]=1**. ChooseReport is the name of the option group control, and 1 is the value of the group when you select the first item in the group.

> TIP *If you are in doubt about the name of the control, look at the Name property on the Other tab of the control's property sheet.*

5. Move to the next row and repeat steps 3 and 4 to open the Alpha Entry report in Print Preview with the condition that the ChooseReport group value is 2.

6. Continue to define macro actions to open the remaining reports in Print Preview. You should have six actions in the PreviewReports macro, each opening a different report in Print Preview.

7. You could add a final action to the macro that closes the Choose Report form so you can see the Print Preview window. Set the following arguments for the Close action:

   ■ Object Type—Form

   ■ Object Name—Choose Report

   ■ Save—No

8. Leave an empty row and create a new macro named PrintReports to print each of the reports using the same conditions. Do not include the Close action with the second macro, so the pop-up dialog box remains on the screen for further selections.

> TIP *An easy way to add the conditions to the PrintReports macro is to copy the [ChooseReport]= part of the condition and paste it in subsequent lines, then add the values.*

The macro command for the Cancel button can be simply Close with the Choose Report form name as the argument. Figure 17-6 shows the completed macro group from the Choose Report form.

Attach the Macros to Form Controls

Once you have created the macros, the next step is to indicate when they should execute by attaching them to the event properties of the controls. To attach the macros to the command buttons:

1. Double-click the Preview command button in the form Design view to open the property sheet.

2. Click the Events tab and choose the macro name from the drop-down list next to the On Click event property. Figure 17-7 shows the PreviewReports macro in the Choose Report macro group as the action to carry out when the button is clicked.

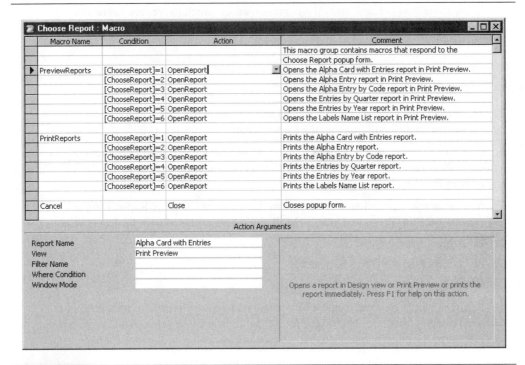

FIGURE 17-6 The macro group for the Choose Report form

3. Repeat steps 1 and 2 to attach the PrintReports macro to the Print button and the Cancel macro to the Cancel button.

Set Form Properties and Style

The last phase of creating a custom dialog box is to change some of the form properties to make it look and act more like a dialog box than a data entry form. A dialog box is a pop-up modal form. *Pop-up* means that it opens and stays on top of other windows even when it no longer is the active window. *Modal* means that you must hide or close the form before you can work in any other object or menu command.

To set these and some other properties, open the form in Design view and double-click the form selector to open the form property sheet. Set the form properties as described in Table 17-2. All of the properties are on the Format tab except PopUp and Modal, which are on the Other tab.

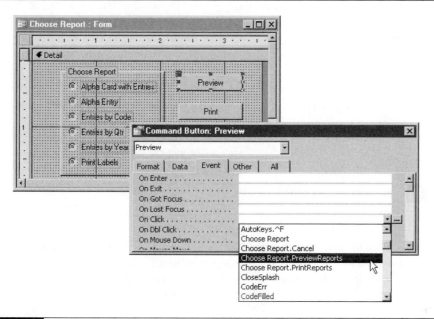

FIGURE 17-7   Attaching a macro to the Preview command button

Property	Setting	Purpose
PopUp	Yes	Form will remain on top of other windows.
Modal	Yes	Form retains focus until it is closed.
Caption	Choose Report	Displays text in the title bar in Form view instead of the form name.
Allow Form View	Yes	Permits the form in Form view.
Allow Datasheet View	No	Prevents switching to Datasheet view.
Allow PivotTable View	No	Prevents switching to PivotTable view.
Allow PivotChart View	No	Prevents switching to PivotChart view.
Scroll Bars	Neither	Removes scroll bars from the form.
Record Selectors	No	Removes record selectors from the form.

TABLE 17-2   Property Settings for a Custom Dialog Box

17

Property	Setting	Purpose
Navigation Buttons	No	Removes navigation buttons from the form.
Dividing Lines	No	Removes horizontal lines from the form.
Auto Center	Yes	Centers the form automatically when it opens. If you want the form to appear in a special place, set to No.
Border Style	Dialog	Form has a thick border and includes only a title bar with a control menu box.
Control Box	Yes	Displays the control menu box in the title bar in Form view so the user can close the form.
MinMax Buttons	None	Prevents the user from resizing the form in Form view.

TABLE 17-2 Property Settings for a Custom Dialog Box *(continued)*

Always leave the user a way to close the form, such as the control menu box, the Close button, or a button that runs a Close macro action. If you accidentally create and display a modal form without a way to close it, you can use ALT-F4 to close the form. Return to the Design view and add a visible option to close the form.

Two additional features that help turn a form into a dialog box are the default and Cancel buttons:

- The command button specified as the default button is pushed automatically when the user presses ENTER. The default button shows with a darker border than the rest of the buttons on the form.

- The command button specified as the Cancel button is pushed automatically when the user presses ESC.

You can assign any one button in the form as the default button and one other as the Cancel button by setting the Default or Cancel control property to Yes.

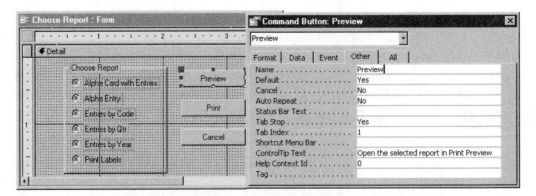

While you are working with the command button properties, you can add ScreenTips that will appear when you rest the mouse pointer over the button. To add ScreenTips, type the text in the button's ControlTip Text property box on the Other tab of the property sheet.

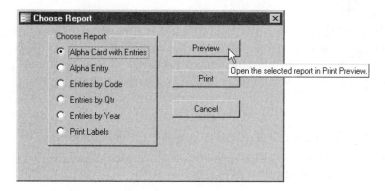

Create a Dialog Box for User Input

In Chapter 8, you saw how to create a parameter query that prompts the user to enter the criteria for the query. You can use a custom dialog box to accomplish the same thing. For example, the dialog box shown in the following illustration prompts the user to enter the DR value of the Alpha Entry records he or she wants to see. It includes instructions to ensure a valid input value.

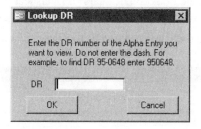

After you enter the DR value and click OK, a parameter query runs using the value as the criteria for the DR field. For this example, make a copy of the Alpha DR Query and name it **Lookup DR.** You can change the criteria of the DR column to get the value from the dialog box instead of a parameter prompt.

Set the Input Form Properties

There are several special features about the Lookup DR form in addition to the properties that make it a dialog box as described in the previous section. These include the following:

■ The DR box is an unbound text box named FindDR.

17

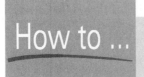 **Reduce Blank Space in a Dialog Box**

If the dialog box you built shows too much blank space in Form view, return to Design view and drag the right border in until it nearly touches the controls. You can't use the Window | Size to Fit Form command with this form because it is modal. This means you can't do anything outside the form while it is open—even click a toolbar button.

- The FindDR text box is first in the tab order with a Tab Index property of 0.
- The OK command button Default property is set to Yes so the user can simply press ENTER after typing the DR value to run the query.
- The Cancel command button Cancel property is set to Yes so the user can press ESC to close the dialog box.

Create the Macros

The LookUpDR macro group contains two macros, one for each command button:

- The Run Query macro, which is attached to the OK button, contains two actions: OpenQuery, which runs the Lookup DR query in Datasheet view in read-only mode, and Close, which closes the Lookup DR form after running the query.
- The CloseForm macro closes the Lookup DR form without running the query.

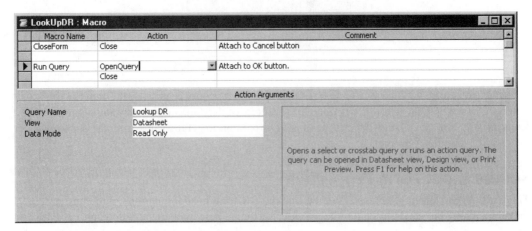

Modify the Query

To pass the DR value from the form to the query, the Criteria must be set to the unbound text box control in the form. To do this, type **[Forms]![Lookup DR]![FindDR]** in the Criteria row of the DR column in the query grid.

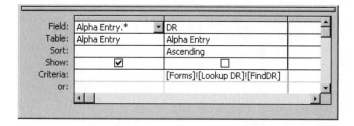

Each of the three parts of the statement is enclosed in square brackets to indicate that it is an identifier that refers to an object or control. The first element defines the object type, Forms; the exclamation point (!) indicates that the element that follows was named by the user. The second element identifies the specific form, Lookup DR, and the third identifies the unbound text box control, FindDR, in the form.

TIP   *Be sure to clear the check box in the Show row of the DR column; otherwise, the query results will have two copies of the DR values.*

Part IV

Exchange Data with Others

Chapter 18

Exchange Database Objects and Text

How to...

- Copy objects from one Access database to another
- Import or link database objects and text files objects
- Use imported or linked tables
- Export database objects and text files

You can get your development work done faster if you don't have to create everything from scratch. Access provides a number of useful functions and tools that enable you to exchange database objects between Access databases. You can even exchange Access objects with other types of databases such as dBASE, Paradox, or SQL tables and databases that support the Open Database Connectivity (ODBC) protocol. You also can make use of text files in Access or send Access data out as text.

Copy Objects among Access Databases

It is often easier to modify an existing object than it is to develop a table, form, or report from scratch. The first step in the modification of existing Access database objects is to copy the objects you want to edit. Standard copy-and-paste operations and drag-and-drop techniques can be used to copy objects from one Access database to another.

Copy and Paste

To copy and paste an Access database object, first select the object you want to copy in the Database window. With the new Office 2003 clipboard, you can copy as many as 24 objects before you need to paste them into their ultimate destination and clear space for more copied objects.

For example, to make a copy of the Alpha Card table in the Police database:

1. Click Tables under Objects in the Database window.

2. Select the Alpha Card table from the list of tables.

3. Use one of the following to copy the table to the clipboard:
   - Click the Copy toolbar button.

   - Choose File | Copy.
   - Right-click the table name and choose Copy from the shortcut menu or press CTRL-C.

If you want to copy the table to the same database, there are three ways to paste the table:

- Click the Paste toolbar button.

- Select Edit | Paste.
- Right-click in the Tables page outside any table name and choose Paste from the shortcut menu or press CTRL-V.

When you copy a table, the Paste Table As dialog box asks for a name for the table and presents the following options:

- Pasting the structure of the table (without its data)
- Pasting the structure of the table and its data
- Appending the data to an existing table

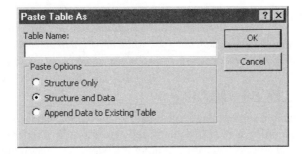

TIP   *If you choose to paste the data to an existing table, you might have problems with duplicate primary key fields or unique index values. You also need to consider differing table structures. See Chapter 8 for information on solving problems with append queries.*

If you want to copy an object to another Access database instead of within its own database with a different name, do the following:

1. Start up a second instance of Access and open the destination database.
2. Choose Windows | Tile Vertically to tile the two Access windows in a split screen format.
3. Copy the object in the source database.
4. Select the object category in the destination Database window and paste it into the destination database.

If you don't want to use two instances of Access, close the source database after you copy the object, then open the corresponding object page in the destination database and click Paste.

NOTE   *Copying an object generates a copy of all the properties of that object. For example, when a form is copied, the format, source data, event specifications, filters, and all other properties are copied with the form.*

Drag and Drop

A drag-and-drop technique can also be used to copy objects between databases. To use drag and drop, you need to have two instances of Access active at the same time.

18

To drag an object from one window to another:

1. Make sure both Database windows are open to the same object page, then select the object you want to copy in the source database.

2. While holding the left mouse button down, drag the item to the destination database.

3. Release the mouse button; the new object appears in the destination database.

When drag-and-drop techniques are used to copy tables, the Paste Table As dialog box does not appear. As a result, when tables are copied this way, the table structure and its data are pasted into the destination database while the original object remains in the source database. If you want just the structure, open the copied table and delete all the records.

Import or Link Access Data

Two other important techniques for adding Access data to an Access database or project are *importing* and *linking*. Importing is used to actually copy Access data or other objects into an Access database from other Access databases. Linking is a way of connecting to and using data in an Access database without actually copying the data from the other database.

You can import or link data from Access versions 2.0, 7.0/95, 8.0/97, 9.0/2000, and 10.0/2002 to Access 2003 databases.

NOTE   *If you are importing or linking a database that requires a password, you must enter the password before you can proceed.*

Import Objects

You can import every object in a database but let's start with the simplest case. The first case to look at is the importing of a couple of objects from one Access database to another. To import the objects:

1. Choose File | Get External Data | Import. The Import dialog box opens (see Figure 18-1) where you locate and select the database file that contains the objects you want to import. You can also right-click in the Database window and choose Import from the shortcut menu. Make sure the Files of Type box in the Import dialog box shows Microsoft Office Access.

2. When you locate the database file from which you want to import objects, select it and click Import. The Import Objects dialog box opens where you choose the objects to import. In this example, the Northwind database is selected from sample Access applications, and the Products and Categories tables are imported.

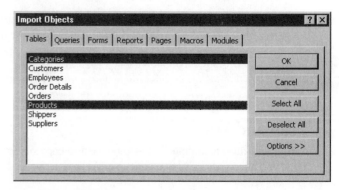

FIGURE 18-1   Choosing a file in the Import dialog box

3. To choose which objects to import, click the desired object tab and do one of the following:

- Select each object name individually.
- Click Select All.
- To remove an object from the import list, select it again, or click Deselect All to remove all selected objects.

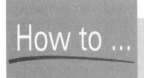

Choose Whether to Import or Link

You should choose to import data into an Access database if you expect to use the data only in Access and not depend on another program to maintain the data. Access is more efficient when working with its own tables and you can modify the data just the same as native-grown data.

You should link with data in another program if you rely on the source program to update the information. Linking is also useful in a multiuser environment where you split an existing database and place the data on a network server. Users can then share the database and create their own forms, reports, and other objects.

4. Repeat step 3 for all the desired object types.

5. After selecting all the objects you want to import, click OK to return to the Database window, where you can see the objects that have been imported.

Figure 18-2 shows the Police Database window with the newly imported Categories and Products tables. The imported tables are now part of the Police database and do not appear different from the native tables.

If you import a table that includes Lookup fields, you must remember to import the tables or queries to which the fields refer and from which they get their values. If you don't want to or can't import the supporting value tables or queries, you can change the imported table design by changing the field Display Control property on the Lookup tab to Text Box for each Lookup field.

If you try to import a table that is already linked to another table, you link to the source table data instead of importing it.

Set Import Options

There are several options you can set to customize the import process. When you click Options in the Import Objects dialog box, the box expands to show a lower pane with three sets of import options.

The first set of options presents other table features that can be imported:

■ The Relationships option is selected by default and includes the relationships you have defined for the tables and queries you import.

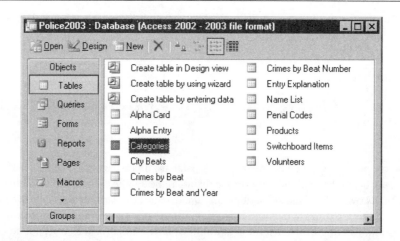

FIGURE 18-2 The Database window includes imported tables.

- The Menus and Toolbars option includes all the custom menus and toolbars in the database from which you are importing. However, Access will not import any menu or toolbar that has the same name as one in the destination database.

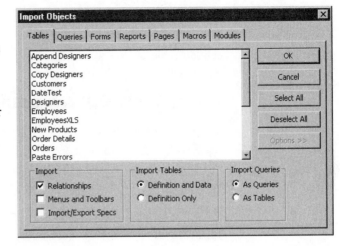

- The Import/Export Specs option includes all the import and export specifications set for the source database. See the section "Import and Link Text Files" for information about setting import specifications.

The second set of options, Import Tables, determines whether to import both the table definition and the data (default) or only the definition. This is useful for creating a copy of the table structures for a new database without including any existing data.

The third set of options, Import Queries, applies to any queries you have selected to import and specifies whether to import queries as queries (the default setting) or run the query and import the resulting recordset as a table.

Once opened, the Options pane remains open as you click other object tabs.

When choosing which objects to import, consider the options carefully. For example, importing a form without importing its underlying tables or queries can result in problems that might be difficult to resolve. Logical, useful groupings of objects should be imported together. This means that tables should be imported to provide the field definitions and data for all the forms, queries, reports, pages, macros, and modules you choose to import.

Link Access Tables

Linking to tables in another Access database makes them available without copying them into the active database. Linking saves space and reduces the need to maintain redundant data. Linking also ensures that you always have access to current information. However, linking also means that you are dependent on an object that actually resides in another environment, where it can be renamed, moved, or deleted.

To link to a table in another Access database:

1. Open the destination database—in this example, Police.

2. Start the linking process by choosing File | Get External Data | Link Tables from any page in the Database window. You can also right-click in the Database window and choose Link Tables from the shortcut menu.

18

3. In the Link dialog box, select the Microsoft Office Access file type and then select the database that you want to link to your active database.

4. Click Link. The Link Tables dialog box opens, showing only a Tables tab because tables are the only Access objects to which you can link.

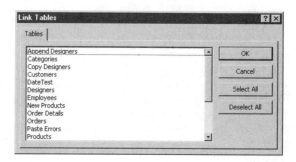

5. Select one or more of the available tables and click OK.

In this example, the Suppliers table is linked to the Police database, as shown by the arrow next to the table icon.

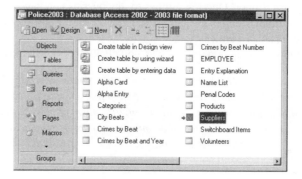

Import from or Link to Other Data Sources

Access can import data or link to existing tables in other database management systems. Access provides specific recognition of some database table formats. Acquiring data and other objects from foreign databases is not much different than importing or linking Access databases.

You can both import and link dBASE III, IV, 5, and 7 files as well as Paradox 3.x, 4.x, 5.0, and 8.0 files. For version dBASE 7 and Paradox 8.0, you need the updated ISAM drivers available from Microsoft Technical Support.

You can also import and link data from ODBC data sources such as the Microsoft SQL Server and Visual FoxPro. You will need a connection to the appropriate ODBC data source and the data source defined.

Data types are generally compatible among these database management systems, although they aren't labeled consistently. For example, dBASE Character and Paradox Alphanumeric data types both become Text fields in Access. dBASE Float and Paradox Currency types become Number fields in Access with the Field Size property set to Double. dBASE calls Yes/No fields Logical.

Use Data from dBASE or Paradox

Importing a dBASE table or a Paradox file into an Access database is similar to importing a table from an Access database. Other database programs such as FileMaker Pro can export .dbf formatted files that you can import into Access the same as an original dBASE file. For example, to import a dBASE table:

1. Choose File | Get External Data | Import or right-click in the Database window and choose Import from the shortcut menu.

2. In the Files of Type box in the Import dialog box, select the database file type—dBASE IV in this example. Locate and select the file you want to import.

3. Select the filename—Employee.dbf in this example—and click Import.

4. After a few seconds, you should see a message indicating Employee.dbf has been successfully imported into the open Access database.

5. Click OK, then locate and import other files as necessary or click Close to close the dialog box and return to the Police database window.

Once the table is imported, it looks and behaves just like an Access table. You use the same procedure to import Paradox files.

Another approach to making use of data from a dBASE or Paradox database is to use the Link Tables operation by choosing File | Get External Data | Link Tables. You can also right-click in the Database window and choose Link Tables from the shortcut menu. The Link dialog box appears, in which you select the appropriate file type and the specific file to be linked.

When you import a dBASE file, Access creates a table with the same name as the .dbf file and imports the data. Conversely, when you link to a dBASE file, Access also requires that the associated dBASE index files be linked. If you choose to link to a dBASE file, the Select Index Files dialog box appears, in which you can choose the indexes (.ndx and .mdx files) that are associated with the .dbf file.

■ If there are none, click Cancel and proceed with the link operation.

■ If you select one or more index files, the Select Unique Record Identifier dialog box prompts you to select the corresponding index field. Your index must have a unique value for each record, or difficulties might occur when you try to update records.

After importing or linking a dBASE file, you can set field properties for the table. If you import a file with no primary index, you can set the index in Access. When you update the file with Access, the index is also automatically updated. If you use dBASE to update the file, you must also update the corresponding index in dBASE before trying to open the file in Access.

18

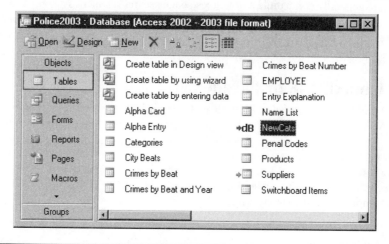

FIGURE 18-3   A linked dBASE file in the Access Database window

Figure 18-3 shows a linked dBASE file in the Database window by displaying the arrow and a dB icon indicating that NewCats is a linked dBASE file.

If you select a Paradox table to link to, you need the index (.px) file and the memo (.mb) file (if the table has any). Without these files you will not be able to open the linked table in Access. If the Paradox table does not have a primary index, you must create one in Paradox to be able to update the table in Access.

Work with Linked or Imported Tables

You can use linked or imported tables the same as any other Access table, with some precautions. Imported tables essentially have become new tables within your Access database. However, linked tables still reside within the environments in which they were created. Thus, issues such as renaming the table or changing its characteristics have implications for relating the linked table to its original source environment.

Rename a Linked Table in Access

The linked table might have a name that is not very meaningful in your Access database. You can give it a more relevant name without disturbing the link. Select the table in the Database window and choose Edit | Rename or right-click the table and choose Rename from the shortcut menu, then edit the old name or enter a new name.

Change Linked Table Properties

The database that owns a table usually sets the table properties of linked tables. The source database also sets the field properties and validation rules. Data entered in the table from within Access must conform to most of the properties set for the originating database fields such as default values, minimum or maximum values, field format, text options, and any other validation requirements.

Field properties that you can change in a linked table from within Access include Format, Decimal Places, Input Mask, and Caption. If you want to change other field properties in a form, set them for the controls that are bound to the fields.

Update Links with the Linked Table Manager

When the location of a linked table is changed, use the Linked Table Manager database utility to reestablish the proper path or link to the table. The Linked Table Manager does not physically move files; it only updates the path leading to the file location. There are two cases in which the Linked Table Manager might be consulted:

- To examine or refresh links
- To change the path or location of linked tables

To refresh links:

1. Select Tools | Database Utilities | Linked Table Manager. The Linked Table Manager dialog box displays a list of all tables linked to the current database with the table name and the current path.

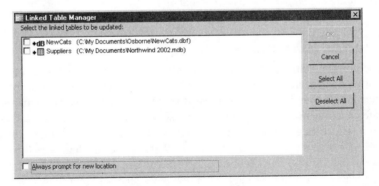

2. Click Select All or check only the table links you want to refresh, then click OK.

3. If the Linked Table Manager is successful in locating the file, it displays a message to that effect. If not, the manager prompts for the location of the table by displaying a Select New Location of *Tablename* dialog box where you can locate the file and change the path.

18

The Linked Table Manager has no way of refreshing links to tables whose names were changed in the source database after linking. Delete the current link and start over.

To change the path to a linked table, open the Linked Table Manager as in the preceding list and do the following:

1. Select the Always Prompt for New Location option in the Linked Table Manager dialog box.

2. Check the tables whose links you want to change, then click OK.

3. Designate their new location in the Select New Location of *Tablename* dialog box, then click Open. The Linked Table Manager verifies that all selected tables were successfully refreshed.

4. Click OK to close the message box, then click Close.

Unlink Tables

Unlinking a table removes the linkage only to a table in another (source) database. The procedure for unlinking a table is identical to that for deleting a table; however, the Delete function does not actually delete the linked table. It deletes only the link to the database.

If your intention is to delete a link to a table in another database and not to actually delete a complete table and its data, be sure to select a table name with the arrow indicating it is a linked table. If you inadvertently select a regular table (as opposed to a linked table) and perform a Delete, the table and its data will be lost.

Import and Link Text Files

Text files are useful when you import or link the data to Access tables. If no other common data format exists between the source of the data and Access, you can create a text file with the source program and then import that file into Access. Most relational, hierarchical, or network-oriented database management systems can generate a text version of the data using some kind of record selection function. Text files are either *fixed-width* (files consisting of rows of data of the same length) or *delimited* text files (files containing records that use special characters to indicate the separation between data fields). Most delimited text files also use a *text qualifier*—usually double quotation marks—to delimit strings. After you have generated text files, you can import or link them to an Access database using the same external data importing and linking functions used for data from any source.

Use Delimited Text Files

Importing or linking a delimited text file begins with the same sequence as other importing and linking operations. However, prior to starting the importing/linking process, you must specify a table ready to receive the data—either a new table structure with the appropriate field definitions or an existing table to which this new data can be appended.

NOTE *You can create a new table to receive the data from delimited text files by using basic table design techniques (see Chapter 3) or by copying the table structure from an existing table. Be careful to account for the proper number of fields, field length, and data type selection to import text data correctly.*

To import a text file, open the Import dialog box as before, then do the following:

1. In the Import window, select Text Files in the Files of Type box.

2. Locate and select the text file that you want to import and click Import.

3. The Import Text Wizard dialog box appears, displaying sample data from the selected text file. The Import Text Wizard analyzes the selected file and determines whether it is a fixed-width text file or a delimited file. Figure 18-4 shows that the text file we are importing, SENIORS.TXT, is a delimited text file.

4. Click Next to see how the file is formatted. In the case illustrated here (see Figure 18-5), the wizard has determined that the fields in this file are delimited by commas, text fields are bounded by quotation marks, and the first row does not contain field names.

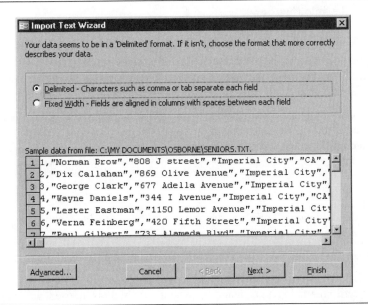

FIGURE 18-4 The Import Text Wizard determines the type of text file.

18

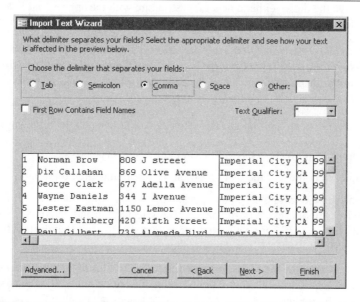

FIGURE 18-5 The Import Text Wizard determines the file's characteristics.

5. Do one of the following:

■ If you agree with the results of the Import Text Wizard's processing, click Next.

■ If you do not agree, adjust the selections (for the delimiting character, the text qualifier, and whether the first row contains field names) until you are satisfied that they are accurate, then click Next.

6. At this point you must decide whether to import the data to a new table or append to an existing table. If you select to append the data to an existing table, select a table name from the drop-down list and click Finish.

> **NOTE** *You can append text files to an existing table only if the first row of the text file matches the table's field names.*

7. Because the field names are not in the first row of the text table, choose to import the data to a new table and click Next.

8. The Import Text Wizard asks you to specify information about each field in the file (see Figure 18-6).

9. Enter or verify the field name, data type, whether the field is indexed, and whether you want to import or skip that field. The wizard names the fields Field1, Field2, and so on, but you can rename them. Click in the field column to make changes.

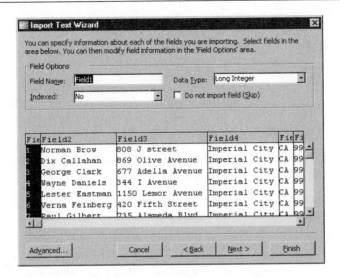

FIGURE 18-6   Setting imported field information

10. After completing the field information, click Next; the wizard suggests specifying a primary key field by letting the wizard add one or by specifying an existing field, or you can choose not to have a primary key (see Figure 18-7). Click Next.

11. Enter a name for the new table and click Finish.

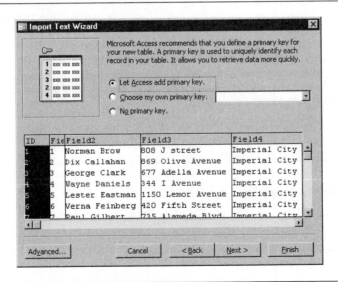

FIGURE 18-7   Adding a primary key

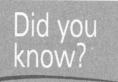

About Import Errors

It is possible that improperly defined data or data of an improper length could cause errors. If this occurs, Access creates an Import Errors table containing descriptions of the errors. The table shows the field names and row numbers of the data that caused the error.

Some of the possible import errors are:

- **Field Truncation**   Occurs when the text value is longer than the Field Size property setting for the destination field.

- **Type Conversion Failure**   Occurs when a value is the wrong data type for the destination field.

- **Key Violation**   Occurs when a duplicate primary key value appears.

- **Validation Rule Failure**   Occurs when a field value breaks the rule defined in the Validation Rule property for the destination field.

- **Null in Required Field**   Occurs when the Required property of the destination field is set to Yes and a Null value occurs.

- **Unparsable Record**   Occurs when a text value contains a character specified as the text delimiter character.

If the problem is with the data, edit the file. If you're trying to append data to an existing table, you may need to change the table definition. After correcting the problems, import the file again. When a value contains the delimiter character, edit each field to repeat the character twice. When you finish, check the destination files to make sure that some of the records do not have duplicate copies.

TIP   *If the import process seems to be taking a long time, errors could be occurring. Press CTRL-BREAK to cancel any time during the process.*

Linking delimited text files with the Link Text Wizard is the same as importing, with two exceptions: you are not asked if you want to link to an existing table or create a new one, and you are not prompted for a primary index because you are not creating a new table.

Use Fixed-Width Text Files

The Import Text Wizard reacts a little differently once fixed-width text files are detected. The second wizard dialog box (see Figure 18-8) shows the fixed-length data with vertical lines between fields and a ruler at the top. The wizard asks you to confirm whether the lines indicate

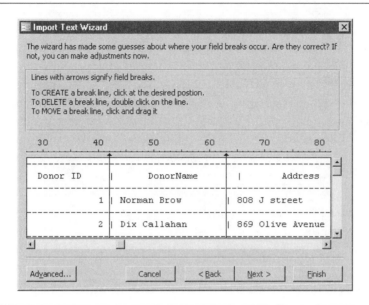

Importing a fixed-width text file

the proper separation point between fields and provides guidance for how to move or reposition the lines:

- To create a line, click at the position where a field separation is desired. Two lines have been added in Figure 18-8.
- To delete a line, double-click the line to remove the field separation.
- To move a line, click and drag the line to the proper position.

Once adjustments are completed, the process of identifying the destination table and completing the import or link is the same as with delimited files.

Change Import Specifications

You can change the import specifications for a text file using the Advanced features of the Import Text Wizard. Click the Advanced button in the Import Text Wizard dialog box to display the Import Specification dialog box (Figure 18-9), which enables you to specify a number of table characteristics, including:

- The file format (delimited or fixed-width)
- If delimited, the field delimiter and text qualifier characters

18

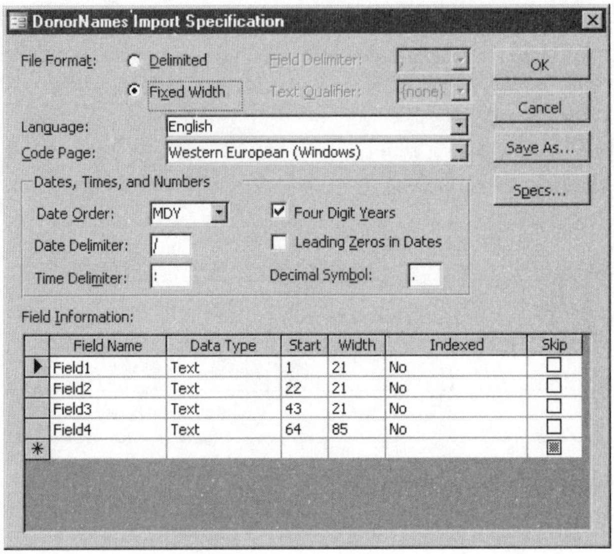

FIGURE 18-9 Setting the import specifications

- The language and code page

- The specifications for dates, times, and numbers

- Information for each incoming field such as name, starting and ending position in the record, data type, whether the field is to be indexed, and whether to omit the field from the import

Once the text file characteristics have been satisfactorily specified, the OK button returns you to the Import Text Wizard dialog box, where clicking the Finish button will complete the text import action and place the table in your Access database.

Export to an Existing Access Database

Exporting data or database objects to another Access database has the same functionality as copying and pasting. Once in their destination database, the objects look and behave like the native objects. The same data formats are supported as with importing.

To export a table:

1. Select the table name in the Database window and choose File | Export or right-click the table name and choose Export from the shortcut menu.

2. In the Export Table To dialog box, locate and select the destination database, and select the export file type in the Save as Type box (see Figure 18-10).

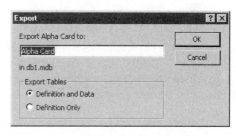

3. Click Export.

4. Accept the existing name or enter a new name for the destination table in the Export dialog box and select to export both the table definition and data or only the definition.

5. Click OK.

When you are exporting database objects other than tables, the basic steps are the same with the exception that the final step is not required because you are exporting only an object design without any data.

You can export only one database object at a time. If you need to export multiple objects to an Access database, it might be quicker to open the destination database and choose File | Get External Data | Import, which can be used to import multiple objects at once.

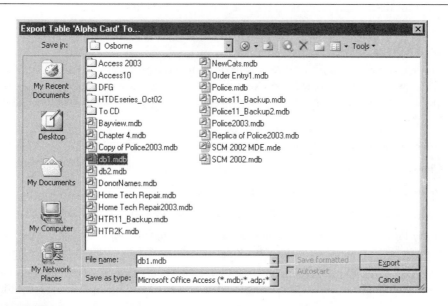

FIGURE 18-10   Choosing a destination in the Export Table To dialog box

18

Export to Another Database Format

Access supports exporting data to the same database, and text formats are acceptable for importing and linking. Access also can export data in the proper formats for other applications such as spreadsheets (Excel and Lotus 1-2-3) and text files such as RTF and Wordfiles as discussed in the next chapter.

 When you export data to older database programs such as dBASE or Paradox, both of which limit table names to eight characters (not including the file extension), the longer table names are truncated to comply with the limitation. This can result in duplicate names. To prevent this, make a copy of your table with a shorter name before exporting the copy.

To export data to these formats:

1. Select the table in your active database and select File | Export, or right-click the table name and choose Export from the shortcut menu.

2. In the Export Table To dialog box, choose the dBASE or Paradox file format in the Save as Type box.

3. Click the arrow next to Save In and select the drive and folder to which to export.

4. Enter the destination filename in the File Name box and click Export.

Export to Text Files

When you want to export data from an Access database to a text file, call upon the Export Text Wizard, which works much like the Import Text Wizard. The wizard helps you specify the format of the exported Access file and determine where to store the output. To export data to a text file using the Export Text Wizard:

1. Select the table containing the data you want to export to a text file.

2. Choose File | Export or right-click the table and choose Export from the shortcut menu.

3. In the Export Table To dialog box, select Text Files in the Save as Type box.

4. In the Save In box, select the folder that will receive the exported text data.

5. In the File Name box, enter the name of the text file that you want to assign to the exported data or select an existing file to receive the data. Click Export.

6. The Export Text Wizard dialog box (see Figure 18-11) displays data from the selected table. You can choose between saving the data as a fixed-width or a delimited text file.

7. Click Next.

8. If you chose Delimited, the next dialog box (see Figure 18-12) contains the specifics of the delimiters, text qualifiers, and other features of each field.

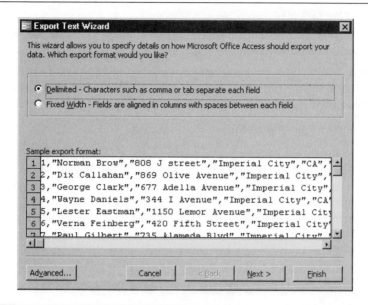

FIGURE 18-11   Selecting the text file type with the Export Text Wizard

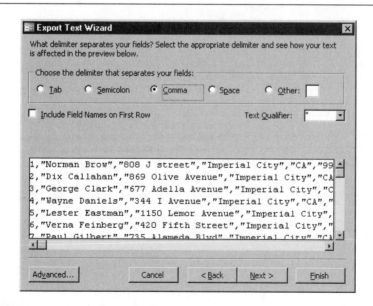

FIGURE 18-12   Setting the text file characteristics with the Export Text Wizard

18

9. If you agree with the default settings, click Next.

10. If you do not agree, adjust the selections (for the delimiting character, the text indicator, and whether the first row contains field names). Click Next.

11. If you chose Fixed Width, the next dialog box asks for verification of the field lengths. Figure 18-13 shows the same table being exported as fixed-width. You can drag the divider lines left or right to adjust the width of the fields.

12. Click Finish to complete the export.

You can also use the Export Text Wizard to customize the export specifications for a text file the same way you set the import specifications with the Import Text Wizard. When you click the Advanced button in the Export Text Wizard, an Export Specification dialog box appears, allowing you to specify the file format (fixed-width or delimited); the language and code page settings; the specifications for dates, times, and numbers; and field information. The options are the same as for importing.

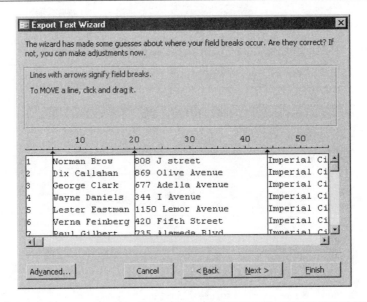

FIGURE 18-13 Exporting the text as fixed-width

Chapter 19

Exchange Data with Outside Sources

How to...

- Copy or move records
- Save Access output as an external file
- Work with Word
- Work with Excel

The last chapter focused on exchanging data within the Access management realm, with other database management systems, and with text files. In this chapter, we investigate how to exchange information between an Access database and an outside source—a word processor or a spreadsheet. A successful exchange of data with these outside sources involves a sequence of steps that ensure that the end result will be useful.

Copy or Move Records

To copy or move records from other applications into Access, you must make sure that the data is arranged in an appropriate format and then use the selection, copy, and paste functions in Access to move the records you want. You can bring data into Access from several different word processors and spreadsheets.

Copy or Move Data from a Word Processor

There are two approaches to copying or moving records from a table created with a word processor. The first approach is to save the desired records to a text file with fixed-length or delimited records and import them into the target table as described in the previous chapter.

The second approach is to perform a copy (or cut)-and-paste operation. For this approach to work properly, you should know two major things:

- The records in the word processing file must already be in a table or be properly separated by tab characters.
- The columns in the word processor table must be in the same order as the fields in the Access table you are targeting.

When you copy and paste the data, you place a copy of that data in the destination file and leave the original data alone in the source file. When you cut and paste the data, you actually delete it from the source and place it in the target file. You can add new records to either a datasheet or a form.

If you are adding records to a datasheet, the columns are not required to have the same names as the fields but the data being copied or moved should be the same data type. If you are adding records to a form, the data is copied or moved to text box controls, which are bound to table fields and have the same names as those of the incoming data columns. If the column names don't match the control names or the columns have no names, the data is moved or copied to the form in the tab order.

On the receiving end, you can replace existing records or add to the records already in the datasheet or form. To replace records in a datasheet, select the same number of records to eliminate as you selected to bring in from the word processor. In a form, you can replace only the current record.

To move or copy word processing data:

1. In the word processor application, select the records that you want to move or copy using the selection method provided by the application, shown here:

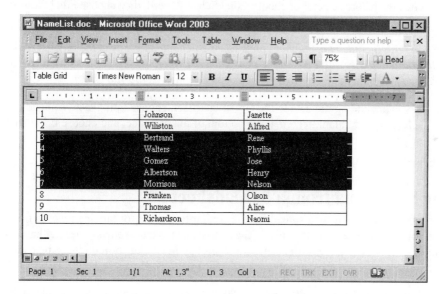

2. Do one of the following, both of which place the selected records on the clipboard:

   ■ If you want to copy the records, choose Edit | Copy or click the Copy toolbar button or press CTRL-C.

   ■ If you actually want to move the records from the word processing file to the Access database, choose Edit | Cut, click the Cut toolbar button, or press CTRL-X.

 In Word, you can also right-click the selection and choose Cut or Copy from the shortcut menu. Other word processing programs have different methods for placing text on the clipboard. If the application from which you are getting the records does not have the Cut and Copy commands, use the comparable commands to place the data on the Windows clipboard.

19

3. Open the Access datasheet or form you want to receive the records, then do one of the following:

■ To replace records in Datasheet view, select the records you want to replace and then choose Edit | Paste, click the Paste toolbar button, or press CTRL-V. If you select fewer records in the target than in the source table, the selected records are replaced and the excess records from the source table are ignored. If you select more records in the target table, they are replaced with the records selected in the source table beginning at the top of the table; the excess selection in the target table is untouched.

■ If you are replacing a record in a form, move to the record you want to replace and click the record selector or choose Edit | Select Record, then choose Edit | Paste, click the Paste toolbar button, or press CTRL-V.

 If you have included the column labels when you copied or moved the records to the clipboard and they don't match the field names in the form, Access asks whether you want to paste the field names in the order you defined as the Tab Order.

■ If you are adding the data to the target datasheet, choose Edit | Paste Append or select the new, blank record at the bottom of the datasheet and choose Edit | Paste or press CTRL-V.

4. Click Yes to confirm the paste operation.

Copy or Move Data from a Spreadsheet

Copying or moving records from a spreadsheet is similar to copying or moving records from a word processor. The advantage in the case of the spreadsheet is that the data does not have to be arranged in or converted to table form because it is already in tabular form on the spreadsheet. The same criteria apply as in the case of the word processor:

■ The columns in the spreadsheet must be in the same order as the data elements in the table for the data copy/move to be useful.

■ If the records are to be added to a form, the column names in the spreadsheet should be the same as the names of the corresponding text box controls on the database form.

Copy or Move Records from Access to Another Application

Copying or moving records from an Access datasheet or a form to another application is similar to bringing new records into Access from a source application. When you paste Access records to a different application, the field names appear in the first row of the table in a word processor or worksheet in a spreadsheet.

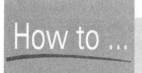

How to ... Drag and Drop Access Objects

You also can use the drag-and-drop method to move database objects among applications. You must have both applications running; then click an Access table or query in the Database window and drag it to a Word document or Excel worksheet. Going in the other direction, you can create an Access table by dragging and dropping a range of cells from an Excel worksheet to the Table page of the Database window.

> **TIP**   *If you are copying from a datasheet that has subdatasheets, only one level is copied at a time. To copy the subdatasheet, open it, then perform the same copy or move operation.*

The same four basic steps are used:

1. Select the Access data you want to copy or move and copy or cut it to the clipboard.

2. Open the other application.

3. If you are replacing existing data, select that data. If you are adding new data to existing data, place the insertion point where you want to begin pasting the new data.

4. Use the other application's command to paste or append the Access data.

If you are pasting Access records into a Word document, place the insertion point where you want the records to appear. The data is pasted in the document as a table. If you are copying from a form, Access includes the form and column names as well as the data.

If you are pasting to Excel, place the insertion point in the cell where you want the first column heading to be. The rest of the Access data fills out columns and rows to the right and down in the Excel worksheet.

Save Access Output as an External File

The previous chapter discusses saving Access data and objects in other database management systems or in text format. You can also export the data from Access tables, queries, forms, and reports to a number of other file formats both within and external to Microsoft Office.

To save the data from an Access table in one of these file formats:

1. In the Database window, select the table that contains the data you want to export.

2. Choose File | Export, or right-click and choose Export from the shortcut menu.

19

3. In the Export Table To dialog box, select a file type in the Save as Type box and click OK. Depending on your choice of file type, the dialog box title bar might show Export Table As.

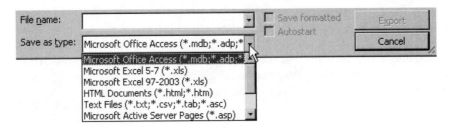

 Scroll down the list in the Save as Type box to see the available export file formats.

4. Use the Save In box to locate the destination folder.

5. Enter a name for the output file and click Export.

If you export the Access object to Excel 5-7 or 97-2003, HTML Documents, or Text Files, you can also check two other options. The first is Save Formatted, which preserves as much of the formatting as possible. The second is Autostart, which becomes available after you check Save Formatted. This option launches the destination application and opens the exported file for viewing or editing when you click Export.

 If you choose Rich Text Format, XML Documents, Microsoft IIS 1-2, or Active Server Pages, the Save Formatted option is checked by default. Autostart is available with Rich Text Format and XML Documents file type but not with IIS or ASP.

Work with Word

Microsoft Office has become so seamless that you almost can't tell one application from another. For example, Word works smoothly with Access to prepare form letters for an address list or helps to transmit Access data in a text format. There are four ways to use Access data in Word other than the simple cut-and-paste or drag process:

- Save the Access data as Rich Text Format, then open with Word.
- Send the Access data to Word as a mail merge source file.
- Load Access data into Word with the Publish It with Microsoft Word Office Link.
- Use the Merge It with Microsoft Word Office Link to include Access data in a mail merge operation.

Office Links is a tool that provides smooth interaction with the other Office programs such as Word and Excel. You can reach the Office Links commands from the Tools menu or by clicking the Office Links toolbar button.

Save in Rich Text Format

Rich Text Format (RTF) is a standard format used by Word and other word processing and desktop publishing programs for Windows. Settings such as fonts and styles are kept intact when files are saved as RTF files.

To save the output of an Access datasheet, form, or report as an RTF file, choose Rich Text Format from the Save as Type box in the Export As dialog box. When you choose the Rich Text Format file type, the Save Formatted option is automatically selected and cannot be cleared. The AutoStart option becomes available. If checked, this option launches Word for editing the file when you click Export to complete the process.

Figure 19-1 shows the Alpha Card table as an RTF file in the Word 2003 window.

Index	Name	DOB	Age	Address	City	State	Zip	Alias
1	ALLEN, FRANK ROGER			4455 CALLA AVE	LITTLE TOWN	NV	42111	
3	AIYER, ROBERT L	10/2/1979		445 G AVE	BAYVIEW	CA	09112	
4	AILLEM, PAUL CALVIN	7/5/1979		454 EBONY AVE	LITTLE TOWN	NV	42111	
5	AIZENBAUM, ESTELA			4780 SOUTHWORTH #4504	BAYVIEW	CA	09112	
6	AKEN, HAILESILASSIE B	1/5/1949		168 W CHESTER DR #4	BIG CITY	CA	09118	MN:BEYENE
8	AKOD, DEAN F			446 J AVE	BAYVIEW	CA	09112	
9	AKKINS, KEVIN MICHAEL	6/10/1975		4441 OCALA AVE	BIG TOWN	NV	42111	
10	AHREN, R JOY	6/15/1972		779 F AVE	BAYVIEW	CA	09112	
11	ADKINS, DALE STEVEN	2/18/1952	51	444 MAIN #4	BAYVIEW	CA	09112	SUCKER
12	APPLE, JAKE VANDEN			118 C AVE	BAYVIEW	CA	09112	
13	ASKOLM, MARIANNE E	6/12/1977		611 GLORIETTA BLVD	BAYVIEW	CA	09112	
14	AL ANON			8404 CLAIRMONT MESA BLVD	BIG PLACE	CA	09113	
15	ALADEN, DOUGLAS M	9/6/1962		41944 NEDDICK	OUTBACK	AZ	05111	
16	RENT A CAR					CA		
17	ALSON, NATHAN DAVID	10/13/1976		7646 CALDY PL	BIG PLACE	CA	09113	
18	ALMAND, JUAN ANGEL SAUCEDO	3/8/1979		1540 B AVE	OUR TOWN	AZ	08111	
19	ADKONS, ABDON HUMBERTO	3/16/1979	24	4444 FOURTH AVE #404	BIG TOWN	NV	42111	CROWN CITY CAB
20	ALANO	7/5/1978		744 MAIN AVE	BAYVIEW	CA	09112	
21	ARENSON, JUSTINO							PIRATA
22	ALIMAN, EDGAR	2/6/1962		4744 C REGENCY WAY	BIG TOWN	NV	42111	

FIGURE 19-1   An Access table saved as an RTF file

Save an Access Table or Query as a Mail Merge Data Source

An easy way to make an Access mailing list available to the Word mail merge process is to save the table or query as a mail merge data source document. In the Export To dialog box, choose Microsoft Word Merge as the file type. When you click Export, Access creates and saves the data source with the Access field names and record data. You can export Access data to any version of Word for use with the Word mail merge feature. The field names in the header row must match the field names placed in the Word mail merge main document. If they don't match, you must edit either the Access data source or the Word main document.

Be sure the Access table or query has no field names longer than 20 characters. Word's mail merge feature truncates excess characters, which can result in duplicate field names. In addition, the feature converts spaces and special characters in field names to underscores.

Publish with Word

You can use an Office Link to save the output of a datasheet, form, or report as an RTF file and load the file into Word automatically. For example, suppose you created a custom form or report that you want to include in your company's annual report, which is being created in Word.

One of the differences between this process and the process of saving a datasheet as a mail merge data source is that forms and reports can be published as well as tables and queries. For mail merge, only tables and queries are accepted.

To publish an Access object into Word:

1. Select the name of the table, query, form, or report you want to save and load into Word. If you want to load only part of a datasheet, open the datasheet first and select the records you want to load.

 2. Choose Tools | Office Links or click the Office Links toolbar button, then click Publish It with Microsoft Office Word.

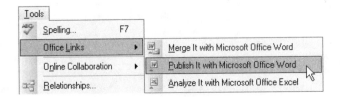

The list of Office Links commands will vary depending on the applications you have installed.

This saves the selected object or data in a file in the current Access folder, opens Word automatically, and opens the file for review and editing. Figure 19-2 shows the result of publishing the Alpha Entry by Code query datasheet in Word.

Use Merge It with Word

An Access database is often an ideal place to store addresses and names of customers, business associates, or friends. Once the link between Access and Word is established, you can open Word any time to print form letters, envelopes, or labels using the current data from Access.

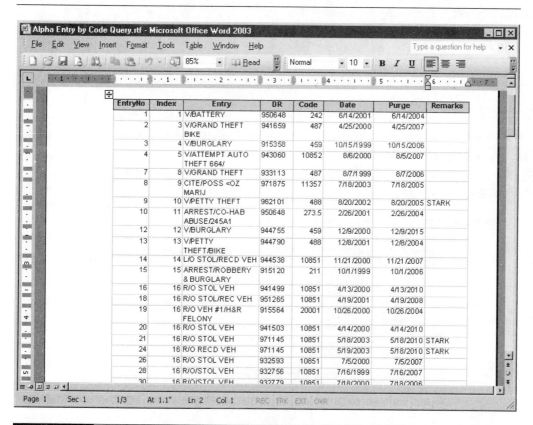

FIGURE 19-2   Results of publishing a query with Microsoft Word

19

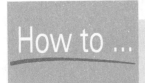

How to ... Prepare for Mail Merge

A query might be the ideal way to simplify Access data structures for this mail merge function. Your table for customer names and addresses might have a number of other fields, such as a telephone number or date of last order, that you don't need to pass on. You can design a query that selects only those fields relevant to addressing correspondence (Name, Title, Company, Street Address, City, State, and Zip). The Word mail merge feature also can do this after receiving the table data, but you should avoid cluttering up the exchange of data with unnecessary fields.

To merge data from an Access table or query using the Microsoft Word mail merge functions:

1. In the Database window, select the table or query containing the data.

2. Choose Tools | Office Links or click the Office Links toolbar button, then select Merge It with Microsoft Office Word.

3. The Microsoft Word Mail Merge Wizard dialog box appears, shown next, offering a choice of linking your data to an existing Microsoft Word document or creating a new one. Select one of these options and click OK. Word starts up and opens either a new document or the specific document you have selected.

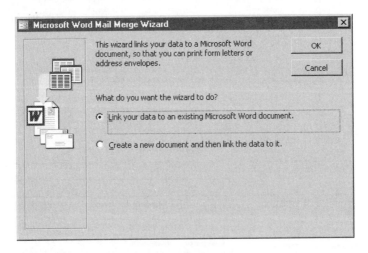

4. When you click the Insert Merge Fields button, the list of fields from the Access table is displayed. Figure 19-3 shows a new Word document with a dialog box listing the fields from the NameList Access table as the data source.

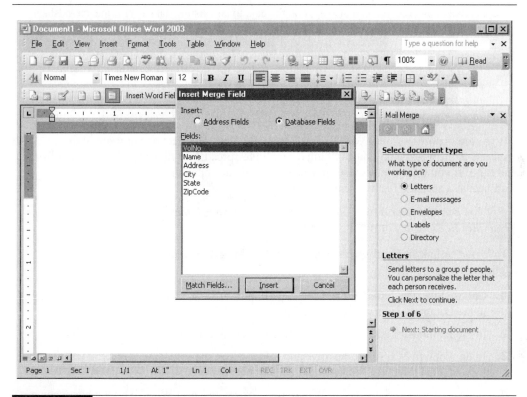

FIGURE 19-3   Using an Access table as the mail merge data source

5. Select the specific fields you want to insert in your document and place them in the
    document. For more information about how mail merge works, consult your Microsoft
    Word documentation.

Work with Excel

Excel is another application of the Microsoft Office suite that can work smoothly with your data
in Access. The association between Excel and Access can also be a two-way street. You can use
Excel data in Access or use Access data in Excel.

Import from and Link to Excel Spreadsheets

Before you try to import or link to data from an Excel or other spreadsheet, make sure the data
is arranged in a tabular format. The spreadsheet must also have the same type of data in each
column as the target Access datasheet and the rows must contain the same field in each position.
     You can choose to import or link an entire spreadsheet or only the data from a named range
of cells within the spreadsheet. Usually, you create a new table from the imported or linked

19

spreadsheet data; however, you can also append the data to an existing datasheet if the spreadsheet column headings are the same as the table field names.

Access tries to assign appropriate data types to the imported data fields, but it does not always make the correct assumption. Before you do any work on the new table, be sure the field data types are what you want. You should also check the assumed field properties and set additional properties, such as formatting, to fit the intended table use in Access. Number field formatting can differ between Excel and Access.

If you are importing from Excel version 5.0 or later, you can select one or more of the worksheets in the workbook. You can't import multiple-spreadsheet files from Excel 4.0 or from Lotus 1-2-3. If you want one of these spreadsheets, you must open the program and save each spreadsheet as a separate file before importing.

You can also import from other spreadsheet programs if they are capable of saving the files in Excel or Lotus 1-2-3 format.

To import or link an Excel spreadsheet, invoke the Import Spreadsheet Wizard by doing the following:

1. Choose File | Get External Data and click Import or Link Tables. You can also right-click in the Database window and choose Import or Link Tables from the shortcut menu.

2. In the Import (or Link) dialog box, select Microsoft Excel in the Files of Type box.

3. In the Look In box, select the drive and folder where the spreadsheet file you want is located, then select the filename and click Import or Link.

4. In the first Import Spreadsheet Wizard (or Link Spreadsheet Wizard) dialog box (shown next), you can choose to import a specific worksheet or a named range of cells, then click Next.

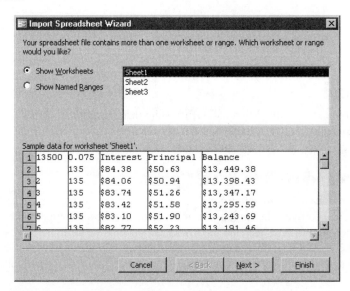

5. In the next wizard dialog box, check First Row Contains Column Headings(shown next), then click Next. Clear the check box if the first row contains field data instead of column headings.

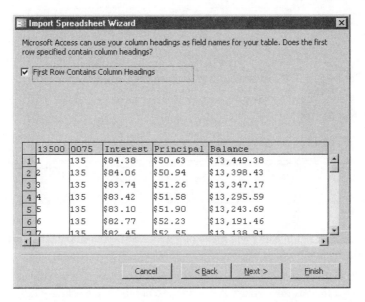

If you indicate that the first row contains the column headings and there are some headings containing data that can't be used for valid Access field names (if, for instance, the heading is blank), Access displays a message to that effect and automatically assigns valid field names.

6. In the third wizard dialog box, choose to store the data in a new table or in an existing one. If you want to store the data in an existing table, select the table name from the list of tables in the current database. If you are linking, enter the name of the table to which to link the spreadsheet data. Click Next.

7. In the next wizard dialog box, you can set the field options for each field in the worksheet:

- Click in the Field Name box and enter a new name for the field.
- Choose Yes in the Indexed box to create an index on that field.
- Change the data type, if applicable, in the Data Type box (this is not always available).
- Choose to skip the field when importing the spreadsheet.

19

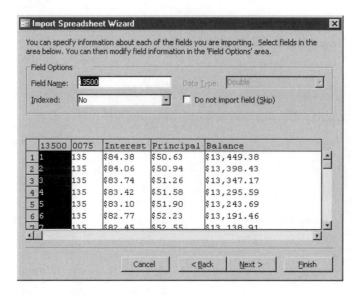

8. Click in the next field header and make other changes. After making the desired changes to each field, click Next.

9. In the next dialog box, choose one of the fields as the primary key. You can also let Access add a field as the primary key or choose not to have a primary key at all. Then click Next.

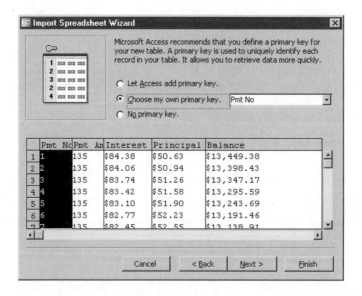

You might need to adjust the column widths.

NOTE

10. In the final wizard dialog box, you can accept the Excel name or enter a new name for the Access table, then click Finish.

The new Payment Table in Access contains the data that was in the Excel range of cells:

Pmt No	Pmt Amt	Interest	Principal	Balance
1	135	$84.38	$50.63	$13,449.38
2	135	$84.06	$50.94	$13,398.43
3	135	$83.74	$51.26	$13,347.17
4	135	$83.42	$51.58	$13,295.59
5	135	$83.10	$51.90	$13,243.69
6	135	$82.77	$52.23	$13,191.46
7	135	$82.45	$52.55	$13,138.91
8	135	$82.12	$52.88	$13,086.03
9	135	$81.79	$53.21	$13,032.82
10	135	$81.46	$53.54	$12,979.27
11	135	$81.12	$53.88	$12,925.39
12	135	$80.78	$54.22	$12,871.18
13	135	$80.44	$54.56	$12,816.62
14	135	$80.78	$54.22	$12,762.40

Record: 1 of 14

The following illustration shows the table design created by the Import Spreadsheet Wizard. Notice that the Pmt No is specified as the primary key field. Now you can change the Pmt Amt data type to Currency to improve the appearance of the table data.

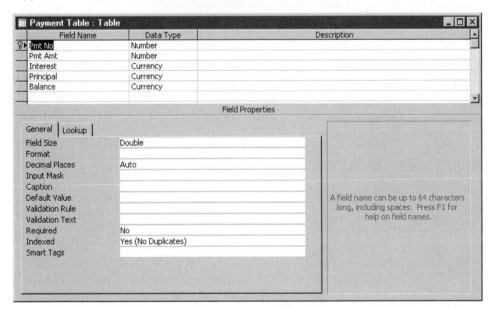

Field Name	Data Type	Description
Pmt No	Number	
Pmt Amt	Number	
Interest	Currency	
Principal	Currency	
Balance	Currency	

Field Properties

General | Lookup

Field Size	Double
Format	
Decimal Places	Auto
Input Mask	
Caption	
Default Value	
Validation Rule	
Validation Text	
Required	No
Indexed	Yes (No Duplicates)
Smart Tags	

A field name can be up to 64 characters long, including spaces. Press F1 for help on field names.

19

Export a Table or Query to Excel

Exporting all or part of a datasheet to an Excel spreadsheet is similar to exporting to other file types. In the Export As dialog box, select the desired Microsoft Excel version or other spreadsheet file type in the Save as Type box. Locate the folder where you want to store the exported data. If you are adding the data to an existing spreadsheet, select the name; otherwise, enter a new filename in the File Name box.

Check the Save Formatted option in the Export To dialog box if you want to keep the same fonts and field width and preserve the data that displays in the Lookup fields. The export process takes a little longer with this option but you won't have to restore the formatting in the spreadsheet. The spreadsheet file created by Access contains the field names in the first row and data in the subsequent rows. If you are exporting a form, the data is saved as a table of data. If you are exporting a report that includes grouped records, the group levels are saved as outline levels in Excel.

When you choose the Save Formatted option, the AutoStart option becomes available. This option automatically launches Excel with the data on the screen when you click Export.

Use Analyze It with Microsoft Excel

The Analyze It with Microsoft Excel Office link is very useful for sending data to Excel for data analysis and charting. Although Access has some charting capabilities, you have more resources when you let Excel do your charting for you. Once you have constructed charts in Excel, you can include them in your Access form or report by placing them into unbound object controls.

To load database information into Microsoft Excel, you use the Analyze It with Microsoft Excel command in the Office Links menu. All the formatting done in Access, such as font styles, field size, and colors, can be transferred to the Excel spreadsheet. Report groups are saved in the worksheet as outline levels, and forms are saved as simple data tables.

To load Access data into an Excel worksheet:

1. In the Database window, select the name of the datasheet, form, or report that you want to load into Excel. If you want to send only part of a table, open the datasheet first and select the records you want to load.

 2. Choose Tools | Office Links or click the Office Links toolbar button and click Analyze It with Microsoft Office Excel.

After a moment, Excel opens showing a new worksheet with the data from the Access object (see Figure 19-4). The selected records are saved as an Excel file (.xls) in the same folder as the Access database.

NOTE *Because some of the number formatting might be different in Excel, when you choose Save Formatted, you might see a warning that some of the formatting might be lost.*

	A	B	C	D	E	F
1	Product ID	Product Name	Supplier	Category	Quantity Per Unit	Unit Pri
2	1	Chai	Exotic Liquids	Beverages	10 boxes x 20 bags	$18
3	2	Chang	Exotic Liquids	Beverages	24 - 12 oz bottles	$19
4	3	Aniseed Syrup	Exotic Liquids	Condiments	12 - 550 ml bottles	$10
5	4	Chef Anton's Cajun Seasoning	New Orleans Cajun Delights	Condiments	48 - 6 oz jars	$22
6	5	Chef Anton's Gumbo Mix	New Orleans Cajun Delights	Condiments	36 boxes	$21
7	6	Grandma's Boysenberry Spread	Grandma Kelly's Homestead	Condiments	12 - 8 oz jars	$25
8	7	Uncle Bob's Organic Dried Pears	Grandma Kelly's Homestead	Produce	12 - 1 lb pkgs.	$30
9	8	Northwoods Cranberry Sauce	Grandma Kelly's Homestead	Condiments	12 - 12 oz jars	$40
10	9	Mishi Kobe Niku	Tokyo Traders	Meat/Poultry	18 - 500 g pkgs.	$97
11	10	Ikura	Tokyo Traders	Seafood	12 - 200 ml jars	$31
12	11	Queso Cabrales	Cooperativa de Quesos 'Las Cabras'	Dairy Products	1 kg pkg.	$21
13	12	Queso Manchego La Pastora	Cooperativa de Quesos 'Las Cabras'	Dairy Products	10 - 500 g pkgs.	$38
14	13	Konbu	Mayumi's	Seafood	2 kg box	$6
15	14	Tofu	Mayumi's	Produce	40 - 100 g pkgs.	$23
16	15	Genen Shouyu	Mayumi's	Condiments	24 - 250 ml bottles	$15
17	16	Pavlova	Pavlova, Ltd.	Confections	32 - 500 g boxes	$17
18	17	Alice Mutton	Pavlova, Ltd.	Meat/Poultry	20 - 1 kg tins	$39
19	18	Carnarvon Tigers	Pavlova, Ltd.	Seafood	16 kg pkg.	$62
20	19	Teatime Chocolate Biscuits	Specialty Biscuits, Ltd.	Confections	10 boxes x 12 pieces	$9
21	20	Sir Rodney's Marmalade	Specialty Biscuits, Ltd.	Confections	30 gift boxes	$81
22	21	Sir Rodney's Scones	Specialty Biscuits, Ltd.	Confections	24 pkgs. x 4 pieces	$10
23	22	Gustaf's Knäckebröd	PB Knäckebröd AB	Grains/Cereals	24 - 500 g pkgs.	$21
24	23	Tunnbröd	PB Knäckebröd AB	Grains/Cereals	12 - 250 g pkgs.	$9
25	24	Guaraná Fantástica	Refrescos Americanas LTDA	Beverages	12 - 355 ml cans	$4
26	25	NuNuCa Nuß-Nougat-Creme	Heli Süßwaren GmbH & Co. KG	Confections	20 - 450 g glasses	$14
27	26	Gumbär Gummibärchen	Heli Süßwaren GmbH & Co. KG	Confections	100 - 250 g bags	$31
28	27	Schoggi Schokolade	Heli Süßwaren GmbH & Co. KG	Confections	100 - 100 g pieces	$43
29	28	Rössle Sauerkraut	Plutzer Lebensmittelgroßmärkte AG	Produce	25 - 825 g cans	$45

FIGURE 19-4 Access data in an Excel worksheet

You Can Mail Objects Right from Access

You can send Access tables, queries, forms, reports, report snapshots, and even modules attached to an e-mail message.

To attach an Access object to an e-mail message:

1. Select the object you want to send in the Database window. If you want to send only some of the records from a table or query, open the table or query in Datasheet view and select the records you want to send.

2. Choose File | Send To or right-click the object and point to Send To in the shortcut menu; then click Mail Recipient (as Attachment).

3. In the Send dialog box, choose the file format you want to use for your e-mail attachment; then click OK.

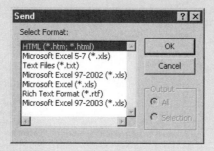

Your e-mail client program opens an e-mail message form where you can address and add text to your message and send it out. The object that you have selected to send is automatically attached to the message.

Chapter 20

Share with Multiple Users

How to...

- Share a database on a network
- Replicate a database for multiple users
- Manage a database in a multiple-user environment

Creating and maintaining a database in a multiple-user environment is not a simple task. When you welcome more users to a database, you open yourself up to a whole new set of complications. Some users might not have up-to-date information; other users can try to update the same information at the same time, causing conflicts. Access includes several tools that can help ensure the integrity and security of the database and other useful features for resolving conflicts.

If the database is accessed through different computers, such as the workplace computer and a laptop, you can create replicas of the database. However, when many copies of the database are on different computers accessed by different users, conflicts can occur when changes are made to the same data. Access includes several tools that can help resolve the conflicts and ensure the integrity and security of the database.

Share a Database on a Network

In a multiple-user environment, there are several ways to share a single database with others. Rather than every user keeping a complete copy of the database, you can provide other means for sharing that can also improve data reliability and consistency. Some of the options for sharing an Access database are as follows:

- Place the database in a central location where all users have access to all objects in it.
- Split the database so that the users share only the table data.
- Create a replicated database whose members can be synchronized so the data they use is identical.
- Place the entire database or part of the database on the Internet.

Share an Entire Database

The easiest way to share data is to put the entire database, tables and all, on the network server or in a folder that can be shared. All users then have access to all the data and use the same database objects. If everyone uses the database for the same activities and you don't want the users to be able to customize their own objects, this is the best strategy. Figure 20-1 shows the model for sharing the entire database among multiple users. The entire database is stored on the network server, and the workstations access all the objects via the LAN.

To share an entire database on a network server, copy the database to the shared folder, then set the Default Open Mode on the Advanced tab of the Options dialog box to Shared. Access must be installed on each computer on the network to share the databases.

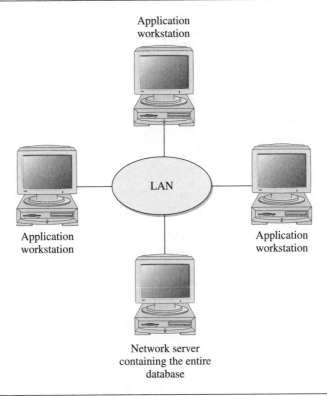

Application
workstation

LAN

Application
workstation

Application
workstation

Network server
containing the entire
database

FIGURE 20-1   Sharing a database among multiple users

Split the Database

A faster method of sharing a database is to put all the tables on the network server and let the users keep the other objects on their own workstations. Only the data is transmitted over the network, thus reducing network traffic. This strategy is useful when the users' jobs and activities are different or the users do not all have the same versions of Access. The users maintain only those objects that directly pertain to their own activities.

The database containing the tables is called the *back-end* database; the one containing the other objects is the *front-end* database. The front-end database contains links to the tables in the back-end database. Access provides the Database Splitter Wizard to separate the tables from the rest of the database. Figure 20-2 illustrates the front-end/back-end model for sharing an Access database. All tables are stored in the back end on the network server. The workstations store all the other objects—queries, forms, reports, macros, and modules.

20

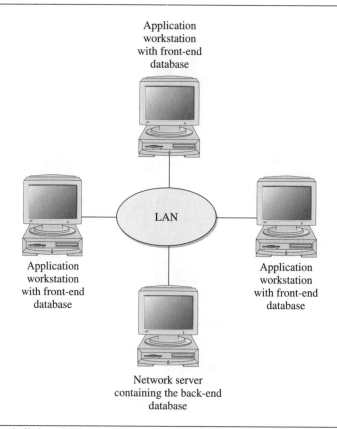

Application
workstation
with front-end
database

LAN

Application
workstation
with front-end
database

Application
workstation
with front-end
database

Network server
containing the back-end
database

FIGURE 20-2   Splitting the database into a front end and back end

TIP

It is not easy to undo what the Database Splitter Wizard does; be sure to make a backup copy of the database before attempting to split it.

To split a database into the front- and back-end elements:

1. Open the database and make sure no objects in the database are open, then choose Tools | Database Utilities | Database Splitter. The Database Splitter Wizard opens with a message describing the process (see Figure 20-3).

2. After reading the message, click Split Database. The next dialog box lets you specify where to place the back-end database.

3. Use the Save In box (see Figure 20-4) to locate the network server on your system. The Network Neighborhood entry in the drop-down list helps you find a computer on the LAN to use as the back-end server.

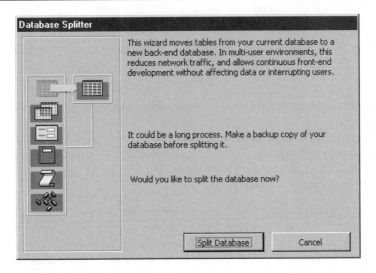

FIGURE 20-3 Starting the Database Splitter

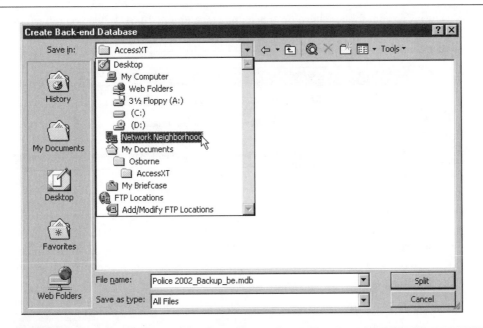

FIGURE 20-4 Selecting the location for the back-end database

20

4. Enter a name for the back-end database or accept the default name (the name of the current database with "_be" added).

5. Click Split. When the process is completed, a message appears announcing the successful split. Click OK to close the message box.

It might take a while to split a large database. The wizard actually is deleting the tables from the current database, creating a new database with the tables, then linking the current database to the new back-end tables.

When you open the Tables tab of the current database after splitting, you can see by the link icons next to the names in the list that all the tables listed are links to another database (see Figure 20-5). If you open the new back-end database, you can see all the tables listed on the Tables tab but all the other tabs are empty.

NOTE
To customize the distributed database environment further, you can reduce network traffic even more by moving relatively static tables—such as lookup tables containing data that doesn't change often—to the front-end databases. If the data in the lookup table changes, you can make the changes in the back-end version and alert the users to copy the data to their own lookup tables. Temporary tables should also be stored locally to prevent conflicts and reduce network traffic.

If you need to change the link to any of the back-end tables, choose Tools | Database Utilities | Linked Table Manager. In the Linked Table Manager dialog box, choose the affected tables and check the "Always prompt for new location" check box (see Figure 20-6). When you refresh the

FIGURE 20-5   Tables are linked to the back-end database.

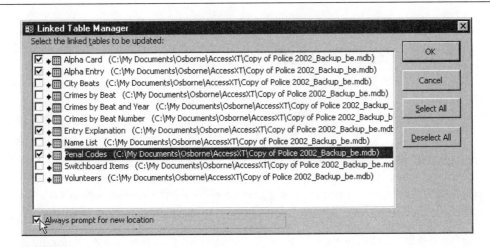

FIGURE 20-6   Setting to prompt for a new table location

link to the table, you will have the opportunity to change the location of the linked table in the standard file location dialog box.

Prevent Exclusive Access

When multiple users are sharing a database, competition for data access can occur. If one user opens the database with exclusive access, no other user can work with it. To prevent or at least discourage this from happening, set the Default Open Mode to Shared in the Advanced tab of the Options dialog box. Then instruct all the users not to open the database in an exclusive mode. See Chapter 21 for information about including security in a multiple-user environment.

You can also set up a security system that prevents certain users from opening a database in exclusive mode but permits others to do so. The database administrator must be able to open the database in exclusive mode to perform duties, such as compacting and backing up the database.

Replicate a Database

Replication makes copies of a database for use in different locations but enables the respective copies to be totally synchronized. Each user can have a separate copy of the database with the master file centrally located where it can be updated with the changes in the remote replicas.

NOTE *Replication is not a good idea if you expect a lot of data entry and editing in the individual replicas. Conflicts can arise when the same data is updated by two users; these conflicts take time to resolve. Replication is also not recommended if your data must be real time and completely up to date at all times. Even if the master database is updated at frequent intervals, it is not 100 percent current between updates.*

There Are Consequences to Replication

Before you decide to replicate your database, it is important to understand certain changes that will significantly increase the size of the database and decrease the flexibility. For example, several new system tables and system fields may be added to the database. If you want to see these system tables and fields, check the System Objects option in the View tab of the Options dialog box.

AutoNumber fields behave differently when you replicate a database. The AutoNumber fields that are set to incremental numbering are changed to random numbering. Existing records retain their values but new records are assigned AutoNumbers randomly. If any applications depend on autonumbering for tracking, you can add a Date/Time field to provide sequential ordering of new records.

Certain size limitations also are the result of the addition of the three system fields. Each record can contain a maximum of 2,048 bytes. The system fields occupy a minimum of 54 bytes to store the identifiers, indexes, and information about changes in the record. This reduces the amount of space left over for actual record data. In addition, an Access table can contain up to 255 fields, 4 of which are taken up by the replication system fields.

Replication is for distributing and resynchronizing the data in tables, but doesn't synchronize changes in queries, forms, reports, macros, and so on, because those contain no data and are uneditable in the replicas.

The master database where all the design changes are implemented is called the *Design Master* and the copies are called *replicas*. The Design Master and the replicas might contain both common replicated objects and unique objects. Each replica can be tailored to a location or a specific type of data, and the common data can be synchronized and shared with the other users.

When you replicate a database, Access offers to make a backup copy. If you respond Yes, the copy is added to the same folder as the original. You can copy it from there to another medium later.

If some of the users need only parts of the database, you can also create a partial replica that contains only those objects they need. For example, a manufacturing company may have several factories in different states. The main headquarters would maintain the master database, while each local factory would have a partial replica containing only the information relating to its location and activities. Partial replicas can reduce network traffic and costs while offering greater security and smaller local databases.

The Briefcase method of creating a database replica was invented for the user who wants to work on the database with a laptop. Once the Briefcase replica is created, it can be synchronized with the Design Master like any other replica.

Manage the Database in a Multiuser Environment

As soon as more than one user can open a database, someone should be assigned as the database administrator (DBA). This person is responsible for ensuring the integrity and security of the database. Among the issues that the DBA needs to address are:

- Controlling read/write access to the data
- Setting up the user groups with the appropriate levels of access and security
- Adding new users to a group and removing users from a group
- Ensuring accurate, up-to-date record data and minimizing data-locking conflicts
- Editing database objects as necessary and ensuring that all users have current versions
- Backing up and compacting the database

Control Data Editing

If two users attempt to edit the same record at the same time, the results can be unpredictable. Some form of data locking is necessary to ensure the integrity of the database. Allowing one user temporary exclusive access to a record is called *record locking.* When a data page (a unit of data storage), recordset (table or query) object, or a database object is locked, it is read-only to all users except the one who is currently entering or editing the data in it.

Access provides three levels of record locking, ranging from no locks at all to locking all the records in the recordset. You can set the default record-locking scheme in the Advanced tab of the Options dialog box (see Figure 20-7). Choose Tools | Options and click the Advanced tab to find the choices.

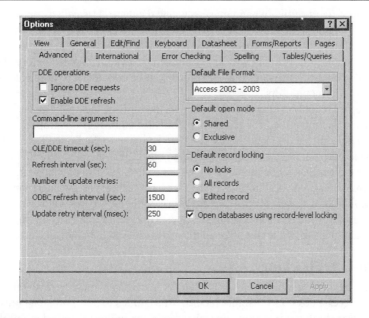

| FIGURE 20-7 | Setting record locking on the Advanced tab of the Options dialog box |

Set Default Record Locking

The "Default Record Locking" setting in the Options dialog box applies only to datasheet views of tables and queries. If you want to set the record locking for forms or reports, set the Record Locks property on the Data tab of the object's property sheet. Setting record locks for a report prevents changes in records in the underlying table or query while the report is being previewed or printed. You can also set the Record Locks property for a query and override the default setting.

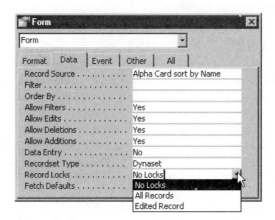

No Locks is the default setting when you start a new database. It is called "optimistic record locking" because it is used where few record write conflicts are expected. Access does not lock the record during editing. The edited record is locked only at the exact moment it is being saved. It is assumed that one user most likely will have completely saved the record before another user tries to edit it. Using No Locks ensures that all records can be edited at any time but it can also cause editing conflicts among users.

The Edited Record record-locking strategy is called "pessimistic locking" because it is assumed that there will be much competition for access to records for editing. If it is important that all editing of a record be completed before another user has access to it, the Edited Record strategy is required. As soon as one user begins to edit a record, no other user can make any changes to it until the first user saves the changes. Other users can view the record, but cannot change it.

The All Records strategy locks all records in the form or datasheet and the underlying tables for the entire time the form or datasheet is open. No one else can edit the records. One case in which this strategy would be useful is when you are running an update query that applies to several different records and you want to make sure all the affected records are locked until the query is completed.

Apply Record-Level Locking

A new option that became available with Access 2000 is *record-level locking*. With this record-level locking in effect, Access locks only a single record. This applies to accessing data only through a form. If you want to disable this option, clear the check box in the Advanced tab of the Options dialog box. The setting takes effect the next time you open the database with File | Open. The record-level locking setting does not affect the record-locking scheme set in the "Default record locking" option group.

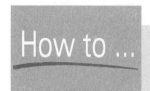

Choose a Locking Strategy

The strategy you choose depends on your data, how many users share the application, and how they use the data. For most multiuser environments, the No Locks strategy can be the most effective even though some brief write conflict errors can occur. The overall performance of the system is more efficient than with the other record-locking strategies.

If there are more imperative reasons for locking records during editing, use one of the other locking strategies.

If the data in a form, report, or query is acquired from an Open Database Connectivity (ODBC) database, Access treats it as if the No Locks setting were selected and disregards the Record Locks property setting.

The setting does not take effect if you open the database by selecting the filename from the list of recently used files at the end of the File menu.

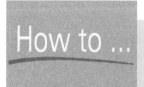

Minimize Conflicts

One way to reduce the number of locking conflicts is to arrange the workload so each user is responsible for different parts of the database. For example, one user updates records for sales in the Western states, another for the Southern area, and so on.

When two users try to update the same record and cause a conflict, Access tries several times to save the record. Access first attempts to free the record from the lock before displaying the Write Conflict message. The Update Retry Interval setting specifies the period of time that elapses between tries. The Number of Update Retries setting determines how many times Access is to try to save the record before giving up. These settings are all on the Advanced tab of the Options dialog box, which you can display by choosing Tools | Options.

You can try different combinations of these two settings. For example, set the Number of Update Retries to 0 for Access to display the Write Conflict message at once. Set both to higher values to reduce the number of write conflicts by allowing Access to try to save the record more times with a longer interval between attempts. However, with this arrangement, users might complain that the system appears slow. Experiment with these settings to settle on the right combination for your application.

20

The setting does not take effect if you open the database by selecting the filename from the list of recently used files at the end of the File menu.

Update Records with Refresh and Requery

If the data in your shared database changes frequently and it is important that the user has up-to-date data, you can use two methods to keep the data current: *refresh* and *requery*.

The refresh method updates only those records already appearing in Datasheet or Form view. When you refresh the datasheet or form, records aren't reordered or deleted; those that no longer meet the filter criteria are also not removed. To update the recordset to reflect these actions, you must requery the records.

To refresh a table, query, or form manually, open the table or query in Datasheet view or the form in Form view, then choose Records | Refresh.

Requerying completely rebuilds the underlying recordset. The easiest way to requery is to press SHIFT-F9.

 *The default interval for refreshing records is 60 seconds, which might be too long in critical situations. You can reset the interval to 10 or 15 seconds. If you set it too low, Access will create a lot of network traffic.*

Edit Shared Database Objects

Even though you do your best to have all the database object designs completed before setting up the database for shared access, there are bound to be changes that must be made later. Any local objects can be modified at any time but the shared objects require special consideration.

Before you begin to make significant design changes to a shared database, be sure you open it in exclusive mode by selecting Open Exclusive from the Open button in the Open Database dialog box. Pick a time to do this when other users do not require access to the database, such as the middle of the night.

If the required design changes are less invasive, you can safely modify the objects while the database is open in shared mode. If the table or any query, form, or report based on the table is open, you can't change the table design. The converse is also true—if you are modifying a table design, the table and any query, form, or report based on it is unavailable to another user. It is a good idea to have the changes well thought-out and specific before opening the table design; then keep it open as briefly as possible.

Other tips that are helpful when you need to edit shared database objects are:

- When you edit a query, form, or report design that is already in use by another user, that user won't see the new version until the object is closed and reopened.

- If the objects you want to change are dependent on each other, be sure to edit them all at the same time so they will be consistent.

- Make sure no one is using the macro you want to edit by opening the database in exclusive mode. If you change a macro that someone is using, you can cause problems.

Chapter 21

Secure a Database

How to...

- Secure a database with a password
- Create a workgroup of users
- Assign and change permissions and ownerships among the workgroup
- Use the User-Level Security Wizard
- Remove user-level security
- Encode/decode a database

The main purpose of database security is to prevent unauthorized access to the information, either for viewing or editing. A second, no less important, goal of database security is to prevent design modifications by unqualified individuals. Even the slightest change in a form design or a data validation rule can cause problems that can be difficult to locate and correct.

Access provides two levels of security for databases:

- Global protection through the use of database passwords
- User-level security based on the Access security model

With these levels you can protect an entire database or single objects in the database, respectively; distinguish between users; and offer different levels of access to each.

Secure a Database with a Password

Protecting a database with a database password is the simplest way to keep the information from prying eyes. However, it is more appropriate for the single-user database than for a networked, multiple-user database. Although this method is secure, it applies only to opening the database. Once open, the data and all the database objects are available to the user for viewing or editing unless other types of security have already been defined as described in the remaining sections of this chapter. In addition, Access stores the password in an unencoded form, which might compromise your database security. To be safe, always make a backup copy of the database before adding the password and store the copy in a secure location.

You must have exclusive use of the database to assign a password. Anyone who knows the password can open the database. To add password protection to a database, make sure all other users have closed the database, then do the following:

1. Open the database in exclusive mode by clicking the down arrow next to the Open button in the Open dialog box and choosing Open Exclusive.

2. Choose Tools | Security | Set Database Password.

3. Enter the password you want to use in the Password box, repeat it in the Verify box, then click OK. If the two entries are not the same, Access asks you to reenter the password in the Verify box.

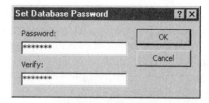

CAUTION *Do not forget your password! You will not be able to open the database and there is no way to bypass the requirement for a password. Always select a word that you can remember, such as the name of your favorite cat. As a backup, write it down in a safe place, just in case.*

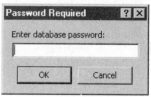

The next time you try to open the database, Access will require you to enter the password.

To remove the password, open the database again in exclusive mode and choose Tools | Security | Unset Database Password. Enter the password in the Unset Database Password dialog box and click OK.

Secure a Multiple-User Database

When a database has multiple users, security becomes more complicated. Not all users require access to all parts of the database, yet someone must be responsible for every object in the database. Organizing users in groups helps simplify the security problem; you can also allow each group to carry out specific actions on specific objects in the database. All the information about the workgroups is stored in a separate file called the Workgroup Information File (WIF) with the file extension .mdw. The default WIF is System.mdw.

Understand the User-Level Security Model

There are two advantages to the user-level security scheme: no user can inadvertently break the application by making design changes, and sensitive data is protected. The Access user-level security model is based on the concept of workgroups consisting of users who share data in a

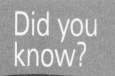

About Security Problems with Linked Tables

Security problems might occur if one of the tables in a password-protected database is linked to a second database that does not require a password. The password for the first database is stored with the linking information in the second database. Any user who can open the second database also can open the linked table in the protected database. The password also is stored in an unencoded form in the unprotected database, making it readable to any user.

multiuser environment. The members of the workgroups are listed in user and group accounts (a group account is a collection of user accounts).

Each member of the workgroup is allowed a specific amount of freedom within the database and its objects. For example, members of one group account might be permitted to enter and edit data but not to modify a form design. Another group might be allowed to view only specific data and be denied access to sensitive information.

The following describes the four elements of the Access security model:

- **User** A person who uses the database. In a secured database, the user must sign on with his or her name and password to be able to use the database. You grant the same permissions to the users in the group. Individual users can belong to more than one group and have additional access to the database.

NOTE *Access user accounts are not related to Windows user accounts.*

- **Group** A set of users who have the same security level and need access to the same areas of the database. You grant the same permissions to the users in the group. Individual users can belong to more than one group and have additional access to the database.

- **Permission** Grants a user or group the right to perform a specific act on a database object. For example, the Open/Run permission gives the user the right to open a database, form, or report or to run a macro.

- **Object** Refers to any of the Access tables, queries, forms, reports, macros, or modules in addition to the database itself.

NOTE *You will see the list of permissions a little later in "Assign or Change Permissions and Ownerships."*

Another concept in the security model is that of ownership. All database objects must be owned by some user. The owner is responsible for the object and has the ultimate authority over its design, use, and availability to other users. The user who creates a new object or imports one from another database is by default the owner of the object and always has Administer permission on the object. However, the owner can transfer ownership to another user or group.

Built-in Groups and Users

An Access database comes equipped with two built-in groups, neither of which can be made secure. Both groups are identical in the workgroup information file for all databases and can't be deleted or renamed. In the Admins group, all members are administrators of the database and have full permissions on all objects in the database. The Users group includes all of the individual user accounts in the database. All members of the Users group by default have permissions on all newly created objects in the database.

An Access database also includes a built-in user, Admin, who is a member of both built-in groups. The Admin user is in every copy of System.mdw, the default WIF file that was created when you installed Access. Each Admin user has permission to open, view, and modify all the data and every object in every Access database, including those on other computers that have Access installed. As a result, the first step in securing a new database is to use the Workgroup Administrator to define new administrator and user accounts that limit these permissions. After the new accounts are established, remove the Admin user account from the Admins group.

What Is Needed to Secure a Database?

To secure a multiple-user database properly, you need to:

- Change the ownership of all the database objects from the default Admin.
- Remove all permissions for the Admin user and the Users group.
- Grant permissions to the new users and groups.

NOTE *As an additional security measure, you can also encode the database so no other program can read it. Encoding a database compacts the database file and helps protect it from being read by a word processor.*

Secure a Database with the User-Level Security Wizard

The User-Level Security Wizard creates a backup copy of the current database with the same name and the .bak file extension, then secures the selected objects in the current database. All relationships and linked tables are retained. The secure database is owned by the user who runs the wizard. The original database remains unchanged.

To secure a database with the User-Level Security Wizard, log on as a member of the Admins group and do the following:

1. Open the database you want to secure and choose Tools | Security | User-Level Security Wizard.

2. The first Security Wizard dialog box opens (see Figure 21-1) with the option of creating a new WIF for the database or, if one already exists, modifying the current WIF. Choose "Create a new workgroup information file" and click Next.

3. Enter a unique workgroup ID (WID) in the second dialog box. The WID is a 4 to 20 character string that is case sensitive. One is already provided for you but you can replace it with your own. You can also include your name and company name if desired. In the lower pane of the dialog box, choose whether you want this to be the default WIF for this database or you would rather create a shortcut that will open the new secured database. Click Next.

NOTE *If you choose to make this the default WIF, any database you open without specifying a WIF will use this one.*

4. The third Security Wizard dialog box (see Figure 21-2) contains seven tabs showing all the objects in the current database. By default, the wizard secures all the objects but if

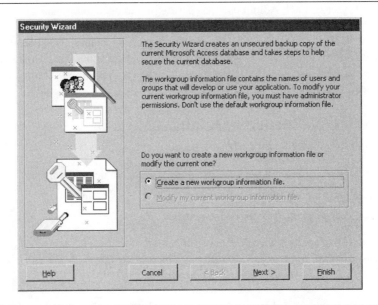

FIGURE 21-1   Starting the Security Wizard

you want to leave some of them as they are now, clear the check marks by the object names. Click Next after setting individual object security.

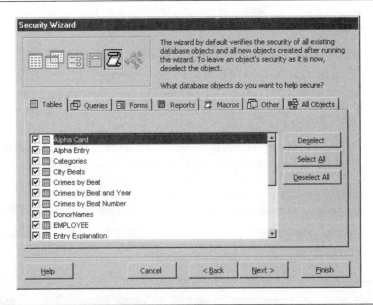

FIGURE 21-2   Specifying individual object security

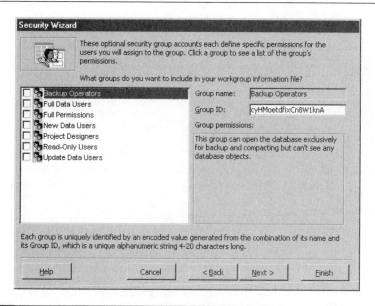

FIGURE 21-3   Including predefined groups in the WIF

5. The next dialog box (see Figure 21-3) enables you to set up the security group accounts you want included in the WIF. To see the specific permissions allowed for each predefined group, select the group name and read the text in the Group permissions box. Each group has a unique group ID. To see what permissions are automatically granted to each group, select the group and read the Group Permissions pane.

> **NOTE** *You don't have to use any of these groups. They are just common groups that Access provides in case you find any of them handy. You can make your own special groups later, too.*

6. In the next dialog box, you can assign some permissions to the Users group. By default, the Security Wizard withholds all permissions from the Users group because anyone who has a copy of Access is a member of the Users group and would be awarded the same permissions. If you choose Yes in this dialog box, the wizard displays a stern warning (see Figure 21-4). So be sure to choose No and click Next.

7. To add new users to the WIF, enter the user name, password, and Personal ID (PID) in the next dialog box (see Figure 21-5). You can also delete a user or edit an existing password or PID by selecting the name from the list on the left. The names, PIDs, and any passwords you have created with the wizard are printed in the report the wizard creates. Click Next to move to the next dialog box.

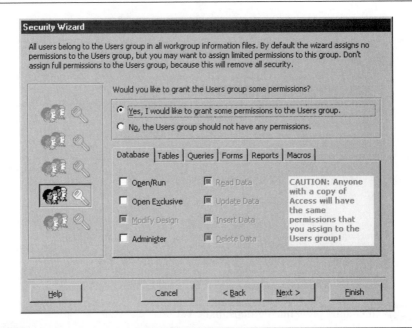

FIGURE 21-4   Granting permissions to the Users group

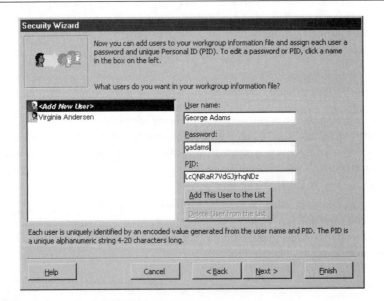

FIGURE 21-5   Adding users to the workgroup information file

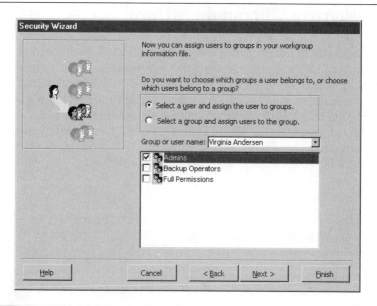

FIGURE 21-6   Assigning users to groups

8. In the next-to-last Security Wizard dialog box (see Figure 21-6), assign the users you added to your workgroup in the previous dialog box to a specific group. Actually, you can work either way in this dialog box—start with the list of users or start with the list of groups:

  ■ If you choose "Select a user and assign the user to groups," the drop-down list contains the list of users and the group names appear below. Check the group name and choose user names to add from the drop-down list.

  ■ If you choose "Select a group and assign users to the group," the drop-down list contains the group names and the user names appear in the box below. Select a group name from the drop-down list, then check all the user names you want assigned to the group.

9. Click Next to move to the final dialog box, where you are prompted for a name for the unsecured backup copy of the database.

10. Click Finish to complete the creation of the new WIF.

After creating the new WIF, the Security Wizard displays a report of the setting used in the file. You can save the report as a report snapshot, then print it and store the hard copy in a safe place. You will need all this information if you ever need to rebuild the WIF.

Create a Workgroup Without the Wizard

The default workgroup is defined in a WIF created by the Access Setup program and stored in the folder where you installed Access. When you want to define user-level security, you create a new WIF to contain the user and group accounts and passwords for all the members of the workgroup. The security accounts in the WIF can be assigned permissions for databases and objects. These permissions are stored in the secure database rather than in the WIF.

You can modify the default WIF, use an existing file, or create a new one. For a secure WIF that can't be duplicated, do not use the default System.mdw file. If you want to use an existing file, be sure it was created with a unique WID.

To create a new WIF, use the Workgroup Administrator, as follows:

1. Close any open database and choose Tools | Security | Workgroup Administrator.

2. The Workgroup Administrator dialog box displays the name and location of the current WIF and explains the purpose of a WIF. It also offers three buttons: Create, Join, and OK. Click Create to start a new WIF.

3. The Workgroup Owner Information dialog box displays the registered owner name and organization. Accept the entries or change them as necessary. The Name and Organization entries can contain up to 39 alphanumeric characters.

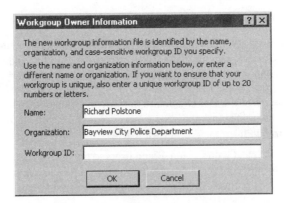

4. Enter a unique string of between 4 and 20 characters in the Workgroup ID box, then click OK. The WID is a form of workgroup password, which is case sensitive.

5. In the next dialog box, type a new name for the WIF. You can change the folder by typing a new path or by clicking Browse to specify the new path. Click OK.

6. The final dialog box (see Figure 21-7) asks you to confirm the workgroup information you have entered. Before clicking OK, copy all the information in the dialog box exactly as it appears. You can click Change to return to the Workgroup Owner Information dialog box and change any of the entries. Click OK when finished. If the file already exists, you are asked to confirm the overwrite.

CAUTION *Be sure to write down the exact entries you made in the Name, Organization, and Workgroup ID boxes in the Workgroup Owner Information dialog box and keep the copy in a safe location away from unauthorized users. You can also press ALT-PRINTSCREEN to capture the Confirm Workgroup Information dialog box on the window clipboard. Then open a new Word file and press CTRL-V to paste it into the document. From there you can print the information. If the WIF is damaged and you need to restore it, you must have the exact information or you will not be able to access the database.*

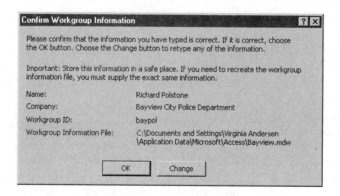

FIGURE 21-7   Confirming the Workgroup Information

After you click OK, the Workgroup Administrator builds the information file and changes the Windows Registry so that the new WIF is used the next time you start Access. Any new accounts you add will be saved in this file. If you want others to be able to join the workgroup, save it to a shared folder in the preceding step 5; now each user can run the Workgroup Administrator to join the file.

After informing you that the file was created successfully, the Administrator returns to the first dialog box. Click OK to leave the program.

Switch to a Different Workgroup

Although only one WIF can be used at a time on the computer, you can switch workgroups on the same computer. This is called joining a workgroup. You can use the Workgroup Administrator to switch from one workgroup to another if you have secured databases from two different sources or if you want to return to the default system WIF.

To do this:

1. Start the Workgroup Administrator as in the preceding steps and click Join in the first dialog box.

2. In the Workgroup Information File dialog box, enter the name of the WIF you want to use or click Browse to locate it.

3. Click OK. The Administrator displays a confirmation message.

4. Click OK again, then click Exit to leave the Workgroup Administrator.

Organize Security Accounts

It is easier to maintain database security if the users are organized by department or function and are assigned to group accounts. Each group is assigned permissions on the basis of its activities and needs. When users log on to a secured database, they log on with their user account, not the group account. After logging on, the users inherit all the permissions of the group plus any permissions assigned specifically to the individual user accounts.

Group accounts are made up of users and can also own database objects. Group accounts are used to assign a common set of permissions to multiple users. A user can belong to more than one group, in which case the user has the sum of all the group permissions. User accounts consist of a single user who might own objects and have permissions for those and other objects in the database. User accounts are stored in the WIF that the users will join when they access the database.

To create any type of security account, you must log on as a member of the Admins group. You can use the User and Group Accounts dialog box (see Figure 21-8) to do the following:

- Create and delete user and group accounts
- Add a user to a group
- Remove a user from a group
- Change or clear a user password

21

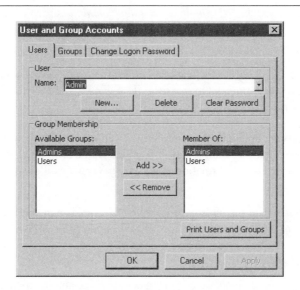

FIGURE 21-8 Working in the User and Group Accounts dialog box

> NOTE
>
> *Every account must have a PID that is saved with the account name. It is not the same as a password, which each user creates later.*

Create and Delete User Accounts

To create a new user account:

1. Start Access with the workgroup in which you want to include the new user account, then open a database.

> TIP
>
> *If you don't know whether you are starting in the right workgroup, use the Workgroup Administrator to see which workgroup is current and change the WIF if necessary.*

2. Choose Tools | Security | User and Group Accounts.

3. In the User and Group Accounts dialog box, click the Users tab and click New. The New User/Group dialog box opens.

4. Type a unique name for the new user account and a PID. The user name can contain up to 20 numbers and letters.

5. Click OK when finished.

For security reasons, the PID should be a unique combination of alphanumeric characters that have no actual meaning and do not form a word.

Be sure to keep a copy of the exact name and PID that you enter for the new account. You will need them if you have to re-create the account. The PIDs are case sensitive but the names are not.

To delete a user account, open the Users tab of the User and Group Accounts dialog box and select the name of the account you want to delete from the Name drop-down list. Click Delete and respond Yes when asked for confirmation. After you have made all the necessary deletions, click OK to close the dialog box.

You can't delete any of the built-in users from the Users group and you must leave at least one user in the Admins group. You also can't delete the Admin user account.

Create and Delete Group Accounts

Creating a new group account is similar to creating a new user account except that you do it in the Groups tab (see Figure 21-9) in the User and Group Accounts dialog box instead of the Users tab.

When you click New, the same New User/Group dialog box opens where you enter the name and PID for the new group. The group name follows the same rules as the user name.

To delete a group, on the Groups tab select the group name from the Name drop-down list and click Delete. Respond Yes to the confirmation request to delete the group, then click OK.

The built-in Admins and Users group accounts can't be deleted.

Add and Remove Users from Groups

As with all activities involving database security, you must log on as a member of the Admins group to add a user to a group or remove one from a group. To add a user to an existing group:

1. Start Access in the workgroup containing the security accounts.

2. Open a database and choose Tools | Security | User and Group Accounts, then click the Users tab.

3. Select the name of the user you want to add to the group from the Name drop-down list.

4. In the Available Groups box, select the group to which you want to add the user and click Add. The group name is added to the Member Of list.

Using the Groups tab of the User and Group Accounts dialog box

5. If you want to add this user to other groups, repeat step 4. If you want to add other users to groups, repeat steps 3 and 4.

6. Click OK when you have finished adding users to the groups.

To delete a user from a security group, open the Users tab of the User and Group Accounts dialog box as before and select the name of the user you want to remove in the Name box. Select the group name in the Member Of box and click Remove. Repeat these steps for all the users you want to remove and click OK when you are finished.

The default Users group is the exception. Because Access automatically adds all users to the group, the only way you can remove a user account from the Users group is to delete the user account altogether.

Create or Change Account Passwords

By default, when you add a new user account to a workgroup, Access assigns a blank password to it. The Admin account is also assigned a blank password. To make sure no one can log on using an existing user name, you should have all users enter a unique password for their accounts.

How to ... Document Security

To document the arrangement of users and the groups to which they belong, click the Print Users and Groups button on the Users tab of the User and Group Accounts dialog box. The Print Security dialog box appears, which gives you the option of printing only the users, only the groups, or both. The list of users includes the user names and the groups to which each user belongs. The list of groups includes the group names and the users who belong to that group.

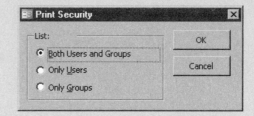

To create or change a security account password:

1. Start Access using the workgroup the account is in and log on with the user account name.

2. Open a database and choose Tools | Security | User and Group Accounts.

3. Click the Change Logon Password tab (see Figure 21-10) and enter the current password in the Old Password box. If no password has been defined for the account, leave that box blank.

FIGURE 21-10   Changing the logon password

4. Enter the new password in the New Password box. The password is case sensitive and can contain up to 20 characters, including any except the ASCII 0 (Null) character.

5. Enter the same characters in the Verify box and click OK.

To clear a password, you must log on as a member of the Admins group, then do the following:

1. Open the User and Group Accounts dialog box and click the Users tab.

2. Select the user account name from the Name drop-down list and click Clear Password.

3. Repeat step 2 to clear other user account passwords and click OK when finished.

Require Logon

All users of a database are automatically logged on as Admin users until you add a password to the Admin user account. Then, when users try to start Access, they must enter their user account names and passwords. To activate the logon procedure:

1. Start Access using the workgroup to which you want to add the logon password.

2. Choose Tools | Security | User and Group Accounts and click the Users tab.

3. With the Admin user account selected in the Name box, click the Change Logon Password tab (refer to Figure 21-10).

4. Leave the Old Password box blank because there is no password yet; then type the new password (up to 20 characters) in the New Password box. Passwords are case sensitive.

5. Type the password in the Verify box, then click OK.

The next time you or another member of the workgroup starts Access, the Logon dialog box appears. Enter the user account name in the Name box and the account password in the Password box. If your password is blank, leave the password box blank. Then click OK.

To turn off the Logon dialog box, start Access using the workgroup whose logon you want to deactivate and return to the Users tab of the User and Group Accounts dialog box. Select Admin in the Name box and click Clear Password. Deactivating the Logon procedure does not remove any user-level security that you have defined for the database; it only lets you start Access without logging on.

Assign or Change Permissions and Ownerships

Permissions are granted to a user either explicitly to the individual user account or implicitly to the group account of which the user is a member. As mentioned previously, the owner of an object is the user who created it. To assign default permissions or to change permissions or ownerships for a database object, you must be one of the following:

■ A member of the Admins group of the WIF that was in use when the database was created

■ The owner of the database object

■ A user who has Administer permission on the object

To view or change the permissions and ownerships, choose Tools | Security | User and Group Permissions. Figure 21-11 shows the User and Group Permissions dialog box with one tab for working with permissions and another for changing object ownership.

In addition to the list of all existing objects in the database, you can select <New Tables/ Queries> to include any yet-to-be-created tables or queries in the permissions. If you have selected a different Object Type from the list, the <New...> option in the Object Name list will show that object type.

Assign and Remove Permissions

To work with permissions, open the database using the WIF that contains the user or group accounts to which you want to assign permissions. Open the Permissions tab of the User and Group Permissions dialog box. In the Permissions tab, you can do any of the following:

■ To see what permissions a user already enjoys with a specific object, click the Users option button, then select the user account name in the User/Group Name box. Select the type of object from the Object Type drop-down list and select the specific object from the Object Name box. The check boxes in the Permission area show which

FIGURE 21-11 Assigning user and group permissions

permissions have been explicitly granted to the user. Implicitly granted permissions will show in the group permissions list.

- To see what permissions a group has on an object, click the Groups option button and select the group account name from the User/Group Name box. Select the object type and name the same way as for user account permissions. The Permission area shows the permissions currently granted to the group account.

- To change permissions, select the user or group account first, then select the object type. Select one or more objects from the Object Name list, then check or clear the permissions.

> **TIP**   *To select multiple contiguous objects in the list, drag the mouse pointer over the names. To select multiple scattered objects, hold down CTRL and click the objects you want.*

After finishing with each object or set of objects, click Apply to keep the dialog box open for more changes. When finished, click OK.

Transfer Object Ownership

To transfer ownership of an object to a different user or group, click the Change Owner tab of the User and Group Permissions dialog box (see Figure 21-12). The list in the upper box displays the objects of the type selected in the Object Type box with their current owners.

About Changing Permissions

Some tips to remember when changing permissions are as follows:

- Some permissions are related and, when granted, automatically grant other permissions. For example, if you click the Update Data permission for a table, the Read Data and Read Design permissions are automatically checked because they will be needed to modify data. Similarly, if you clear the Update Data or Read Data permission for a table, the Modify Design permission also is automatically cleared.

- If you modify an object and save it with the same name, the permissions are unchanged. If you copy it or save it with a different name, you must reassign the permissions.

- When you change permissions on objects containing Visual Basic code, such as forms, reports, or modules, the permissions don't take effect until you close and reopen the database.

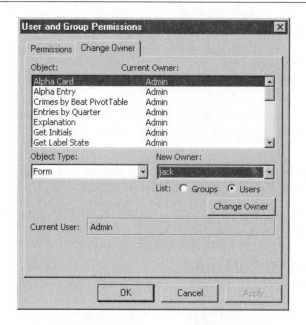

FIGURE 21-12 Changing object ownership

To change ownership of an object:

1. Select the object type in the Object Type box.

2. Select one or more objects in the list. You can select them by dragging over the names or holding CTRL as you click the names.

3. Click Groups to see a list of group accounts in the New Owner drop-down list or click Users to see the user accounts.

4. Select the group or user name from the New Owner list and click Change Owner. Ownership is transferred to the group or user selected in the New Owner list.

5. Make any other changes in ownership and click OK when finished.

> TIP *When you transfer ownership of an object to a group account, all members of the group are automatically granted ownership permissions on the object.*

You can also transfer ownership of a complete database to another administrator. Start Access using the new administrator's workgroup ID and create a new blank database, then import all the objects from the original database to the new one.

Remove User-Level Security

Removing the user-level security that has been created for a database involves returning ownership of the database and all the objects in it to the default Admin user. To do this, you must be able to log on as the workgroup administrator who is a member of the Admins group. After logging on to the database, give the default Users group full permissions on all objects. Exit Access and log on again as Admin and create a blank database in which to import all the objects from the original database.

CAUTION   *The result of this process is a completely unsecured database. Be aware that any workgroup or user can open the new database. The workgroup information file that is in effect when you import the objects from the original database is the one used for the Admin group with the new database. All imported objects are owned by the user that imported them.*

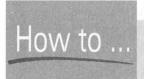

How to ... Repair a Damaged Workgroup Information File

Everyone hopes it won't happen, but sometimes the workgroup information file becomes damaged and you will not be able to open the database that relies on that WIF. How you solve this problem depends on whether you used the Workgroup Administrator to create the WIF in the first place and whether you saved a backup copy of the file.

■ No matter how you created the WIF, if you saved a backup copy, use Windows Explorer or another utility program to copy the most recent copy of the file to the folder where Access is installed or to the original path.

■ If you used the default WIF and did not make a backup copy, you must reinstall Access to re-create the default WIF.

■ If you used the Workgroup Administrator to create the file and did not save a backup copy, you must use the Administrator to re-create the file. Start the Administrator by typing in the same case sensitive name, organization, and workgroup ID you used before.

■ If you used the Workgroup Administrator to join a file on a path other than the folder where Access is installed and did not save a backup copy, create a new copy using the same method you used to create the original file and type the same case sensitive name, organization, and workgroup ID entries as before.

The security account information is stored in the WIF, so if you have to create a new file, you must re-create the security accounts with the same names and personal ID entries. The permissions and object ownership are stored in the secure database and don't need to be redefined but they must be connected with the same accounts as in the original database.

Other Security Measures

Encoding is another, less rigorous way of securing a database. Encoding a database renders it unreadable with a program other than Access (for example, with a debugger or a text editor). Hiding specific objects from user view can prevent sensitive data from leaking to unauthorized users.

Encode and Decode a Database

When you encode a database, it is compacted and rendered completely unreadable by a word processor or any utility program. Encoding a database does not restrict access to database objects. Decoding the database reverses the process and restores its original form.

You must be the owner of the WIF and you must be able to open the database in exclusive mode. The database also must be closed before you can encode it. In addition, you must have enough storage space for both the original and the encoded versions of the database file. To encode a database:

1. In an empty Access window, choose Tools | Security | Encode/Decode Database.

2. In the Encode/Decode Database dialog box, select the database you want to encode and click OK.

3. In the Encode Database As dialog box, specify the drive and folder where you want to store the encoded database and click OK. You can even save the encoded database in a Web folder by choosing Web Folders from the Save In drop-down list.

If you choose to store the encoded database with the same name and in the same folder as the original database, Access asks for confirmation before replacing the original file. If you confirm this, Access automatically replaces the original file with the successfully encoded version. If the encoding fails, the original database is not deleted. Once the database is encoded, you use it just like normal.

To decode an encoded database, repeat the same steps as for encoding and specify the drive and folder for storing the decoded file from the Decode Database As dialog box.

Hide Database Objects

If you have objects in your database that you want to keep from view, you can prevent them from appearing in the Database window. Hiding the objects doesn't provide more security than simply removing them from view. To hide an object:

1. Select the object in the Database window and click the properties toolbar button, or right-click the object name and choose Properties from the shortcut menu.

2. Click the Hidden option at the bottom of the General tab of the Properties dialog box and click OK.

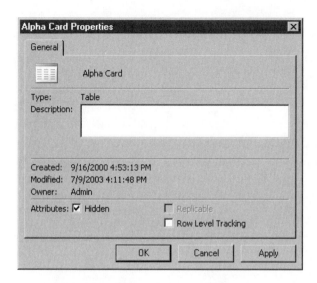

When you return to the Database window, the object no longer appears. To see the names of objects that have been hidden, choose Tools | Options and click the View tab. Click the Hidden Objects option in the Show group and then click OK. The hidden objects appear dimmed in the Database window, but they can still be opened.

To remove the Hidden property, open the object's property dialog box again and clear the Hidden option.

Appendix

Convert to Access 2003

You can convert from an earlier version of Access with the information presented here, but you might want to keep the database in the earlier version and just run it with Access 2003 instead. This is important if your database is used by more than one user and not all of the users have upgraded to Access 2003. You can convert an Access database that was created in Access 2.0 or later to Access 2000 or 2002-2003 format. You can also convert an Access 2002-2003 format back to 2000 or 97 file format.

Secured databases present a special problem during conversion because they are associated with a user-level security workgroup information file. You may want to re-create the WIF after converting the database.

Decide on a Conversion Strategy

If necessary, you can enable the database to run in Access 2003 without conversion. *Enabling* a database allows you to view and edit data but you will not be able to save changes in the design of any of the objects. If you want to modify an object, you must open the database in the original version.

If your database is shared among several users and not all of them can convert to Access 2000 or 2002-2003 format, you can split the database and convert part of it, and leave other parts unchanged. This way the database can be shared by users on different versions of Access.

Once the database is converted, you will no longer be able to open it with the original version of Access. If you convert an Access 97 or 2000 database to 2002-2003, you can't open it in the original version but you can convert it back. You can also convert an Access 2000 or 2002-2003 database to Access 97 but not to version 2.0 or 95.

Convert a Database

Before you convert the database, be sure to make a backup copy. Keep this copy until you are satisfied that the database has converted correctly and you have mastered Access 2003.

To convert the database to Access 2002-2003 file format:

1. Close the database you want to convert. If you are operating in a multiple-user environment, make sure all other users have also closed the database.

2. In an empty Access 2003 window, choose Tools | Database Utilities | Convert Database | To Access 2002-2003 File Format.

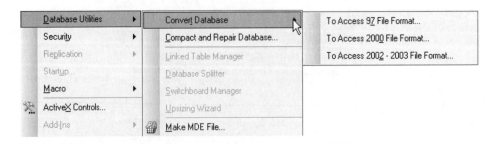

A

3. The Database to Convert From dialog box opens where you select the database you want to convert, then click Convert.

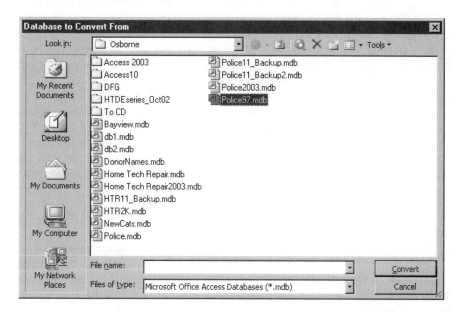

4. In the Convert Database Into dialog box, which is similar to the previous dialog box, enter a new name for the converted database or choose a different location. You can use the same name or enter a new one. Click Save.

You can convert the file to a different name in the same folder or use the same name in a different folder.

As the file is converted, you might see messages about compile errors during the conversion because some of the Visual Basic commands might no longer be valid. You can correct the code after conversion.

If the database you are converting has linked tables, make sure the tables remain in the original folder so the converted database can find them. If Access can't find them, the converted database won't work properly. After you have converted the database, you can move the linked tables to another location and use the Linked Table Manager to restore the links. The linked tables are not automatically converted; you must convert them separately.

When you convert a version 2.0 or 95 database to Access 2000 or 2002-2003, the built-in toolbars and custom toolbars are automatically converted to the new toolbar style. Custom menu bars created in Access 95 with the Menu Builder or with macros using the AddMenu action are interpreted as the new style menu bars but not automatically converted. You can use the Tools | Macro command to create new style menus, toolbars, and shortcut menus from the macros created in the earlier version; then you can modify them with the Customize dialog box.

Convert a Workgroup Information File

If you want to take advantage of the new security and performance improvements with Access 2000 or 2002-2003, re-create the Workgroup Information File (WIF) after the database has been converted. If some users are still using a pre-2000 version of Access, keep the original WIF. Create the new WIF by entering the exact, case sensitive name, company, and workgroup ID that you used in the previous version. If you don't get them exactly right, the Admins group will be invalid.

If you are upgrading from version 2.0, you must convert the WIF that is stored as an .mda file to the new .mdw file type. If you are upgrading from Access 95 or 97, you don't need to convert the WIF but you should compact it after converting the database. Tell the users to join the compacted WIF before opening the database.

Next, re-create the group and user accounts in the new WIF, again making sure to enter the exact group or user name and Personal ID for each group. When the new WIF is complete, instruct the users to use the Workgroup Administrator to join the new WIF. See Chapters 20 and 21 for more information about multiple-user environments and workgroups.

Convert a Secured Database

To convert or even enable a secured database, you must meet specific requirements and log on with certain permissions. Access 2003 creates a new WIF and makes it the current file when first installed. You must join this new WIF, which defines the users of the database before you can convert it. If a different file was in use when the database was secured, join that WIF instead of the default Access WIF.

When you log on to convert the database, you must have the following permissions:

- Open/Run and Open Exclusive permissions for the database
- Administer permissions for the MSysACEs and MSysObjects system tables
- Modify Design permissions for all the tables in the database, or you must be the owner of the tables
- Read Design permissions for all objects in the database

 If you log on as Admin or a member of the Admins group, Access will automatically grant you these permissions.

The conversion process is the same as for unsecured databases once you have logged on with sufficient permissions.

Convert a Replicated Database

When all users of the replicated database have upgraded to Access 2003, you can convert the replica set. The process involves making a complete test set including a Design Master and several replicas for use in Access 2003. Be sure to synchronize all the replicas in the set to make sure you have complete data. The test set must be kept completely isolated from the original set to be entirely safe, preferably on a separate computer.

After creating several replicas from the new test Design Master, choose Tools | Database Utilities | Convert Database to convert the test Design Master and the test replicas to Access 2003. Synchronize the converted Design Master with the newly converted replicas and operate the database as it is intended. After you are satisfied that the test set works as planned with Access 2003, delete all the members of the test set and convert the original replica set. Once the replica set is converted to Access 2003, you can no longer open it with Access 97, 2000, or 2002.

Enable a Database

If you are not converting the database because not all users have yet upgraded to Access 2003, you can still use the database created in an earlier version with your version 2003. By enabling a database, you can view database objects and add, delete, or modify records but you cannot modify any existing object design or add new objects to an enabled database from Access 2003. You must open the database using the version with which it was created to be able to modify object designs or add new objects.

The first time you open an Access 97 or earlier database with Access 2003, the Convert/Open dialog box asks if you want to convert it to Access 2002-2003 or simply open it in the original format.

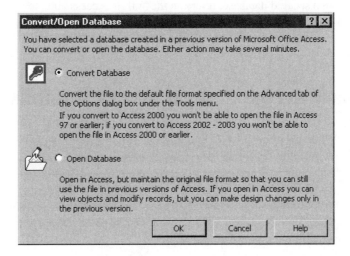

When you choose Open Database and click OK, a message appears explaining the database was created by an earlier version and that you won't be able to make any changes to the database objects. You can still edit the data but not make any design changes. It also gives you instructions for converting the database to Access 2003 if you want. You see the same message each subsequent time you open the database created with the earlier version.

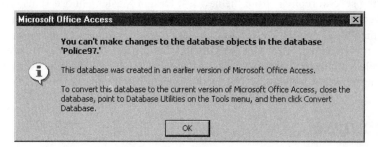

You can't link or import an Access 2002-2003 table into an enabled database but you can go the other way and open the version 2002-2003 database and export tables to the previous-version database. You can also cut, copy, and paste data from version 2002-2003 tables to previous-version tables.

When you enable a previous-version database in Access 2003, any custom toolbars are converted to the new style for consistency of viewing but the conversion isn't saved when you close the database. Custom menu bars are also interpreted as the new version 2002-2003 style. Menu bar macros are not converted but are still supported.

If you are enabling a secured database, re-create the WIF in Access 2003 to make sure it retains its security. If that is not possible, use the Workgroup Administrator to join the previous-version secure WIF. Using the previous-version WIF keeps all the security except the protection for the Visual Basic code.

Share a Database Across Several Access Versions

To use a database with several versions of Access, you can create a front-end/back-end database out of it. Leave the data in the oldest version as the back end and convert the other objects to a later-version front end. To build the single-file Access database:

1. Convert the entire database to the Access 2002-2003 file format.

2. Open the converted database and choose Tools | Database Utilities | Database Splitter.

3. Split the database into a front end and back end, then delete the back-end database created by the Database Splitter Wizard.

4. Choose Tools | Database Utilities | Linked Table Manager to link the new Access 2002-2003 front end to the tables in the previous-version database.

If the database is already a front-end/back-end application, you need to convert only the front end and leave the back end alone. Run the Linked Table Manager to link the converted front end to the original back-end database.

Convert from Access 2002-2003 to Access 97

If you need to use an Access 2002-2003 database on an Access 97 system, you can convert it if it is not a member of a replica set. Some special conditions need to be considered when converting an Access 2002-2003 database to Access 97:

- If the database is protected by user-level security, remove it before trying to convert. After it is converted, you can secure the database in Access 97.
- If it is protected with a password, you don't need to remove the password before converting the database.
- You must log on with Open/Run and Open Exclusive permissions for the database and Read Design permissions for all the objects in the database.

To convert an Access 2002-2003 database to Access 97, open the database and make sure no other user has it open, then do the following:

1. If you have protected the code with a password, open the Visual Basic Editor window and choose Tools | Properties, then enter the password in the Password box on the Protection tab of the Project Properties dialog box.
2. Return to the Access window and choose Tools | Database Utilities | Convert Databases | To Access 97 File Format.
3. In the Convert Database Into dialog box, enter a name for the previous-version database you want to create from the Access 2002-2003 version and click Save.

Convert from Access 2002-2003 to Access 2000

An Access 2002-2003 file can be easily converted to Access 2000 file format. Some features that are available only in 2002 are not available in the converted database. For example, Visual Basic procedures that use objects, functions, or other elements that are new to Access 2003 will cause compile errors when you open the file in Access 2000.

NOTE *For more information about converting Access files, see the Help topics, "Converting an Access File," "About Converting an Access File," and "Troubleshooting Converting an Access File."*

Index

G

N

INTERNATIONAL CONTACT INFORMATION

AUSTRALIA
McGraw-Hill Book Company
Australia Pty. Ltd.
TEL +61-2-9900-1800
FAX +61-2-9878-8881
http://www.mcgraw-hill.com.au
books-it_sydney@mcgraw-hill.com

CANADA
McGraw-Hill Ryerson Ltd.
TEL +905-430-5000
FAX +905-430-5020
http://www.mcgraw-hill.ca

GREECE, MIDDLE EAST, & AFRICA
(Excluding South Africa)
McGraw-Hill Hellas
TEL +30-210-6560-990
TEL +30-210-6560-993
TEL +30-210-6560-994
FAX +30-210-6545-525

MEXICO (Also serving Latin America)
McGraw-Hill Interamericana Editores
S.A. de C.V.
TEL +525-1500-5108
FAX +525-117-1589
http://www.mcgraw-hill.com.mx
carlos_ruiz@mcgraw-hill.com

SINGAPORE (Serving Asia)
McGraw-Hill Book Company
TEL +65-6863-1580
FAX +65-6862-3354
http://www.mcgraw-hill.com.sg
mghasia@mcgraw-hill.com

SOUTH AFRICA
McGraw-Hill South Africa
TEL +27-11-622-7512
FAX +27-11-622-9045
robyn_swanepoel@mcgraw-hill.com

SPAIN
McGraw-Hill/
Interamericana de España, S.A.U.
TEL +34-91-180-3000
FAX +34-91-372-8513
http://www.mcgraw-hill.es
professional@mcgraw-hill.es

UNITED KINGDOM, NORTHERN,
EASTERN, & CENTRAL EUROPE
McGraw-Hill Education Europe
TEL +44-1-628-502500
FAX +44-1-628-770224
http://www.mcgraw-hill.co.uk
emea_queries@mcgraw-hill.com

ALL OTHER INQUIRIES Contact:
McGraw-Hill/Osborne
TEL +1-510-420-7700
FAX +1-510-420-7703
http://www.osborne.com
omg_international@mcgraw-hill.com

Sound Off!

Visit us at **www.osborne.com/bookregistration** and let us know what you thought of this book. While you're online you'll have the opportunity to register for newsletters and special offers from McGraw-Hill/Osborne.

We want to hear from you!

Sneak Peek

Visit us today at **www.betabooks.com** and see what's coming from McGraw-Hill/Osborne tomorrow!

Based on the successful software paradigm, Bet@Books™ allows computing professionals to view partial and sometimes complete text versions of selected titles online. Bet@Books™ viewing is free, invites comments and feedback, and allows you to "test drive" books in progress on the subjects that interest you the most.

Know How

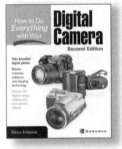

How to Do Everything with Your Digital Camera
Second Edition
ISBN: 0-07-222555-6

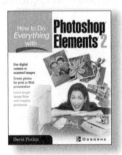

How to Do Everything with Photoshop Elements 2
ISBN: 0-07-222638-2

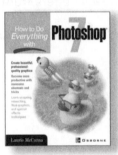

How to Do Everything with Photoshop 7
ISBN: 0-07-219554-1

How to Do Everything with Your Sony CLIÉ
ISBN: 0-07-222659-5

How to Do Everything with Macromedia Contribute
0-07-222892-X

How to Do Everything with Your eBay Business
0-07-222948-9

How to Do Everything with Your Tablet PC
ISBN: 0-07-222771-0

How to Do Everything with Your iPod
ISBN: 0-07-222700-1

How to Do Everything with Your iMac,
Third Edition
ISBN: 0-07-213172-1

How to Do Everything with Your iPAQ Pocket P
Second Edition
ISBN: 0-07-222950-0